Peter Singer's remarkably clear and comprehensive *Practical Ethics* has become a classic introduction to applied ethics since its publication in 1979 and has been translated into many languages. For this second edition the author has revised all the existing chapters, added two new ones, and updated the bibliography. He has also added an appendix describing some of the deep misunderstanding of, and consequent violent reaction to, the book in Germany, Austria, and Switzerland where the book has tested the limits of freedom of speech.

The focus of the book is the application of ethics to difficult and controversial social questions: equality and discrimination by race, sex, ability, or species; abortion, euthanasia, and embryo experimentation; the Moral Status of animals; political violence and civil disobedience; overseas aid and the obligation to assist others; responsibility for the environment; the treatment of refugees. Singer explains and assesses relevant arguments in a perspicuous, nondoctrinaire way. He structures the book to show how contemporary controversies often have deep philosophical roots; and he presents an ethical theory of his own that can be applied consistently and convincingly to all the practical cases.

The book's primary readership remains teachers and students of ethics whether in philosophy or some other branch of the humanities or social sciences. However, such is the clarity of the book's style and structure that it should interest any thinking person concerned with the most difficult social problems facing us as we approach the twenty-first century.

"Singer's book is packed with admirably marshaled and detailed information, social, medical, and economic, and has a splendid appendix of notes and references to further reading. The utility of this utilitarian's book to students of its subject can hardly be exaggerated."
   — H.L.A. Hart, New York Review of Books

"Peter Singer has provided us with a good example of the fruits of a major and by now established extension of philosophical interest. He succeeds in being straightforward, clear, and forceful without oversimplifying the technical aspects of the problems he discusses or trivializing the underlying philosophical issues."
   — The Times Higher Education Supplement

"This book is concentrated fare. The masterly and lively writing, rich with brief and telling examples, is devoted to close reasoning on some basic issues confronting the human community."
   — The Humanist

"Excellent and highly provocative."
   — Choice

PRACTICAL ETHICS – SECOND EDITION

Practical Ethics

Second Edition

PETER SINGER

Centre for Human Bioethics
Monash University

CAMBRIDGE
UNIVERSITY PRESS

Published by the Press Syndicate of the University of Cambridge
The Pitt Building, Trumpington Street, Cambridge CB2 1RP
40 West 20th Street, New York, NY 10011-4211, USA
10 Stamford Road, Oakleigh, Victoria 3166, Australia

© Cambridge University Press 1993

First published 1993

Printed in the United States of America

Library of Congress Cataloging-in-Publication Data
Singer, Peter.
Practical ethics / Peter Singer. – 2nd ed.
p. cm.
Includes bibliographical references.
ISBN 0-521-43363-0 (hc). – ISBN 0-521-43971-X (pb)
1. Ethics. 2. Social ethics. I. Title.
BJ1012.S49 1993
170–dc20 92–12319
CIP

A catalog record for this book is available from the British Library.

ISBN 0-521-43363-0 hardback
ISBN 0-521-43971-X paperback

CONTENTS

v

PREFACE

Practical ethics covers a wide area. We can find ethical ramifications in most of our choices, if we look hard enough. This book does not attempt to cover this whole area. The problems it deals with have been selected on two grounds: their relevance, and the extent to which philosophical reasoning can contribute to a discussion of them.

I regard an ethical issue as relevant if it is one that any thinking person must face. Some of the issues discussed in this book confront us daily: what are our personal responsibilities towards the poor? Are we justified in treating animals as nothing more than machines producing flesh for us to eat? Should we be using paper that is not recycled? And why should we bother about acting in accordance with moral principles anyway? Other problems, like abortion and euthanasia, fortunately are not everyday decisions for most of us; but they are issues that can arise at some time in our lives. They are also issues of current concern about which any active participant in our society's decision-making process needs to reflect.

The extent to which an issue can usefully be discussed philosophically depends on the kind of issue it is. Some issues are controversial largely because there are facts in dispute. For example, whether the release of new organisms created by the use of recombinant DNA ought to be permitted seems to hang largely on whether the organisms pose a serious risk to the environment. Although philosophers may lack the expertise to tackle this question, they may still be able to say something useful about whether it is acceptable to run a given risk of environmental damage. In other cases, however, the facts are clear and accepted by both sides; it is conflicting ethical views that give rise to disagreement over what to do. Then the kind of reasoning and analysis that philosophers practise really can make a difference. The issues discussed in this book are ones in which ethical, rather than factual, disagreement determines the positions people take. The potential contribution of philosophers to discussions of these issues is therefore considerable.

This book has played a central role in events that must give pause to anyone who thinks that freedom of thought and expression can be taken for granted in liberal democracies today. Since its first publication in 1979, it has been widely read and used in many courses at universities and colleges. It has been translated into German, Italian, Japanese, Spanish, and Swedish. The response has generally been positive. There are, of course, many who disagree with the arguments presented in the book, but the disagreement has almost always been at the level of reasoned debate. The only exception has been the reaction in German-speaking countries. In Germany, Austria, and Switzerland opposition to the views contained in this book reached such a peak that conferences or lectures at which I was invited to speak have been cancelled, and courses at German universities in which the book was to be used have been subjected to such repeated disruption that they could not continue. For readers interested in further details of this sorry story a fuller account is reprinted as an appendix.

Naturally, the German opposition to this book has made me reflect on whether the views I have expressed really are, as at least some Germans appear to believe, so erroneous or so dangerous that they must not be uttered. Although much of the German opposition is simply misinformed about what I am saying, there is an underlying truth to the claim that the book breaks a taboo – or perhaps more than one taboo. In Germany since the defeat of Hitler it has not been possible openly to discuss the question of euthanasia, nor the issue of whether a human life may be so full of misery as not to be worth living. More fundamental still, and not limited to Germany, is the taboo on comparing the value of human and nonhuman lives. In the commotion that followed the cancellation of a conference in Germany at which I had been invited to speak, the German sponsoring organisation, to disassociate itself from my views, passed a series of motions, one of which read: 'The uniqueness of human life forbids any comparison – or more specifically, equation – of human existence with other living beings, with their forms of life or interests.' Comparing, and in some cases equating, the lives of humans and animals is exactly what this book is about; in fact it could be said that if there is any single aspect of this book that distinguishes it from other approaches to such issues as human equality, abortion, euthanasia, and the environment, it is the fact that these topics are approached with a conscious disavowal of any assumption that all members of our own species have, merely because they are members of our species, any distinctive worth or inherent value that puts them above members of other species. The belief in human superiority is a very fundamental one, and it underlies our thinking in many sensitive areas. To challenge it is no trivial matter, and that such a challenge should provoke a strong reaction ought not to suprise us. Nevertheless, once we have understood that the breaching of this taboo on comparing humans and animals is partly responsible for the protests, it becomes clear that there is no going back. For reasons that are developed in subsequent chapters, to prohibit any cross-species comparisons would be philosophically indefensible. It would also make it impossible to overcome the wrongs we are now doing to nonhuman animals, and would reinforce attitudes that have done immense irreparable damage to the environment of this planet that we share with members of other species.

So I have not backed away from the views that have caused so much controversy in German-speaking lands. If these views have their dangers, the dangers of attempting to continue to maintain the present crumbling taboos are greater still. Needless to say, many will disagree with what I have to say. Objections and counter-arguments are welcome. Since the days of Plato, philosophy has advanced dialectically as philosophers have offered reasons for disagreeing with the views of other philosophers. Disagreement is good, because it is the way to a more defensible position; the suggestion that the views I have advanced should not even be discussed is, however, a totally different matter, and one that I am quite content to leave to readers, after they have read and reflected upon the chapters that follow.

Though I have not changed my views on the issues that have aroused the most fanatical opposition, this revised edition contains many other changes. I have added two new chapters on important ethical questions that were not covered in the previous edition: Chapter 9 on the refugee question and chapter 10 on the environment. Chapter 2 has a new section on equality and disability. The sections of Chapter 6 on embryo experimentation and fetal tissue use are also new. Every chapter has been reworked, factual material has been updated, and where my position has been misunderstood by my critics, I have tried to make it clearer.

As far as my underlying ethical views are concerned, some of my friends and colleagues will no doubt be distressed to find that countless hours spent discussing these matters with me have served only to reinforce my conviction that the consequentialist approach to ethics taken in the first edition is fundamentally sound. There have been two significant changes to the form of consequentialism espoused. The first is that I make use of the distinction drawn by R. M. Hare, in his book Moral Thinking, between two distinct levels of moral reasoning – the everyday intuitive level and the more reflective, critical level. The second is that I have dropped the suggestion – which I advanced rather tentatively in the fifth chapter of the first edition – that one might try to combine both the 'total' and 'prior existence' versions of utilitarianism, applying the former to sentient beings who are not self-conscious and the latter to those who are. I now think that preference utilitarianism draws a sufficiently sharp distinction between these two categories of being to enable us to apply one version of utilitarianism to all sentient beings. Nevertheless, I am still not entirely satisfied with my treatment of this whole question of how we should deal with ethical choices that involve bringing a being or beings into existence. As Chapters 4–7 make clear, the way in which we answer this perplexing question has implications for the issues of abortion, the treatment of severely disabled newborn infants, and for the killing of animals. The period between editions of this book has seen the publication of by far the most intricate and far-sighted analysis to date of this problem: Derek Parfit's *Reasons and Persons*. Unfortunately, Parfit himself remains baffled by the questions he has raised, and his conclusion is that the search for 'Theory X' – a satisfactory way of answering the question – must continue. So perhaps it is hardly to be expected that a satisfactory solution can emerge in this, both slimmer and more wide-ranging, volume.

In writing this book I have made extensive use of my own previously published articles and books. Thus Chapter 3 is based on *Animal Liberation* (New York Review/Random House, 2d edition, 1990), although it takes into account objections made since the book first appeared in 1975. The sections of Chapter 6 on such topics as in vitro fertilisation, the argument from potential, embryo experimentation, and the use of fetal tissue, all draw on work I wrote jointly with Karen Dawson, which was published as 'IVF and the Argument From Potential' in *Philosophy and Public Affairs*, vol. 17 (1988), and in Peter Singer, Helga Kuhse, and others, *Embryo Experimentation* (Cambridge University Press, 1990). In this revised edition, Chapter 7 includes points reached together with Helga Kuhse in working on our much fuller treatment of the issue of euthanasia for severely disabled infants, *Should the Baby Live?* (Oxford University Press, 1985). Chapter 8 restates arguments from 'Famine, Affluence and Morality', *Philosophy and Public Affairs*, vol. 1 (1972) and from 'Reconsidering the Famine Relief Argument' in Peter Brown and Henry Shue (eds.) *Food Policy: The Responsibility of the United States in the Life and Death Choices* (New York, The Free Press, 1977). Chapter 9 again draws on a co-authored piece, this time written with my wife, Renata Singer, and first published as 'The Ethics of Refugee Policy' in M. Gibney (ed.), *Open Borders? Closed Societies?* (Greenwood Press, New York, 1988). Chapter 10 is based on 'Environmental Values', a chapter that I contributed to Ian Marsh (ed.), *The Environmental Challenge* (Longman Cheshire, Melbourne, 1991). Parts of Chapter 11 draw on my first book, *Democracy and Disobedience* (Oxford, Clarendon Press, 1973).

H. J. McCloskey, Derek Parfit, and Robert Young provided useful comments on a draft version of the first edition of this book. Robert Young's ideas also entered into my thinking at an earlier stage, when we jointly taught a course on these topics at La Trobe University. The chapter on euthanasia, in particular, owes much to his ideas, though he may not agree with everything in it. Going back further still, my interest in ethics was stimulated by H. J. McCloskey, whom I was fortunate to have as a teacher during my undergraduate years; while the mark left by R. M. Hare, who taught me at Oxford, is apparent in the ethical foundations underlying the positions taken in this book. Jeremy Mynott, of Cambridge University Press, encouraged me to write the book and helped to shape and improve it as it went along.

For assistance with the revised edition, I must thank those with whom I have worked jointly on material that has been included in this book: Karen Dawson, Helga Kuhse, and Renata Singer. Helga Kuhse, in particular, has been a close colleague for the past ten years, and during that period I have learned much by discussing most of the topics in this book with her.

She also read and commented on several chapters of this revised edition. Paola Cavalieri gave me detailed comments and criticism on the entire draft, and I thank her for suggesting several improvements. There are, of course, many others who have challenged what I wrote in the first edition and forced me to think about these issues again, but to thank them all is impossible, and to thank a few would be unjust. This time it was Terence Moore, at Cambridge University Press, whose enthusiasm for the book provided the stimulus for me to carry out the revisions.

To give an uncluttered text, the notes, references, and suggested further reading are grouped together at the end of the book.

1

ABOUT ETHICS

THIS book is about practical ethics, that is, the application of ethics or morality – I shall use the words interchangeably – to practical issues like the treatment of ethnic minorities, equality for women, the use of animals for food and research, the preservation of the natural environment, abortion, euthanasia, and the obligation of the wealthy to help the poor. No doubt the reader will want to get on to these issues without delay; but there are some preliminaries that must be dealt with at the start. In order to have a useful discussion within ethics, it is necessary to say a little *about* ethics, so that we have a clear understanding of what we are doing when we discuss ethical questions. This first chapter therefore sets the stage for the remainder of the book. In order to prevent it from growing into an entire volume itself, I have kept it brief. If at times it is dogmatic, that is because I cannot take the space properly to consider all the different conceptions of ethics that might be opposed to the one I shall defend; but this chapter will at least serve to reveal the assumptions on which the remainder of the book is based.

WHAT ETHICS IS NOT

Some people think that morality is now out of date. They regard morality as a system of nasty puritanical prohibitions, mainly designed to stop people having fun. Traditional moralists claim to be the defenders of morality in general, but they are really defending a particular moral code. They have been allowed to preempt the field to such an extent that when a newspaper headline reads BISHOP ATTACKS DECLINING MORAL STANDARDS, we expect to read yet again about promiscuity, homosexuality, pornography, and so on, and not about the puny amounts we give as overseas aid to poorer nations, or our reckless indifference to the natural environment of our planet.

So the first thing to say about ethics is that it is not a set of prohibitions particularly concerned with sex. Even in the era of AIDS, sex raises no unique moral issues at all. Decisions about sex may involve considerations of honesty, concern for others, prudence, and so on, but there is nothing special about sex in this respect, for the same could be said of decisions about driving a car. (In fact, the moral issues raised by driving a car, both from an environmental and from a safety point of view, are much more serious than those raised by sex.) Accordingly, this book contains no discussion of sexual morality. There are more important ethical issues to be considered.

Second, ethics is not an ideal system that is noble in theory but no good in practice. The reverse of this is closer to the truth: an ethical judgment that is no good in practice must suffer from a theoretical defect as well, for the whole point of ethical judgments is to guide practice.

Some people think that ethics is inapplicable to the real world because they regard it as a system of short and simple rules like 'Do not lie', 'Do not steal', and 'Do not kill'. It is not surprising that those who hold this view of ethics should also believe that ethics is not suited to life's complexities. In unusual situations, simple rules conflict; and even when they do not, following a rule can lead to disaster. It may normally be wrong to lie, but if you were living in Nazi Germany and the Gestapo came to your door looking for Jews, it would surely be right to deny the existence of the Jewish family hiding in your attic.

Like the failure of a restrictive sexual morality, the failure of an ethic of simple rules must not be taken as a failure of ethics as a whole. It is only a failure of one view of ethics, and not even an irremediable failure of that view. The deontologists – those who think that ethics is a system of rules – can rescue their position by finding more complicated and more specific rules that do not conflict with each other, or by ranking the rules in some hierarchical structure to resolve conflicts between them. Moreover, there is a long-standing approach to ethics that is quite untouched by the complexities that make simple rules difficult to apply. This is the consequentialist view. Consequentialists start not with moral rules but with goals. They assess actions by the extent to which they further these goals. The best-known, though not the only, consequentialist theory is utilitarianism. The classical utilitarian regards an action as right if it produces as much or more of an increase in the happiness of all affected by it than any alternative action, and wrong if it does not.

The consequences of an action vary according to the circumstances in which it is performed. Hence a utilitarian can never properly be accused of a lack of realism, or of a rigid adherence to ideals in defiance of practical experience. The utilitarian will judge lying bad in some circumstances and good in others, depending on its consequences.

Third, ethics is not something intelligible only in the context of religion. I shall treat ethics as entirely independent of religion.

Some theists say that ethics cannot do without religion because the very meaning of 'good' is nothing other than 'what God approves'. Plato refuted a similar claim more than two thousand years ago by arguing that if the gods approve of some actions it must be because those actions are good, in which case it cannot be the gods' approval that makes them good. The alternative view makes divine approval entirely arbitrary: if the gods had happened to approve of torture and disapprove of helping our neighbours, torture would have been good and helping our neighbours bad. Some modern theists have attempted to extricate themselves from this type of dilemma by maintaining that God is good and so could not possibly approve of torture; but these theists are caught in a trap of their own making, for what can they possibly mean by the assertion that God is good? That God is approved of by God?

Traditionally, the more important link between religion and ethics was that religion was thought to provide a reason for doing what is right, the reason being that those who are virtuous will be rewarded by an eternity of bliss while the rest roast in hell. Not all religious thinkers have accepted this argument: Immanuel Kant, a most pious Christian, scorned anything that smacked of a self-interested motive for obeying the moral law. We must obey it, he said, for its own sake. Nor do we have to be Kantians to dispense with the motivation offered by traditional religion. There is a long line of thought that finds the source of ethics in the attitudes of benevolence and sympathy for others that most people have. This is, however, a complex topic, and since it is the subject of the final chapter of this book I shall not pursue it here. It is enough to say that our everyday observation of our fellow human beings clearly shows that ethical behaviour does not require belief in heaven and hell.

The fourth, and last, claim about ethics that I shall deny in this opening chapter is that ethics is relative or subjective. At least, I shall deny these claims in some of the senses in which they are often made. This point requires a more extended discussion than the other three.

Let us take first the oft-asserted idea that ethics is relative to the society one happens to live in. This is true in one sense and false in another. It is true that, as we have already seen in discussing consequentialism, actions that are right in one situation because of their good consequences may be wrong in another situation because of their bad consequences. Thus casual sexual intercourse may be wrong when it leads to the existence of children who cannot be adequately cared for, and not wrong when, because of the existence of effective contraception, it does not lead to reproduction at all. But this is only a superficial form of relativism. While it suggests that the applicability of a specific principle like 'Casual sex is wrong' may be relative to time and place, it says nothing against such a principle being objectively valid in specific circumstances, or against the universal applicability of a more general principle like 'Do what increases happiness and reduces suffering.'

The more fundamental form of relativism became popular in the nineteenth century when data on the moral beliefs and practices of far-flung societies began pouring in. To the strict reign of Victorian prudery the knowledge that there were places where sexual relations between unmarried people were regarded as perfectly wholesome brought the seeds of a revolution in sexual attitudes. It is not surprising that to some the new knowledge suggested, not merely that the moral code of nineteenth-century Europe was not objectively valid, but that no moral judgment can do more than reflect the customs of the society in which it is made.

Marxists adapted this form of relativism to their own theories. The ruling ideas of each period, they said, are the ideas of its ruling class, and so the morality of a society is relative to its dominant economic class, and thus indirectly relative to its economic basis. So they triumphantly refuted the claims of feudal and bourgeois morality to objective, universal validity. But this raises a problem: if all morality is relative, what is so special about communism? Why side with the proletariat rather than the bourgeoisie?

Engels dealt with this problem in the only way possible, by abandoning relativism in favour of the more limited claim that the morality of a society divided into classes will always be relative to the ruling class, although the morality of a society without class antagonisms could be a 'really human' morality. This is no longer relativism at all. Nevertheless, Marxism, in a confused sort of way, still provides the impetus for a lot of woolly relativist ideas.

The problem that led Engels to abandon relativism defeats ordinary ethical relativism as well. Anyone who has thought through a difficult ethical decision knows that being told what our society thinks we ought to do does not settle the quandary. We have to reach our own decision. The beliefs and customs we were brought up with may exercise great influence on us, but once we start to reflect upon them we can decide whether to act in accordance with them, or to go against them.

The opposite view – that ethics is always relative to a particular society – has most implausible consequences. If our society disapproves of slavery, while another society approves of it, we have no basis to choose between these conflicting views. Indeed, on a relativist analysis there is really no conflict – when I say slavery is wrong I am really only saying that my society disapproves of slavery, and when the slaveowners from the other society say that slavery is right, they are only saying that their society approves of it. Why argue? Obviously we could both be speaking the truth.

Worse still, the relativist cannot satisfactorily account for the nonconformist. If 'slavery is wrong' means 'my society disapproves of slavery', then someone who lives in a society that does not disapprove of slavery is, in claiming that slavery is wrong, making a simple factual error. An opinion poll could demonstrate the error of an ethical judgment. Would-be reformers are therefore in a parlous situation: when they set out to change the ethical views of their fellow-citizens they are *necessarily* mistaken; it is only when they succeed in winning most of the society over to their own views that those views become right.

These difficulties are enough to sink ethical relativism; ethical subjectivism at least avoids making nonsense of the valiant efforts of would-be moral reformers, for it makes ethical judgments depend on the approval or disapproval of the person making the judgment, rather than that person's society. There are other difficulties, though, that at least some forms of ethical subjectivism cannot overcome.

If those who say that ethics is subjective mean by this that when I say that cruelty to animals is wrong I am really only saying that I disapprove of cruelty to animals, they are faced with an aggravated form of one of the difficulties of relativism: the inability to account for ethical disagreement. What was true for the relativist of disagreement between people from different societies is for the subjectivist true of disagreement between any two people. I say cruelty to animals is wrong: someone else says it is not wrong. If this means that I disapprove of cruelty to animals and someone else does not, both statements may be true and so there is nothing to argue about.

Other theories often described as 'subjectivist' are not open to this objection. Suppose someone maintains that ethical judgments are neither true nor false because they do not describe anything – neither objective moral facts, nor one's own subjective states of mind. This theory might hold that, as C. L. Stevenson suggested, ethical judgments express attitudes, rather than describe them, and we disagree about ethics because we try, by expressing our own attitude, to bring our listeners to a similar attitude. Or it might be, as R. M. Hare has urged, that ethical judgments are prescriptions and therefore more closely related to commands than to statements of fact. On this view we disagree because we care about what people do. Those features of ethical argument that imply the existence of objective moral standards can be explained away by maintaining that this is some kind of error – perhaps the legacy of the belief that ethics is a God-given system of law, or perhaps just another example of our tendency to objectify our personal wants and preferences. J. L. Mackie has defended this view.

Provided they are carefully distinguished from the crude form of subjectivism that sees ethical judgments as descriptions of the speaker's attitudes, these are plausible accounts of ethics. In their denial of a realm of ethical facts that is part of the real world, existing quite independently of us, they are no doubt correct; but does it follow from this that ethical judgments are immune from criticism, that there is no role for reason or argument in ethics, and that, from the standpoint of reason, any ethical judgment is as good as any other? I do not think it does, and none of the three philosophers referred to in the previous paragraph denies reason and argument a role in ethics, though they disagree as to the significance of this role.

This issue of the role that reason can play in ethics is the crucial point raised by the claim that ethics is subjective. The non-existence of a mysterious realm of objective ethical facts does not imply the non-existence of ethical reasoning. It may even help, since if we could arrive at ethical judgments only by intuiting these strange ethical facts, ethical argument would be more difficult still. So what has to be shown to put practical ethics on a sound basis is that ethical reasoning is possible. Here the temptation is to say simply that the proof of the pudding lies in the eating, and the proof that reasoning is possible in ethics is to be found in the remaining chapters of this book; but this is not entirely satisfactory. From a theoretical point of view it is unsatisfactory because we might find ourselves reasoning about ethics without really understanding how this can happen; and from a practical point of view it is unsatisfactory because our reasoning is more likely to go astray if we lack a grasp of its foundations. I shall therefore attempt to say something about how we can reason in ethics.

WHAT ETHICS IS: ONE VIEW

What follows is a sketch of a view of ethics that allows reason an important role in ethical decisions. It is not the only possible view of ethics, but it is a plausible view. Once again, however, I shall have to pass over qualifications and objections worth a chapter to themselves. To those who think these undiscussed objections defeat the position I am advancing, I can only say, again, that this whole chapter may be treated as no more than a statement of the assumptions on which this book is based. In that way it will at least assist in giving a clear view of what I take ethics to be.

What is it to make a moral judgment, or to argue about an ethical issue, or to live according to ethical standards? How do moral judgments differ from other practical judgments? Why do we regard a woman's decision to have an abortion as raising an ethical issue, but not her decision to change her job? What is the difference between a person who lives by ethical standards and one who doesn't?

All these questions are related, so we only need to consider one of them; but to do this we need to say something about the nature of ethics. Suppose that we have studied the lives of a number of different people, and we know a lot about what they do, what they believe, and so on. Can we then decide which of them are living by ethical standards and which are not?

We might think that the way to proceed here is to find out who believes it wrong to lie, cheat, steal, and so on and does not do any of these things, and who has no such beliefs, and shows no such restraint in their actions. Then those in the first group would be living according to ethical standards and those in the second group would not be. But this procedure mistakenly assimilates two distinctions: the first is the distinction between living according to (what we judge to be) the right ethical standards and living according to (what we judge to be) mistaken ethical standards; the second is the distinction between living according to some ethical standards, and living according to no ethical standards at all. Those who lie and cheat, but do not believe what they are doing to be wrong, may be living according to ethical standards. They may believe, for any of a number of possible reasons, that it is right to lie, cheat, steal, and so on. They are not living according to conventional ethical standards, but they may be living according to some other ethical standards.

This first attempt to distinguish the ethical from the non-ethical was mistaken, but we can learn from our mistakes. We found that we must concede that those who hold unconventional ethical beliefs are still living according to ethical standards, *if they believe, for any reason, that it is right to do as they are doing.* The italicised condition gives us a clue to the answer we are seeking. The notion of living according to ethical standards is tied up with the notion of defending the way one is living, of giving a reason for it, of justifying it. Thus people may do all kinds of things we regard as wrong, yet still be living according to ethical standards, if they are prepared to defend and justify what they do. We may find the justification inadequate, and may hold that the actions are wrong, but the attempt at justification, whether successful or not, is sufficient to bring the person's conduct within the domain of the ethical as opposed to the non-ethical. When, on the other hand, people cannot put forward any justification for what they do, we may reject their claim to be living according to ethical standards, even if what they do is in accordance with conventional moral principles.

We can go further. If we are to accept that a person is living according to ethical standards, the justification must be of a certain kind. For instance, a justification in terms of self-interest alone will not do. When Macbeth, contemplating the murder of Duncan, admits that only 'vaulting ambition' drives him to do it, he is admitting that the act cannot be justified ethically. 'So that I can be king in his place' is not a weak attempt at an ethical justification for assassination; it is not the sort of reason that counts as an ethical justification at all. Self-interested acts must be shown to be compatible with more broadly based ethical principles if they are to be ethically defensible, for the notion of ethics carries with it the idea of something bigger than the individual. If I am to defend my conduct on ethical grounds, I cannot point only to the benefits it brings me. I must address myself to a larger audience.

From ancient times, philosophers and moralists have expressed the idea that ethical conduct is acceptable from a point of view that is somehow universal. The 'Golden Rule' attributed to Moses, to be found in the book of Leviticus and subsequently repeated by Jesus, tells us to go beyond our own personal interests and 'love thy neighbour as thyself' – in other words, give the same weight to the interests of others as one gives to one's own interests. The same idea of putting oneself in the position of another is involved in the other Christian formulation of the commandment, that we do to others as we would have them do to us. The Stoics held that ethics derives from a universal natural law. Kant developed this idea into his famous formula: 'Act only on that maxim through which you can at the same time will that it should become a universal law.' Kant's theory has itself been modified and developed by R. M. Hare, who sees universalisability as a logical feature of moral judgments. The eighteenth -century British philosophers Hutcheson, Hume, and Adam Smith appealed to an imaginary 'impartial spectator' as the test of a moral judgment, and this theory has its modern version in the Ideal Observer theory. Utilitarians, from Jeremy Bentham to J. J. C. Smart, take it as axiomatic that in deciding moral issues 'each counts for one and none for more than one'; while John Rawls, a leading contemporary critic of utilitarianism, incorporates essentially the same axiom into his own theory by deriving basic ethical principles from an imaginary choice in which those choosing do not know whether they will be the ones who gain or lose by the principles they select. Even Continental European philosophers like the existentialist Jean -Paul Sartre and the critical theorist Jürgen Habermas, who differ in many ways from their English-speaking colleagues – and from each other – agree that ethics is in some sense universal.

One could argue endlessly about the merits of each of these characterisations of the ethical; but what they have in common is more important than their differences. They agree that an ethical principle cannot be justified in relation to any partial or sectional group. Ethics takes a universal point of view. This does not mean that a particular ethical judgment must be universally applicable. Circumstances alter causes, as we have seen. What it does mean is that in making ethical judgments we go beyond our own likes and dislikes. From an ethical point of view, the fact that it is I who benefit from, say, a more equal distribution of income and you who lose by it, is irrelevant. Ethics requires us to go beyond 'I' and 'you' to the universal law, the universalisable judgment, the standpoint of the impartial spectator or ideal observer, or whatever we choose to call it.

Can we use this universal aspect of ethics to derive an ethical theory that will give us guidance about right and wrong? Philosophers from the Stoics to Hare and Rawls have attempted this. No attempt has met with general acceptance. The problem is that if we describe the universal aspect of ethics in bare, formal terms, a wide range of ethical theories, including quite irreconcilable ones, are compatible with this notion of universality; if, on the other hand, we build up our description of the universal aspect of ethics so that it leads us ineluctably to one particular ethical theory, we shall be accused of smuggling our own ethical beliefs into our definition of the ethical – and this definition was supposed to be broad enough, and neutral enough, to encompass all serious candidates for the status of 'ethical theory'. Since so many others have failed to overcome this obstacle to deducing an ethical theory from the universal aspect of ethics, it would be foolhardy to attempt to do so in a brief introduction to a work with a quite different aim. Nevertheless I shall propose something only a little less ambitious. The universal aspect of ethics, I suggest, does provide a persuasive, although not conclusive, reason for taking a broadly utilitarian position.

My reason for suggesting this is as follows. In accepting that ethical judgments must be made from a universal point of view, I am accepting that my own interests cannot, simply because they are my interests, count more than the interests of anyone else. Thus my very natural concern that my own interests be looked after must, when I think ethically, be extended to the interests of others. Now, imagine that I am trying to decide between two possible courses of action – perhaps whether to eat all the fruits I have collected myself, or to share them with others. Imagine, too, that I am deciding in a complete ethical vacuum, that I know nothing of any ethical considerations – I am, we might say, in a pre-ethical stage of thinking. How would I make up my mind? One thing that would be still relevant would be how the possible courses of action will affect my interests. Indeed, if we define 'interests' broadly enough, so that we count anything people desire as in their interests (unless it is incompatible with another desire or desires), then it would seem that at this pre-ethical stage, *only* one's own interests can be relevant to the decision.

Suppose I then begin to think ethically, to the extent of re-cognising that my own interests cannot count for more, simply because they are my own, than the interests of others. In place of my own interests, I now have to take into account the in-terests of all those affected by my decision. This requires me to weigh up all these interests and adopt the course of action most likely to maximise the interests of those affected. Thus at least at some level in my moral reasoning I must choose the course of action that has the best consequences, on balance, for all affected. (I say 'at some level in my moral reasoning' because, as we shall see later, there are utilitarian reasons for believing that we ought not to try to calculate these consequences for every ethical decision we make in our daily lives, but only in very unusual circumstances, or perhaps when we are reflecting on our choice of general principles to guide us in future. In other words, in the specific example given, at first glance one might think it obvious that sharing the fruit that I have gathered has better consequences for all affected than not sharing them. This may in the end also be the best general principle for us all to adopt, but before we can have grounds for believing this to be the case, we must also consider whether the effect of a general practice of sharing gathered fruits will benefit all those affected, by bringing about a more equal distribution, or whether it will reduce the amount of food gathered, because some will cease to gather anything if they know that they will get sufficient from their share of what others gather.)

The way of thinking I have outlined is a form of utilitarianism. It differs from classical utilitarianism in that 'best consequences' is understood as meaning what, on balance, furthers the interests of those affected, rather than merely what increases pleasure and reduces pain. (It has, however, been suggested that classical utilitarians like Bentham and John Stuart Mill used 'pleasure' and 'pain' in a broad sense that allowed them to include achieving what one desired as a 'pleasure' and the reverse as a 'pain'. If this interpretation is correct, the difference between classical utilitarianism and utilitarianism based on interests disappears.)

What does this show? It does not show that utilitarianism can be deduced from the universal aspect of ethics. There are other ethical ideals – like individual rights, the sanctity of life, justice, purity, and so on – that are universal in the required sense, and are, at least in some versions, incompatible with utilitarianism. It does show that we very swiftly arrive at an initially utilitarian position once we apply the universal aspect of ethics to simple, pre-ethical decision making. This, I believe, places the onus of proof on those who seek to go beyond utilitarianism. The utilitarian position is a minimal one, a first base that we reach by universalising self-interested decision making. We cannot, if we are to think ethically, refuse to take this step. If we are to be persuaded that we should go beyond utilitarianism and accept non-utilitarian moral rules or ideals, we need to be provided with good reasons for taking this further step. Until such reasons are produced, we have some grounds for remaining utilitarians.

This tentative argument for utilitarianism corresponds to the way in which I shall discuss practical issues in this book. I am inclined to hold a utilitarian position, and to some extent the book may be taken as an attempt to indicate how a consistent utilitarianism would deal with a number of controversial problems. But I shall not take utilitarianism as the only ethical position worth considering. I shall try to show the bearing of other views, of theories of rights, of justice, of the sanctity of life, and so on, on the problems discussed. In this way readers will be able to come to their own conclusions about the relative merits of utilitarian and non-utilitarian approaches, and about the whole issue of the role of reason and argument in ethics.

2

EQUALITY AND ITS IMPLICATIONS

THE present century has seen dramatic changes in moral attitudes. Most of these changes are still controversial. Abortion, almost everywhere prohibited thirty years ago, is now legal in many countries (though it is still opposed by substantial and respected sections of the population). The same is true of changes in attitudes to sex outside marriage, homosexuality, pornography, euthanasia, and suicide. Great as the changes have been, no new consensus has been reached. The issues remain controversial and it is possible to defend either side without jeopardising one's intellectual or social standing.

Equality seems to be different. The change in attitudes to inequality – especially racial inequality – has been no less sudden and dramatic than the change in attitudes to sex, but it has been more complete. Racist assumptions shared by most Europeans at the turn of the century are now totally unacceptable, at least in public life. A poet could not now write of 'lesser breeds without the law', and retain – indeed enhance – his reputation, as Rudyard Kipling did in 1897. This does not mean that there are no longer any racists, but only that they must disguise their racism if their views and policies are to have any chance of general acceptance. Even South Africa has abandoned apartheid. The principle that all humans are equal is now part of the prevailing political and ethical orthodoxy. But what, exactly, does it mean and why do we accept it?

Once we go beyond the agreement that blatant forms of racial

16

discrimination are wrong, once we question the basis of the principle that all humans are equal and seek to apply this principle to particular cases, the consensus starts to weaken. One sign of this was the furor that occurred during the 1970s over the claims made by Arthur Jensen, professor of educational psychology at the University of California, Berkeley, and H. J. Eysenck, professor of psychology at the University of London, about genetically based variations in intelligence between different races. Many of the most forceful opponents of Jensen and Eysenck assume that these claims, if sound, would justify racial discrimination. Are they right? Similar questions can be asked about research into differences between males and females.

Another issue requiring us to think about the principle of equality is 'affirmative action'. Some philosophers and lawyers have argued that the principle of equality requires that when allocating jobs or university places we should favour members of disadvantaged minorities. Others have contended that the same principle of equality rules out any discrimination on racial grounds, whether for or against the worst-off members of society.

We can only answer these questions if we are clear about what it is we intend to say, and can justifiably say, when we assert that all humans are equal – hence the need for an inquiry into the ethical foundations of the principle of equality.

When we say that all humans are equal, irrespective of race or sex, what exactly are we claiming? Racists, sexists, and other opponents of equality have often pointed out that, by whatever test we choose, it simply is not true that all humans are equal. Some are tall, some are short; some are good at mathematics, others are poor at it; some can run 100 metres in ten seconds, some take fifteen or twenty; some would never intentionally hurt another being, others would kill a stranger for $100 if they could get away with it; some have emotional lives that touch the heights of ecstasy and the depths of despair, while others

17

live on a more even plane, relatively untouched by what goes on around them. And so we could go on. The plain fact is that humans differ, and the differences apply to so many characteristics that the search for a factual basis on which to erect the principle of equality seems hopeless.

John Rawls has suggested, in his influential book *A Theory of Justice*, that equality can be founded on the natural characteristics of human beings, provided we select what he calls a 'range property'. Suppose we draw a circle on a piece of paper. Then all points within the circle – this is the 'range' – have the property of being within the circle, and they have this property equally, Some points may be closer to the centre and others nearer the edge, but all are, equally, points inside the circle. Similarly, Rawls suggests, the property of 'moral personality' is a property that virtually all humans possess, and all humans who possess this property possess it equally. By 'moral personality' Rawls does not mean 'morally good personality'; he is using 'moral' in contrast to 'amoral'. A moral person, Rawls says, must have a sense of justice. More broadly, one might say that to be a moral person is to be the kind of person to whom one can make moral appeals, with some prospect that the appeal will be heeded.

Rawls maintains that moral personality is the basis of human equality, a view that derives from his 'contract' approach to justice. The contract tradition sees ethics as a kind of mutually beneficial agreement – roughly, 'Don't hit me and I won't hit you.' Hence only those capable of appreciating that they are not being hit, and of restraining their own hitting accordingly, are within the sphere of ethics.

There are problems with using moral personality as the basis of equality. One objection is that having a moral personality is a matter of degree. Some people are highly sensitive to issues of justice and ethics generally; others, for a variety of reasons, have only a limited awareness of such principles. The suggestion that being a moral person is the minimum necessary for coming within the scope of the principle of equality still leaves it open just where this minimal line is to be drawn. Nor is it intuitively obvious why, if moral personality is so important, we should not have grades of moral status, with rights and duties corresponding to the degree of refinement of one's sense of justice.

Still more serious is the objection that it is not true that all humans are moral persons, even in the most minimal sense. Infants and small children, along with some intellectually disabled humans, lack the required sense of justice. Shall we then say that all humans are equal, except for very young or intellectually disabled ones? This is certainly not what we ordinarily understand by the principle of equality. If this revised principle implies that we may disregard the interests of very young or intellectually disabled humans in ways that would be wrong if they were older or more intelligent, we would need far stronger arguments to induce us to accept it. (Rawls deals with infants and children by including *potential* moral persons along with actual ones within the scope of the principle of equality. But this is an ad hoc device, confessedly designed to square his theory with our ordinary moral intuitions, rather than something for which independent arguments can be produced. Moreover although Rawls admits that those with irreparable intellectual disabilities 'may present a difficulty' he offers no suggestions towards the solution of this difficulty.)

So the possession of 'moral personality' does not provide a satisfactory basis for the principle that all humans are equal. I doubt that any natural characteristic, whether a 'range property' or not, can fulfil this function, for I doubt that there is any morally significant property that all humans possess equally.

There is another possible line of defence for the belief that there is a factual basis for a principle of equality that prohibits racism and sexism. We can admit that humans differ as individuals, and yet insist that there are no morally significant differences between the races and sexes. Knowing that someone is of African or European descent, female or male, does not enable us to draw conclusions about her or his intelligence, sense of justice, depth of feelings, or anything else that would entitle us to treat her or him as less than equal. The racist claim that people of European descent are superior to those of other races in these capacities is in this sense false. The differences between individuals in these respects are not captured by racial boundaries. The same is true of the sexist stereotype that sees women as emotionally deeper and more caring, but also less rational, less aggressive, and less enterprising than men. Obviously this is not true of women as a whole. Some women are emotionally shallower, less caring, and more rational, more aggressive and, more enterprising than some men.

The fact that humans differ as individuals, not as races or sexes, is important, and we shall return to it when we come to discuss the implications of the claims made by Jensen, Eysenck, and others; yet it provides neither a satisfactory principle of equality nor an adequate defence against a more sophisticated opponent of equality than the blatant racist or sexist. Suppose that someone proposes that people should be given intelligence tests and then classified into higher or lower status categories on the basis of the results. Perhaps those who scored above 125 would be a slave-owning class; those scoring between 100 and 125 would be free citizens but lack the right to own slaves; while those scoring below 100 would be made the slaves of those who had scored above 125. A hierarchical society of this sort seems as abhorrent as one based on race or sex; but if we base our support for equality on the factual claim that differences between individuals cut across racial and sexual boundaries, we have no grounds for opposing this kind of inegalitarianism. For this hierarchical society would be based on real differences between people.

We can reject this 'hierarchy of intelligence' and similar fantastic schemes only if we are clear that the claim to equality does not rest on the possession of intelligence, moral personality, rationality, or similar matters of fact. There is no logically compelling reason for assuming that a difference in ability between two people justifies any difference in the amount of consideration we give to their interests. Equality is a basic ethical principle, not an assertion of fact. We can see this if we return to our earlier discussion of the universal aspect of ethical judgments.

We saw in the previous chapter that when I make an ethical judgment I must go beyond a personal or sectional point of view and take into account the interests of all those affected. This means that we weigh up interests, considered simply as interests and not as my interests, or the interests of Australians, or of people of European descent. This provides us with a basic principle of equality: the principle of equal consideration of interests.

The essence of the principle of equal consideration of interests is that we give equal weight in our moral deliberations to the like interests of all those affected by our actions. This means that if only X and Y would be affected by a possible act, and if X stands to lose more than Y stands to gain, it is better not to do the act. We cannot, if we accept the principle of equal consideration of interests, say that doing the act is better, despite the facts described, because we are more concerned about Y than we are about X. What the principle really amounts to is this: an interest is an interest, whoever's interest it may be.

We can make this more concrete by considering a particular interest, say the interest we have in the relief of pain. Then the principle says that the ultimate moral reason for relieving pain is simply the undesirability of pain as such, and not the undesirability of X's pain, which might be different from the undesirability of Y's pain. Of course, X's pain might be more undesirable than Y's pain because it is more painful, and then the principle of equal consideration would give greater weight to the relief of X's pain. Again, even where the pains are equal, other factors might be relevant, especially if others are affected. If there has been an earthquake we might give priority to the relief of a doctor's pain so she can treat other victims. But the doctor's pain itself counts only once, and with no added weighting. The principle of equal consideration of interests acts like a pair of scales, weighing interests impartially. True scales favour the side where the interest is stronger or where several interests combine to outweigh a smaller number of similar interests; but they take no account of whose interests they are weighing.

From this point of view race is irrelevant to the consideration of interests; for all that counts are the interests themselves. To give less consideration to a specified amount of pain because that pain was experienced by a member of a particular race would be to make an arbitrary distinction. Why pick on race? Why not on whether a person was born in a leap year? Or whether there is more than one vowel in her surname? All these characteristics are equally irrelevant to the undesirability of pain from the universal point of view. Hence the principle of equal consideration of interests shows straightforwardly why the most blatant forms of racism, like that of the Nazis, are wrong. For the Nazis were concerned only for the welfare of members of the 'Aryan' race, and the sufferings of Jews, Gypsies, and Slavs were of no concern to them.

The principle of equal consideration of interests is sometimes thought to be a purely formal principle, lacking in substance and too weak to exclude any inegalitarian practice. We have already seen, however, that it does exclude racism and sexism, at least in their most blatant forms. If we look at the impact of the principle on the imaginary hierarchical society based on intelligence tests we can see that it is strong enough to provide a basis for rejecting this more sophisticated form of inegalitarianism, too.

The principle of equal consideration of interests prohibits making our readiness to consider the interests of others depend on their abilities or other characteristics, apart from the characteristic of having interests. It is true that we cannot know where equal consideration of interests will lead us until we know what interests people have, and this may vary according to their abilities or other characteristics. Consideration of the interests of mathematically gifted children may lead us to teach them advanced mathematics at an early age, which for different children might be entirely pointless or positively harmful. But the basic element, the taking into account of the person's interests, whatever they may be, must apply to everyone, irrespective of race, sex, or scores on an intelligence test. Enslaving those who score below a certain line on an intelligence test would not – barring extraordinary and implausible beliefs about human nature – be compatible with equal consideration. Intelligence has nothing to do with many important interests that humans have, like the interest in avoiding pain, in developing one's abilities, in satisfying basic needs for food and shelter, in enjoying friendly and loving relations with others, and in being free to pursue one's projects without unnecessary interference from others. Slavery prevents the slaves from satisfying these interests as they would want to; and the benefits it confers on the slave-owners are hardly comparable in importance to the harm it does to the slaves.

So the principle of equal consideration of interests is strong enough to rule out an intelligence-based slave society as well as cruder forms of racism and sexism. It also rules out discrimination on the grounds of disability, whether intellectual or physical, in so far as the disability is not relevant to the interests under consideration (as, for example, severe intellectual disability might be if we are considering a person's interest in voting in an election). The principle of equal consideration of interests therefore may be a defensible form of the principle that all humans are equal, a form that we can use in discussing more controversial issues about equality. Before we go on to these topics, however, it will be useful to say a little more about the nature of the principle.

Equal consideration of interests is a minimal principle of equality in the sense that it does not dictate equal treatment. Take a relatively straightforward example of an interest, the interest in having physical pain relieved. Imagine that after an earthquake I come across two victims, one with a crushed leg, in agony, and one with a gashed thigh, in slight pain. I have only two shots of morphine left. Equal treatment would suggest that I give one to each injured person, but one shot would not do much to relieve the pain of the person with the crushed leg. She would still be in much more pain than the other victim, and even after I have given her one shot, giving her the second shot would bring greater relief than giving a shot to the person in slight pain. Hence equal consideration of interests in this situation leads to what some may consider an inegalitarian result: two shots of morphine for one person, and none for the other.

There is a still more controversial inegalitarian implication of the principle of equal consideration of interests. In the case above, although equal consideration of interests leads to unequal treatment, this unequal treatment is an attempt to produce a more egalitarian result. By giving the double dose to the more seriously injured person, we bring about a situation in which there is less difference in the degree of suffering felt by the two victims than there would be if we gave one dose to each. Instead of ending up with one person in considerable pain and one in no pain, we end up with two people in slight pain. This is in line with the principle of declining marginal utility, a principle well-known to economists, which states that for a given individual, a set amount of something is more useful when people have little of it than when they have a lot. If I am struggling to survive on 200 grams of rice a day, and you provide me with an extra fifty grams per day, you have improved my position significantly; but if I already have a kilo of rice per day, I won't care much about the extra fifty grams. When marginal utility is taken into account the principle of equal consideration of interests inclines us towards an equal distribution of income, and to that extent the egalitarian will endorse its conclusions. What is likely to trouble the egalitarian about the principle of equal consideration of interests is that there are circumstances in which the principle of declining marginal utility does not hold or is overridden by countervailing factors.

We can vary the example of the earthquake victims to illustrate this point. Let us say, again, that there are two victims, one more severely injured than the other, but this time we shall say that the more severely injured victim, A, has lost a leg and is in danger of losing a toe from her remaining leg; while the less severely injured victim, B, has an injury to her leg, but the limb can be saved. We have medical supplies for only one person. If we use them on the more severely injured victim the most we can do is save her toe, whereas if we use them on the less severely injured victim we can save her leg. In other words, we assume that the situation is as follows: without medical treatment, A loses a leg and a toe, while B loses only a leg; if we give the treatment to A, A loses a leg and B loses a leg; if we give the treatment to B, A loses a leg and a toe, while B loses nothing.

Assuming that it is worse to lose a leg than it is to lose a toe (even when that toe is on one's sole remaining foot) the principle of declining marginal utility does not suffice to give us the right answer in this situation. We will do more to further the interests, impartially considered, of those affected by our actions if we use our limited resources on the less seriously injured victim than on the more seriously injured one. Therefore this is what the principle of equal consideration of interests leads us to do. Thus equal consideration of interests can, in special cases, widen rather than narrow the gap between two people at different levels of welfare. It is for this reason that the principle is a minimal principle of equality, rather than a thoroughgoing egalitarian principle. A more thoroughgoing form of egalitarianism would, however, be difficult to justify, both in general terms and in its application to special cases of the kind just described.

Minimal as it is, the principle of equal consideration of interests can seem too demanding in some cases. Can any of us really give equal consideration to the welfare of our family and the welfare of strangers? This question will be dealt with in Chapter 9, when we consider our obligations to assist those in need in poorer parts of the world. I shall try to show then that it does not force us to abandon the principle, although the principle may force us to abandon some other views we hold. Meanwhile we shall see how the principle assists us in discussing some of the controversial issues raised by demands for equality.

EQUALITY AND GENETIC DIVERSITY

In 1969 Arthur Jensen published a long article in the *Harvard Educational Review* entitled 'How Much Can We Boost IQ and Scholastic Achievement?' One short section of the article discussed the probable causes of the undisputed fact that – on average – African Americans do not score as well as most other Americans in standard IQ tests. Jensen summarised the upshot of this section as follows:

> All we are left with are various lines of evidence, no one of which is definitive alone, but which, viewed altogether, make it a not unreasonable hypothesis that genetic factors are strongly implicated in the average negro–white intelligence difference. The preponderance of evidence is, in my opinion, less consistent with a strictly environmental hypothesis than with a genetic hypothesis, which, of course, does not exclude the influence of environment or its interaction with genetic factors.

This heavily qualified statement comes in the midst of a detailed review of a complex scientific subject, published in a scholarly journal. It would hardly have been surprising if it passed unnoticed by anyone but scientists working in the area of psychology or genetics. Instead it was widely reported in the popular press as an attempt to defend racism on scientific grounds. Jensen was accused of spreading racist propaganda and likened to Hitler. His lectures were shouted down and students demanded that he be dismissed from his university post. H. J. Eysenck, a British professor of psychology who supported Jensen's theories received similar treatment, in Britain and Australia as well as in the United States. Interestingly, Eysenck's argument did not suggest that those of European descent have the highest average intelligence among Americans; instead, he noted some evidence that Americans of Japanese and Chinese descent do better on tests of abstract reasoning (despite coming from backgrounds lower on the socioeconomic scale) than Americans of European descent.

The opposition to genetic explanations of alleged racial differences in intelligence is only one manifestation of a more general opposition to genetic explanations in other socially sensitive areas. It closely parallels, for instance, initial feminist hostility to the idea that there are biological factors behind male dominance. (The second wave of the feminist movement seems to be more willing to entertain the idea that biological differences between the sexes are influential in, for example, greater male aggression and stronger female caring behaviour.) The opposition to genetic explanations also has obvious links with the intensity of feeling aroused by sociobiological approaches to the study of human behaviour. The worry here is that if human social behaviour is seen as deriving from that of other social mammals, we shall come to think of hierarchy, male dominance, and inequality as part of our evolved nature, and as unchangeable. More recently, the commencement of the international scientific project that is designed to map the human genome – that is, to provide a detailed scientific description of the genetic code typical of human beings – has attracted protests because of apprehension over what such a map might reveal about genetic differences between humans, and the use to which such information might be put.

It would be inappropriate for me to attempt to assess the scientific merits of biological explanations of human behaviour in general, or of racial or sexual differences in particular. My concern is rather with the implications of these theories for the ideal of equality. For this purpose it is not necessary for us to establish whether the theories are right. All we have to ask is: suppose that one ethnic group does turn out to have a higher average IQ than another, and that part of this difference has a genetic basis. Would this mean that racism is defensible, and we have to reject the principle of equality? A similar question can be asked about the impact of theories of biological differences between the sexes. In neither case does the question assume that the theories are sound. It would be most unfortunate if our scepticism about such things led us to neglect these questions and then unexpected evidence turned up confirming the theories, with the result that a confused and unprepared public took the theories to have implications for the ideal of equality that they do not have.

I shall begin by considering the implications of the view that there is a difference in the average IQ of two different ethnic groups, and that genetic factors are responsible for at least a part of this difference. I shall then consider the impact of alleged differences in temperament and ability between the sexes.

Racial Differences and Racial Equality

Let us suppose, just for the sake of exploring the consequences, that evidence accumulates supporting the hypothesis that there are differences in intelligence between the different ethnic groups of human beings. (We should not assume that this would mean that Europeans come out on top. As we have already seen, there is some evidence to the contrary.) What significance would this have for our views about racial equality?

First a word of caution. When people talk of differences in intelligence between ethnic groups, they are usually referring to differences in scores on standard IQ tests. Now 'IQ' stands for 'intelligence quotient' but this does not mean that an IQ test really measures what we mean by 'intelligence' in ordinary contexts. Obviously there is some correlation between the two: if schoolchildren regarded by their teachers as highly intelligent did not generally score better on IQ tests than schoolchildren regarded as below normal intelligence, the tests would have to be changed – as indeed they were changed in the past. But this does not show how close the correlation is, and since our ordinary concept of intelligence is vague, there is no way of telling. Some psychologists have attempted to overcome this difficulty by simply defining 'intelligence' as 'what intelligence tests measure', but this merely introduces a new concept of 'intelligence', which is easier to measure than our ordinary notion but may be quite different in meaning. Since 'intelligence' is a word in everyday use, to use the same word in a different sense is a sure path to confusion. What we should talk about, then, is differences in IQ, rather than differences in intelligence, since this is all that the available evidence could support.

The distinction between intelligence and scores on IQ tests has led some to conclude that IQ is of no importance; this is the opposite, but equally erroneous, extreme to the view that IQ is identical with intelligence. IQ is important in our society. One's IQ is a factor in one's prospects of improving one's occupational status, income, or social class. If there are genetic factors in racial differences in IQ, there will be genetic factors in racial differences in occupational status, income, and social class. So if we are interested in equality, we cannot ignore IQ.

When people of different racial origin are given IQ tests, there tend to be differences in the average scores they get. The existence of such differences is not seriously disputed, even by those who most vigorously opposed the views put forward by Jensen and Eysenck. What is hotly disputed is whether the differences are primarily to be explained by heredity or by environment – in other words, whether they reflect innate differences between different groups of human beings, or whether they are due to the different social and educational situations in which these groups find themselves. Almost everyone accepts that environmental factors do play a role in IQ differences between groups; the debate is over whether they can explain all or virtually all of the differences.

Let us suppose that the genetic hypothesis turns out to be correct (making this supposition, as I have said, not because we believe it is correct but in order to explore its implications); what would be the implications of genetically based differences in IQ between different races? I believe that the implications of this supposition are less drastic than they are often supposed to be and give no comfort to genuine racists. I have three reasons for this view.

First, the genetic hypothesis does not imply that we should reduce our efforts to overcome other causes of inequality between people, for example, in the quality of housing and schooling available to less well-off people. Admittedly, if the genetic hypothesis is correct, these efforts will not bring about a situation in which different racial groups have equal IQs. But this is no reason for accepting a situation in which any people are hindered by their environment from doing as well as they can. Perhaps we should put special efforts into helping those who start from a position of disadvantage, so that we end with a more egalitarian result.

Second, the fact that the average IQ of one racial group is a few points higher than that of another does not allow anyone to say that all members of the higher IQ group have higher IQs than all members of the lower IQ group – this is clearly false for any racial group – or that any particular individual in the higher IQ group has a higher IQ than a particular individual in the lower IQ group – this will often be false. The point is that these figures are averages and say nothing about individuals. There will be a substantial overlap in IQ scores between the two groups. So whatever the cause of the difference in average IQs, it will provide no justification for racial segregation in education or any other field. It remains true that members of different racial groups must be treated as individuals, irrespective of their race.

The third reason why the genetic hypothesis gives no support for racism is the most fundamental of the three. It is simply that, as we saw earlier, the principle of equality is not based on any actual equality that all people share. I have argued that the only defensible basis for the principle of equality is equal consideration of interests, and I have also suggested that the most important human interests – such as the interest in avoiding pain, in developing one's abilities, in satisfying basic needs for food and shelter, in enjoying warm personal relationships, in being free to pursue one's projects without interference, and many others – are not affected by differences in intelligence. We can be even more confident that they are not affected by differences in IQ. Thomas Jefferson, who drafted the ringing assertion of equality with which the American Declaration of Independence begins, knew this. In reply to an author who had endeavoured to refute the then common view that Africans lack intelligence, he wrote:

> Be assured that no person living wishes more sincerely than I do, to see a complete refutation of the doubts I have myself entertained and expressed on the grade of understanding allotted to them by nature, and to find that they are on a par with ourselves . . . but whatever be their degree of talent, it is no measure of their rights. Because Sir Isaac Newton was superior to others in understanding, he was not therefore lord of the property or person of others.

Jefferson was right. Equal status does not depend on intelligence. Racists who maintain the contrary are in peril of being forced to kneel before the next genius they encounter.

These three reasons suffice to show that claims that for genetic reasons one racial group is not as good as another at IQ tests do not provide grounds for denying the moral principle that all humans are equal. The third reason, however, has further ram-

31

ifications that we shall follow up after discussing differences between the sexes.

Sexual Differences and Sexual Equality

The debates over psychological differences between females and males are not about IQ in general. On general IQ tests there are no consistent differences in the average scores of females and males. But IQ tests measure a range of different abilities, and when we break the results down according to the type of ability measured, we do find significant differences between the sexes. There is some evidence suggesting that females have greater verbal ability than males. This involves being better able to understand complex pieces of writing and being more creative with words. Males, on the other hand, appear to have greater mathematical ability, and also do better on tests involving what is known as 'visual-spatial' ability. An example of a task requiring visual-spatial ability is one in which the subject is asked to find a shape, say a square, which is embedded or hidden in a more complex design.

We shall discuss the significance of these relatively minor differences in intellectual abilities shortly. The sexes also differ markedly in one major non-intellectual characteristic: aggression. Studies conducted on children in several different cultures have borne out what parents have long suspected: boys are more likely to play roughly, attack each other and fight back when attacked, than girls. Males are readier to hurt others than females; a tendency reflected in the fact that almost all violent criminals are male. It has been suggested that aggression is associated with competitiveness and the drive to dominate others and get to the top of whatever pyramid one is a part of. In contrast, females are readier to adopt a role that involves caring for others.

These are the major psychological differences that have repeatedly been observed in many studies of females and males.

What is the origin of these differences? Once again the rival explanations are environmental versus biological, nurture versus nature. Although this question of origin is important in some special contexts, it was given too much weight by the first wave of feminists who assumed that the case for women's liberation rested on acceptance of the environmental side of the controversy. What is true of racial discrimination holds here, too: discrimination can be shown to be wrong whatever the origin of the known psychological differences. But first let us look briefly at the rival explanations.

Anyone who has had anything to do with children will know that in all sorts of ways children learn that the sexes have different roles. Boys get trucks or guns for their birthday presents; girls get dolls or brush and comb sets. Girls are put into dresses and told how nice they look; boys are dressed in jeans and praised for their strength and daring. Children's books almost invariably used to portray fathers going out to work while mothers clean the house and cook the dinner; some still do, although in many countries feminist criticisms of this type of literature have had some impact.

Social conditioning exists, certainly, but does it explain the differences between the sexes? It is, at best, an incomplete explanation. We still need to know *why* our society – and not just ours, but practically every human society – should shape children in this way. One popular answer is that in earlier, simpler societies, the sexes had different roles because women had to breast-feed their children during the long period before weaning. This meant that the women stayed closer to home while the men went out to hunt. As a result females evolved a more social and emotional character, while males became tougher and more aggressive. Because physical strength and aggression were the ultimate forms of power in these simple societies, males became dominant. The sex roles that exist today are, on this view, an inheritance from these simpler circumstances, an inheritance that became obsolete once technology made it possible for the weakest person to operate a crane that lifts fifty tons, or fire a missile that kills millions. Nor do women have to be tied to home and children in the way they used to be, since a woman can now combine motherhood and a career.

The alternative view is that while social conditioning plays some role in determining psychological differences between the sexes, biological factors are also at work. The evidence for this view is particularly strong in respect of aggression. In *The Psychology of Sex Differences*, Eleanor Emmons Maccoby and Carol Nagy Jacklin give four grounds for their belief that the greater aggression of males has a biological component:

1 Males are more aggressive than females in all human societies in which the difference has been studied.
2 Similar differences are found in humans and in apes and other closely related animals.
3 The differences are found in very young children, at an age when there is no evidence of any social conditioning in this direction (indeed Maccoby and Jacklin found some evidence that boys are more severely punished for showing aggression than girls).
4 Aggression has been shown to vary according to the level of sex hormones, and females become more aggressive if they receive male hormones.

The evidence for a biological basis of the differences in visual-spatial ability is a little more complicated, but it consists largely of genetic studies that suggest that this ability is influenced by a recessive sex-linked gene. As a result, it is estimated, approximately 50 per cent of males have a genetic advantage in situations demanding visual-spatial ability, but only 25 per cent of females have this advantage.

Evidence for and against a biological factor in the superior verbal ability of females and the superior mathematical ability of males is, at present, too weak to suggest a conclusion one way or the other.

Adopting the strategy we used before in discussing race and IQ, I shall not go further into the evidence for and against these biological explanations of differences between males and females. Instead I shall ask what the implications of the biological hypotheses would be.

The differences in the intellectual strengths and weaknesses of the sexes cannot explain more than a minute proportion of the difference in positions that males and females hold in our society. It might explain why, for example, there should be more males than females in professions like architecture and engineering, professions that may require visual-spatial ability; but even in these professions, the magnitude of the differences in numbers cannot be explained by the genetic theory of visual-spatial ability. This theory suggests that half as many females are as genetically advantaged in this area as males, which would account for the lower average scores of females in tests of visual-spatial ability, but cannot account for the fact that in most countries there are not merely twice as many males as females in architecture and engineering, but at least ten times as many. Moreover, if superior visual-spatial ability explains the male dominance of architecture and engineering, why isn't there a corresponding female advantage in professions requiring high verbal ability? It is true that there are more women journalists than engineers, and probably more women have achieved lasting fame as novelists than in any other area of life; yet female journalists and television commentators continue to be outnumbered by males, outside specifically 'women's subjects' such as cookery and child care. So even if one accepts biological explanations for the patterning of these abilities, one can still argue that women do not have the same opportunities as men to make the most of the abilities they have.

What of differences in aggression? One's first reaction might be that feminists should be delighted with the evidence on this point – what better way could there be of showing the superiority of females than by demonstrating their greater reluctance to hurt others? But the fact that most violent criminals are male may be only one side of greater male aggression. The other side could be greater male competitiveness, ambition, and drive to achieve power. This would have different, and for feminists less welcome, implications. Some years ago an American sociologist, Steven Goldberg, built a provocatively entitled book, *The Inevitability of Patriarchy*, around the thesis that the biological basis of greater male aggression will always make it impossible to bring about a society in which women have as much political power as men. From this claim it is easy to move to the view that women should accept their inferior position in society and not strive to compete with males, or to bring up their daughters to compete with males in these respects; instead women should return to their traditional sphere of looking after the home and children. This is just the kind of argument that has aroused the hostility of some feminists to biological explanations of male dominance.

As in the case of race and IQ, the moral conclusions alleged to follow from the biological theories do not really follow from them at all. Similar arguments apply.

First, whatever the origin of psychological differences between the sexes, social conditioning can emphasise or soften these differences. As Maccoby and Jacklin stress, the biological bias towards, say, male visual-spatial superiority is really a greater natural readiness to learn these skills. Where women are brought up to be independent, their visual-spatial ability is much higher than when they are kept at home and dependent on males. This is no doubt true of other differences as well. Hence feminists may well be right to attack the way in which we encourage girls and boys to develop in distinct directions, even if this encouragement is not itself responsible for creating psychological differences between the sexes, but only reinforces innate predispositions.

Second, whatever the origin of psychological differences between the sexes, they exist only when averages are taken, and some females are more aggressive and have better visual-spatial ability than some males. We have seen that the genetic hypothesis offered in explanation of male visual-spatial superiority itself suggests that a quarter of all females will have greater natural visual-spatial ability than half of all males. Our own observations should convince us that there are females who are also more aggressive than some males. So, biological explanations or not, we are never in a position to say: 'You're a woman, so you can't become an engineer', or 'Because you are female, you will not have the drive and ambition needed to succeed in politics.' Nor should we assume that no male can possibly have sufficient gentleness and warmth to stay at home with the children while their mother goes out to work. We must assess people as individuals, not merely lump them into 'female' and 'male' if we are to find out what they are really like; and we must keep the roles occupied by females and males flexible if people are to be able to do what they are best suited for.

The third reason is, like the previous two, parallel to the reasons I have given for believing that a biological explanation of racial differences in IQ would not justify racism. The most important human interests are no more affected by differences in aggression than they are by differences in intelligence. Less aggressive people have the same interest in avoiding pain, developing their abilities, having adequate food and shelter, enjoying good personal relationships, and so on, as more aggressive people. There is no reason why more aggressive people ought to be rewarded for their aggression with higher salaries and the ability to provide better for these interests.

Since aggression, unlike intelligence, is not generally regarded as a desirable trait, the male chauvinist is hardly likely to deny that greater aggression in itself provides no ethical justification of male supremacy. He may, however, offer it as an explanation, rather than a justification, of the fact that males hold most of the leading positions in politics, business, the universities and other areas in which people of both sexes compete for power and status. He may then go on to suggest that this shows that the present situation is merely the result of competition between males and females under conditions of equal opportunity. Hence, it is not, he may say, unfair. This suggestion raises the further ramifications of biological differences between people that, as I said at the close of our discussion of the race and IQ issue, need to be followed up in more depth.

FROM EQUALITY OF OPPORTUNITY TO EQUALITY OF CONSIDERATION

In most Western societies large differences in income and social status are commonly thought to be all right, as long as they were brought into being under conditions of equal opportunity. The idea is that there is no injustice in Jill earning $200,000 and Jack earning $20,000, as long as Jack had his chance to be where Jill is today. Suppose that the difference in income is due to the fact that Jill is a doctor whereas Jack is a farm worker. This would be acceptable if Jack had the same opportunity as Jill to be a doctor, and this is taken to mean that Jack was not kept out of medical school because of his race, or religion, or a disability that was irrelevant to his ability to be a doctor, or something similar – in effect, if Jack's school results had been as good as Jill's, he would have been able to study medicine, become a doctor, and earn $200,000 a year. Life, on this view, is a kind of race in which it is fitting that the winners should get the prizes, as long as all get an equal start. The equal start represents equality of opportunity and this, some say, is as far as equality should go.

To say that Jack and Jill had equal opportunities to become a doctor, because Jack would have got into medical school if his results had been as good as Jill's, is to take a superficial view of equal opportunity that will not stand up to further probing. We need to ask why Jack's results were not as good as Jill's. Perhaps his education up to that point had been inferior – bigger classes, less qualified teachers, inadequate resources, and so on. If so, he was not competing on equal terms with Jill after all.

Genuine equality of opportunity requires us to ensure that schools give the same advantages to everyone.

Making schools equal would be difficult enough, but it is the easiest of the tasks that await a thoroughgoing proponent of equal opportunity. Even if schools are the same, some children will be favoured by the kind of home they come from. A quiet room to study, plenty of books, and parents who encourage their child to do well at school could explain why Jill succeeds where Jack, forced to share a room with two younger brothers and put up with his father's complaints that he is wasting his time with books instead of getting out and earning his keep, does not. But how does one equalise a home? Or parents? Unless we are prepared to abandon the traditional family setting and bring up our children in communal nurseries, we can't.

This might be enough to show the inadequacy of equal opportunity as an ideal of equality, but the ultimate objection – the one that connects with our previous discussion of equality – is still to come. Even if we did rear our children communally, as on a kibbutz in Israel, they would inherit different abilities and character traits, including different levels of aggression and different IQs. Eliminating differences in the child's environment would not affect differences in genetic endowment. True, it might reduce the disparity between, say, IQ scores, since it is likely that, at present, social differences accentuate genetic differences; but the genetic differences would remain and on most estimates they are a major component of the existing differences in IQ. (Remember that we are now talking of *individuals*. We do not know if race affects IQ, but there is little doubt that differences in IQ between individuals of the same race are, in part, genetically determined.)

So equality of opportunity is not an attractive ideal. It rewards the lucky, who inherit those abilities that allow them to pursue interesting and lucrative careers. It penalises the unlucky, whose genes make it very hard for them to achieve similar success.

We can now fit our earlier discussion of race and sex differences into a broader picture. Whatever the facts about the social or genetic basis of racial differences in IQ, removing social disadvantages will not suffice to bring about an equal or a just distribution of income – not an equal distribution, because those who inherit the abilities associated with high IQ will continue to earn more than those who do not; and not a just distribution because distribution according to the abilities one inherits is based on an arbitrary form of selection that has nothing to do with what people deserve or need. The same is true of visual-spatial ability and aggression, if these do lead to higher incomes or status. If, as I have argued, the basis of equality is equal consideration of interests, and the most important human interests have little or nothing to do with these factors, there is something questionable about a society in which income and social status correlate to a significant degree with them.

When we pay people high salaries for programming computers and low salaries for cleaning offices, we are, in effect, paying people for having a high IQ, and this means that we are paying people for something determined in part before they are born and almost wholly determined before they reach an age at which they are responsible for their actions. From the point of view of justice and utility there is something wrong here. Both would be better served by a society that adopted the famous Marxist slogan: 'From each according to his ability, to each according to his needs.' If this could be achieved, the differences between the races and sexes would lose their social significance. Only then would we have a society truly based on the principle of equal consideration of interests.

Is it realistic to aim at a society that rewards people according to their needs rather than their IQ, aggression, or other inherited abilities? Don't we have to pay people more to be doctors or lawyers or university professors, to do the intellectually demanding work that is essential for our well-being?

There are difficulties in paying people according to their needs rather than their inherited abilities. If one country attempts to introduce such a scheme while others do not, the result is likely to be some kind of 'brain drain'. We have already seen this, on a small scale, in the number of scientists and doctors who have left Britain to work in the United States – not because Britain does pay people according to need rather than inherited abilities, but because these sections of the community, though relatively well-paid by British standards, were much better paid in the United States. If any one country were to make a serious attempt to equalise the salaries of doctors and manual workers, there can be no doubt that the number of doctors emigrating would greatly increase. This is part of the problem of 'socialism in one country'. Marx expected the socialist revolution to be a world-wide one. When the Russian Marxists found that their revolution had not sparked off the anticipated world revolution, they had to adapt Marxist ideas to this new situation. They did so by harshly restricting freedom, including the freedom to emigrate. Without these restrictions, during the communist period in the Soviet Union and other communist states, and despite the considerable pay differentials that still did exist in those nations when under communist rule, and that continue to exist in the remaining communist countries, there would have been a crippling outflow of skilled people to the capitalist nations, which rewarded skill more highly.[1] But if 'socialism in one country' requires making the country an armed camp, with border guards keeping watch on the citizens within as well as the enemy without, socialism may not be worth the price.

To allow these difficulties to lead us to the conclusion that we can do nothing to improve the distribution of income that now exists in capitalist countries would, however, be too pessimistic. There is, in the more affluent Western nations, a good

---

1 According to one observer, salary differentials in China are quite steep, in some areas steeper than in Western nations. For instance, a full professor gets almost seven times as much as a junior lecturer, whereas in Britain, Australia, or the United States, the ratio is more like three to one. See Simon Leys, *Chinese Shadows* (New York, 1977).

deal of scope for reducing pay differentials before the point is reached at which significant numbers of people begin to think of emigrating. This is, of course, especially true of those countries, like the United States, where pay differentials are presently very great. It is here that pressure for a more equitable distribution can best be applied.

What of the problems of redistribution within a single nation? There is a popular belief that if we did not pay people a lot of money to be doctors or university professors, they would not undertake the studies required to achieve these positions. I do not know what evidence there is in support of this assumption, but it seems to me highly dubious. My own salary is considerably higher than the salaries of the people employed by the university to mow the lawns and keep the grounds clean, but if our salaries were identical I would still not want to swap positions with them – although their jobs are a lot more pleasant than some lowly paid work. Nor do I believe that my doctor would jump at a chance to change places with his receptionist if their salaries did not differ. It is true that my doctor and I have had to study for several years to get where we are, but I at least look back on my student years as one of the most enjoyable periods of my life.

Although I do not think it is because of the money that people choose to become doctors rather than receptionists, there is one qualification to be made to the suggestion that payment should be based on need rather than ability. It must be admitted that the prospect of earning more money sometimes leads people to make greater efforts to use the abilities they have, and these greater efforts can benefit patients, customers, students, or the public as a whole. It might therefore be worth trying to reward *effort*, which would mean paying people more if they worked near the upper limits of their abilities, whatever those abilities might be. This, however, is quite different from paying people for the level of ability they happen to have, which is something they cannot themselves control. As Jeffrey Gray, a British professor of psychology, has written, the evidence for genetic control of IQ suggests that to pay people differently for 'upper-class' and 'lower-class' jobs is 'a wasteful use of resources in the guise of "incentives" that either tempt people to do what is beyond their powers or reward them more for what they would do anyway'.

We have, up to now, been thinking of people such as university professors, who (at least in some countries) are paid by the government, and doctors, whose incomes are determined either by government bodies, where there is some kind of national health service, or by the government protection given to professional associations like a medical association, which enables the profession to exclude those who might seek to advertise their services at a lower cost. These incomes are therefore already subject to government control and could be altered without drastically changing the powers of government. The private business sector of the economy is a different matter. Business people who are quick to seize an opportunity will, under any private enterprise system, make more money than their rivals or, if they are employed by a large corporation, may be promoted faster. Taxation can help to redistribute some of this income, but there are limits to how effective a steeply progressive tax system can be – there almost seems to be a law to the effect that the higher the rate of tax, the greater the amount of tax avoidance.

So do we have to abolish private enterprise if we are to eliminate undeserved wealth? That suggestion raises issues too large to be discussed here; but it can be said that private enterprise has a habit of reasserting itself under the most inhospitable conditions. As the Russians and East Europeans soon found, communist societies still had their black markets, and if you wanted your plumbing fixed swiftly it was advisable to pay a bit extra on the side. Only a radical change in human nature – a decline in acquisitive and self-centred desires – could overcome the tendency for people to find a way around any system that suppresses private enterprise. Since no such change in human nature is in sight, we shall probably continue to pay most to those with inherited abilities, rather than those who have the greatest needs. To hope for something entirely different is unrealistic. To work for wider recognition of the principle of payment according to needs and effort rather than inherited ability is both realistic and, I believe, right.

AFFIRMATIVE ACTION

The preceding section suggested that moving to a more egalitarian society in which differences of income are reduced is ethically desirable but likely to prove difficult. Short of bringing about general equality, we might at least attempt to ensure that where there are important differences in income, status, and power, women and racial minorities should not be on the worse end in numbers disproportionate to their numbers in the community as a whole. Inequalities among members of the same ethnic group may be no more justifiable than those between ethnic groups, or between males and females, but when these inequalities coincide with an obvious difference between people like the differences between African Americans and Americans of European descent, or between males and females, they do more to produce a divided society with a sense of superiority on the one side and a sense of inferiority on the other. Racial and sexual inequality may therefore have a more divisive effect than other forms of inequality. It may also do more to create a feeling of hopelessness among the inferior group, since their sex or their race is not the product of their own actions and there is nothing they can do to change it.

How are racial and sexual equality to be achieved within an inegalitarian society? We have seen that equality of opportunity is practically unrealisable, and if it could be realised might allow innate differences in aggression or IQ unfairly to determine membership of the upper strata. One way of overcoming these obstacles is to go beyond equality of opportunity and give preferential treatment to members of disadvantaged groups. This is affirmative action (sometimes also called 'reverse discrimination'). It may be the best hope of reducing long-standing inequalities; yet it appears to offend against the principle of equality itself. Hence it is controversial.

Affirmative action is most often used in education and employment. Education is a particularly important area, since it has an important influence on one's prospects of earning a high income, holding a satisfying job, and achieving power and status in the community. Moreover in the United States education has been at the centre of the dispute over affirmative action because of Supreme Court cases over university admission procedures favouring disadvantaged groups. These cases have arisen because males of European descent were denied admission to courses although their academic records and admission test scores were better than those of some African American students admitted. The universities did not deny this; they sought to justify it by explaining that they operated admission schemes intended to help disadvantaged students.

The leading case, as far as United States law is concerned, is *Regents of the University of California* v. *Bakke*. Alan Bakke applied for admission to the medical school of the University of California at Davis. In an attempt to increase the number of members of minority groups who attended medical school, the university reserved 16 out of every 100 places for students belonging to a disadvantaged minority. Since these students would not have won so many places in open competition, fewer students of European descent were admitted than there would have been without this reservation. Some of these students denied places would certainly have been offered them if, scoring as they did on the admission tests, they had been members of a disadvantaged minority. Bakke was among these rejected European

American students and on being rejected he sued the university. Let us take this case as a standard case of affirmative action. Is it defensible?

I shall start by putting aside one argument sometimes used to justify discrimination in favour of members of disadvantaged groups. It is sometimes said that if, say, 20 per cent of the population is a racial minority, and yet only 2 per cent of doctors are from this minority, this is sufficient evidence that, somewhere along the line, our community discriminates on the basis of race. (Similar arguments have been mounted in support of claims of sexual discrimination.) Our discussion of the genetics-versus-environment debate indicates why this argument is inconclusive. It *may* be the case that members of the under-represented group are, *on average*, less gifted for the kind of study one must do to become a doctor. I am not saying that this is true, or even probable, but it cannot be ruled out at this stage. So a disproportionately small number of doctors from a particular ethnic minority is not in itself proof of discrimination against members of that minority. (Just as the disproportionately large number of African American athletes in the U.S. Olympic athletic team is not in itself proof of discrimination against European Americans.) There might, of course, be other evidence suggesting that the small number of doctors from the minority group really is the result of discrimination; but this would need to be shown. In the absence of positive evidence of discrimination, it is not possible to justify affirmative action on the grounds that it merely redresses the balance of discrimination existing in the community.

Another way of defending a decision to accept a minority student in preference to a student from the majority group who scored higher in admission tests would be to argue that standard tests do not give an accurate indication of ability when one student has been severely disadvantaged. This is in line with the point made in the last section about the impossibility of achieving equal opportunity. Education and home background presumably influence test scores. A student with a background of deprivation who scores 55 per cent in an admission test may have better prospects of graduating in minimum time than a more privileged student who scores 70 per cent. Adjusting test scores on this basis would not mean admitting disadvantaged minority students in preference to better-qualified students. It would reflect a decision that the disadvantaged students really were better qualified than the others. This is not racial discrimination.

The University of California could not attempt this defence, for its medical school at Davis had simply reserved 16 per cent of places for minority students. The quota did not vary according to the ability displayed by minority applicants. This may be in the interests of ultimate equality, but it is undeniably racial discrimination.

In this chapter we have seen that the only defensible basis for the claim that all humans are equal is the principle of equal consideration of interests. That principle outlaws forms of racial and sexual discrimination which give less weight to the interests of those discriminated against. Could Bakke claim that in rejecting his application the medical school gave less weight to his interests than to those of African American students?

We have only to ask this question to appreciate that university admission is not normally a result of consideration of the interests of each applicant. It depends rather on matching the applicants against standards that the university draws up with certain policies in mind. Take the most straightforward case: admission rigidly governed by scores on an intelligence test. Suppose those rejected by this procedure complained that their interests had been given less consideration than the interests of applicants of higher intelligence. The university would reply that its procedure did not take the applicants' interests into account at all, and so could hardly give less consideration to the interests of one applicant than it gave to others. We could then ask the university why it used intelligence as the criterion of admission.

It might say, first, that to pass the examinations required for graduation takes a high level of intelligence. There is no point in admitting students unable to pass, for they will not be able to graduate. They will waste their own time and the university's resources. Secondly, the university may say, the higher the intelligence of our graduates, the more useful they are likely to be to the community. The more intelligent our doctors, the better they will be at preventing and curing disease. Hence the more intelligent the students a medical school selects, the better value the community gets for its outlay on medical education.

This particular admission procedure is of course one-sided; a good doctor must have other qualities in addition to a high degree of intelligence. It is only an example, however, and that objection is not relevant to the point I am using the example to make. This point is that no one objects to intelligence as a criterion for selection in the way that they object to race as a criterion; yet those of higher intelligence admitted under an intelligence-based scheme have no more of an intrinsic right to admission than those admitted by reverse discrimination. Higher intelligence, I have argued before, carries with it no right or justifiable claim to more of the good things our society offers. If a university admits students of higher intelligence it does so not in consideration of their greater interest in being admitted, nor in recognition of their right to be admitted, but because it favours goals that it believes will be advanced by this admission procedure. So if this same university should adopt new goals and use affirmative action to promote them, applicants who would have been admitted under the old procedure cannot claim that the new procedure violates their right to be admitted, or treats them with less respect than others. They had no special claim to be admitted in the first place; they were the fortunate beneficiaries of the old university policy. Now that this policy has changed others benefit, not they. If this seems unfair, it is only because we had become accustomed to the old policy.

So affirmative action cannot justifiably be condemned on the grounds that it violates the rights of university applicants, or treats them with less than equal consideration. There is no inherent right to admission, and equal consideration of the interests of applicants is not involved in normal admission tests. If affirmative action is open to objection it must be because the goals it seeks to advance are bad, or because it will not really promote these goals.

The principle of equality might be a ground for condemning the goals of a racially discriminatory admissions procedure. When universities discriminate against already disadvantaged minorities we suspect that the discrimination really does result from less concern for the interests of the minority. Why else did universities in the American South excluded African Americans until segregation was held to be unconstitutional? Here, in contrast to the affirmative action situation, those rejected could justifiably claim that their interests were not being weighed equally with the interests of European Americans who were admitted. Other explanations may have been offered, but they were surely specious.

Opponents of affirmative action have not objected to the goals of social equality and greater minority representation in the professions. They would be hard put to do so. Equal consideration of interests supports moves towards equality because of the principle of diminishing marginal utility, because it relieves the feeling of hopeless inferiority that can exist when members of one race or sex are always worse off than members of another race or the other sex, and because severe inequality between races means a divided community with consequent racial tension.

Within the overall goal of social equality, greater minority representation in professions like law and medicine is desirable for several reasons. Members of minority groups are more likely to work among their own people than those who come from the mainstream ethnic groups, and this may help to overcome the scarcity of doctors and lawyers in poor neighbourhoods where most members of disadvantaged minorities live. They may also have a better understanding of the problems disadvantaged people face than any outsider would have. Minority and female doctors and lawyers can serve as role models to other members of minority groups, and to women, breaking down the unconscious mental barriers against aspiring to such positions. Finally, the existence of a diverse student group will help members of the dominant ethnic group to learn more about the attitudes of African Americans and women, and thus become better able, as doctors and lawyers, to serve the whole community.

Opponents of affirmative action are on stronger ground when they claim that affirmative action will not promote equality. As Justice Lewis F. Powell, Jr., said, in the *Bakke* case, 'Preferential programs may only reinforce common stereotypes holding that certain groups are unable to achieve success without special protection.' To achieve real equality, it might be said, members of minority groups and women must win their places on their merits. As long as they get into law school more easily than others, law graduates from disadvantaged minority groups – including those who would have got in under open competition – will be regarded as inferior.

There is also a long-term objection to affirmative action as a means to equality. In the present social climate we may be confident that race will be taken into account only to benefit disadvantaged minorities; but will this climate last? Should old -fashioned racism return, won't our approval of racial quotas now make it easier to turn them against minority groups? Can we really expect the introduction of racial distinctions to advance the goal of the elimination of racial distinctions?

These practical objections raise difficult factual issues. Though they were referred to in the *Bakke* case, they have not been central in the American legal battles over affirmative action. Judges are properly reluctant to decide cases on factual grounds on which they have no special expertise. Alan Bakke won his case chiefly on the grounds that the U.S. Civil Rights Act of 1964 provides that no person shall, on the grounds of colour, race, or national origin, be excluded from any activity receiving federal financial assistance. A bare majority of the judges held that this excluded all discrimination, benign or not. They added, however, that there would be no objection to a university including race as one among a number of factors, like athletic or artistic ability, work experience, demonstrated compassion, a history of overcoming disadvantage, or leadership potential. The court thus effectively allowed universities to choose their student body in accord with their own goals, as long as they did not use quotas.

That may be the law in the United States, but in other countries – and in general, when we look at the issue with an eye to ethics, rather than the law – the distinction between quotas and other ways of giving preference to disadvantaged groups may be less significant. The important point is that affirmative action, whether by quotas or some other method, is not contrary to any sound principle of equality and does not violate any rights of those excluded by it. Properly applied, it is in keeping with equal consideration of interests, in its aspirations at least. The only real doubt is whether it will work. In the absence of more promising alternatives it seems worth a try.

A CONCLUDING NOTE: EQUALITY AND DISABILITY

In this chapter we have been concerned with the interplay of the moral principle of equality and the differences, real or alleged, between groups of people. Perhaps the clearest way of seeing the irrelevance of IQ, or specific abilities, to the moral principle of equality, is to consider the situation of people with disabilities, whether physical or intellectual. When we consider how such people are to be treated, there is no argument about whether they are as able as people without disabilities. By definition, they are lacking at least some ability that normal people have. These disabilities will sometimes mean that they should be treated differently from others. When we are looking for fire-fighters, we can justifiably exclude someone who is confined to a wheelchair; and if we are seeking a proof-reader, a blind person need not apply. But the fact that a specific disability may rule a person out of consideration for a particular position does not mean that that person's interests should be given less consideration than those of anyone else. Nor does it justify discrimination against disabled people in any situation in which the particular disability a person has is not relevant to the employment or service offered.

For centuries, disabled people have been subjected to prejudice, in some cases no less severe than those under which racial minorities have suffered. Intellectually disabled people were locked up, out of sight of the public, in appalling conditions. Some were virtual slaves, exploited for cheap labour in households or factories. Under a so-called "euthanasia program" the Nazis murdered tens of thousands of intellectually disabled people who were quite capable of wanting to continue living and enjoying their lives. Even today, some businesses will not hire a person in a wheelchair for a job that she could do as well as anyone else. Others seeking a salesperson will not hire someone whose appearance is abnormal, for fear that sales will fall. (Similar arguments were used against employing members of racial minorities; we can best overcome such prejudices by becoming used to people who are different from us.)

We are now just starting to think about the injustice that has been done to disabled people, and to consider them as a disadvantaged group. That we have been slow in doing so may well be due to the confusion between factual equality and moral equality discussed earlier in this chapter. Because disabled people are different, in some respects, we have not seen it as discriminatory to treat them differently. We have overlooked the fact that, as in the examples given above, the disabled person's disability has been irrelevant to the different – and disadvantageous – treatment. There is therefore a need to ensure that legislation that prohibits discrimination on grounds of race, ethnicity or gender also prohibits discrimination on the grounds of disability, unless the disability can be shown to be relevant to the employment or service offered.

Nor is that all. Many of the arguments for affirmative action in the case of those disadvantaged by race or gender apply even more strongly to disabled people. Mere equality of opportunity will not be enough in situations in which a disability makes it impossible to become an equal member of the community. Giving disabled people equal opportunity to attend university is not much use if the library is accessible only by a flight of stairs that they cannot use. Many disabled children are capable of benefitting from normal schooling, but are prevented from taking part because additional resources are required to cope with their special needs. Since such needs are often very central to the lives of disabled people, the principle of equal consideration of interests will give them much greater weight than more minor needs of others. For this reason, it will generally be justifiable to spend more on behalf of disabled people than we spend on behalf of others. Just how much more is, of course, a difficult question. Where resources are scarce, there must be some limit. By giving equal consideration to the interests of those with disabilities, and empathetically imagining ourselves in their situation, we can, in principle, reach the right answer; but it will not be easy to determine what exactly, in each particular situation, that answer should be.

Some will claim to find a contradiction between this recognition of disabled people as a group that has been subjected to unjustifiable discrimination, and arguments that appear later in this book defending abortion and infanticide in the case of a fetus or an infant with a severe disability. For these later arguments presuppose that life is better without a disability than with one; and is this not itself a form of prejudice, held by people without disabilities, and parallel to the prejudice that it is better to be a member of the European race, or a man, than to be of African descent, or a woman?

The error in this argument is not difficult to detect. It is one thing to argue that people with disabilities who want to live their lives to the full should be given every possible assistance in doing so. It is another, and quite different thing, to argue that if we are in a position to choose, for our next child, whether that child shall begin life with or without a disability, it is mere prejudice or bias that leads us to choose to have a child without a disability. If disabled people who must use wheelchairs to get around were suddenly offered a miracle drug that would, with no side effects, give them full use of their legs, how many of them would refuse to take it on the grounds that life with a disability is in no way inferior to life without a disability? In seeking medical assistance to overcome and eliminate disability, when it is available, disabled people themselves show that the preference for a life without disability is no mere prejudice. Some disabled people might say that they make this choice only because society puts so many obstacles in the way of disabled people. They claim that it is social conditions that disable them, not their physical or intellectual condition. This assertions twists the more limited truth, that social conditions make the lives of the disabled much more difficult than they need be, into a sweeping falsehood. To be able to walk, to see, to hear, to be relatively free from pain and discomfort, to communicate effectively – all these are, under virtually any social conditions, genuine benefits. To say this is not to deny that people lacking these abilities may triumph over their disabilities and have lives of astonishing richness and diversity. Nevertheless, we show no prejudice against disabled people if we prefer, whether for ourselves or for our children, not to be faced with hurdles so great that to surmount them is in itself a triumph.

3

EQUALITY FOR ANIMALS?

IN Chapter 2, I gave reasons for believing that the fundamental principle of equality, on which the equality of all human beings rests, is the principle of equal consideration of interests. Only a basic moral principle of this kind can allow us to defend a form of equality that embraces all human beings, with all the differences that exist between them. I shall now contend that while this principle does provide an adequate basis for human equality, it provides a basis that cannot be limited to humans. In other words I shall suggest that, having accepted the principle of equality as a sound moral basis for relations with others of our own species, we are also committed to accepting it as a sound moral basis for relations with those outside our own species – the non-human animals.

This suggestion may at first seem bizarre. We are used to regarding discrimination against members of racial minorities, or against women, as among the most important moral and political issues facing the world today. These are serious matters, worthy of the time and energy of any concerned person. But animals? Isn't the welfare of animals in a different category altogether, a matter for people who are dotty about dogs and cats? How can anyone waste their time on equality for animals when so many humans are denied real equality?

This attitude reflects a popular prejudice against taking the interests of animals seriously – a prejudice no better founded than the prejudice of white slaveowners against taking the interests of their African slaves seriously. It is easy for us to criticise the prejudices of our grandfathers, from which our fathers freed themselves. It is more difficult to distance ourselves from our own views, so that we can dispassionately search for prejudices among the beliefs and values we hold. What is needed now is a willingness to follow the arguments where they lead, without a prior assumption that the issue is not worth our attention.

The argument for extending the principle of equality beyond our own species is simple, so simple that it amounts to no more than a clear understanding of the nature of the principle of equal consideration of interests. We have seen that this principle implies that our concern for others ought not to depend on what they are like, or what abilities they possess (although precisely what this concern requires us to do may vary according to the characteristics of those affected by what we do). It is on this basis that we are able to say that the fact that some people are not members of our race does not entitle us to exploit them, and similarly the fact that some people are less intelligent than others does not mean that their interests may be disregarded. But the principle also implies that the fact that beings are not members of our species does not entitle us to exploit them, and similarly the fact that other animals are less intelligent than we are does not mean that their interests may be disregarded.

We saw in Chapter 2 that many philosophers have advocated equal consideration of interests, in some form or other, as a basic moral principle. Only a few have recognised that the principle has applications beyond our own species, one of the few being Jeremy Bentham, the founding father of modern utilitarianism. In a forward-looking passage, written at a time when African slaves in the British dominions were still being treated much as we now treat nonhuman animals, Bentham wrote:

> The day may come when the rest of the animal creation may acquire those rights which never could have been withholden from them but by the hand of tyranny. The French have already discovered that the blackness of the skin is no reason why a

human being should be abandoned without redress to the caprice of a tormentor. It may one day come to be recognised that the number of the legs, the villosity of the skin, or the termination of the *os sacrum*, are reasons equally insufficient for abandoning a sensitive being to the same fate. What else is it that should trace the insuperable line? Is it the faculty of reason, or perhaps the faculty of discourse? But a fullgrown horse or dog is beyond comparison a more rational, as well as a more conversable animal, than an infant of a day, or a week, or even a month, old. But suppose they were otherwise, what would it avail? The question is not, Can they *reason*? nor Can they *talk*? but, *Can they suffer?*

In this passage Bentham points to the capacity for suffering as the vital characteristic that entitles a being to equal consideration. The capacity for suffering – or more strictly, for suffering and/or enjoyment or happiness – is not just another characteristic like the capacity for language, or for higher mathematics. Bentham is not saying that those who try to mark 'the insuperable line' that determines whether the interests of a being should be considered happen to have selected the wrong characteristic. The capacity for suffering and enjoying things is a prerequisite for having interests at all, a condition that must be satisfied before we can speak of interests in any meaningful way. It would be nonsense to say that it was not in the interests of a stone to be kicked along the road by a schoolboy. A stone does not have interests because it cannot suffer. Nothing that we can do to it could possibly make any difference to its welfare. A mouse, on the other hand, does have an interest in not being tormented, because mice will suffer if they are treated in this way.

If a being suffers, there can be no moral justification for refusing to take that suffering into consideration. No matter what the nature of the being, the principle of equality requires that the suffering be counted equally with the like suffering – in so far as rough comparisons can be made – of any other being. If a being is not capable of suffering, or of experiencing enjoyment or happiness, there is nothing to be taken into account. This is why the limit of sentience (using the term as a convenient, if not strictly accurate, shorthand for the capacity to suffer or experience enjoyment or happiness) is the only defensible boundary of concern for the interests of others. To mark this boundary by some characteristic like intelligence or rationality would be to mark it in an arbitrary way. Why not choose some other characteristic, like skin colour?

Racists violate the principle of equality by giving greater weight to the interests of members of their own race when there is a clash between their interests and the interests of those of another race. Racists of European descent typically have not accepted that pain matters as much when it is felt by Africans, for example, as when it is felt by Europeans. Similarly those I would call 'speciesists' give greater weight to the interests of members of their own species when there is a clash between their interests and the interests of those of other species. Human speciesists do not accept that pain is as bad when it is felt by pigs or mice as when it is felt by humans.

That, then, is really the whole of the argument for extending the principle of equality to nonhuman animals; but there may be some doubts about what this equality amounts to in practice. In particular, the last sentence of the previous paragraph may prompt some people to reply: 'Surely pain felt by a mouse just is not as bad as pain felt by a human. Humans have much greater awareness of what is happening to them, and this makes their suffering worse. You can't equate the suffering of, say, a person dying slowly from cancer, and a laboratory mouse undergoing the same fate.'

I fully accept that in the case described the human cancer victim normally suffers more than the nonhuman cancer victim. This in no way undermines the extension of equal consideration of interests to nonhumans. It means, rather, that we must take care when we compare the interests of different species. In some situations a member of one species will suffer more than a member of another species. In this case we should still apply the principle of equal consideration of interests but the result of so doing is, of course, to give priority to relieving the greater suffering. A simpler case may help to make this clear.

If I give a horse a hard slap across its rump with my open hand, the horse may start, but it presumably feels little pain. Its skin is thick enough to protect it against a mere slap. If I slap a baby in the same way, however, the baby will cry and presumably does feel pain, for the baby's skin is more sensitive. So it is worse to slap a baby than a horse, if both slaps are administered with equal force. But there must be some kind of blow – I don't know exactly what it would be, but perhaps a blow with a heavy stick – that would cause the horse as much pain as we cause a baby by a simple slap. That is what I mean by 'the same amount of pain' and if we consider it wrong to inflict that much pain on a baby for no good reason then we must, unless we are speciesists, consider it equally wrong to inflict the same amount of pain on a horse for no good reason.

There are other differences between humans and animals that cause other complications. Normal adult human beings have mental capacities that will, in certain circumstances, lead them to suffer more than animals would in the same circumstances. If, for instance, we decided to perform extremely painful or lethal scientific experiments on normal adult humans, kidnapped at random from public parks for this purpose, adults who entered parks would become fearful that they would be kidnapped. The resultant terror would be a form of suffering additional to the pain of the experiment. The same experiments performed on nonhuman animals would cause less suffering since the animals would not have the anticipatory dread of being kidnapped and experimented upon. This does not mean, of course, that it would be *right* to perform the experiment on animals, but only that there is a reason, and one that is not speciesist, for preferring to use animals rather than normal adult humans, if the experiment is to be done at all. Note, however, that this same argument gives us a reason for preferring to use human infants – orphans perhaps – or severely intellectually disabled humans for experiments, rather than adults, since infants and severely intellectually disabled humans would also have no idea of what was going to happen to them. As far as this argument is concerned, nonhuman animals and infants and severely intellectually disabled humans are in the same category; and if we use this argument to justify experiments on nonhuman animals we have to ask ourselves whether we are also prepared to allow experiments on human infants and severely intellectually disabled adults. If we make a distinction between animals and these humans, how can we do it, other than on the basis of a morally indefensible preference for members of our own species?

There are many areas in which the superior mental powers of normal adult humans make a difference: anticipation, more detailed memory, greater knowledge of what is happening, and so on. These differences explain why a human dying from cancer is likely to suffer more than a mouse. It is the mental anguish that makes the human's position so much harder to bear. Yet these differences do not all point to greater suffering on the part of the normal human being. Sometimes animals may suffer more because of their more limited understanding. If, for instance, we are taking prisoners in wartime we can explain to them that while they must submit to capture, search, and confinement they will not otherwise be harmed and will be set free at the conclusion of hostilities. If we capture wild animals, however, we cannot explain that we are not threatening their lives. A wild animal cannot distinguish an attempt to overpower and confine from an attempt to kill; the one causes as much terror as the other.

It may be objected that comparisons of the sufferings of different species are impossible to make, and that for this reason when the interests of animals and humans clash, the principle of equality gives no guidance. It is true that comparisons of suffering between members of different species cannot be made precisely. Nor, for that matter, can comparisons of suffering between different human beings be made precisely. Precision is not essential. As we shall see shortly, even if we were to prevent the infliction of suffering on animals only when the interests of humans will not be affected to anything like the extent that animals are affected, we would be forced to make radical changes in our treatment of animals that would involve our diet, the farming methods we use, experimental procedures in many fields of science, our approach to wildlife and to hunting, trapping and the wearing of furs, and areas of entertainment like circuses, rodeos, and zoos. As a result, the total quantity of suffering caused would be greatly reduced; so greatly that it is hard to imagine any other change of moral attitude that would cause so great a reduction in the total sum of suffering in the universe.

So far I have said a lot about the infliction of suffering on animals, but nothing about killing them. This omission has been deliberate. The application of the principle of equality to the infliction of suffering is, in theory at least, fairly straightforward. Pain and suffering are bad and should be prevented or minimised, irrespective of the race, sex, or species of the being that suffers. How bad a pain is depends on how intense it is and how long it lasts, but pains of the same intensity and duration are equally bad, whether felt by humans or animals. When we come to consider the value of life, we cannot say quite so confidently that a life is a life, and equally valuable, whether it is a human life or an animal life. It would not be speciesist to hold that the life of a self-aware being, capable of abstract thought, of planning for the future, of complex acts of communication, and so on, is more valuable than the life of a being without these capacities. (I am not saying whether this view is justifiable or not; only that it cannot simply be rejected as speciesist, because it is not on the basis of species itself that one life is held to be more valuable than another.) The value of life is a notoriously difficult ethical question, and we can only arrive at a reasoned conclusion about the comparative value of human and animal life after we have discussed the value of life in general. This is a topic for a separate chapter. Meanwhile there are important conclusions to be derived from the extension beyond our own species of the principle of equal consideration of interests, irrespective of our conclusions about the value of life.

SPECIESISM IN PRACTICE

Animals as Food

For most people in modern, urbanised societies, the principal form of contact with nonhuman animals is at meal times. The use of animals for food is probably the oldest and the most widespread form of animal use. There is also a sense in which it is the most basic form of animal use, the foundation stone on which rests the belief that animals exist for our pleasure and convenience.

If animals count in their own right, our use of animals for food becomes questionable – especially when animal flesh is a luxury rather than a necessity. Eskimos living in an environment where they must kill animals for food or starve might be justified in claiming that their interest in surviving overrides that of the animals they kill. Most of us cannot defend our diet in this way. Citizens of industrialised societies can easily obtain an adequate diet without the use of animal flesh. The overwhelming weight of medical evidence indicates that animal flesh is not necessary for good health or longevity. Nor is animal production in industrialised societies an efficient way of producing food, since most of the animals consumed have been fattened on grains and other foods that we could have eaten directly. When we feed these grains to animals, only about 10 per cent of the nutritional value remains as meat for human consumption. So, with the exception of animals raised entirely on grazing land unsuitable for crops, animals are eaten neither for health, nor to increase our food supply. Their flesh is a luxury, consumed because people like its taste.

In considering the ethics of the use of animal flesh for human food in industrialised societies, we are considering a situation in which a relatively minor human interest must be balanced against the lives and welfare of the animals involved. The principle of equal consideration of interests does not allow major interests to be sacrificed for minor interests.

The case against using animals for food is at its strongest when animals are made to lead miserable lives so that their flesh can be made available to humans at the lowest possible cost. Modern forms of intensive farming apply science and technology to the attitude that animals are objects for us to use. In order to have meat on the table at a price that people can afford, our society tolerates methods of meat production that confine sentient animals in cramped, unsuitable conditions for the entire duration of their lives. Animals are treated like machines that convert fodder into flesh, and any innovation that results in a higher 'conversion ratio' is liable to be adopted. As one authority on the subject has said, 'Cruelty is acknowledged only when profitability ceases.' To avoid speciesism we must stop these practices. Our custom is all the support that factory farmers need. The decision to cease giving them that support may be difficult, but it is less difficult than it would have been for a white Southerner to go against the traditions of his society and free his slaves; if we do not change our dietary habits, how can we censure those slaveholders who would not change their own way of living?

These arguments apply to animals who have been reared in factory farms – which means that we should not eat chicken, pork, or veal, unless we know that the meat we are eating was not produced by factory farm methods. The same is true of beef that has come from cattle kept in crowded feedlots (as most beef does in the United States). Eggs will come from hens kept in small wire cages, too small even to allow them to stretch their wings, unless the eggs are specifically sold as 'free range' (or unless one lives in a relatively enlightened country like Switzerland, which has prohibited the cage system of keeping hens).

These arguments do not take us all the way to a vegetarian diet, since some animals, for instance sheep, and in some countries cattle, still graze freely outdoors. This could change. The American pattern of fattening cattle in crowded feedlots is spreading to other countries. Meanwhile, the lives of free-ranging animals are undoubtedly better than those of animals reared in factory farms. It is still doubtful if using them for food is compatible with equal consideration of interests. One problem is, of course, that using them as food involves killing them – but this is an issue to which, as I have said, we shall return when we have discussed the value of life in the next chapter. Apart from taking their lives there are also many other things done to animals in order to bring them cheaply to our dinner table. Castration, the separation of mother and young, the breaking up of herds, branding, transporting, and finally the moments of slaughter – all of these are likely to involve suffering and do not take the animals' interests into account. Perhaps animals could be reared on a small scale without suffering in these ways, but it does not seem economical or practical to do so on the scale required for feeding our large urban populations. In any case, the important question is not whether animal flesh *could* be produced without suffering, but whether the flesh we are considering buying was produced without suffering. Unless we can be confident that it was, the principle of equal consideration of interests implies that it was wrong to sacrifice important interests of the animal in order to satisfy less important interests of our own; consequently we should boycott the end result of this process.

For those of us living in cities where it is difficult to know

how the animals we might eat have lived and died, this conclusion brings us close to a vegetarian way of life. I shall consider
some objections to it in the final section of this chapter.

Experimenting on Animals

Perhaps the area in which speciesism can most clearly be observed is the use of animals in experiments. Here the issue stands
out starkly, because experimenters often seek to justify experimenting on animals by claiming that the experiments lead us
to discoveries about humans; if this is so, the experimenter must
agree that human and nonhuman animals are similar in crucial
respects. For instance, if forcing a rat to choose between starving
to death and crossing an electrified grid to obtain food tells us
anything about the reactions of humans to stress, we must assume that the rat feels stress in this kind of situation.

People sometimes think that all animal experiments serve
vital medical purposes, and can be justified on the grounds that
they relieve more suffering than they cause. This comfortable
belief is mistaken. Drug companies test new shampoos and cos-
metics they are intending to market by dripping concentrated
solutions of them into the eyes of rabbits, in a test known as
the Draize test. (Pressure from the animal liberation movement
has led several cosmetic companies to abandon this practice.
An alternative test, not using animal, has now been found.
Nevertheless, many companies, including some of the largest,
still continue to perform the Draize test.) Food additives, including artificial colourings and preservatives, are tested by what
is known as the LD50 – a test designed to find the 'lethal dose',
or level of consumption that will make 50 per cent of a sample
of animals die. In the process nearly all of the animals are made
very sick before some finally die and others pull through. These
tests are not necessary to prevent human suffering: even if there
were no alternative to the use of animals to test the safety of
the products, we already have enough shampoos and food col-

ourings. There is no need to develop new ones that might be dangerous.

In many countries, the armed forces perform atrocious experiments on animals that rarely come to light. To give just one example: at the U.S. Armed Forces Radiobiology Institute, in Bethesda, Maryland, rhesus monkeys have been trained to run inside a large wheel. If they slow down too much, the wheel slows down, too, and the monkeys get an electric shock. Once the monkeys are trained to run for long periods, they are given lethal doses of radiation. Then, while sick and vomiting, they are forced to continue to run until they drop. This is supposed to provide information on the capacities of soldiers to continue to fight after a nuclear attack.

Nor can all university experiments be defended on the grounds that they relieve more suffering than they inflict. Three experimenters at Princeton University kept 256 young rats without food or water until they died. They concluded that young rats under conditions of fatal thirst and starvation are much more active than normal adult rats given food and water. In a well-known series of experiments that went on for more than fifteen years, H. F. Harlow of the Primate Research Center, Madison, Wisconsin, reared monkeys under conditions of maternal deprivation and total isolation. He found that in this way he could reduce the monkeys to a state in which, when placed among normal monkeys, they sat huddled in a corner in a condition of persistent depression and fear. Harlow also produced monkey mothers so neurotic that they smashed their infant's face into the floor and rubbed it back and forth. Although Harlow himself is no longer alive, some of his former students at other U.S. universities continue to perform variations on his experiments.

In these cases, and many others like them, the benefits to humans are either nonexistent or uncertain, while the losses to members of other species are certain and real. Hence the experiments indicate a failure to give equal consideration to the interests of all beings, irrespective of species.

In the past, argument about animal experimentation has often missed this point because it has been put in absolutist terms: would the opponent of experimentation be prepared to let thousands die from a terrible disease that could be cured by experimenting on one animal? This is a purely hypothetical question, since experiments do not have such dramatic results, but as long as its hypothetical nature is clear, I think the question should be answered affirmatively – in other words, if one, or even a dozen animals had to suffer experiments in order to save thousands, I would think it right and in accordance with equal consideration of interests that they should do so. This, at any rate, is the answer a utilitarian must give. Those who believe in absolute rights might hold that it is always wrong to sacrifice one being, whether human or animal, for the benefit of another. In that case the experiment should not be carried out, whatever the consequences.

To the hypothetical question about saving thousands of people through a single experiment on an animal, opponents of speciesism can reply with a hypothetical question of their own: would experimenters be prepared to perform their experiments on orphaned humans with severe and irreversible brain damage if that were the only way to save thousands? (I say 'orphaned' in order to avoid the complication of the feelings of the human parents.) If experimenters are not prepared to use orphaned humans with severe and irreversible brain damage, their readiness to use nonhuman animals seems to discriminate on the basis of species alone, since apes, monkeys, dogs, cats, and even mice and rats are more intelligent, more aware of what is happening to them, more sensitive to pain, and so on, than many severely braindamaged humans barely surviving in hospital wards and other institutions. There seems to be no morally relevant characteristic that such humans have that nonhuman animals lack. Experimenters, then, show bias in favour of their own species whenever they carry out experiments on nonhuman animals for purposes that they would not think justified them in using human beings at an equal or lower level of sentience, awareness, sensitivity, and so on. If this bias were eliminated, the number of experiments performed on animals would be greatly reduced.

Other Forms of Speciesism

I have concentrated on the use of animals as food and in research, since these are examples of large-scale, systematic speciesism. They are not, of course, the only areas in which the principle of equal consideration of interests, extended beyond the human species, has practical implications. There are many other areas that raise similar issues, including the fur trade, hunting in all its different forms, circuses, rodeos, zoos, and the pet business. Since the philosophical questions raised by these issues are not very different from those raised by the use of animals as food and in research, I shall leave it to the reader to apply the appropriate ethical principles to them.

SOME OBJECTIONS

I first put forward the views outlined in this chapter in 1973. At that time there was no animal liberation or animal rights movement. Since then a movement has sprung up, and some of the worst abuses of animals, like the Draize and LD50 tests, are now less widespread, even though they have not been eliminated. The fur trade has come under attack, and as a result fur sales have declined dramatically in countries like Britain, the Netherlands, Australia, and the United States. Some countries are also starting to phase out the most confining forms of factory farming. As already mentioned, Switzerland has prohibited the cage system of keeping laying hens. Britain has outlawed the raising of calves in individual stalls, and is phasing out individual stalls for pigs. Sweden, as in other areas of social reform, is in the lead here, too: in 1988 the Swedish Parliament passed a law that will, over a ten-year period, lead to the elimination of all systems of factory farming that confine animals for long periods and prevent them carrying out their natural behaviour.

Despite this increasing acceptance of many aspects of the case for animal liberation, and the slow but tangible progress made on behalf of animals, a variety of objections have emerged, some straightforward and predictable, some more subtle and unexpected. In this final section of the chapter I shall attempt to answer the most important of these objections. I shall begin with the more straightforward ones.

How Do We Know That Animals Can Feel Pain?

We can never directly experience the pain of another being, whether that being is human or not. When I see my daughter fall and scrape her knee, I know that she feels pain because of the way she behaves – she cries, she tells me her knee hurts, she rubs the sore spot, and so on. I know that I myself behave in a somewhat similar – if more inhibited – way when I feel pain, and so I accept that my daughter feels something like what I feel when I scrape my knee.

The basis of my belief that animals can feel pain is similar to the basis of my belief that my daughter can feel pain. Animals in pain behave in much the same way as humans do, and their behaviour is sufficient justification for the belief that they feel pain. It is true that, with the exception of those apes who have been taught to communicate by sign language, they cannot actually say that they are feeling pain – but then when my daughter was very young she could not talk, either. She found other ways to make her inner states apparent, thereby demonstrating that we can be sure that a being is feeling pain even if the being cannot use language.

To back up our inference from animal behaviour, we can point to the fact that the nervous systems of all vertebrates, and especially of birds and mammals, are fundamentally similar. Those parts of the human nervous system that are concerned with feeling pain are relatively old, in evolutionary terms. Unlike the cerebral cortex, which developed fully only after our ancestors diverged from other mammals, the basic nervous system evolved in more distant ancestors common to ourselves and the other 'higher' animals. This anatomical parallel makes it likely that the capacity of animals to feel is similar to our own.

It is significant that none of the grounds we have for believing that animals feel pain hold for plants. We cannot observe behaviour suggesting pain – sensational claims to the contrary have not been substantiated – and plants do not have a centrally organised nervous system like ours.

Animals Eat Each Other, So Why Shouldn't We Eat Them?

This might be called the Benjamin Franklin Objection. Franklin recounts in his *Autobiography* that he was for a time a vegetarian but his abstinence from animal flesh came to an end when he was watching some friends prepare to fry a fish they had just caught. When the fish was cut open, it was found to have a smaller fish in its stomach. 'Well', Franklin said to himself, 'if you eat one another, I don't see why we may not eat you' and he proceeded to do so.

Franklin was at least honest. In telling this story, he confesses that he convinced himself of the validity of the objection only after the fish was already in the frying pan and smelling 'admirably well'; and he remarks that one of the advantages of being a 'reasonable creature' is that one can find a reason for whatever one wants to do. The replies that can be made to this objection are so obvious that Franklin's acceptance of it does testify more to his love of fried fish than to his powers of reason.

For a start, most animals who kill for food would not be able to survive if they did not, whereas we have no need to eat animal flesh. Next, it is odd that humans, who normally think of the behaviour of animals as 'beastly' should, when it suits them, use an argument that implies that we ought to look to animals for moral guidance. The most decisive point, however, is that nonhuman animals are not capable of considering the alternatives open to them or of reflecting on the ethics of their diet. Hence it is impossible to hold the animals responsible for what they do, or to judge that because of their killing they 'deserve' to be treated in a similar way. Those who read these lines, on the other hand, must consider the justifiability of their dietary habits. You cannot evade responsibility by imitating beings who are incapable of making this choice.

Sometimes people point to the fact that animals eat each other in order to make a slightly different point. This fact suggests, they think, not that animals deserve to be eaten, but rather that there is a natural law according to which the stronger prey upon the weaker, a kind of Darwinian 'survival of the fittest' in which by eating animals we are merely playing our part.

This interpretation of the objection makes two basic mistakes, one a mistake of fact and the other an error of reasoning. The factual mistake lies in the assumption that our own consumption of animals is part of the natural evolutionary process. This might be true of a few primitive cultures that still hunt for food, but it has nothing to do with the mass production of domestic animals in factory farms.

Suppose that we did hunt for our food, though, and this was part of some natural evolutionary process. There would still be an error of reasoning in the assumption that because this process is natural it is right. It is, no doubt, 'natural' for women to produce an infant every year or two from puberty to menopause, but this does not mean that it is wrong to interfere with this process. We need to know the natural laws that affect us in order to estimate the consequences of what we do; but we do not have to assume that the natural way of doing something is incapable of improvement.

Differences between Humans and Animals

That there is a huge gulf between humans and animals was unquestioned for most of the course of Western civilisation. The basis of this assumption has been undermined by Darwin's discovery of our animal origins and the associated decline in the credibility of the story of our Divine Creation, made in the image of God with an immortal soul. Some have found it difficult to accept that the differences between us and the other animals are differences of degree rather than kind. They have searched for ways of drawing a line between humans and animals. To date these boundaries have been shortlived. For instance, it used to be said that only humans used tools. Then it was observed that the Galapagos woodpecker used a cactus thorn to dig insects out of crevices in trees. Next it was suggested that even if other animals used tools, humans are the only toolmaking animals. But Jane Goodall found that chimpanzees in the jungles of Tanzania chewed up leaves to make a sponge for sopping up water, and trimmed the leaves off branches to make tools for catching insects. The use of language was another boundary line – but now chimpanzees, gorillas, and an orangutan have learnt Ameslan, the sign language of the deaf, and there is some evidence suggesting that whales and dolphins may have a complex language of their own.

If these attempts to draw the line between humans and animals had fitted the facts of the situation, they would still not carry any moral weight. As Bentham pointed out, the fact that a being does not use language or make tools is hardly a reason for ignoring its suffering. Some philosophers have claimed that there is a more profound difference. They have claimed that animals cannot think or reason, and that accordingly they have no conception of themselves, no self-consciousness. They live from instant to instant, and do not see themselves as distinct entities with a past and a future. Nor do they have autonomy, the ability to choose how to live one's life. It has been suggested that autonomous, self-conscious beings are in some way much more valuable, more morally significant, than beings who live from moment to moment, without the capacity to see themselves as distinct beings with a past and a future. Accordingly, on this view, the interests of autonomous, self-conscious beings ought normally to take priority over the interests of other beings.

I shall not now consider whether some nonhuman animals are self-conscious and autonomous. The reason for this omission is that I do not believe that, in the present context, much depends on this question. We are now considering only the application of the principle of equal consideration of interests. In the next chapter, when we discuss questions about the value of life, we shall see that there are reasons for holding that self-consciousness is crucial in debates about whether a being has a right to life; and we shall then investigate the evidence for self-consciousness in nonhuman animals. Meanwhile the more important issue is: does the fact that a being is self-conscious entitle that being to some kind of priority of consideration?

The claim that self-conscious beings are entitled to prior consideration is compatible with the principle of equal consideration of interests if it amounts to no more than the claim that something that happens to self-conscious beings can be contrary to their interests while similar events would not be contrary to the interests of beings who were not self-conscious. This might be because the self-conscious creature has greater awareness of what is happening, can fit the event into the overall framework of a longer time period, has different desires, and so on. But this is a point I granted at the start of this chapter, and provided that it is not carried to ludicrous extremes – like insisting that if I am self-conscious and a veal calf is not, depriving me of veal causes more suffering than depriving the calf of his freedom to walk, stretch and eat grass – it is not denied by the criticisms I made of animal experimentation and factory farming.

It would be a different matter if it were claimed that, even when a self-conscious being did not suffer more than a being that was merely sentient, the suffering of the self-conscious being is more important because these are more valuable types of being. This introduces nonutilitarian claims of value – claims that do not derive simply from taking a universal standpoint in the manner described in the final section of Chapter 1. Since the argument for utilitarianism developed in that section was admittedly tentative, I cannot use that argument to rule out all nonutilitarian values. Nevertheless we are entitled to ask *why* self-conscious beings should be considered more valuable and in particular why the alleged greater value of a self-conscious being should result in preferring the lesser interests of a self-conscious being to the greater interests of a merely sentient being, even where the self-consciousness of the former being is not itself at stake. This last point is an important one, for we are not now considering cases in which the lives of self-conscious beings are at risk but cases in which self-conscious beings will go on living, their faculties intact, whatever we decide. In these cases, if the existence of self-consciousness does not affect the nature of the interests under comparison, it is not clear why we should drag self-consciousness into the discussion at all, any more than we should drag species, race or sex into similar discussions. Interests are interests, and ought to be given equal consideration whether they are the interests of human or nonhuman animals, self-conscious or non–self-conscious animals.

There is another possible reply to the claim that self-consciousness, or autonomy, or some similar characteristic, can serve to distinguish human from nonhuman animals: recall that there are intellectually disabled humans who have less claim to be regarded as self-conscious or autonomous than many nonhuman animals. If we use these characteristics to place a gulf between humans and other animals, we place these less able humans on the other side of the gulf; and if the gulf is taken to mark a difference in moral status, then these humans would have the moral status of animals rather than humans.

This reply is forceful, because most of us find horrifying the idea of using intellectually disabled humans in painful experiments, or fattening them for gourmet dinners. But some philosophers have argued that these consequences would not really follow from the use of a characteristic like self-consciousness or autonomy to distinguish humans from other animals. I shall consider three of these attempts.

The first suggestion is that severely intellectually disabled humans who do not possess the capacities that mark the normal human off from other animals should nevertheless be treated as if they did possess these capacities, since they belong to a species, members of which normally do possess them. The suggestion is, in other words, that we treat individuals not in accordance with their actual qualities, but in accordance with the qualities normal for their species.

It is interesting that this suggestion should be made in defence of treating members of our species better than members of another species, when it would be firmly rejected if it were used to justify treating members of our race or sex better than members of another race or sex. In the previous chapter, when discussing the impact of possible differences in IQ between members of different ethnic groups, I made the obvious point that whatever the difference between the *average* scores for different groups, some members of the group with the lower average score will do better than some members of groups with the higher average score, and so we ought to treat people as individuals and not according to the average score for their ethnic group, whatever the explanation of that average might be. If we accept this we cannot consistently accept the suggestion that when dealing with severely intellectually disabled humans we should grant them the status or rights normal for their species. For what is the significance of the fact that this time the line is to be drawn around the species rather than around the race or sex? We cannot insist that beings be treated as individuals in the one case, and as members of a group in the other. Membership of a species is no more relevant in these circumstances than membership of a race or sex.

A second suggestion is that although severely intellectually disabled humans may not possess higher capacities than other animals, they are nonetheless human beings, and as such we have special relations with them that we do not have with other animals. As one reviewer of *Animal Liberation* put it: 'Partiality for our own species, and within it for much smaller groupings is, like the universe, something we had better accept . . . The danger in an attempt to eliminate partial affections is that it may remove the source of all affections.'

This argument ties morality too closely to our affections. Of course some people may have a closer relationship with the most profoundly intellectually disabled human than they do with any nonhuman animal, and it would be absurd to tell them that they should not feel this way. They simply do, and as such there is nothing good or bad about it. The question is whether our moral obligations to a being should be made to depend on our feelings in this manner. Notoriously, some human beings have a closer relationship with their cat than with their neighbours. Would those who tie morality to affections accept that these people are justified in saving their cats from a fire before they save their neighbours? And even those who are prepared to answer this question affirmatively would, I trust, not want to go along with racists who could argue that if people have more natural relationships with, and greater affection towards, others of their own race, it is all right for them to give preference to the interests of other members of their own race. Ethics does not demand that we eliminate personal relationships and partial affections, but it does demand that when we act we assess the moral claims of those affected by our actions with some degree of independence from our feelings for them.

The third suggestion invokes the widely used 'slippery slope' argument. The idea of this argument is that once we take one step in a certain direction we shall find ourselves on a slippery slope and shall slither further than we wished to go. In the present context the argument is used to suggest that we need a clear line to divide those beings we can experiment upon, or fatten for dinner, from those we cannot. Species membership makes a nice sharp dividing line, whereas levels of self-consciousness, autonomy, or sentience do not. Once we allow that an intellectually disabled human being has no higher moral status than an animal, the argument goes, we have begun our descent down a slope, the next level of which is denying rights to social misfits, and the bottom of which is a totalitarian government disposing of any groups it does not like by classifying them as subhuman.

The slippery slope argument may serve as a valuable warning in some contexts, but it cannot bear too much weight. If we believe that, as I have argued in this chapter, the special status we now give to humans allows us to ignore the interests of billions of sentient creatures, we should not be deterred from trying to rectify this situation by the mere possibility that the principles on which we base this attempt will be misused by evil rulers for their own ends. And it is no more than a possibility. The change I have suggested might make no difference to our treatment of humans, or it might even improve it.

In the end, no ethical line that is arbitrarily drawn can be secure. It is better to find a line that can be defended openly and honestly. When discussing euthanasia in Chapter 7 we shall see that a line drawn in the wrong place can have unfortunate results even for those placed on the higher, or human side of the line.

It is also important to remember that the aim of my argument is to elevate the status of animals rather than to lower the status of any humans. I do not wish to suggest that intellectually disabled humans should be force-fed with food colourings until half of them die – although this would certainly give us a more accurate indication of whether the substance was safe for humans than testing it on rabbits or dogs does. I would like our conviction that it would be wrong to treat intellectually disabled humans in this way to be transferred to nonhuman animals at similar levels of self-consciousness and with similar capacities for suffering. It is excessively pessimistic to refrain from trying to alter our attitudes on the grounds that we might start treating intellectually disabled humans with the same lack of concern we now have for animals, rather than give animals the greater concern that we now have for intellectually disabled humans.

Ethics and Reciprocity

In the earliest surviving major work of moral philosophy in the Western tradition, Plato's *Republic*, there is to be found the following view of ethics:

> They say that to do injustice is, by nature, good; to suffer injustice, evil; but that there is more evil in the latter than good in the former. And so when men have both done and suffered injustice and have had experience of both, any who are not able to avoid the one and obtain the other, think that they had better agree among themselves to have neither; hence they begin to establish laws and mutual covenants; and that which is ordained by law is termed by them lawful and just. This, it is claimed, is the origin and nature of justice – it is a mean or compromise, between the best of all, which is to do injustice and not be punished, and the worst of all, which is to suffer injustice without the power of retaliation.

This was not Plato's own view; he put it into the mouth of Glaucon in order to allow Socrates, the hero of his dialogue, to refute it. It is a view that has never gained general acceptance, but has not died away either. Echoes of it can be found in the ethical theories of contemporary philosophers like John Rawls and David Gauthier; and it has been used, by these philosophers and others, to justify the exclusion of animals from the sphere of ethics, or at least from its core. For if the basis of ethics is that I refrain from doing nasty things to others as long as they don't do nasty things to me, I have no reason against doing nasty things to those who are incapable of appreciating my restraint and controlling their conduct towards me accordingly. Animals, by and large, are in this category. When I am surfing far out from shore and a shark attacks, my concern for animals will not help; I am as likely to be eaten as the next surfer, though he may spend every Sunday afternoon taking potshots at sharks from a boat. Since animals cannot reciprocate, they are, on this view, outside the limits of the ethical contract.

In assessing this conception of ethics we should distinguish between *explanations* of the origin of ethical judgments, and *justifications* of these judgments. The explanation of the origin of ethics in terms of a tacit contract between people for their mutual benefit has a certain plausibility (though in view of the quasi-ethical social rules that have been observed in the societies of other mammals, it is obviously a historical fantasy). But we could accept this account, as a historical explanation, without thereby committing ourselves to any views about the rightness or wrongness of the ethical system that has resulted. No matter how self-interested the origins of ethics may be, it is possible that once we have started thinking ethically we are led beyond these mundane premises. For we are capable of reasoning, and reason is not subordinate to self-interest. When we are reasoning about ethics, we are using concepts that, as we saw in the first chapter of this book, take us beyond our own personal interest, or even the interest of some sectional group. According to the contract view of ethics, this universalising process should stop at the boundaries of our community; but once the process has begun we may come to see that it would not be consistent with our other convictions to halt at that point. Just as the first

79

mathematicians, who may have started counting in order to keep track of the number of people in their tribe, had no idea that they were taking the first steps along a path that would lead to the infinitesimal calculus, so the origin of ethics tells us nothing about where it will end.

When we turn to the question of justification, we can see that contractual accounts of ethics have many problems. Clearly, such accounts exclude from the ethical sphere a lot more than nonhuman animals. Since severely intellectually disabled humans are equally incapable of reciprocating, they must also be excluded. The same goes for infants and very young children; but the problems of the contractual view are not limited to these special cases. The ultimate reason for entering into the ethical contract is, on this view, self-interest. Unless some additional universal element is brought in, one group of people has no reason to deal ethically with another if it is not in their interest to do so. If we take this seriously we shall have to revise our ethical judgments drastically. For instance, the white slave traders who transported African slaves to America had no self-interested reason for treating Africans any better than they did. The Africans had no way of retaliating. If they had only been contractualists, the slave traders could have rebutted the abolitionists by explaining to them that ethics stops at the boundaries of the community, and since Africans are not part of their community they have no duties to them.

Nor is it only past practices that would be affected by taking the contractual model seriously. Though people often speak of the world today as a single community, there is no doubt that the power of people in, say, Chad, to reciprocate either good or evil that is done to them by, say, citizens of the United States is limited. Hence it does not seem that the contract view provides for any obligations on the part of wealthy nations to poorer nations.

Most striking of all is the impact of the contract model on

our attitude to future generations. 'Why should I do anything for posterity? What has posterity ever done for me?' would be the view we ought to take if only those who can reciprocate are within the bounds of ethics. There is no way in which those who will be alive in the year 2100 can do anything to make our lives better or worse. Hence if obligations only exist where there can be reciprocity, we need have no worries about problems like the disposal of nuclear waste. True, some nuclear wastes will still be deadly for a quarter of a million years; but as long as we put it in containers that will keep it away from us for 100 years, we have done all that ethics demands of us.

These examples should suffice to show that, whatever its origin, the ethics we have now does go beyond a tacit understanding between beings capable of reciprocity. The prospect of returning to such a basis will, I trust, not be appealing. Since no account of the origin of morality compels us to base our morality on reciprocity, and since no other arguments in favour of this conclusion have been offered, we should reject this view of ethics.

At this point in the discussion some contract theorists appeal to a looser view of the contract idea, urging that we include within the moral community all those who have or will have the *capacity* to take part in a reciprocal agreement, irrespective of whether they are in fact able to reciprocate, and irrespective, too, of when they will have this capacity. Plainly, this view is no longer based on reciprocity at all, for (unless we care greatly about having our grave kept tidy or our memory preserved for ever) later generations plainly cannot enter into reciprocal relationships with us, even though they will one day have the capacity to reciprocate. If contract theorists abandon reciprocity in this manner, however, what is left of the contract account? Why adopt it at all? And why limit morality to those who have the capacity to enter into agreements with us, if in fact there is no possibility of them ever doing so? Rather than cling to the husk of a contract view that has lost its kernel, it would be better to abandon it altogether, and consider, on the basis of universalisability, which beings ought to be included within morality.

4

WHAT'S WRONG WITH KILLING?

A N oversimplified summary of the first three chapters of this book might read like this: the first chapter sets up a conception of ethics from which, in the second chapter, the principle of equal consideration of interests is derived; this principle is then used to illuminate problems about the equality of humans and, in the third chapter, applied to non-human animals.

Thus the principle of equal consideration of interests has been behind much of our discussion so far; but as I suggested in the previous chapter, the application of this principle when lives are at stake is less clear than when we are concerned with interests like avoiding pain and experiencing pleasure. In this chapter we shall look at some views about the value of life, and the wrongness of taking life, in order to prepare the ground for the following chapters in which we shall turn to the practical issues of killing animals, abortion, euthanasia, and environmental ethics.

HUMAN LIFE

People often say that life is sacred. They almost never mean what they say. They do not mean, as their words seem to imply, that life itself is sacred. If they did, killing a pig or pulling up a cabbage would be as abhorrent to them as the murder of a human being. When people say that life is sacred, it is human life they have in mind. But why should human life have special value?

In discussing the doctrine of the sanctity of human life I shall not take the term 'sanctity' in a specifically religious sense. The doctrine may well have a religious origin, as I shall suggest later in this chapter, but it is now part of a broadly secular ethic, and it is as part of this secular ethic that it is most influential today. Nor shall I take the doctrine as maintaining that it is always wrong to take human life, for this would imply absolute pacifism, and there are many supporters of the sanctity of human life who concede that we may kill in self-defence. We may take the doctrine of the sanctity of human life to be no more than a way of saying that human life has some special value, a value quite distinct from the value of the lives of other living things.

The view that human life has unique value is deeply rooted in our society and is enshrined in our law. To see how far it can be taken, I recommend a remarkable book: *The Long Dying of Baby Andrew*, by Robert and Peggy Stinson. In December 1976 Peggy Stinson, a Pennsylvania schoolteacher, was twenty-four weeks pregnant when she went into premature labor. The baby, whom Robert and Peggy named Andrew, was marginally viable. Despite a firm statement from both parents that they wanted 'no heroics', the doctors in charge of their child used all the technology of modern medicine to keep him alive for nearly six months. Andrew had periodic fits. Towards the end of that period, it was clear that if he survived at all, he would be seriously and permanently impaired. Andrew was also suffering considerably: at one point his doctor told the Stinsons that it must 'hurt like hell' every time Andrew drew a breath. Andrew's treatment cost $104,000, at 1977 cost levels – today it could easily be three times that, for intensive care for extremely premature babies costs at least $1,500 per day.

Andrew Stinson was kept alive, against the wishes of his parents, at a substantial financial cost, notwithstanding evident suffering, and despite the fact that, after a certain point it was clear that he would never be able to live an independent life, or to think and talk in the way that most humans do. Whether such treatment of an infant human being is or is not the right thing to do – and I come back to this question in Chapter 7 – it makes a striking contrast with the casual way in which we take the lives of stray dogs, experimental monkeys, and beef cattle. What justifies the difference?

In every society known to us there has been some prohibition on the taking of life. Presumably no society can survive if it allows its members to kill one another without restriction. Precisely who is protected, however, is a matter on which societies have differed. In many tribal societies the only serious offence is to kill an innocent member of the tribe itself – members of other tribes may be killed with impunity. In more sophisticated nation-states protection has generally extended to all within the nation's territorial boundaries, although there have been cases – like slave-owning states – in which a minority was excluded. Nowadays most agree, in theory if not in practice, that, apart from special cases like self-defence, war, possibly capital punishment, and one or two other doubtful areas, it is wrong to kill human beings irrespective of their race, religion, class, or nationality. The moral inadequacy of narrower principles, limiting the respect for life to a tribe, race, or nation, is taken for granted; but the argument of the preceding chapter must raise doubts about whether the boundary of our species marks a more defensible limit to the protected circle.

At this point we should pause to ask what we mean by terms like 'human life' or 'human being'. These terms figure prominently in debates about, for example, abortion. 'Is the fetus a human being?' is often taken as the crucial question in the abortion debate; but unless we think carefully about these terms such questions cannot be answered.

It is possible to give 'human being' a precise meaning. We can use it as equivalent to 'member of the species Homo sapiens'. Whether a being is a member of a given species is something that can be determined scientifically, by an examination of the nature of the chromosomes in the cells of living organisms. In this sense there is no doubt that from the first moments of its existence an embryo conceived from human sperm and eggs is a human being; and the same is true of the most profoundly and irreparably intellectually disabled human being, even of an infant who is born anencephalic – literally, without a brain.

There is another use of the term 'human', one proposed by Joseph Fletcher, a Protestant theologian and a prolific writer on ethical issues. Fletcher has compiled a list of what he calls 'indicators of humanhood' that includes the following: self-awareness, self-control, a sense of the future, a sense of the past, the capacity to relate to others, concern for others, communication, and curiosity. This is the sense of the term that we have in mind when we praise someone by saying that she is 'a real human being' or shows 'truly human qualities'. In saying this we are not, of course, referring to the person's membership in the species Homo sapiens which as a matter of biological fact is rarely in doubt; we are implying that human beings characteristically possess certain qualities, and this person possesses them to a high degree.

These two senses of 'human being' overlap but do not coincide. The embryo, the later fetus, the profoundly intellectually disabled child, even the newborn infant – all are indisputably members of the species Homo sapiens, but none are self-aware, have a sense of the future, or the capacity to relate to others. Hence the choice between the two senses can make an important difference to how we answer questions like 'Is the fetus a human being?'

When choosing which words to use in a situation like this we should choose terms that will enable us to express our meaning clearly, and that do not prejudge the answer to substantive questions. To stipulate that we shall use 'human' in, say, the first of the two senses just described, and that therefore the fetus is a human being and abortion is immoral would not do. Nor would it be any better to choose the second sense and argue on this basis that abortion is acceptable. The morality of abortion is a substantive issue, the answer to which cannot depend on a stipulation about how we shall use words. In order to avoid begging any questions, and to make my meaning clear, I shall for the moment put aside the tricky term 'human' and substitute two different terms, corresponding to the two different senses of 'human'. For the first sense, the biological sense, I shall simply use the cumbersome but precise expression 'member of the species Homo sapiens' while for the second sense I shall use the term 'person'.

This use of 'person' is itself, unfortunately, liable to mislead, since 'person' is often used as if it meant the same as 'human being'. Yet the terms are not equivalent; there could be a person who is not a member of our species. There could also be members of our species who are not persons. The word 'person' has its origin in the Latin term for a mask worn by an actor in classical drama. By putting on masks the actors signified that they were acting a role. Subsequently 'person' came to mean one who plays a role in life, one who is an agent. According to the *Oxford Dictionary*, one of the current meanings of the term is 'a self-conscious or rational being'. This sense has impeccable philosophical precedents. John Locke defines a person as 'A thinking intelligent being that has reason and reflection and can consider itself as itself, the same thinking thing, in different times and places.'

This definition makes 'person' close to what Fletcher meant by 'human', except that it selects two crucial characteristics – rationality and self-consciousness – as the core of the concept. Quite possibly Fletcher would agree that these two are central, and the others more or less follow from them. In any case, I propose to use 'person', in the sense of a rational and self-conscious being, to capture those elements of the popular sense of 'human being' that are not covered by 'member of the species Homo sapiens'.

The Value of the Life of Members of the Species Homo Sapiens

With the clarification gained by our terminological interlude, and the argument of the preceding chapter to draw upon, this section can be very brief. The wrongness of inflicting pain on a being cannot depend on the being's species: nor can the wrongness of killing it. The biological facts upon which the boundary of our species is drawn do not have moral significance. To give preference to the life of a being simply because that being is a member of our species would put us in the same position as racists who give preference to those who are members of their race.

To those who have read the preceding chapters of this book, this conclusion may seem obvious, for we have worked towards it gradually; but it differs strikingly from the prevailing attitude in our society, which as we have seen treats as sacred the lives of all members of our species. How is it that our society should have come to accept a view that bears up so poorly under critical scrutiny? A short historical digression may help to explain.

If we go back to the origins of Western civilisation, to Greek or Roman times, we find that membership of Homo sapiens was not sufficient to guarantee that one's life would be protected. There was no respect for the lives of slaves or other 'barbarians'; and even among the Greeks and Romans themselves, infants had no automatic right to life. Greeks and Romans killed deformed or weak infants by exposing them to the elements on a hilltop. Plato and Aristotle thought that the state should enforce the killing of deformed infants. The celebrated legislative codes said to have been drawn up by Lycurgus and Solon contained similar provisions. In this period it was thought better to end a life that had begun inauspiciously than to attempt to prolong that life, with all the problems it might bring.

Our present attitudes date from the coming of Christianity. There was a specific theological motivation for the Christian insistence on the importance of species membership: the belief that all born of human parents are immortal and destined for an eternity of bliss or for everlasting torment. With this belief, the killing of Homo sapiens took on a fearful significance, since it consigned a being to his or her eternal fate. A second Christian doctrine that led to the same conclusion was the belief that since we are created by God we are his property, and to kill a human being is to usurp God's right to decide when we shall live and when we shall die. As Thomas Aquinas put it, taking a human life is a sin against God in the same way that killing a slave would be a sin against the master to whom the slave belonged. Non-human animals, on the other hand, were believed to have been placed by God under man's dominion, as recorded in the Bible (Genesis 1:29 and 9:1–3). Hence humans could kill non-human animals as they pleased, as long as the animals were not the property of another.

During the centuries of Christian domination of European thought the ethical attitudes based on these doctrines became part of the unquestioned moral orthodoxy of European civilisation. Today the doctrines are no longer generally accepted, but the ethical attitudes to which they gave rise fit in with the deep-seated Western belief in the uniqueness and special privileges of our species, and have survived. Now that we are reassessing our speciesist view of nature, however, it is also time to reassess our belief in the sanctity of the lives of members of our species.

The Value of a Person's Life

We have broken down the doctrine of the sanctity of human life into two separate claims, one that there is special value in the life of a member of our species, and the other that there is special value in the life of a person. We have seen that the former claim cannot be defended. What of the latter? Is there special value in the life of a rational and self-conscious being, as distinct from a being that is merely sentient?

One line of argument for answering this question affirmatively runs as follows. A self-conscious being is aware of itself as a distinct entity, with a past and a future. (This, remember, was Locke's criterion for being a person.) A being aware of itself in this way will be capable of having desires about its own future. For example, a professor of philosophy may hope to write a book demonstrating the objective nature of ethics; a student may look forward to graduating; a child may want to go for a ride in an aeroplane. To take the lives of any of these people, without their consent, is to thwart their desires for the future. Killing a snail or a day-old infant does not thwart any desires of this kind, because snails and newborn infants are incapable of having such desires.

It may be said that when a person is killed we are not left with a thwarted desire in the same sense in which I have a thwarted desire when I am hiking through dry country and, pausing to ease my thirst, discover a hole in my waterbottle. In this case I have a desire that I cannot fulfil, and I feel frustration and discomfort because of the continuing and unsatisfied desire for water. When I am killed the desires I have for the future do not continue after my death, and I do not suffer from their non-fulfilment. But does this mean that preventing the fulfilment of these desires does not matter?

Classical utilitarianism, as expounded by the founding father of utilitarianism, Jeremy Bentham, and refined by later philosophers like John Stuart Mill and Henry Sidgwick, judges actions by their tendency to maximise pleasure or happiness and minimise pain or unhappiness. Terms like 'pleasure' and 'happiness' lack precision, but it is clear that they refer to something that is experienced, or felt – in other words, to states of consciousness. According to classical utilitarianism, therefore, there is no direct significance in the fact that desires for the future go unfulfilled when people die. If you die instantaneously, whether you have any desires for the future makes no difference to the amount of pleasure or pain you experience. Thus for the classical utilitarian the status of 'person' is not *directly* relevant to the wrongness of killing.

Indirectly, however, being a person may be important for the classical utilitarian. Its importance arises in the following manner. If I am a person, I have a conception of myself. I know that I have a future. I also know that my future existence could be cut short. If I think that this is likely to happen at any moment, my present existence will be fraught with anxiety, and will presumably be less enjoyable than if I do not think it is likely to happen for some time. If I learn that people like myself are very rarely killed, I will worry less. Hence the classical utilitarian can defend a prohibition on killing persons on the *indirect* ground that it will increase the happiness of people who would otherwise worry that they might be killed. I call this an *indirect* ground because it does not refer to any direct wrong done to the person killed, but rather to a consequence of it for other people. There is, of course, something odd about objecting to murder, not because of the wrong done to the victim, but because of the effect that the murder will have on others. One has to be a tough-minded classical utilitarian to be untroubled by this oddness. (Remember, though, that we are now only considering what is *especially* wrong about killing a *person*. The classical utilitarian can still regard killing as wrong because it eliminates the happiness that the victim would have experienced, had she lived. This objection to murder will apply to any being likely to have a happy future, irrespective of whether the being is a person.) For present purposes, however, the main point is that this indirect ground does provide a reason for taking the killing of a person, under certain conditions, more seriously than the killing of a non-personal being. If a being is incapable of conceiving of itself as existing over time, we need not take into account the possibility of it worrying about the prospect of its future existence being cut short. It can't worry about this, for it has no conception of its own future.

I said that the indirect classical utilitarian reason for taking the killing of a person more seriously than the killing of a non-person holds 'under certain conditions'. The most obvious of these conditions is that the killing of the person may become known to other persons, who derive from this knowledge a more gloomy estimate of their own chances of living to a ripe old age, or simply become fearful of being murdered. It is of course possible that a person could be killed in complete secrecy, so that no one else knew a murder had been committed. Then this indirect reason against killing would not apply.

To this last point, however, a qualification must be made. In the circumstances described in the last paragraph, the indirect classical utilitarian reason against killing would not apply *in so far as we judge this individual case*. There is something to be said, however, against applying utilitarianism only or primarily at the level of each individual case. It may be that in the long run, we will achieve better results – greater overall happiness – if we urge people not to judge each individual action by the standard of utility, but instead to think along the lines of some broad principles that will cover all or virtually all of the situations that they are likely to encounter.

Several reasons have been offered in support of this approach. R.M. Hare has suggested a useful distinction between two levels of moral reasoning: the intuitive and the critical. To consider, in theory, the possible circumstances in which one might maximise utility by secretly killing someone who wants to go on living is to reason at the critical level. As philosophers, or just as reflective, self-critical people, it can be interesting and helpful to our understanding of ethical theory to think about such unusual hypothetical cases. Everyday moral thinking, however, must be more intuitive. In real life we usually cannot foresee all the complexities of our choices. It is simply not practical to try to calculate the consequences, in advance, of every choice we make. Even if we were to limit ourselves to the more significant choices, there would be a danger that in many cases we would be calculating in less than ideal circumstances. We could be hurried, or flustered. We might be feeling angry, or hurt, or competitive. Our thoughts could be coloured by greed, or sexual desire, or thoughts of vengeance. Our own interests, or the interests of those we love, might be at stake. Or we might just not be very good at thinking about such complicated issues as the likely consequences of a significant choice. For all these reasons, Hare suggests, it will be better if, for our everyday ethical life, we adopt some broad ethical principles and do not deviate from them. These principles should include those that experience has shown, over the centuries, to be generally conducive to producing the best consequences: and in Hare's view that would include many of the standard moral principles, for example, telling the truth, keeping promises, not harming others, and so on. Respecting the lives of people who want to go on living would presumably be among these principles. Even though, at the critical level, we can conceive of circumstances in which better consequences would flow from acting against one or more of these principles, people will do better on the whole if they stick to the principles than if they do not.

On this view, soundly chosen intuitive moral principles should be like a good tennis coach's instructions to a player. The instructions are given with an eye to what will pay off most of the time; they are a guide to playing "percentage tennis". Occasionally an individual player might go for a freak shot, and pull off a winner that has everyone applauding; but if the coach is any good at all, deviations from the instructions laid down will, more often than not, lose. So it is better to put the thought of going for those freak shots out of one's mind. Similarly, if we are guided by a set of well-chosen intuitive principles, we may do better if we do not attempt to calculate the consequences of each significant moral choice we must make, but instead consider what principles apply to it, and act accordingly. Perhaps very occasionally we will find ourselves in circumstances in which it is absolutely plain that departing from the principles will produce a much better result than we will obtain by sticking to them, and then we may be justified in making the departure. But for most of us, most of the time, such circumstances will not arise and can be excluded from our thinking. Therefore even though at the critical level the classical utilitarian must concede the possibility of cases in which it would be better not to respect a person's desire to continue living, because the person could be killed in complete secrecy, and a great deal of unalleviated misery could thereby be prevented, this kind of thinking has no place at the intuitive level that should guide our everyday actions. So, at least, a classical utilitarian can argue.

That is, I think, the gist of what the classical utilitarian would say about the distinction between killing a person and killing some other type of being. There is, however, another version of utilitarianism that gives greater weight to the distinction. This other version of utilitarianism judges actions, not by their tendency to maximise pleasure or minimise pain, but by the extent to which they accord with the preferences of any beings affected by the action or its consequences. This version of utilitarianism is known as 'preference utilitarianism'. It is preference utilitarianism, rather than classical utilitarianism, that we reach by universalising our own interests in the manner described in the opening chapter of this book – if, that is, we make the plausible move of taking a person's interests to be what, on balance and after reflection on all the relevant facts, a person prefers.

According to preference utilitarianism, an action contrary to the preference of any being is, unless this preference is outweighed by contrary preferences, wrong. Killing a person who prefers to continue living is therefore wrong, other things being equal. That the victims are not around after the act to lament the fact that their preferences have been disregarded is irrelevant. The wrong is done when the preference is thwarted.

For preference utilitarians, taking the life of a person will normally be worse than taking the life of some other being, since persons are highly future-oriented in their preferences. To kill a person is therefore, normally, to violate not just one, but a wide range of the most central and significant preferences a being can have. Very often, it will make nonsense of everything that the victim has been trying to do in the past days, months, or even years. In contrast, beings who cannot see themselves as entities with a future cannot have any preferences about their own future existence. This is not to deny that such beings might struggle against a situation in which their lives are in danger, as a fish struggles to get free of the barbed hook in its mouth; but this indicates no more than a preference for the cessation of a state of affairs that is perceived as painful or frightening. Struggle against danger and pain does not suggest that fish are capable of preferring their own future existence to non-existence. The behaviour of a fish on a hook suggests a reason for not killing fish by that method, but does not in itself suggest a preference utilitarian reason against killing fish by a method that brings about death instantly, without first causing pain or distress. (Again, remember that we are here considering what is especially wrong about killing a person; I am not saying that there are never any preference utilitarian reasons against killing conscious beings who are not persons.)

Does a Person Have a Right to Life?

Although preference utilitarianism does provide a direct reason for not killing a person, some may find the reason – even when coupled with the important indirect reasons that any form of utilitarianism will take into account – not sufficiently stringent. Even for preference utilitarianism, the wrong done to the person killed is merely one factor to be taken into account, and the preference of the victim could sometimes be outweighed by the preferences of others. Some say that the prohibition on killing people is more absolute than this kind of utilitarian calculation implies. Our lives, we feel, are things to which we have a *right*, and rights are not to be traded off against the preferences or pleasures of others.

I am not convinced that the notion of a moral right is a helpful or meaningful one, except when it is used as a shorthand way of referring to more fundamental moral considerations. Nevertheless, since the idea that we have a 'right to life' is a popular one, it is worth asking whether there are grounds for attributing rights to life to persons, as distinct from other living beings.

Michael Tooley, a contemporary American philosopher, has argued that the only beings who have a right to life are those who can conceive of themselves as distinct entities existing over time – in other words, persons, as we have used the term. His argument is based on the claim that there is a conceptual connection between the desires a being is capable of having and the rights that the being can be said to have. As Tooley puts it:

> The basic intuition is that a right is something that can be violated and that, in general, to violate an individual's right to something is to frustrate the corresponding desire. Suppose, for example, that you own a car. Then I am under a prima facie obligation not to take it from you. However, the obligation is not unconditional: it depends in part upon the existence of a corresponding desire in you. If you do not care whether I take your car, then I generally do not violate your right by doing so.

Tooley admits that it is difficult to formulate the connections between rights and desires precisely, because there are problem cases like people who are asleep or temporarily unconscious. He does not want to say that such people have no rights because they have, at that moment, no desires. Nevertheless, Tooley holds, the possession of a right must in some way be linked with the capacity to have the relevant desires, if not with having the actual desires themselves.

The next step is to apply this view about rights to the case of the right to life. To put the matter as simply as possible – more simply than Tooley himself does and no doubt *too* simply – if the right to life is the right to continue existing as a distinct entity, then the desire relevant to possessing a right to life is the desire to continue existing as a distinct entity. But only a being who is capable of conceiving herself as a distinct entity existing over time – that is, only a person – could have this desire. Therefore only a person could have a right to life.

This is how Tooley first formulated his position, in a striking article entitled "Abortion and Infanticide", first published in 1972. The problem of how precisely to formulate the connections between rights and desires, however, led Tooley to alter his position in a subsequent book with the same title, *Abortion and Infanticide*. He there argues that an individual cannot at a given time – say, now – have a right to continued existence unless the individual is of a kind such that it can now be in its interests that it continue to exist. One might think that this makes a dramatic difference to the outcome of Tooley's position, for while a newborn infant would not seem to be capable of conceiving itself as a distinct entity existing over time, we commonly think that it can be in the interests of an infant to be saved from death, even if the death would have been entirely without pain or suffering. We certainly do this in retrospect: I might say, if I know that I nearly died in infancy, that the person who snatched my pram from the path of the speeding train is my greatest benefactor, for without her swift thinking I would never have had the happy and fulfilling life that I am now living. Tooley argues, however, that the retrospective attribution of an interest in living to the infant is a mistake. I am not the infant from whom I developed. The infant could not look forward to developing into the kind of being I am, or even into any intermediate being, between the being I now am and the infant. I cannot even recall being the infant; there are no mental links between us. Continued existence cannot be in the interests of a being who *never* has had the concept of a continuing self – that is, never has been able to conceive of itself as existing over time. If the train had instantly killed the infant, the death would not have been contrary to the interests of the infant, because the infant would never have had the concept of existing over time. It is true that I would then not be alive, but I can say that it is in my interests to be alive only because I do have the concept of a continuing self. I can with equal truth say that it is in my interests that my parents met, because if they had never met, they could not have created the embryo from which I developed, and so I would not be alive. This does not mean that the creation of this embryo was in the interests of any potential being who was lurking around, waiting to be brought into existence. There was no such being, and had I not been brought into existence, there would not have been anyone who missed out on the life I have enjoyed living. Similarly, we make a mistake if we now construct an interest in future life in the infant, who in the first days following birth can have no concept of continued existence, and with whom I have no mental links.

Hence in his book Tooley reaches, though by a more circuitous route, a conclusion that is practically equivalent to the conclusion he reached in his article. To have a right to life, one must have, or at least at one time have had, the concept of having a continued existence. Note that this formulation avoids any problems in dealing with sleeping or unconscious people; it is enough that they have had, at one time, the concept of continued existence for us to be able to say that continued life may be in their interests. This makes sense: my desire to continue living – or to complete the book I am writing, or to travel around the world next year – does not cease whenever I am not consciously thinking about these things. We often desire things without the desire being at the forefront of our minds. The fact that we have the desire is apparent if we are reminded of it, or suddenly confronted with a situation in which we must choose between two courses of action, one of which makes the fulfilment of the desire less likely. In a similar way, when we go to sleep our desires for the future have not ceased to exist.

They will still be there, when we wake. As the desires are still part of us, so, too, our interest in continued life remains part of us while we are asleep or unconscious.

People and Respect for Autonomy

To this point our discussion of the wrongness of killing people has focused on their capacity to envisage their future and have desires related to it. Another implication of being a person may also be relevant to the wrongness of killing. There is a strand of ethical thought, associated with Kant but including many modern writers who are not Kantians, according to which respect for autonomy is a basic moral principle. By 'autonomy' is meant the capacity to choose, to make and act on one's own decisions. Rational and self-conscious beings presumably have this ability, whereas beings who cannot consider the alternatives open to them are not capable of choosing in the required sense and hence cannot be autonomous. In particular, only a being who can grasp the difference between dying and continuing to live can autonomously choose to live. Hence killing a person who does not choose to die fails to respect that person's autonomy; and as the choice of living or dying is about the most fundamental choice anyone can make, the choice on which all other choices depend, killing a person who does not choose to die is the gravest possible violation of that person's autonomy.

Not everyone agrees that respect for autonomy is a basic moral principle, or a valid moral principle at all. Utilitarians do not respect autonomy for its own sake, although they might give great weight to a person's desire to go on living, either in a preference utilitarian way, or as evidence that the person's life was on the whole a happy one. But if we are preference utilitarians we must allow that a desire to go on living can be outweighed by other desires, and if we are classical utilitarians we must recognise that people may be utterly mistaken in their expectations of happiness. So a utilitarian, in objecting to the killing of a person, cannot place the same stress on autonomy as those who take respect for autonomy as an independent moral principle. The classical utilitarian might have to accept that in some cases it would be right to kill a person who does not choose to die on the grounds that the person will otherwise lead a miserable life. This is true, however, only on the critical level of moral reasoning. As we saw earlier, utilitarians may encourage people to adopt, in their daily lives, principles that will in almost all cases lead to better consequences when followed than any alternative action. The principle of respect for autonomy would be a prime example of such a principle. We shall discuss actual cases that raise this issue shortly, in the discussion of euthanasia in Chapter 7.

It may be helpful here to draw together our conclusions about the value of a person's life. We have seen that there are four possible reasons for holding that a person's life has some distinctive value over and above the life of a merely sentient being: the classical utilitarian concern with the effects of the killing on others; the preference utilitarian concern with the frustration of the victim's desires and plans for the future; the argument that the capacity to conceive of oneself as existing over time is a necessary condition of a right to life; and respect for autonomy. Although at the level of critical reasoning a classical utilitarian would accept only the first, indirect, reason, and a preference utilitarian only the first two reasons, at the intuitive level utilitarians of both kinds would probably advocate respect for autonomy too. The distinction between critical and intuitive levels thus leads to a greater degree of convergence, at the level of everyday moral decision making, between utilitarians and those who hold other moral views than we would find if we took into account only the critical level of reasoning. In any case, none of the four reasons for giving special protection to the lives of persons can be rejected out of hand. We shall therefore bear all four in mind when we turn to practical issues involving killing.

Before we do turn to practical questions about killing, however, we have still to consider claims about the value of life that are based neither on membership of our species, nor on being a person.

CONSCIOUS LIFE

There are many beings who are sentient and capable of experiencing pleasure and pain, but are not rational and self-conscious and so not persons. I shall refer to these beings as conscious being. Many non-human animals almost certainly fall into this category; so must newborn infants and some intellectually disabled humans. Exactly which of these lack self-consciousness is something we shall consider in the next chapters. If Tooley is right, those beings who do lack self-consciousness cannot be said to have a right to life, in the full sense of 'right'. Still, for other reasons, it might be wrong to kill them. In the present section we shall ask if the life of a being who is conscious but not self-conscious has value, and if so, how the value of such a life compares with the value of a person's life.

Should We Value Conscious Life?

The most obvious reason for valuing the life of a being capable of experiencing pleasure or pain is the pleasure it can experience. If we value our own pleasures – like the pleasures of eating, of sex, of running at full speed and of swimming on a hot day – then the universal aspect of ethical judgments requires us to extend our positive evaluation of our own experience of these pleasures to the similar experiences of all who can experience them. But death is the end of all pleasurable experiences. Thus the fact that beings will experience pleasure in the future is a reason for saying that it would be wrong to kill them. Of course, a similar argument about pain points in the opposite direction, and it is only when we believe that the pleasure that beings are likely to experience outweighs the pain they are likely to suffer, that this argument counts against killing. So what this argument amounts to is that we should not cut short a pleasant life.

This seems simple enough: we value pleasure, killing those who lead pleasant lives eliminates the pleasure they would otherwise experience, therefore such killing is wrong. But stating the argument in this way conceals something that, once noticed, makes the issue anything but simple. There are two ways of reducing the amount of pleasure in the world: one is to eliminate pleasures from the lives of those leading pleasant lives; the other is to eliminate those leading pleasant lives. The former leaves behind beings who experience less pleasure than they otherwise would have. The latter does not. This means that we cannot move automatically from a preference for a pleasant life rather than an unpleasant one, to a preference for a pleasant life rather than no life at all. For, it might be objected, being killed does not make us worse off; it makes us cease to exist. Once we have ceased to exist, we shall not miss the pleasure we would have experienced.

Perhaps this seems sophistical – an instance of the ability of academic philosophers to find distinctions where there are no significant differences. If that is what you think, consider the opposite case: a case not of reducing pleasure, but of increasing it. There are two ways of increasing the amount of pleasure in the world: one is to increase the pleasure of those who now exist; the other is to increase the number of those who will lead pleasant lives. If killing those leading pleasant lives is bad because of the loss of pleasure, then it would seem to be good to increase the number of those leading pleasant lives. We could do this by having more children, provided we could reasonably expect their lives to be pleasant, or by rearing large numbers of animals under conditions that would ensure that their lives would be pleasant. But would it really be good to create more pleasure by creating more pleased beings?

There seem to be two possible approaches to these perplexing issues. The first approach is simply to accept that it is good to increase the amount of pleasure in the world by increasing the number of pleasant lives, and bad to reduce the amount of pleasure in the world by reducing the number of pleasant lives. This approach has the advantage of being straightforward and clearly consistent, but it requires us to hold that if we could increase the number of beings leading pleasant lives without making others worse off, it would be good to do so. To see whether you are troubled by this conclusion, it may be helpful to consider a specific case. Imagine that a couple are trying to decide whether to have children. Suppose that as far as their own happiness is concerned, the advantages and disadvantages balance out. Children will interfere with their careers at a crucial stage of their professional lives, and they will have to give up their favourite recreation, cross-country skiing, for a few years at least. At the same time, they know that, like most parents, they will get joy and fulfilment from having children and watching them develop. Suppose that if others will be affected, the good and bad effects will cancel each other out. Finally, suppose that since the couple could provide their children with a good start in life, and the children would be citizens of a developed nation with a high living standard, it is probable that their children will lead pleasant lives. Should the couple count the likely future pleasure of their children as a significant reason for having children? I doubt that many couples would, but if we accept this first approach, they should.

I shall call this approach the 'total' view since on this view we aim to increase the total amount of pleasure (and reduce the total amount of pain) and are indifferent whether this is done by increasing the pleasure of existing beings, or increasing the number of beings who exist.

The second approach is to count only beings who already exist, prior to the decision we are taking, or at least will exist independently of that decision. We can call this the 'prior existence' view. It denies that there is value in increasing pleasure by creating additional beings. The prior existence view is more in harmony with the intuitive judgment most people have (I think) that couples are under no moral obligation to have children when the children are likely to lead pleasant lives and no one else is adversely affected. But how do we square the prior existence view with our intuitions about the reverse case, when a couple are considering having a child who, perhaps because it will inherit a genetic defect, would lead a thoroughly miserable life and die before its second birthday? We would think it wrong for a couple knowingly to conceive such a child; but if the pleasure a possible child will experience is not a reason for bringing it into the world, why is the pain a possible child will experience a reason *against* bringing it into the world? The prior existence view must either hold that there is nothing wrong with bringing a miserable being into the world, or explain the asymmetry between cases of possible children who are likely to have pleasant lives, and possible children who are likely to have miserable lives. Denying that it is bad knowingly to bring a miserable child into the world is hardly likely to appeal to those who adopted the prior existence view in the first place because it seemed more in harmony with their intuitive judgments than the total view; but a convincing explanation of the asymmetry is not easy to find. Perhaps the best one can say – and it is not very good – is that there is nothing directly wrong in conceiving a child who will be miserable, but once such a child exists, since its life can contain nothing but misery, we should reduce the amount of pain in the world by an act of euthanasia. But euthanasia is a more harrowing process for the parents and others involved than non-conception. Hence we have an indirect reason for not conceiving a child bound to have a miserable existence.

So is it wrong to cut short a pleasant life? We can hold that it is, on either the total view or the prior existence view, but our answers commit us to different things in each case. We can only take the prior existence approach if we accept that it is not wrong to bring a miserable being into existence – or else offer an explanation for why this should be wrong, and yet it not be wrong to fail to bring into existence a being whose life will be pleasant. Alternatively we can take the total approach, but then we must accept that it is also good to create more beings whose lives will be pleasant – and this has some odd practical implications. Some of these implications we have already seen. Others will become evident in the next chapter.

Comparing the Value of Different Lives

If we can give an affirmative – albeit somewhat shaky – answer to the question whether the life of a being who is conscious but not self-conscious has some value, can we also compare the value of different lives, at different levels of consciousness or self-consciousness? We are not, of course, going to attempt to assign numerical values to the lives of different beings, or even to produce an ordered list. The best that we could hope for is some idea of the principles that, when supplemented with the appropriate detailed information about the lives of different beings, might serve as the basis for such a list. But the most fundamental issue is whether we can accept the idea of ordering the value of different lives at all.

Some say that it is anthropocentric, even speciesist, to order the value of different lives in a hierarchical manner. If we do so we shall, inevitably, be placing ourselves at the top and other beings closer to us in proportion to the resemblance between them and ourselves. Instead we should recognise that from the points of view of the different beings themselves, each life is of equal value. Those who take this view recognise, of course, that a person's life may include the study of philosophy while a mouse's life cannot; but they say that the pleasures of a mouse's life are all that the mouse has, and so can be presumed to mean as much to the mouse as the pleasures of a person's life mean to the person. We cannot say that the one is more or less valuable than the other.

Is it speciesist to judge that the life of a normal adult member of our species is more valuable than the life of a normal adult mouse? It would be possible to defend such a judgment only if we can find some neutral ground, some impartial standpoint from which we can make the comparison.

The difficulty of finding neutral ground is a very real practical difficulty, but I am not convinced that it presents an insoluble theoretical problem. I would frame the question we need to ask in the following manner. Imagine that I have the peculiar property of being able to turn myself into an animal, so that like Puck in *A Midsummer-Night's Dream,* 'Sometimes a horse I'll be, sometimes a hound.' And suppose that when I am a horse, I really am a horse, with all and only the mental experiences of a horse, and when I am a human being I have all and only the mental experiences of a human being. Now let us make the additional supposition that I can enter a third state in which I remember exactly what it was like to be a horse and exactly what it was like to be a human being. What would this third state be like? In some respects – the degree of self-awareness and rationality involved, for instance – it might be more like a human existence than an equine one, but it would not be a human existence in every respect. In this third state, then, I could compare horse-existence with human-existence. Suppose that I were offered the opportunity of another life, and given the choice of life as a horse or as a human being, the lives in question being in each case about as good as horse or human lives can reasonably be expected to be on this planet. I would then be deciding, in effect, between the value of the life of a horse (to the horse) and the value of the life of a human (to the human).

Undoubtedly this scenario requires us to suppose a lot of things that could never happen, and some things that strain our imagination. The coherence of an existence in which one is neither a horse nor a human, but remembers what it was like to be both, might be questioned. Nevertheless I think I can make some sense of the idea of choosing from this position; and I am fairly confident that from this position, some forms of life would be seen as preferable to others.

If it is true that we can make sense of the choice between existence as a mouse and existence as a human, then – whichever way the choice would go – we can make sense of the idea that the life of one kind of animal possesses greater value than the life of another; and if this is so, then the claim that the life of every being has equal value is on very weak ground. We cannot defend this claim by saying that every being's life is all-important for it, since we have now accepted a comparison that takes a more objective – or at least intersubjective – stance and thus goes beyond the value of the life of a being considered solely from the point of view of that being.

So it would not necessarily be speciesist to rank the value of different lives in some hierarchical ordering. How we should go about doing this is another question, and I have nothing better to offer than the imaginative reconstruction of what it would be like to be a different kind of being. Some comparisons may be too difficult. We may have to say that we have not the slightest idea whether it would be better to be a fish or a snake; but then, we do not very often find ourselves forced to choose between killing a fish or a snake. Other comparisons might not be so difficult. In general it does seem that the more highly developed the conscious life of the being, the greater the degree of self-awareness and rationality and the broader the range of possible experiences, the more one would prefer that kind of life, if one were choosing between it and a being at a lower level of awareness. Can utilitarians defend such a preference? In a famous passage John Stuart Mill attempted to do so:

> Few human creatures would consent to be changed into any of the lower animals, for a promise of the fullest allowance of a beast's pleasures; no intelligent human being would consent to

be a fool, no instructed person would be an ignoramus, no person of feeling and conscience would be selfish and base, even though they should be persuaded that the fool, the dunce, or the rascal is better satisfied with his lot than they are with theirs . . . It is better to be a human being dissatisfied than a pig satisfied; better to be Socrates dissatisfied than a fool satisfied. And if the fool, or the pig, are of a different opinion, it is because they only know their own side of the question. The other party to the comparison knows both sides.

As many critics have pointed out, this argument is weak. Does Socrates really know what it is like to be a fool? Can he truly experience the joys of idle pleasure in simple things, untroubled by the desire to understand and improve the world? We may doubt it. But another significant aspect of this passage is less often noticed. Mill's argument for preferring the life of a human being to that of an animal (with which most modern readers would be quite comfortable) is exactly paralleled by his argument for preferring the life of an intelligent human being to that of fool. Given the context and the way in which the term "fool" was commonly used in his day, it seems likely that by this he means what we would now refer to as a person with an intellectual disability. With this further conclusion some modern readers will be distinctly uncomfortable; but as Mill's argument suggests, it is not easy to embrace the preference for the life of a human over that of a non-human, without at the same time endorsing a preference for the life of a normal human being over that of another human at a similar intellectual level to that of the non-human in the first comparison.

Mill's argument is difficult to reconcile with classical utilitarianism, because it just does not seem true that the more intelligent being necessarily has a greater capacity for happiness; and even if we were to accept that the capacity is greater, the fact that, as Mill acknowledges, this capacity is less often filled (the fool is satisfied, Socrates is not) would have to be taken into consideration. Would a preference utilitarian have a better prospect of defending the judgments Mill makes? That would depend on how we compare different preferences, held with differing degrees of awareness and self-consciousness. It does not seem impossible that we should find ways of ranking such different preferences, but at this stage the question remains open.

This chapter has focussed on the killing of conscious beings. Whether there is anything wrong about taking non-conscious life – the lives of trees or plants, for instance – will be taken up in Chapter 10, on environmental ethics.

5

TAKING LIFE: ANIMALS

IN Chapter 4 we examined some general principles about the
value of life. In this and the following two chapters we shall
draw from that discussion some conclusions about three cases
of killing that have been the subject of heated debate: abortion,
euthanasia, and killing animals. Of these three, the question of
killing animals has probably aroused the least controversy;
nevertheless, for reasons that will become clear later, it is impossible to defend a position on abortion and euthanasia without taking some view about the killing of non-human animals.
So we shall look at that question first.

CAN A NON-HUMAN ANIMAL BE A PERSON?

We have seen that there are reasons for holding that the killing
of a person is more seriously wrong than the killing of a being
who is not a person. This is true whether we accept preference
utilitarianism, Tooley's argument about the right to life, or the
principle of respect for autonomy. Even a classical utilitarian
would say that there may be indirect reasons why it is worse
to kill a person. So in discussing the wrongness of killing non-
human animals it is important to ask if any of them are persons.

It sounds odd to call an animal a person. This oddness may
be no more than a symptom of our habit of keeping our own
species sharply separated from others. In any case, we can avoid
the linguistic oddness by rephrasing the question in accordance
with our definition of 'person'. What we are really asking
is whether any non-human animals are rational and self-

conscious beings, aware of themselves as distinct entities with a past and a future.

Are animals self-conscious? There is now solid evidence that some are. Perhaps the most dramatic evidence comes from apes who can communicate with us using a human language. The ancient dream of teaching our language to another species was realised when two American scientists, Allen and Beatrice Gardner, guessed that the failure of previous attempts to teach chimpanzees to talk was due to the chimpanzees' lacking, not the intelligence required for using language, but the vocal equipment needed to reproduce the sounds of human language. The Gardners therefore decided to treat a young chimpanzee as if she were a human baby without vocal chords. They communicated with her, and with each other when in her presence, by using American Sign Language, a language widely used by deaf people.

The technique was a striking success. The chimpanzee, whom they called 'Washoe', learned to understand about 350 different signs, and to use about 150 of them correctly. She put signs together to form simple sentences. As for self-consciousness, Washoe does not hesitate, when shown her own image in a mirror and asked 'Who is that?' to reply: 'Me, Washoe.' Later Washoe moved to Ellensburg, Washington, where she lived with other chimpanzees under the care of Roger and Deborah Fouts. Here she adopted an infant chimpanzee and soon began not only signing to him, but even deliberately teaching him signs, for example, by moulding his hands into the sign for 'food' in an appropriate context.

Gorillas appear to be as good as chimpanzees at learning sign language. Almost twenty years ago Francine Patterson began signing and also speaking English with Koko, a lowland gorilla. Koko now has a working vocabulary of over 500 signs, and she has used about 1000 signs correctly on one or more occasions. She understands an even larger number of spoken English words. Her companion Michael, who began to be exposed to signs at a later age, has used about 400 signs. In front of a mirror, Koko will make faces, or examine her teeth. When asked: 'What's a smart gorilla?' Koko responded: 'Me.' When someone remarked of Koko, in her presence, 'She's a goofball!' Koko (perhaps not understanding the term) signed: 'No, gorilla.'

An orangutan, Chantek, has been taught sign language by Lyn Miles. When shown a photograph of a gorilla pointing to her nose, Chantek was able to imitate the gorilla by pointing to his own nose. This implies that he has an image of his own body and can transfer that image from the two-dimensional plane of the visual image to perform the necessary bodily action.

Apes also use signs to refer to past or future events, thus showing a sense of time. Koko, for example, when asked, six days after the event, what had happened on her birthday, signed 'sleep eat'. Even more impressive is the evidence of temporal sense shown by the regular festivities held by the Fouts for the chimpanzees at Ellensburg. Each year, after Thanksgiving, Roger and Deborah Fouts set up a Christmas tree, covered with edible ornaments. The chimpanzees use the sign combination 'candy tree' to refer to the Christmas tree. In 1989, when snow began to fall just after Thanksgiving but the tree had not yet appeared, a chimpanzee named Tatu asked 'Candy tree?' The Fouts interpret this as showing not only that Tatu remembered the tree, but also that she knew that this was the season for it. Later Tatu also remembered that the birthday of one of the chimpanzees, Dar, followed closely on that of Deborah Fouts. The chimpanzees got ice cream for their birthdays; and after the festivities for Deborah's birthday were over, Tatu asked: 'Dar ice cream?'

Suppose that on the basis of such evidence we accept that the signing apes are self-conscious. Are they exceptional among all the non-human animals in this respect, precisely because they can use language? Or is it merely that language enables these animals to demonstrate to us a characteristic that they, and other animals, possessed all along?

Some philosophers have argued that thinking requires language: one cannot think without formulating one's thoughts in words. The Oxford philosopher Stuart Hampshire, for example, has written:

> The difference here between a human being and an animal lies in the possibility of the human being expressing his intention and putting into words his intention to do so-and-so, for his own benefit or for the benefit of others. The difference is not merely that an animal in fact has no means of communicating, or of recording for itself, its intention, with the effect that no one can ever know what the intention was. It is a stronger difference, which is more correctly expressed as the senselessness of attributing intentions to an animal which has not the means to reflect upon, and to announce to itself or to others, its own future behaviour... It would be senseless to attribute to an animal a memory that distinguished the order of events in the past, and it would be senseless to attribute to it an expectation of an order of events in the future. It does not have the concepts of order, or any concepts at all.

Obviously Hampshire was wrong to distinguish so crudely between humans and animals; for as we have just seen, the signing apes have clearly shown that they do have 'an expectation of an order of events in the future.' But Hampshire wrote before apes had learned to use sign language, so this lapse may be excusable. The same cannot be said for the much later defence of the same view by another English philosopher, Michael Leahy, in a book entitled *Against Liberation*. Like Hampshire, Leahy argues that animals, lacking language, cannot have intentions, or act 'for a reason.'

Suppose that such arguments were to be re-phrased so that they referred to animals who have not learned to use a language, rather than all animals. Would they then be correct? If so, no being without language can be a person. This applies, presumably, to young humans as well as to non-signing animals. It might be argued that many species of animals do use language, just not our language. Certainly most social animals have some means of communicating with each other, whether it be the melodious songs of the humpback whales, the buzzes and whistles of dolphins, the howls and barks of dogs, the songs of birds, and even the dance performed by honey bees returning to the hive, from which other bees learn the distance and direction of the food source from which the bee has come. But whether any of these amount to language, in the required sense, is doubtful; and since it would take us too far from our topic to pursue that issue, I shall assume that they do not, and consider what can be learned from the non-linguistic behaviour of animals.

Is the line of argument that denies intentional behaviour to animals sound when it is limited to animals without language? I do not believe that it is. Hampshire's and Leahy's arguments are typical of those of many philosophers who have written along similar lines, in that they are attempts to do philosophy from the armchair, on a topic that demands investigation in the real world. There is nothing altogether inconceivable about a being possessing the capacity for conceptual thought without having a language and there are instances of animal behaviour that are extraordinarily difficult, if not downright impossible, to explain except under the assumption that the animals are thinking conceptually. In one experiment, for example, German researchers presented a chimpanzee named Julia with two series of five closed and transparent containers. At the end of one series was a box with a banana; the box at the end of the other series was empty. The box containing the banana could only be opened with a distinctively shaped key; this was apparent from looking at the box. This key could be seen inside another locked box; and to open that box, Julia needed another distinctive key, which had to be taken out of a third box which could only be opened with its own key, which was inside a fourth locked box. Finally, in front of Julia, were two initial boxes, open and each containing a distinctive key. Julia was able to choose the correct initial key, by which she could open the next box in the series that led, eventually, to the box with the banana. To do this, she must have been able to reason backwards from her desire to open the box with the banana to her need to have the key that would open it, to her need for the key that would open that box, and so on. Since Julia had not been taught any form of language, her behaviour proves that beings without language can think in quite complex ways.

Nor is it only in laboratory experiments that the behaviour of animals points to the conclusion that they possess both memory of the past and expectations about the future, and that they are self-aware, that they form intentions and act on them. Frans de Waal and his colleagues have for several years watched chimpanzees living in semi-natural conditions in two acres of forest at Amsterdam Zoo. They have often observed co-operating activity that requires planning. For example, the chimpanzees like to climb the trees and break off branches, so that they can eat the leaves. To prevent the rapid destruction of the small forest, the zookeepers have placed electric fencing around the trunk of the trees. The chimpanzees overcome this by breaking large branches from dead trees (which have no fences around them) and dragging them to the base of a live tree. One chimpanzee then holds the dead branch while another climbs up it, over the fence and into the tree. The chimpanzee who gets into the tree in this way shares the leaves thus obtained with the one holding the branch.

De Waal has also observed deliberately deceptive behaviour that clearly shows both self-consciousness and an awareness of the consciousness of another. Chimpanzees live in groups in which one male will be dominant and will attack other males who mate with receptive females. Despite this, a good deal of sexual activity goes on when the dominant male is not watching. Male chimpanzees often seek to interest females in sexual activity by sitting with their legs apart, displaying their erect penis. (Human males who expose themselves in a similar way are continuing a form of chimpanzee behaviour that has become socially inappropriate.) On one occasion a junior male was enticing a female in this manner when the dominant male walked over. The junior male covered his erection with his hands so that the dominant male could not see it.

Jane Goodall has described an incident showing forward planning by Figan, a young wild chimpanzee in the Gombe region of Tanzania. In order to bring the animals closer to her observation post, Goodall had hidden some bananas in a tree:

> One day, sometime after the group had been fed, Figan spotted a banana that had been overlooked – but Goliath [an adult male ranking above Figan in the group's hierarchy] was resting directly underneath it. After no more than a quick glance from the fruit to Goliath, Figan moved away and sat on the other side of the tent so that he could no longer see the fruit. Fifteen minutes later, when Goliath got up and left, Figan without a moment's hesitation went over and collected the banana. Quite obviously he had sized up the whole situation: if he had climbed for the fruit earlier, Goliath would almost certainly have snatched it away. If he had remained close to the banana, he would probably have looked at it from time to time. Chimps are very quick to notice and interpret the eye movements of their fellows, and Goliath would possibly, therefore, have seen the fruit himself. And so Figan had not only refrained from instantly gratifying his desire but had also gone away so that he could not 'give the game away' by looking at the banana.

Goodall's description of this episode does, of course, attribute to Figan a complex set of intentions, including the intention to avoid 'giving the game away' and the intention to obtain the banana after Goliath's departure. It also attributes to Figan an 'expectation of an order of events in the future', namely the expectation that Goliath would move away, that the banana would still be there, and that he, Figan, would then go and get it. Yet there seems nothing at all 'senseless' about these attributions, despite the fact that Figan cannot put his intentions or expectations into words. If an animal can devise a careful plan for obtaining a banana, not now but at some future time, and can take precautions against his own propensity to give away the object of the plan, that animal must be aware of himself as a distinct entity, existing over time.

KILLING NON-HUMAN PERSONS

Some non-human animals are persons, as we have defined the term. To judge the significance of this we must set it in the context of our earlier discussion, in which I argued that the only defensible version of the doctrine of the sanctity of human life was what we might call the 'doctrine of the sanctity of personal life'. I suggested that if human life does have special value or a special claim to be protected, it has it in so far as most human beings are persons. But if some non-human animals are persons, too, the lives of those animals must have the same special value or claim to protection. Whether we base these special moral features of the lives of human persons on preferential utilitarianism, on a right to life deriving from their capacity to see themselves as continuing selves, or on respect for autonomy, these arguments must apply to non-human persons as well. Only the indirect utilitarian reason for not killing persons – the fear that such acts are likely to arouse in other persons – applies less readily to non-human persons since non-humans are less likely than humans to learn about killings that take place at a distance from them. But then, this reason does not apply to all killings of human persons either, since it is possible to kill in such a way that no one learns that a person has been killed.

Hence we should reject the doctrine that places the lives of members of our species above the lives of members of other species. Some members of other species are persons: some members of our own species are not. No objective assessment can support the view that it is always worse to kill members of our species who are not persons than members of other species who are. On the contrary, as we have seen there are strong arguments for thinking that to take the lives of persons is, in itself, more serious than taking the lives of non-persons. So it seems that

117

killing, say, a chimpanzee is worse than the killing of a human being who, because of a congenital intellectual disability, is not and never can be a person.

At present the killing of a chimpanzee is not regarded as a serious matter. Large numbers of chimpanzees are used in scientific research, and many of them die in the course of this research. For many years, because chimpanzees were difficult to breed in captivity, the corporations that supplied these animals captured them in African jungles. The standard method was to shoot a female with an infant by her side. The infant was then captured and shipped to Europe and the United States. Jane Goodall has estimated that for every infant who reached his or her destination alive, six chimpanzees died. Although chimpanzees have been placed on the threatened list, and this trade has now been banned, illegal killing and trading of chimpanzees, and of gorillas and orangutans, still continues.

The great apes – chimpanzees, gorillas, and orangutans – may be the clearest cases of non-human persons, but there are almost certainly others. Systematic observation of whales and dolphins has, for obvious reasons, lagged far behind that of apes, and it is quite possible that these large-brained mammals will turn out to be rational and self-conscious. Despite an official moratorium, the whaling industry slaughters thousands of whales annually in the name of 'research', and the whaling nations are seeking to overturn the International Whaling Commission's moratorium so that they can return to full-scale commercial whaling. Closer to home, many of those who live with dogs and cats are convinced that these animals are self-conscious and have a sense of the future. They begin to expect their companion human being to come home at a certain time. In her book *Emma and I*, Sheila Hocken relates how her guide-dog spontaneously began to take her, every Friday, to the places where she did her weekend shopping, without needing to be told the day. People who feed feral cats on a weekly basis have found that they, too, will turn up on the right day of the week. Such observations may be 'unscientific', but to those who know dogs and cats well they are plausible and in the absence of better studies they should be taken seriously. According to official United States Department of Agriculture figures, approximately 140,000 dogs and 42,000 cats die in laboratories in the United States each year, and smaller but still sizeable numbers are used in every 'developed' nation. And if dogs and cats qualify as persons, the mammals we use for food cannot be far behind. We think of dogs as being more like people than pigs; but pigs are highly intelligent animals and if we kept pigs as pets and reared dogs for food, we would probably reverse our order of preference. Are we turning persons into bacon?

Admittedly, all this is speculative. It is notoriously difficult to establish when another being is self-conscious. But if it is wrong to kill a person when we can avoid doing so, and there is real doubt about whether a being we are thinking of killing is a person, we should give that being the benefit of the doubt. The rule here is the same as that among deer hunters: if you see something moving in the bushes and are not sure if it is a deer or a hunter, don't shoot! (We may think the hunters shouldn't shoot in either case, but the rule is a sound one within the ethical framework hunters use.) On these grounds, a great deal of the killing of non-human animals must be condemned.

KILLING OTHER ANIMALS

Arguments against killing based on the capacity to see oneself as an individual existing over time apply to some non-human animals, but there are others who, though presumably conscious, cannot plausibly be said to be persons. Of those animals that humans regularly kill in large numbers, fish appear to be the clearest case of animals who are conscious but not persons. The rightness or wrongness of killing these animals seems to rest on utilitarian considerations, for they are not autonomous and – at least if Tooley's analysis of rights is correct – do not qualify for a right to life.

Before we discuss the utilitarian approach to killing itself, we should remind ourselves that a wide variety of indirect reasons will figure in the utilitarian's calculations. Many modes of killing used on animals do not inflict an instantaneous death, so there is pain in the process of dying. There is also the effect of the death of one animal on his or her mate or other members of the animal's social group. There are many species of birds in which the bond between male and female lasts for a lifetime. The death of one member of this pair presumably causes distress, and a sense of loss and sorrow for the survivor. The mother–child relationship in mammals can be a source of intense suffering if either is killed or taken away. (Dairy farmers routinely remove calves from their mothers at an early age, so that the milk will be available for humans; anyone who has lived on a dairy farm will know that, for days after the calves have gone, the cows keep calling for them.) In some species the death of one animal may be felt by a larger group – as the behaviour of wolves and elephants suggests. All these factors would lead the utilitarian to oppose a lot of killing of animals, whether or not the animals are persons. These factors would not, however, be reasons for opposing killing non-persons in itself, apart from the pain and suffering it may cause.

The utilitarian verdict on killing that is painless and causes no loss to others is more complicated, because it depends on how we choose between the two versions of utilitarianism outlined in the previous chapter. If we take what I called the 'prior existence' view, we shall hold that it is wrong to kill any being whose life is likely to contain, or can be brought to contain, more pleasure than pain. This view implies that it is normally wrong to kill animals for food, since usually we could bring it about that these animals had a few pleasant months or even years before they died – and the pleasure we get from eating them would not outweigh this.

The other version of utilitarianism – the 'total' view – can lead to a different outcome that has been used to justify meat-eating. The nineteenth-century British political philosopher Leslie Stephen once wrote:

'Of all the arguments for Vegetarianism none is so weak as the argument from humanity. The pig has a stronger interest than anyone in the demand for bacon. If all the world were Jewish, there would be no pigs at all.'

Stephen views animals as if they were replaceable, and with this those who accept the total view must agree. The total version of utilitarianism regards sentient beings as valuable only in so far as they make possible the existence of intrinsically valuable experiences like pleasure. It is as if sentient beings are receptacles of something valuable and it does not matter if a receptacle gets broken, so long as there is another receptacle to which the contents can be transferred without any getting spilt. (This metaphor should not be taken too seriously, however; unlike precious liquids, experiences like pleasure cannot exist independently from a conscious being, and so even on the total view, sentient beings cannot properly be thought of merely as receptacles.) Stephen's argument is that although meat-eaters are responsible for the death of the animal they eat and for the loss of pleasure experienced by that animal, they are also responsible for the creation of more animals, since if no one ate meat there would be no more animals bred for fattening. The loss meat-eaters inflict on one animal is thus balanced, on the total view, by the benefit they confer on the next. We may call this 'the replaceability argument'.

The first point to note about the replaceability argument is that even if it is valid when the animals in question have a pleasant life it would not justify eating the flesh of animals reared in modern factory farms, where the animals are so crowded together and restricted in their movements that their lives seem to be more of a burden than a benefit to them.

A second point is that if it is good to create happy life, then presumably it is good for there to be as many happy beings on our planet as it can possibly hold. Defenders of meat-eating had better hope that they can find a reason why it is better for there to be happy people rather than just the maximum possible number of happy beings, because otherwise the argument might imply that we should eliminate almost all human beings in order to make way for much larger numbers of smaller happy animals. If, however, the defenders of meat-eating do come up with a reason for preferring the creation of happy people to, say, happy mice, then their argument will not support meat-eating at all. For with the possible exception of arid areas suitable only for pasture, the surface of our globe can support more people if we grow plant foods than if we raise animals.

These two points greatly weaken the replaceability argument as a defence of meat-eating, but they do not go to the heart of the matter. Are some sentient beings really replaceable? The response to the first edition of this book suggests that the replaceability argument is probably the most controversial, and widely criticised, argument in this book. Unfortunately none of the critics have offered satisfactory alternative solutions to the underlying problems to which replaceability offers one – if not very congenial – answer.

Henry Salt, a nineteenth-century English vegetarian and author of a book called *Animals' Rights* thought that the argument rested on a simple philosophical error:

> The fallacy lies in the confusion of thought that attempts to compare existence with non-existence. A person who is already in existence may feel that he would rather have lived than not, but he must first have the *terra firma* of existence to argue from: the moment he begins to argue as if from the abyss of the non-existent, he talks nonsense, by predicating good or evil, happiness or unhappiness, of that of which we can predicate nothing.

When I wrote the first edition of *Animal Liberation* I accepted Salt's view. I thought that it was absurd to talk as if one conferred a favour on a being by bringing it into existence, since at the time one confers this favour, there is no being at all. But now I am less confident. After all, as we saw in Chapter 4, we do seem to do something bad if we knowingly bring a miserable being into existence, and if this is so, it is difficult to explain why we do not do something good when we knowingly bring a happy being into existence.

Derek Parfit has described another hypothetical situation that amounts to an even stronger case for the replaceability view. He asks us to imagine that two women are each planning to have a child. The first woman is already three months pregnant when her doctor gives her both bad and good news. The bad news is that the fetus she is carrying has a defect that will significantly diminish the future child's quality of life – although not so adversely as to make the child's life utterly miserable, or not worth living at all. The good news is that this defect is easily treatable. All the woman has to do is take a pill that will have no side-effects, and the future child will not have the defect. In this situation, Parfit plausibly suggests, we would all agree that the woman should take the pill, and that she does wrong if she refuses to take it.

The second woman sees her doctor before she is pregnant, when she is about to stop using contraception, and also receives bad and good news. The bad news is that she has a medical condition that has the effect that if she conceives a child within the next three months, that child will have a significant defect – with exactly the same impact on the child's quality of life as the defect described in the previous paragraph. This defect is not treatable, but the good news is that the woman's condition is a temporary one, and if she waits three months before becoming pregnant, her child will not have the defect. Here too, Parfit suggests, we would all agree that the woman should wait before becoming pregnant, and that she does wrong if she does not wait.

Suppose that the first woman does not take the pill, and the second woman does not wait before becoming pregnant, and that as a result each has a child with a significant disability. It would seem that they have each done something wrong. Are their wrong-doings of equal magnitude? If we assume that it would have been no greater hardship for the second woman to wait three months before becoming pregnant than it would have been for the first woman to take the pill, it would seem that the answer is yes, what each has done is equally wrong. But now consider what this answer implies. The first woman has harmed her child. That child can say to her mother: 'You should have taken the pill. If you had done so, I would not now have this disability, and my life would be significantly better.' But if the child of the second woman tries to make the same claim, her mother has a devastating response. She can say: 'If I had waited three months before becoming pregnant you would never have existed. I would have produced another child, from a different egg and different sperm. Your life, even with your disability, is definitely above the point at which life is so miserable that it ceases to be worth living. You never had a chance of existing without the disability. So I have not harmed you at all.' This reply seems a complete defence to the charge of having harmed the child now in existence. If, despite this, we persist in our belief that it was wrong of the woman not to postpone her pregnancy, where does the wrongness lie? It cannot lie in bringing into existence the child to whom she gave birth, for that child has an adequate quality of life. Could it lie in not bringing a possible being into existence – to be precise, in not bringing into existence the child she would have had if she had waited three months? This is one possible answer, but it commits us to the total view, and implies that, other things being equal, it is good to bring into existence children without disabilities. A third possibility is that the wrong-doing lies, not in harming an identifiable child, nor simply in omitting to bring a possible child into existence, but in bringing into existence a child with a less satisfactory quality of life than another child whom one could have brought into existence. In other words, we have failed to bring about the best possible outcome. This last seems the most plausible answer, but it too suggests that at least possible people are replaceable. The question then becomes this: At what stage in the process that passes from possible people to actual people does replaceability cease to apply? What characteristic makes the difference?

If we think of living creatures – human or non-human – as self-conscious individuals, leading their own lives and wanting to go on living, the replaceability argument holds little appeal. It is possible that when Salt so emphatically rejected the idea of replaceability, he was thinking of such beings, for he concludes the essay quoted above by claiming that Lucretius long ago refuted Stephen's 'vulgar sophism' in the following passage of *De Rerum Natura*:

> What loss were ours, if we had known not birth?
> Let living men to longer life aspire,
> While fond affection binds their hearts to earth:
> But who never hath tasted life's desire,
> Unborn, impersonal, can feel no dearth.

This passage supports the claim that there is a difference between killing living beings who 'to longer life aspire' and failing to create a being who, unborn and impersonal, can feel no loss of life. But what of beings who, though alive, cannot aspire to longer life, because they lack the conception of themselves as living beings with a future? These being are, in a sense, 'impersonal'. Perhaps, therefore, in killing them, one does them no personal wrong, although one does reduce the quantity of happiness in the universe. But this wrong, if it is wrong, can be counter-balanced by bringing into existence similar beings who will lead equally happy lives. So perhaps the capacity to see oneself as existing over time, and thus to aspire to longer life (as well as to have other non-momentary, future-directed interests) is the characteristic that marks out those beings who cannot be considered replaceable.

Although we shall return to this topic in the next two chapters, we can note here that this conclusion is in harmony with Tooley's views about what it takes to have a right to life. For a preference utilitarian, concerned with the satisfaction of preferences rather than experiences of suffering or happiness, there is a similar fit with the distinction already drawn between killing those who are rational and self-conscious beings, and those who are not. Rational, self-conscious beings are individuals, leading lives of their own and cannot in any sense be regarded merely as receptacles for containing a certain quantity of happiness. They have, in the words of the American philosopher James Rachels, a life that is biographical, and not merely biological. In contrast, beings who are conscious, but not self-conscious, more nearly approximate the picture of receptacles for experiences of pleasure and pain, because their preferences will be of a more immediate sort. They will not have desires that project their images of their own existence into the future. Their conscious states are not internally linked over time. We can presume that if fish become unconscious, then before the loss of consciousness they would have no expectations or desires for anything that might happen subsequently, and if they regain consciousness, they have no awareness of having previously existed. Therefore if the fish were killed while unconscious and replaced by a similar number of other fish who could be created only because the first group of fish were killed, there would, from the perspective of fishy awareness, be no difference between that and the same fish losing and regaining consciousness.

For a non–self-conscious being death is the cessation of experiences, in much the same way that birth is the beginning of experiences. Death cannot be contrary to an interest in continued life, any more than birth could be in accordance with an interest in commencing life. To this extent, with non–self-conscious life, birth and death cancel each other out; whereas with self-conscious beings the fact that once self-conscious one may desire to continue living means that death inflicts a loss for which the birth of another is insufficient compensation.

The test of universalisability supports this view. If I imagine myself in turn as a self-conscious being and a conscious but not self-conscious being, it is only in the former case that I could have forward-looking desires that extend beyond periods of sleep or temporary unconsciousness, for example a desire to complete my studies, a desire to have children, or simply a desire to go on living, in addition to desires for immediate satisfaction or pleasure, or to get out of painful or distressing situations. Hence it is only in the former case that my death involves a greater loss than just a temporary loss of consciousness, and is not adequately compensated for by the creation of a being with similar prospects of pleasurable experiences.

In reviewing the first edition of this book H. L. A. Hart, formerly professor of jurisprudence at the University of Oxford, suggested that for a utilitarian, self-conscious beings must be replaceable in just the same way as non–self-conscious beings are. Whether one is a preference utilitarian or a classical utilitarian will, in Hart's view, make no difference here, because

> preference Utilitarianism is after all a form of maximizing utilitarianism: it requires that the overall satisfaction of different persons' preferences be maximized just as Classical Utilitarianianism requires overall experienced happiness to be maximized . . . If preferences, even the desire to live, may be outweighed by the preferences of others, why cannot they be outweighed by new preferences created to take their place?

It is of course true that preference utilitarianism is a form of maximising utilitarianism in the sense that it directs us to maximise the satisfaction of preferences, but Hart is on weaker ground when he suggests that this must mean that existing preferences can be outweighed by new preferences created to take their place. For while the satisfaction of an existing preference is a good thing, the package deal that involves creating and then satisfying a preference need not be thought of as equivalent to it. Again, universalisability supports this way of conceiving preference utilitarianism. If I put myself in the place of another with an unsatisfied preference, and ask myself if I want that preference satisfied, the answer is (tautologically) yes. If, however, I ask myself whether I wish to have a new preference created that can then be satisfied, I will be quite uncertain. If I think of a case in which the satisfaction of the preference will be highly pleasurable, I may say yes. (We are glad that we are hungry if delicious food is on the table before us, and strong sexual desires are fine when we are able to satisfy them.) But if I think of the creation of a preference that is more like a privation, I will say no. (We don't cause ourselves headaches simply in order to be able to take aspirin and thus satisfy our desire to be free of the pain.) This suggests that the creation and satisfaction of a preference is in itself neither good nor bad: our response to the idea of the creation and satisfaction of a preference varies according to whether the experience as a whole will be desirable or undesirable, in terms of other, long-standing preferences we may have, for example for pleasure rather than pain.

Exactly how preference utilitarianism ought to evaluate the creation and satisfaction of a preference, as distinct from the satisfaction of an existing preference, is a difficult issue. In my initial response to Hart's criticism, I suggested that we think of the creation of an unsatisfied preference as putting a debit in a kind of moral ledger that is merely cancelled out by the satisfaction of the preference. (Some will see in this model confirmation of Marx's scornful remark that Bentham's utilitarianism is a philosophy suitable for a nation of shopkeepers!) The 'moral ledger' model has the advantage of explaining the puzzling asymmetry mentioned in the previous chapter, in connection with the difference between the total and the prior existence interpretations of utilitarianism. We consider it wrong to bring into existence a child who, because of a genetic defect, will lead a thoroughly miserable existence for a year or two and then die; yet we do not consider it good or obligatory to bring into existence a child who, in all probability, will lead a happy life. The 'debit' view of preferences just outlined would explain why this should be so: to bring into existence a child, most of whose preferences we will be unable to satisfy, is to create a debit that we cannot cancel. This is wrong. To create a child whose preferences will be able to be satisfied, is to create a debit that can be cancelled. This is, in itself, I thought, ethically neutral. The model can also explain why, in Parfit's example, what the two women do is equally wrong – for both quite unnecessarily bring into existence a child who is likely to have a larger negative balance in the ledger than a child they could have brought into existence.

Unfortunately, this same view carries a less desirable implication: it makes it wrong, other things being equal, to bring into existence a child who will on the whole be very happy, and will be able to satisfy nearly all of her preferences, but will still have some preferences unsatisfied. For if the creation of each preference is a debit that is cancelled only when the desire is satisfied, even the best life will, taken in itself, leave a small debit in the ledger. Since everyone has some unsatisfied desires, the conclusion to be drawn is that it would have been better if none of us had been born. Thus the moral ledger model of creating and satisfying a preference will not do. It might be saved by attaching to it a stipulation that sets a given level of preference satisfaction, below complete satisfaction, as a minimum for overcoming the negative entry opened by the creation of a being with unsatisfied preferences. This might be the level at which we consider a life ceases to be worth living, from the perspective of the person leading that life. Such a solution seems a little ad hoc, but it may be possible to incorporate it into a plausible version of preference utilitarianism.

Another possibility is to take our model from Shakespeare, who speaks of 'life's uncertain voyage', and see the lives of self-conscious beings as arduous and uncertain journeys, at different stages, in which various amounts of hope and desire, as well as time and effort have been invested in order to reach particular goals or destinations. Suppose that I am thinking of travelling to Nepal, where I plan to trek to Thyangboche Monastery, at the base of Mt. Everest. I have always loved high mountains, and I know that I would enjoy being in the Himalayas for the first time. If during these early days of musing on the possibility of such a trip an insuperable obstacle arises – perhaps the Nepalese government bans tourism on the grounds that it is an environmental hazard – I will be a little put out, naturally, but my disappointment will be nothing compared with what it would have been if I had already arranged to take the necessary time off work, perhaps bought a non-refundable plane ticket to Kathmandu, or even trekked a long distance towards my destination, before being barred from reaching my goal. Similarly, one can regard a decision not to bring an infant into the world as akin to preventing a journey from getting underway, but this is not in itself seriously wrong, for the voyager has made no plans and set no goals. Gradually, as goals are set, even if tentatively, and a lot is done in order to increase the probability of the goals being reached, the wrongness of bringing the journey to a premature end increases. Towards the end of life, when most things that might have been achieved have either been done, or are now unlikely to be accomplished, the loss of life may again be less of tragedy than it would have been at an earlier stage of life.

The great virtue of this 'journey' model of a life is that it can explain why beings who can conceive of their own future existence and have embarked on their life journey are not replaceable, while at the same it can account for why it is wrong to bring a miserable being into existence. To do so is to send a being out on a journey that is doomed to disappointment and frustration. The model also offers a natural explanation of why Parfit's two women both do wrong, and to an equal degree:

they both quite unnecessarily send out voyagers with fewer prospects of making a successful journey than other voyagers whom they might have placed at the starting line. The women's children can be thought of as replaceable before the journey begins, but this does not require us to hold that there is an obligation to bring more children into existence, let alone to regard people as replaceable once life's journey has properly begun.

Both the modified moral ledger model and the journey model are metaphors, and should not be taken too literally. At best they suggest ways of thinking about when beings might be considered replaceable, and when they might not be so considered. As I indicated in the Preface, this is an area in which fully satisfactory answers are still to be found.

Before we leave the topic of killing non–self-conscious beings, I should emphasise that to take the view that non–self-conscious beings are replaceable is not to say that their interests do not count. I hope that the third chapter of this book makes it clear that their interests do count. As long as sentient beings are conscious, they have an interest in experiencing as much pleasure and as little pain as possible. Sentience suffices to place a being within the sphere of equal consideration of interests; but it does not mean that the being has a personal interest in continuing to live.

CONCLUSIONS

If the arguments in this chapter are correct, there is no single answer to the question: 'Is it normally wrong to take the life of an animal?' The term 'animal' – even in the restricted sense of 'non-human animal' – covers too diverse a range of lives for one principle to apply to all of them.

Some non-human animals appear to be rational and self-conscious, conceiving themselves as distinct beings with a past and a future. When this is so, or to the best of our knowledge

131

may be so, the case against killing is strong, as strong as the case against killing permanently intellectually disabled human beings at a similar mental level. (I have in mind here the direct reasons against killing; the effects on relatives of the intellectually disabled human will sometimes – but not always – constitute additional indirect reasons against killing the human. For further discussion of this issue, see Chapter 7.)

In the present state of our knowledge, this strong case against killing can be invoked most categorically against the slaughter of chimpanzees, gorillas, and orangutans. On the basis of what we now know about these near-relatives of ours, we should immediately extend to them the same full protection against being killed that we extend now to all human beings. A case can also be made, though with varying degrees of confidence, on behalf of whales, dolphins, monkeys, dogs, cats, pigs, seals, bears, cattle, sheep and so on, perhaps even to the point at which it may include all mammals – much depends on how far we are prepared to go in extending the benefit of the doubt, where a doubt exists. Even if we stopped at the species I have named, however – excluding the remainder of the mammals – our discussion has raised a very large question mark over the justifiability of a great deal of killing of animals carried out by humans, even when this killing takes place painlessly and without causing suffering to other members of the animal community. (Most of this killing, of course, does not take place under such ideal conditions.)

When we come to animals who, as far as we can tell, are not rational and self-conscious beings, the case against killing is weaker. When we are not dealing with beings aware of themselves as distinct entities, the wrongness of painless killing derives from the loss of pleasure it involves. Where the life taken would not, on balance, have been pleasant, no direct wrong is done. Even when the animal killed would have lived pleasantly, it is at least arguable that no wrong is done if the animal killed will, as a result of the killing, be replaced by another animal living an equally pleasant life. Taking this view involves holding that a wrong done to an existing being can be made up for by a benefit conferred on an as yet non-existent being. Thus it is possible to regard non–self-conscious animals as interchangeable with each other in a way that self-conscious beings are not. This means that in some circumstances – when animals lead pleasant lives, are killed painlessly, their deaths do not cause suffering to other animals, and the killing of one animal makes possible its replacement by another who would not otherwise have lived – the killing of non–self-conscious animals may not be wrong.

Is it possible, along these lines, to justify raising chickens for their meat, not in factory farm conditions but roaming freely around a farmyard? Let us make the questionable assumption that chickens are not self-conscious. Assume also that the birds can be killed painlessly, and the survivors do not appear to be affected by the death of one of their numbers. Assume, finally, that for economic reasons we could not rear the birds if we did not eat them. Then the replaceability argument appears to justify killing the birds, because depriving them of the pleasures of their existence can be offset against the pleasures of chickens who do not yet exist, and will exist only if existing chickens are killed.

As a piece of critical moral reasoning, this argument may be sound. Even at that level, it is important to realise how limited it is in its application. It cannot justify factory farming, where animals do not have pleasant lives. Nor does it normally justify the killing of wild animals. A duck shot by a hunter (making the shaky assumption that ducks are not self-conscious, and the almost certainly false assumption that the shooter can be relied upon to kill the duck instantly) has probably had a pleasant life, but the shooting of a duck does not lead to its replacement by another. Unless the duck population is at the maximum that can be sustained by the available food supply, the killing of a duck ends a pleasant life without starting another, and is for that reason wrong on straightforward utilitarian grounds. So although there are situations in which it is not wrong to kill animals, these situations are special ones, and do not cover very many of the billions of premature deaths humans inflict, year after year, on animals.

In any case, at the level of practical moral principles, it would be better to reject altogether the killing of animals for food, unless one must do so to survive. Killing animals for food makes us think of them as objects that we can use as we please. Their lives then count for little when weighed against our mere wants. As long as we continue to use animals in this way, to change our attitudes to animals in the way that they should be changed will be an impossible task. How can we encourage people to respect animals, and have equal concern for their interests, if they continue to eat them for their mere enjoyment? To foster the right attitudes of consideration for animals, including non–self-conscious ones, it may be best to make it a simple principle to avoid killing them for food.

6

TAKING LIFE: THE EMBRYO
AND THE FETUS

FEW ethical issues are as bitterly fought over today as abortion, and, while the pendulum has swung back and forth, neither side has had much success in altering the opinions of its opponents. Until 1967, abortion was illegal in almost all the Western democracies except Sweden and Denmark. Then Britain changed its law to allow abortion on broad social grounds, and in the 1973 case of *Roe* v *Wade*, the United States Supreme Court held that women have a constitutional right to an abortion in the first six months of pregnancy. Western European nations, including Roman Catholic countries like Italy, Spain and France, all liberalised their abortion laws. Only the Republic of Ireland held out against the trend.

Opponents of abortion did not give up. In the United States, conservative Presidents have changed the composition of the Supreme Court, which in turn has nibbled around the margins of the *Roe* v *Wade* decision, allowing states to restrict, in various ways, access to abortion. Outside the United States, the issue of abortion re-surfaced in Eastern Europe after the collapse of communism. The communist states had allowed abortion, but as nationalist and religious forces gathered strength, there were strong moves in countries like Poland for the re-introduction of restrictive laws. Since West Germany had more restrictive laws than East Germany, the need to introduce a single law for a united Germany also caused an intense debate.

In 1978 the birth of Louise Brown raised a new issue about

the status of early human life. For Louise Brown was the first human to have been born from an embryo that had been fertilised outside a human body. The success of Robert Edwards and Patrick Steptoe in demonstrating the possibility of in vitro fertilization, or IVF, was based on several years of experimentation on early human embryos – none of which had survived. IVF is now a routine procedure for certain types of infertility, and has given rise to thousands of healthy babies. To reach this point, however, many more embryos had to be destroyed in experiments, and further improvement of IVF techniques will require continued experimentation. Perhaps more significant still, for the long-term, are the possibilities for other forms of experimentation opened up by the existence of a viable embryo outside the human body. Embryos can now be frozen and stored for many years before being thawed and implanted in a woman. Normal children develop from these embryos, but the technique means that there are large numbers of embryos now preserved in special freezers around the world. (At the time of writing there were about 11,000 frozen embryos in Australia alone.) Because the IVF procedure often produces more embryos than can safely be transferred to the uterus of the woman from whom the egg came, many of these frozen embryos will never be wanted, and presumably will either be destroyed, be donated for research, or given to other infertile couples.

Other new technologies loom just a little way ahead. Embryos can be screened for genetic abnormalities, and then discarded if such abnormalities are found. Edwards has predicted that it will become scientifically feasible to grow embryos in vitro to the point at which, about 17 days after fertilisation, they develop blood stem cells, which could be used to treat various now-lethal blood diseases. Others, speculating about the further future, have asked if one day we will have banks of embryos or fetuses to provide organs for those who need them.

Abortion and destructive embryo experimentation pose difficult ethical issues because the development of the human being is a gradual process. If we take the fertilised egg immediately after conception, it is hard to get upset about its death. The fertilised egg is a single cell. After several days, it is still only a tiny cluster of cells without a single anatomical feature of the being it will later become. The cells that will eventually become the embryo proper are at this stage indistinguishable from the cells that will become the placenta and amniotic sac. Up to about 14 days after fertilisation, we cannot even tell if the embryo is going to be one or two individuals, because splitting can take place, leading to the formation of identical twins. At 14 days, the first anatomical feature, the so-called primitive streak, appears in the position in which the backbone will later develop. At this point the embryo could not possibly be conscious or feel pain. At the other extreme is the adult human being. To kill a human adult is murder, and, except in some special circumstances like those to be discussed in the next chapter, is unhesitatingly and universally condemned. Yet there is no obvious sharp line that divides the fertilised egg from the adult. Hence the problem.

Most of this chapter will be concerned with the problem of abortion, but the discussion of the status of the fetus will have obvious implications for two related issues: embryo experimentation, and the use of fetal tissue for medical purposes. I begin the discussion of abortion stating the position of those opposed to abortion, which I shall refer to as the conservative position. I shall then examine some of the standard liberal responses, and show why they are inadequate. Finally I shall use our earlier discussion of the value of life to approach the issue from a broader perspective. In contrast to the common opinion that the moral question about abortion is a dilemma with no solution, I shall show that, at least within the bounds of non-religious ethics, there is a clear-cut answer and those who take a different view are simply mistaken.

THE CONSERVATIVE POSITION

The central argument against abortion, put as a formal argument, would go something like this:

> First premise: It is wrong to kill an innocent human being.
> Second premise: A human fetus is an innocent human being.
> Conclusion: Therefore it is wrong to kill a human fetus.

The usual liberal response is to deny the second premise of this argument. So it is on whether the fetus is a human being that the issue is joined, and the dispute about abortion is often taken to be a dispute about when a human life begins.

On this issue the conservative position is difficult to shake. The conservative points to the continuum between the fertilised egg and child, and challenges the liberal to point to any stage in this gradual process that marks a morally significant dividing line. Unless there is such a line, the conservative says, we must either upgrade the status of the earliest embryo to that of the child, or downgrade the status of the child to that of the embryo; but no one wants to allow children to be dispatched on the request of their parents, and so the only tenable position is to grant the fetus the protection we now grant the child.

Is it true that there is no morally significant dividing line between fertilised egg and child? Those commonly suggested are: birth, viability, quickening, and the onset of consciousness. Let us consider these in turn.

Birth

Birth is the most visible possible dividing line, and the one that would suit liberals best. It coincides to some extent with our sympathies – we are less disturbed at the destruction of a fetus we have never seen than at the death of a being we can all see, hear and cuddle. But is this enough to make birth the line that decides whether a being may or may not be killed? The conservative can plausibly reply that the fetus/baby is the same entity, whether inside or outside the womb, with the same human features (whether we can see them or not) and the same degree of awareness and capacity for feeling pain. A prematurely born infant may well be *less* developed in these respects than a fetus nearing the end of its normal term. It seems peculiar to hold that we may not kill the premature infant, but may kill the more developed fetus. The location of a being – inside or outside the womb – should not make that much difference to the wrongness of killing it.

Viability

If birth does not mark a crucial moral distinction, should we push the line back to the time at which the fetus could survive outside the womb? This overcomes one objection to taking birth as the decisive point, for it treats the viable fetus on a par with the infant, born prematurely, at the same stage of development. Viability is where the United States Supreme Court drew the line in *Roe* v. *Wade*. The Court held that the state has a legitimate interest in protecting potential life, and this interest becomes 'compelling' at viability 'because the fetus then presumably has the capability of meaningful life outside the mother's womb'. Therefore statutes prohibiting abortion after viability would not, the Court said, be unconstitutional. But the judges who wrote the majority decision gave no indication why the mere capacity to exist outside the womb should make such a difference to the state's interest in protecting potential life. After all, if we talk, as the Court does, of *potential* human life, then the nonviable fetus is as much a potential adult human as the viable fetus. (I shall return to this issue of potentiality shortly; but it is a different issue from the conservative argument we are now discussing, which claims that the fetus is a human being, and not just a potential human being.)

There is another important objection to making viability the cut-off point. The point at which the fetus can survive outside the mother's body varies according to the state of medical technology. Thirty years ago it was generally accepted that a baby born more than two months premature could not survive. Now a six-month fetus – three months premature – can often be pulled through, thanks to sophisticated medical techniques, and fetuses born after as little as five and a half months of gestation have survived. This threatens to undermine the Supreme Court's neat division of pregnancy into trimesters, with the boundary of viability lying between the second and third trimesters.

In the light of these medical developments, do we say that a six-month-old fetus should not be aborted now, but could have been aborted without wrongdoing thirty years ago? The same comparison can also be made, not between the present and the past, but between different places. A six-month-old fetus might have a fair chance of survival if born in a city where the latest medical techniques are used, but no chance at all if born in a remote village in Chad or New Guinea. Suppose that for some reason a woman, six months pregnant, was to fly from New York to a New Guinea village and that, once she had arrived in the village, there was no way she could return quickly to a city with modern medical facilities. Are we to say that it would have been wrong for her to have an abortion before she left New York, but now that she is in the village she may go ahead? The trip does not change the nature of the fetus, so why should it remove its claim to life?

The liberal might reply that the fact that the fetus is totally dependent on the mother for its survival means that it has no right to life independent of her wishes. In other cases, however, we do not hold that total dependence on another person means that that person may decide whether one lives or dies. A newborn baby is totally dependent on its mother, if it happens to

140

be born in an isolated area in which there is no other lactating woman, nor the means for bottle feeding. An elderly woman may be totally dependent on her son looking after her, and a hiker who breaks her leg five days' walk from the nearest road may die if her companion does not bring help. We do not think that in these situations the mother may take the life of her baby, the son of his aged mother, or the hiker of her injured companion. So it is not plausible to suggest that the dependence of the nonviable fetus on its mother gives her the right to kill it; and if dependence does not justify making viability the dividing line, it is hard to see what does.

Quickening

If neither birth nor viability marks a morally significant distinction, there is less still to be said for a third candidate, quickening. Quickening is the time when the mother first feels the fetus move, and in traditional Catholic theology, this was thought to be the moment at which the fetus gained its soul. If we accepted that view, we might think quickening important, since the soul is, on the Christian view, what marks humans off from animals. But the idea that the soul enters the fetus at quickening is an outmoded piece of superstition, discarded now even by Catholic theologians. Putting aside these religious doctrines makes quickening insignificant. It is no more than the time when the fetus is first felt to move of its own accord; the fetus is alive before this moment, and ultrasound studies have shown that fetuses do in fact start moving as early as six weeks after fertilization, long before they can be felt to move. In any case, the capacity for physical motion – or the lack of it – has nothing to do with the seriousness of one's claim for continued life. We do not see the lack of such a capacity as negating the claims of paralysed people to go on living.

141

Consciousness

Movement might be thought to be indirectly of moral significance, in so far as it is an indication of some form of awareness
– and as we have already seen, consciousness, and the capacity
to feel pleasure or pain, are of real moral significance. Despite
this, neither side in the abortion debate has made much mention of the development of consciousness in the fetus. Those
opposed to abortion may show films about the 'silent scream'
of the fetus when aborted, but the intention behind such films
is merely to stir the emotions of the uncommitted. Opponents
of abortion really want to uphold the right to life of the human
being from conception, irrespective of whether it is conscious
or not. For those in favour of abortion, to appeal to the absence
of a capacity for consciousness has seemed a risky strategy.
On the basis of the studies showing that movement takes place
as early as six weeks after fertilization, coupled with other
studies that have found some brain activity as early as the
seventh week, it has been suggested that the fetus could be
capable of feeling pain at this early stage of pregnancy. That
possibility has made liberals very wary of appealing to the
onset of consciousness as a point at which the fetus has a
right to life. We shall return to the issue of consciousness in
the fetus later in this chapter, because it is relevant to the
issue of embryo and fetal experimentation. We will also then
consider an earlier marker that could be relevant to embryo
experimentation, but not to the abortion debate. As far as
abortion is concerned, the discussion up to now has shown
that the liberal search for a morally crucial dividing line between the newborn baby and the fetus has failed to yield any
event or stage of development that can bear the weight of
separating those with a right to life from those who lack such
a right, in a way that clearly shows fetuses to be in the latter
category at the stage of development when most abortions
take place. The conservative is on solid ground in insisting

that the development from the embryo to the infant is a gradual process.

SOME LIBERAL ARGUMENTS

Some liberals do not challenge the conservative claim that the fetus is an innocent human being, but argue that abortion is nonetheless permissible. I shall consider three arguments for this view.

The Consequences of Restrictive Laws

The first argument is that laws prohibiting abortion do not stop abortions, but merely drive them underground. Women who want to have abortions are often desperate. They will go to backyard abortionists or try folk remedies. Abortion performed by a qualified medical practitioner is as safe as any medical operation, but attempts to procure abortions by unqualified people often result in serious medical complications and sometimes death. Thus the effect of prohibiting abortion is not so much to reduce the number of abortions performed as to increase the difficulties and dangers for women with unwanted pregnancies.

This argument has been influential in gaining support for more liberal abortion laws. It was accepted by the Canadian Royal Commission on the Status of Women, which concluded that: 'A law that has more bad effects than good ones is a bad law...As long as it exists in its present form thousands of women will break it.'

The main point to note about this argument is that it is an argument against laws prohibiting abortion, and not an argument against the view that abortion is wrong. This is an important distinction, often overlooked in the abortion debate. The present argument well illustrates the distinction, because one could quite consistently accept it and advocate that the law should allow abortion on request, while at the same time deciding oneself – if one were pregnant – or counselling another who was pregnant, that it would be wrong to have an abortion. It is a mistake to assume that the law should always enforce morality. It may be that, as alleged in the case of abortion, attempts to enforce right conduct lead to consequences no one wants, and no decrease in wrong-doing; or it may be that, as is proposed by the next argument we shall consider, there is an area of private ethics with which the law ought not to interfere.

So this first argument is an argument about abortion law, not about the ethics of abortion. Even within those limits, however, it is open to challenge, for it fails to meet the conservative claim that abortion is the deliberate killing of an innocent human being, and in the same ethical category as murder. Those who take this view of abortion will not rest content with the assertion that restrictive abortion laws do no more than drive women to backyard abortionists. They will insist that this situation can be changed, and the law properly enforced. They may also suggest measures to make pregnancy easier to accept for those women who become pregnant against their wishes. This is a perfectly reasonable response, given the initial ethical judgment against abortion, and for this reason the first argument does not succeed in avoiding the ethical issue.

Not the Law's Business?

The second argument is again an argument about abortion laws rather than the ethics of abortion. It uses the view that, as the report of a British government committee inquiring into laws about homosexuality and prostitution put it: 'There must remain a realm of private morality and immorality that is, in brief and crude terms, not the law's business.' This view is widely accepted among liberal thinkers, and can be traced back to John Stuart Mill's *On Liberty*. The'one very simple principle' of this work is, in Mill's words:

> That the only purpose for which power can be rightfully exercised
> over any member of a civilised community, against his will, is
> to prevent harm to others ... He cannot rightfully be compelled
> to do or forbear because it will be better for him to do so, because
> it will make him happier, because in the opinions of others, to
> do so would be wise or even right.

Mill's view is often and properly quoted in support of the repeal
of laws that create 'victimless crimes' – like laws prohibiting
homosexual relations between consenting adults, the use of
marijuana and other drugs, prostitution, gambling and so on.
Abortion is often included in this list, for example by the crim-
inologist Edwin Schur in his book *Crimes Without Victims*. Those
who consider abortion a victimless crime say that, while everyone is entitled to hold and act on his or her own view about
the morality of abortion, no section of the community should
try to force others to adhere to its own particular view. In a
pluralist society, we should tolerate others with different moral
views and leave the decision to have an abortion up to the
woman concerned.

The fallacy involved in numbering abortion among the victimless crimes should be obvious. The dispute about abortion
is, largely, a dispute about whether or not abortion does have
a 'victim'. Opponents of abortion maintain that the victim of
abortion is the fetus. Those not opposed to abortion may deny
that the fetus counts as a victim in any serious way. They might,
for instance, say that a being cannot be a victim unless it has
interests that are violated, and the fetus has no interests. But
however this dispute may go, one cannot simply ignore it on
the grounds that people should not attempt to force others to
follow their own moral views. My view that what Hitler did to
the Jews is wrong is a moral view, and if there were any prospect
of a revival of Nazism I would certainly do my best to force
others not to act contrary to this view. Mill's principle is defensible only if it is restricted, as Mill restricted it, to acts that do
not harm others. To use the principle as a means of avoiding

the difficulties of resolving the ethical dispute over abortion is to take it for granted that abortion does not harm an 'other' – which is precisely the point that needs to be proven before we can legitimately apply the principle to the case of abortion.

A Feminist Argument

The last of the three arguments that seek to justify abortion without denying that the fetus is an innocent human being is that a woman has a right to choose what happens to her own body. This argument became prominent with the rise of the women's liberation movement and has been elaborated by American philosophers sympathetic to feminism. An influential argument has been presented by Judith Jarvis Thomson by means of an ingenious analogy. Imagine, she says, that you wake up one morning and find yourself in a hospital bed, somehow connected to an unconscious man in an adjacent bed. You are told that this man is a famous violinist with kidney disease. The only way he can survive is for his circulatory system to be plugged into the system of someone else with the same blood type, and you are the only person whose blood is suitable. So a society of music lovers kidnapped you, had the connecting operation performed, and there you are. Since you are now in a reputable hospital you could, if you choose, order a doctor to disconnect you from the violinist; but the violinist will then certainly die. On the other hand, if you remain connected for only (only?) nine months, the violinist will have recovered and you can be unplugged without endangering him.

Thomson believes that if you found yourself in this unexpected predicament you would not be morally required to allow the violinist to use your kidneys for nine months. It might be generous or kind of you to do so, but to say this is, Thomson claims, quite different from saying that you would be doing wrong if you did not do it.

Note that Thomson's conclusion does not depend on denying that the violinist is an innocent human being, with the same right to life as any other innocent human being. On the contrary, Thomson affirms that the violinist does have a right to life – but to have a right to life does not, she says, entail a right to the use of another's body, even if without that use one will die.

The parallel with pregnancy, especially pregnancy due to rape should be obvious. A woman pregnant through rape finds herself, through no choice of her own, linked to a fetus in much the same way as the person is linked to the violinist. True, a pregnant woman does not normally have to spend nine months in bed, but opponents of abortion would not regard this as a sufficient justification for abortion. Giving up a newborn baby for adoption might be more difficult, psychologically, than parting from the violinist at the end of his illness; but this in itself does not seem a sufficient reason for killing the fetus. Accepting for the sake of the argument that the fetus does count as a fully-fledged human being, having an abortion when the fetus is not viable has the same moral significance as unplugging oneself from the violinist. So if we agree with Thomson that it would not be wrong to unplug oneself from the violinist, we must also accept that, whatever the status of the fetus, abortion is not wrong – at least not when the pregnancy results from rape.

Thomson's argument can probably be extended beyond cases of rape. Suppose that you found yourself connected to the violinist, not because you were kidnapped by music lovers, but because you had intended to enter the hospital to visit a sick friend, and when you got into the elevator, you carelessly pressed the wrong button, and ended up in a section of the hospital normally visited only by those who have volunteered to be connected to patients who would not otherwise survive. A team of doctors, waiting for the next volunteer, assumed you were it, jabbed you with an anaesthetic, and connected you. If Thomson's argument was sound in the kidnap case it is probably sound here too, since nine months unwillingly sup-

porting another is a high price to pay for ignorance or carelessness. In this way the argument might apply beyond rape
cases to the much larger number of women who become pregnant through ignorance, carelessness, or contraceptive failure.

But is the argument sound? The short answer is this: It is
sound if the particular theory of rights that lies behind it is
sound; and it is unsound if that theory of rights is unsound.

The theory of rights in question can be illustrated by another
of Thomson's fanciful examples: suppose I am desperately ill
and the only thing that can save my life is the touch of my
favourite film star's cool hand on my fevered brow. Well, Thomson says, even though I have a right to life, this does not mean
that I have a right to force the film star to come to me, or that
he is under any, moral obligation to fly over and save me —
although it would be frightfully nice of him to do so. Thus
Thomson does not accept that we are always obliged to take
the best course of action, all things considered, or to do what
has the best consequences. She accepts, instead, a system of
rights and obligations that allows us to justify our actions independently of their consequences.

I shall say more about this conception of rights in Chapter 8.
At this stage it is enough to notice that a utilitarian would reject
this theory of rights, and would reject Thomson's judgment in
the case of the violinist. The utilitarian would hold that, however
outraged I may be at having been kidnapped, if the consequences of disconnecting myself from the violinist are, on balance, and taking into account the interests of everyone affected,
worse than the consequences of remaining connected, I ought
to remain connected. This does not necessarily mean that utilitarians would regard a woman who disconnected herself as
wicked or deserving of blame. They might recognize that she
has been placed in an extraordinarily difficult situation, one in
which to do what is right involves a considerable sacrifice. They
might even grant that most people in this situation would follow

self-interest rather than do the right thing. Nevertheless, they would hold that to disconnect oneself is wrong.

In rejecting Thomson's theory of rights, and with it her judgment in the case of the violinist, the utilitarian would also be rejecting her argument for abortion. Thomson claimed that her argument justified abortion even if we allowed the life of the fetus to count as heavily as the life of a normal person. The utilitarian would say that it would be wrong to refuse to sustain a person's life for nine months, if that was the only way the person could survive. Therefore if the life of the fetus is given the same weight as the life of a normal person, the utilitarian would say that it would be wrong to refuse to carry the fetus until it can survive outside the womb.

This concludes our discussion of the usual liberal replies to the conservative argument against abortion. We have seen that liberals have failed to establish a morally significant dividing line between the newborn baby and the fetus, and their arguments — with the possible exception of Thomson's argument if her theory of rights can be defended — also fail to justify abortion in ways that do not challenge the conservative claim that the fetus is an innocent human being. Nevertheless, it would be premature for conservatives to assume that their case against abortion is sound. It is now time to bring into this debate some more general conclusions about the value of life.

THE VALUE OF FETAL LIFE

Let us go back to the beginning. The central argument against abortion from which we started was:

> First premise: It is wrong to kill an innocent human being.
> Second premise: A human fetus is an innocent human being.
> Conclusion: Therefore it is wrong to kill a human fetus.

The first set of replies we considered accepted the first premise of this argument but objected to the second. The second set of replies rejected neither premise, but objected to drawing the conclusion from these premises (or objected to the further conclusion that abortion should be prohibited by law). None of the replies questioned the first premise of the argument. Given the widespread acceptance of the doctrine of the sanctity of human life, this is not surprising; but the discussion of this doctrine in the preceding chapters shows that this premise is less secure than many people think.

The weakness of the first premise of the conservative argument is that it relies on our acceptance of the special status of *human* life. We have seen that 'human' is a term that straddles two distinct notions: being a member of the species Homo sapiens, and being a person. Once the term is dissected in this way, the weakness of the conservative's first premise becomes apparent. If 'human' is taken as equivalent to 'person', the second premise of the argument, which asserts that the fetus is a human being, is clearly false; for one cannot plausibly argue that a fetus is either rational or self-conscious. If, on the other hand, 'human' is taken to mean no more than 'member of the species Homo sapiens', then the conservative defence of the life of the fetus is based on a characteristic lacking moral significance and so the first premise is false. The point should by now be familiar: whether a being is or is not a member of our species is, in itself no more relevant to the wrongness of killing it than whether it is or is not a member of our race. The belief that mere membership of our species, irrespective of other characteristics, makes a great difference to the wrongness of killing a being is a legacy of religious doctrines that even those opposed to abortion hesitate to bring into the debate.

Recognising this simple point transforms the abortion issue. We can now look at the fetus for what it is – the actual characteristics it possesses – and can value its life on the same scale as the lives of beings with similar characteristics who are not members of our species. It now becomes apparent that the 'Pro Life' or 'Right to Life' movement is misnamed. Far from having concern for all life, or a scale of concern impartially based on the nature of the life in question, those who protest against abortion but dine regularly on the bodies of chickens, pigs and calves, show only a biased concern for the lives of members of our own species. For on any fair comparison of morally relevant characteristics, like rationality, self-consciousness, awareness, autonomy, pleasure and pain, and so on, the calf, the pig and the much derided chicken come out well ahead of the fetus at any stage of pregnancy – while if we make the comparison with a fetus of less than three months, a fish would show more signs of consciousness.

My suggestion, then, is that we accord the life of a fetus no greater value than the life of a nonhuman animal at a similar level of rationality, self-consciousness, awareness, capacity to feel, etc. Since no fetus is a person, no fetus has the same claim to life as a person. We have yet to consider at what point the fetus is likely to become capable of feeling pain. For now it will be enough to say that until that capacity exists, an abortion terminates an existence that is of no "intrinsic" value at all. Afterwards, when the fetus may be conscious, though not self-conscious, abortion should not be taken lightly (if a woman ever does take abortion lightly). But a woman's serious interests would normally override the rudimentary interests even of a conscious fetus. Indeed, even an abortion late in pregnancy for the most trivial reasons is hard to condemn unless we also condemn the slaughter of far more developed forms of life for the taste of their flesh.

The comparison between the fetus and other animals leads us to one more point. Where the balance of conflicting interests does make it necessary to kill a sentient creature, it is important that the killing be done as painlessly as possible. In the case of nonhuman animals the importance of humane killing is widely accepted; oddly, in the case of abortion little attention is paid to it. This is not because abortion is known to kill the fetus swiftly and humanely. Late abortions – which are the very ones in which the fetus may be able to suffer – are sometimes performed by injecting a salt solution into the amniotic sac that surrounds the fetus. It has been claimed that the effect of this is to cause the fetus to have convulsions and die between one and three hours later. Afterwards the dead fetus is expelled from the womb. If there are grounds for thinking that a method of abortion causes the fetus to suffer, that method should be avoided.

THE FETUS AS POTENTIAL LIFE

One likely objection to the argument I have offered in the preceding section is that it takes into account only the actual characteristics of the fetus, and not its potential characteristics. On the basis of its actual characteristics, some opponents of abortion will admit, the fetus compares unfavourably with many non-human animals; it is when we consider its potential to become a mature human being that membership of the species Homo sapiens becomes important, and the fetus far surpasses any chicken, pig or calf.

Up to this point I have not raised the question of the potential of the fetus because I thought it best to concentrate on the central argument against abortion; but it is true that a different argument, based on the potential of the fetus, can be mounted. Now is the time to look at this other argument. We can state it as follows:

> First premise: It is wrong to kill a potential human being.
> Second premise: A human fetus is a potential human being.
> Conclusion: Therefore it is wrong to kill a human fetus.

The second premise of this argument is stronger than the second premise of the preceding argument. Whereas it is problematic whether a fetus actually *is* a human being – it depends on what we mean by the term – it cannot be denied that the fetus is a potential human being. This is true whether by 'human being' we mean 'member of the species Homo sapiens' or a rational and self-conscious being, a person. The strong second premise of the new argument is, however, purchased at the cost of a weaker first premise, for the wrongness of killing a potential human being – even a potential person – is more open to challenge than the wrongness of killing an actual human being.

It is of course true that the potential rationality, self-consciousness and so on of a fetal Homo sapiens surpasses that of a cow or pig; but it does not follow that the fetus has a stronger claim to life. There is no rule that says that a potential X has the same value as an X, or has all the rights of an X. There are many examples that show just the contrary. To pull out a sprouting acorn is not the same as cutting down a venerable oak. To drop a live chicken into a pot of boiling water would be much worse than doing the same to an egg. Prince Charles is a potential King of England, but he does not now have the rights of a king.

In the absence of any general inference from 'A is a potential X' to 'A has the rights of an X', we should not accept that a potential person should have the rights of a person, unless we can be given some specific reason why this should hold in this particular case. But what could that reason be? This question becomes especially pertinent if we recall the grounds on which, in the previous chapter, it was suggested that the life of a person merits greater protection than the life of a being who is not a person. These reasons – from the indirect classical utilitarian concern with not arousing in others the fear that they may be the next killed, the weight given by the preference utilitarian to a person's desires, Tooley's link between a right to life and the capacity to see oneself as a continuing mental subject, and the principle of respect for autonomy – are all based on the fact that persons see themselves as distinct entities with a past and future. They do not apply to those who are not now and never have been capable of seeing themselves in this way. If these are the grounds for not killing persons, the mere potential for becoming a person does not count against killing.

It might be said that this reply misunderstands the relevance of the potential of the human fetus, and that this potential is important, not because it creates in the fetus a right or claim to life, but because anyone who kills a human fetus deprives the world of a future rational and self-conscious being. If rational and self-conscious beings are intrinsically valuable, to kill a human fetus is to deprive the world of something intrinsically valuable, and so wrong. The chief problem with this as an argument against abortion – apart from the difficulty of establishing that rational and self-conscious beings are of intrinsic value – is that it does not stand up as a reason for objecting to all abortions, or even to abortions carried out merely because the pregnancy is inconveniently timed. Moreover the argument leads us to condemn practices other than abortion that most anti-abortionists accept.

The claim that rational and self-conscious beings are intrinsically valuable is not a reason for objecting to all abortions because not all abortions deprive the world of a rational and self-conscious being. Suppose a woman has been planning to join a mountain-climbing expedition in June, and in January she learns that she is two months pregnant. She has no children at present, and firmly intends to have a child within a year or two. The pregnancy is unwanted only because it is inconveniently timed. Opponents of abortion would presumably think an abortion in these circumstances particularly outrageous, for neither the life nor the health of the mother is at stake – only the enjoyment she gets from climbing mountains. Yet if abortion is wrong only because it deprives the world of a future person, this abortion is not wrong; it does no more than delay the entry of a person into the world.

On the other hand this argument against abortion does lead us to condemn practices that reduce the future human population: contraception, whether by 'artificial' means or by 'natural' means such as abstinence on days when the woman is likely to be fertile; and also celibacy. This argument has, in fact, all the difficulties of the 'total' form of utilitarianism, discussed in the previous two chapters, and it does not provide any reason for thinking abortion worse than any other means of population control. If the world is already overpopulated, the argument provides no reason at all against abortion.

Is there any other significance in the fact that the fetus is a potential person? If there is I have no idea what it could be. In writings against abortion we often find reference to the fact that each human fetus is unique. Paul Ramsey, a former Professor of Religion at Princeton University, has said that modern genetics, by teaching us that the first fusion of sperm and ovum creates a 'never-to-be-repeated' informational speck, seems to lead us to the conclusion that 'all destruction of fetal life should be classified as murder'. But why should this fact lead us to this conclusion? A canine fetus is also, no doubt, genetically unique. Does this mean that it is as wrong to abort a dog as a human? When identical twins are conceived, the genetic information is repeated. Would Ramsey therefore think it permissible to abort one of a pair of identical twins? The children that my wife and I would produce if we did not use contraceptives would be genetically unique. Does the fact that it is still indeterminate precisely what genetically unique character those children would have make the use of contraceptives less evil than abortion? Why should it? And if it does could the looming prospect of successful cloning – a technique in which the cells of one individual are used to reproduce a fetus that is a genetic carbon copy of the original – diminish the seriousness of abortion? Suppose the woman who wants to go mountain climbing were able to have her abortion, take a cell from the aborted fetus and then reimplant that cell in her womb so that an exact genetic replica of the aborted fetus would develop – the only difference being that the pregnancy would now come to term six months later, and thus she could still join the expedition. Would that make the abortion acceptable? I doubt that many opponents of abortion would think so.

THE STATUS OF THE EMBRYO IN THE LABORATORY

It is now time to turn to the debate about experimenting on early human embryos, kept alive in a special fluid, outside the human body. This is a relatively new debate, because the possibility of keeping an embryo alive outside the body is new; but in many respects it goes over the same ground as the abortion debate. Although one central argument for abortion – the claim that a woman has the right to control her own body – is not directly applicable in the newer context, the argument against embryo experimentation relies on one of the two claims we have already examined: either that the embryo is entitled to protection because it is a human being, or that the embryo is entitled to protection because it is a potential human being.

One might therefore think that the case against embryo experimentation is stronger than the case for abortion. For one argument in favour of abortion does not apply, while the major arguments against abortion do. In fact, however, the two arguments against abortion do not apply as straightforwardly as one might imagine to the embryo in the laboratory.

First, is the embryo already a human being? We have already seen that claims for a right to life should not be based on species membership, so the fact that the embryo is of the species Homo sapiens does not show that the embryo is a human being in any morally relevant sense. And if the fetus is not a person, it is even more apparent that the embryo cannot be one. But there is a further interesting point to be made against the claim that the early embryo is a human being: human beings are individuals, and the early embryo is not even an individual. At any time up to about 14 days after fertilisation – and that is longer than human embryos have so far been kept alive outside the

body – the embryo can split into two or more genetically identical embryos. This happens naturally and leads to the formation
of identical twins. When we have an embryo prior to this point,
we cannot be sure if what we are looking at is the precursor of
one or two individuals.

This poses a problem for those who stress the continuity of
our existence from conception to adulthood. Suppose we have
an embryo in a dish on a laboratory bench. If we think of this
embryo as the first stage of an individual human being, we might
call it Mary. But now suppose the embryo divides into two
identical embryos. Is one of them still Mary, and the other Jane?
If so, which one is Mary? There is nothing to distinguish the
two, no way of saying that the one we call Jane split off from
the one we call Mary, rather than vice versa. So should we say
that Mary is no longer with us, and instead we have Jane and
Helen? But what happened to Mary? Did she die? Should we
grieve for her? There is something absurd about these speculations. The absurdity stems from thinking of the embryo as an
individual at a time at which it is only a cluster of cells. So,
until the possibility of twinning is past, it is even more difficult
to maintain that the embryo is a human being, in any morally
significant sense, than it is to maintain that the fetus is a human
being in a morally significant sense. This provides some basis
for the laws and guidelines in Britain and various other countries
that allow experimentation on the embryo up to 14 days after
fertilisation. But for reasons already given, and others that we
are about to discuss, this is still an unnecessarily restrictive limit.

What of the argument from potential? Can the familiar claims
about the potential of the embryo in the uterus be applied to
the embryo in a dish in the laboratory? Before Robert Edwards
began the research that led to the IVF procedure, no-one had
observed a viable human embryo prior to the stage at which it
implants in the wall of the uterus. In the normal process of
reproduction inside the body, the embryo, or 'pre-embryo' as
it is now sometimes called, remains unattached for the first

seven to fourteen days. As long as such embryos existed only inside the woman's body, there was no way of observing them during that period. The very existence of the embryo could not be established until after implantation. Under these circumstances, once the existence of an embryo was known, that embryo had a good chance of becoming a person, unless its development was deliberately interrupted. The probability of such an embryo becoming a person was therefore very much greater than the probability of an egg in a fertile woman uniting with sperm from that woman's partner and leading to a child.

There was also, in those pre-IVF days, a further important distinction between the embryo and the egg and sperm. Whereas the embryo inside the female body has some definite chance (we shall consider later how great a chance) of developing into a child *unless* a deliberate human act interrupts its growth, the egg and sperm can only develop into a child if there *is* a deliberate human act. So in the one case, all that is needed for the embryo to have a prospect of realising its potential is for those involved to refrain from stopping it; in the other case, they have to carry out a positive act. The development of the embryo inside the female body can therefore be seen as a mere unfolding of a potential that is inherent in it. (Admittedly, this is an over-simplification, for it takes no account of the positive acts involved in childbirth; but it is close enough.) The development of the separated egg and sperm is more difficult to regard in this way, because no further development will take place unless the couple have sexual intercourse or use artificial insemination.

Now consider what has happened as a result of the success of IVF. The procedure involves removing one or more eggs from a woman's ovary, placing them in the appropriate fluid in a glass dish, and then adding sperm to the dish. In the more proficient laboratories, this leads to fertilisation in about 80% of the eggs thus treated. The embryo can then be kept in the dish for two to three days, while it grows and divides into two, four, and then eight cells. At about this stage the embryo is usually transferred to a woman's uterus. Although the transfer itself is a simple procedure, it is after the transfer that things are most likely to go wrong: for reasons that are not fully understood, with even the most successful IVF teams, the probability of a given embryo that has been transferred to the uterus actually implanting there, and leading to a continuing pregnancy, is always less than 20%, and generally no more than 10%. In summary, then, before the advent of IVF, in every instance in which we knew of the existence of a normal human embryo, it would have been true to say of that embryo that, unless it was deliberately interfered with, it would most likely develop into a person. The process of IVF, however, leads to the creation of embryos that cannot develop into a person unless there is some deliberate human act (the transfer to the uterus) and that even then, in the best of circumstances, will most likely not develop into a person.

The upshot of all this is that IVF has reduced the difference between what can be said about the embryo, and what can be said about the egg and sperm, when still separate, but considered as a pair. Before IVF, any normal human embryo known to us had a far greater chance of becoming a child than any egg plus sperm prior to fertilisation taking place. But with IVF, there is a much more modest difference in the probability of a child resulting from a 2-cell embryo in a glass dish, and the probability of a child resulting from an egg and some sperm in a glass dish. To be specific, if we assume that the laboratory's fertilisation rate is 80% and its rate of pregnancy per embryo transferred is 10%, then the probability of a child resulting from a given embryo is 10%, and the probability of a child resulting from an egg that has been placed in a fluid to which sperm has been added is 8%. So if the embryo is a potential person, why are not the egg-and-sperm, considered jointly, also a potential person? Yet no member of the pro-life movement wants to rescue eggs and sperm in order to save the lives of the people that they have the potential to become.

Consider the following, not *too* improbable scenario. In the IVF laboratory, a woman's egg has been obtained. It sits in one dish on the bench. The sperm from her partner sits in an adjacent dish, ready to be mixed into the solution containing the egg. Then some bad news arrives: the woman is bleeding from the uterus, and will not be in a suitable condition to receive an embryo for at least a month. There is therefore no point in going ahead with the procedure. A laboratory assistant is told to dispose of the egg and sperm. She does so by tipping them down the sink. So far, so good; but a few hours later, when the assistant returns to prepare the laboratory for the next procedure, she notices that the sink is blocked. The egg and its fluid are still there, in the bottom of the sink. She is about to clear the blockage, when she realizes that the sperm has been tipped into the sink too. Quite possibly, the egg has been fertilised! Now what is she to do? Those who draw a sharp distinction between the egg-and-sperm and the embryo must hold that, while the assistant was quite entitled to pour the egg and sperm down the sink, it would be wrong to clear the blockage now. This is difficult to accept. Potentiality seems not to be such an all-or-nothing concept; the difference between the egg-and-sperm and the embryo is one of degree, related to the probability of development into a person.

Traditional defenders of the right to life of the embryo have been reluctant to introduce degrees of potential into the debate, because once the notion is accepted, it seems undeniable that the early embryo is less of a potential person than the later embryo or the fetus. This could easily be understood as leading to the conclusion that the prohibition against destroying the early embryo is less stringent than the prohibition against destroying the later embryo or fetus. Nevertheless, some defenders of the argument from potential have invoked probability. Among these has been the Roman Catholic theologian John Noonan:

As life itself is a matter of probabilities, as most moral reasoning is an estimate of probabilities, so it seems in accord with the structure of reality and the nature of moral thought to found a moral judgment on the change in probabilities at conception... Would the argument be different if only one out of ten children conceived came to term? Of course this argument would be different. This argument is an appeal to probabilities that actually exist, not to any and all states of affairs which may be imagined ... If a spermatozoon is destroyed, one destroys a being which had a chance of far less than 1 in 200 million of developing into a reasoning being, possessed of the genetic code, a heart and other organs, and capable of pain. If a fetus is destroyed, one destroys a being already possessed of the genetic code, organs and sensitivity to pain, and one which had an 80 per cent chance of developing further into a baby outside the womb who, in time, would reason.

The article from which this quotation is taken has been influential in the abortion debate, and has often been quoted and reprinted by those opposed to abortion, but the development of our understanding of the reproductive process has made Noonan's position untenable. The initial difficulty is that Noonan's figures for embryo survival even in the uterus are no longer regarded as accurate. At the time Noonan wrote, the estimate of pregnancy loss was based on clinical recognition of pregnancies at six to eight weeks after fertilisation. At this stage, the chance of losing the pregnancy through spontaneous abortion is about 15%. Recent technical advances allowing earlier recognition of pregnancy, however, provide startlingly different figures. If pregnancy is diagnosed before implantation (within 14 days of fertilisation) the probability of a birth resulting is 25 to 30%. Post-implantation this increases initially to 46 to 60%, and it is not until six weeks gestation that the chance of birth occurring increases to 85 to 90%.

Noonan claimed that his argument is 'an appeal to probabilities that actually exist, not to any and all states of affairs which may be imagined'. But once we substitute the real probabilities of embryos, at various stages of their existence, becoming persons, Noonan's argument no longer supports the moment of fertilisation as the time at which the embryo gains a significantly different moral status. Indeed, if we were to require an 80% probability of further development into a baby – the figure Noonan himself mentions – we would have to wait until nearly six weeks after fertilisation before the embryo would have the significance Noonan wants to claim for it.

At one point in his argument Noonan refers to the number of sperm involved in a male ejaculation, and says that there is only one chance in 200,000,000 of a sperm becoming part of a living being. This focus on the sperm rather than the egg is a curious instance of male bias, but even if we let that pass, new technology provides still one more difficulty for the argument. There now exists a means of overcoming male infertility caused by a low sperm count. The egg is removed as in the normal in vitro procedure; but instead of adding a drop of seminal fluid to the dish with the egg, a single sperm is picked up with a fine needle and micro-injected under the outer layer of the egg. So if we compare the probability of the embryo becoming a person with the probability of the egg, together with the single sperm that has been picked up by the needle and is about to be micro-injected into the egg, becoming a person, we will be unable to find any sharp distinction between the two. Does that mean that it would be wrong to stop the procedure, once the sperm has been picked up? Noonan's argument from probabilities would seem to commit him either to this implausible claim, or to accepting that we may destroy human embryos. This procedure also undermines Ramsey's claim about the importance of the unique genetic blueprint – that '"never-to-be-repeated" informational speck' having been determined in the case of the embryo but not in the case of the egg and sperm. For that too is here determined before fertilisation.

In this section I have tried to show how the special circumstances of the embryo in the laboratory affect the application of the arguments discussed elsewhere in this chapter about the status of the embryo or fetus. I have not attempted to cover all aspects of in vitro fertilisation and embryo experimentation. To do that it would be necessary to investigate several other issues, including the appropriateness of allocating scarce medical resources to this area at a time when the world has a serious problem of overpopulation, and the speculation that the new techniques will be misused to produce children 'made-to order', either at the behest of parents or, worse still, of some mad dictator. To cover these important but disparate matters would take us too far from the main themes of this book. Brief mention must, however, be made of one other aspect of embryo experimentation: the role of the couple from whose gametes the embryo has developed.

Feminists have played a valuable role in pointing out how vulnerable a couple may be to pressure from the medical team to donate an embryo for research purposes. They may be desperate for a child. The IVF team represent their last hope of achieving this goal. They know that there are many other couples seeking treatment. All this means that they are likely to be prepared to go to great lengths in order to please the medical team. When they are asked to donate eggs or embryos, can they really make a free choice? Only, I think, if it is quite clear that their answer will not affect their IVF treatment in any way. Wherever experimentation on embryos is carried out, there is a need to develop safeguards and forms of oversight to ensure that this is always the case.

MAKING USE OF THE FETUS

The prospects of using human fetuses for medical purposes has created a further controversial issue related to abortion. Research carried out specifically on fetuses has led to the hope of finding cures for many serious illnesses by the transplantation of tissue or cells from the fetus. Compared with adult tissue, fetal tissue appears to grow better after transplantation, and to be less likely to be rejected by the patient. The example that has received the most publicity to date is Parkinson's disease, but the use of fetal tissue has also been suggested in the treatment of Alzheimer's Disease, Huntington's Disease, and diabetes; and fetal transplants have been used to save the life of another fetus, in a case in which a 30 week old fetus, in utero, suffering from a fatal immune system disorder was given fetal cells from aborted fetuses.

Do fetuses have rights or interests that may be violated or harmed by using them for these purposes? I have already argued that the fetus has no right to, nor strictly speaking even an interest in, life. But we have seen that, in the case of animals, to say that a being has no right to life does not mean that the being has no rights or interests at all. If the fetus is capable of feeling pain, then, like animals, the fetus has an interest in not suffering pain, and that interest should be given equal consideration with the similar interests of any other being. It is easy to imagine that keeping a fetus alive after an abortion in order to preserve the tissue of the fetus in the best possible condition could cause pain and suffering to a fetus capable of feeling pain. So we must now return to a more detailed investigation of a topic touched upon earlier in this chapter: When does the fetus become conscious?

Fortunately it is now possible to give a reasonably definite answer to this question. The part of the brain associated with sensations of pain, and more generally with consciousness, is the cerebral cortex. Until 18 weeks of gestation, the cerebral cortex is not sufficiently developed for synaptic connections to take place within it – in other words, the signals that give rise to pain in an adult are not being received. Between 18 and 25 weeks, the brain of the fetus reaches a stage at which there is some nerve transmission in those parts associated with consciousness. Even then, however, the fetus appears to be in a persistent state of sleep, and therefore may not be able to perceive pain. The fetus begins to 'wake up' at a gestational age of around 30 weeks. This is, of course, well beyond the stage of viability, and a 'fetus' that was alive and outside the womb at this stage would be a premature baby, and not a fetus at all.

In order to give the fetus the benefit of the doubt, it would be reasonable to take the earliest possible time at which the fetus might be able to feel anything as the boundary after which the fetus should be protected. Thus we should disregard the uncertain evidence about wakefulness, and take as a more definite line, the time at which the brain is physically capable of receiving signals necessary for awareness. This suggests a boundary at 18 weeks of gestation. Prior to that time, there is no good basis for believing that the fetus needs protection from harmful research, because the fetus cannot be harmed. After that time, the fetus does need protection from harm, on the same basis as sentient, but not self-conscious, nonhuman animals need it.

There is, however, one qualification that must be added to this statement. While the fetus prior to 18 weeks may, strictly speaking, be unable to be harmed, if the fetus is allowed to develop into a child, the future child could be very seriously harmed by an experiment that caused the child to be born in a disabled state. Therefore research that allows the fetus to survive beyond 18 weeks does not come under the permissive rule suggested in the previous paragraph.

In discussions of the use of fetal tissue there is often mention of the risk of 'complicity' in the immoral act of abortion. Those wishing to defend the use of fetal tissue therefore go to great lengths in order to show that the use of fetal tissue can be kept entirely separate from the decision to carry out the abortion, and so does not serve to 'legitimise' abortions. For the same reason, many countries now have, or are developing, laws or guidelines for the use of fetal tissue from induced abortions, and many of these laws or guidelines are drawn up on the basis of the assumption, implicit or explicit, that it is important to separate the decision for the abortion from the use of the fetal tissue, lest the use of fetal tissue serve to increase the incidence of abortions. There may be, for example, a requirement that the donation has to be an entirely anonymous one. This prevents a woman having an abortion in order to donate tissue that might save the life of a relative, perhaps one of her existing children. It is possible that the motivation for such requirements is to protect the woman from pressure to have an abortion. Whether that is a valid ground for requiring anonymity is something I shall consider shortly. Here I wish only to point out that if it is the premise that abortion is immoral that supplies the motive for seeking to prevent any 'complicity' between the use of the fetal tissue and the carrying out of the abortion, or to ensure that fetal tissue use does not contribute to a higher incidence of abortions, then the arguments presented in this chapter count against that view. At least when carried out before 18 weeks, abortion is in itself morally neutral. Even later abortions, when some pain may be involved, could be justified if the outcome were to prevent much greater suffering by saving the life of a child suffering from an immune system disorder, or to cure Parkinson's or Alzheimer's disease in an older person. If the requirement that we separate the act of abortion from the donation of fetal tissue cannot be soundly based on the need to protect the fetus, can it be founded instead on a need to protect the parents, in particular the woman? Different aspects of this separation need to be considered. If the doctor counselling the pregnant woman about her abortion and the doctor seeking fetal tissue for a dying patient are one and the same, the conflict of interest is clear, and there seems a real risk that the doctor will not be able to give disinterested advice to the pregnant woman. So this separation is an important aspect of protecting the position of the pregnant woman.

What, though, of the view that the pregnant woman must

be separated from the recipient by a veil of anonymity? This, of course, prevents her having an abortion in order to provide tissue to someone she knows. Is this restriction justified by consideration of her own interests? On the one hand, without this protection it is easy to imagine scenarios in which a pregnant woman would find herself under great pressure to abort a pregnancy in order to save the life of a dying relative; or a woman who is not pregnant might feel that she has to become pregnant and then terminate the pregnancy to provide the needed fetal tissue. Feminists may well feel that in a society in which men are dominant, the prospects for further intensifying the oppression of women in this way is reason enough to exclude the designation of tissue for a particular known person.

Yet the argument for the opposite conclusion is also strong. It is neither unusual nor unreasonable for a parent to make great sacrifices for a child. We allow both men and women to work long hours doing meaningless factory labor in order to save enough money to ensure that their children receive a good education. This suggests that sacrifice for the sake of a relative or loved one is not in itself wrong or something we need to prohibit. In many countries, we also allow women to have abortions for reasons that are far less important than the saving of a life. This indicates that we do not regard an abortion as something so bad (from the point of view of the fetus, or of the woman) that it should be prohibited, or even restricted to situations in which it is necessary to save a life. If we accept the assumptions that underly both these attitudes, we can scarcely criticise a woman who decides to have an abortion in order to provide fetal tissue that could save the life of her child. Not every woman may want to do this, but those who do may well be making a perfectly reasonable, autonomous decision. It is highly paternalistic for the law to step in and say that a doctor must not give effect to such decisions. From this perspective it is odd that some feminists, whom one might expect to find upholding the right of women to autonomy, should be among those who think that women need special laws to protect them against the effects of their own freely chosen actions.

There is considerable force in both of these opposed arguments, but we should favour autonomy unless there is clear evidence that the results of doing so are very bad indeed. I know of no evidence to that effect. I suspect, in fact, that much (though certainly not all) of the motivation for prohibiting designated donations of tissue derives from a desire to avoid causing more abortions, and in particular, to avoid women becoming pregnant in order to make fetal tissue available. But for the reasons already given, I see nothing inherently wrong with more abortions, or with pregnancies being undertaken in order to provide fetal tissue, as long as the women involved are freely choosing to do this, and the additional abortions really do make some contribution to saving the lives of others. If the chief objection is that the women's actions might be coerced rather than freely chosen, the solution would be not to prohibit *all* choices for abortion to provide fetal tissue, but rather to set up procedures to ensure that those who do this have chosen freely, in the light of all the available relevant information.

At this point commerce is bound to rear its head. Someone will ask: What if women become pregnant and terminate their pregnancies not in order to save the lives of those they care about, but because they will be paid for the fetal tissue? Do not arguments from autonomy suggest that this, too, should be up to the woman to decide? Is it really worse to become pregnant and terminate the pregnancy in order to receive, say, $10,000 than to spend six months doing repetitious labour in a noisy, polluted, hazardous factory for the same amount of money?

Despite my willingness to facilitate fetal tissue use, I am much more reluctant to embrace the free market. This is not because I think that women would be unable to protect themselves from the exploitation of the market; it really does not seem to me a worse form of exploitation than those that we accept in more common forms of employment. Rather, I dislike the idea of a free market in fetal tissue because, as R.M. Titmuss argued many years ago in the case of blood supplies for medical purposes, when we choose between a social policy based on altruism and one based on commerce, we are choosing between two different types of society. It may well be better, for a variety of reasons, that there are some things that money cannot buy; some circumstances in which we must rely on the altruism of those we love, or even of strangers in our society. I support efforts to resist the creeping commercialisation of every aspect of our lives, and so I would resist the commercialisation of fetal tissue.

ABORTION AND INFANTICIDE

There remains one major objection to the argument I have advanced in favour of abortion. We have already seen that the strength of the conservative position lies in the difficulty liberals have in pointing to a morally significant line of demarcation between an embryo and a newborn baby. The standard liberal position needs to be able to point to some such line, because liberals usually hold that it is permissible to kill an embryo or fetus but not a baby. I have argued that the life of a fetus (and even more plainly, of an embryo) is of no greater value than the life of a nonhuman animal at a similar level of rationality, self-consciousness, awareness, capacity to feel, etc., and that since no fetus is a person no fetus has the same claim to life as a person. Now it must be admitted that these arguments apply to the newborn baby as much as to the fetus. A week-old baby is not a rational and self-conscious being, and there are many nonhuman animals whose rationality, self-consciousness, awareness, capacity to feel, and so on, exceed that of a human baby a week or a month old. If the fetus does not have the same claim to life as a person, it appears that the newborn baby does not either, and the life of a newborn baby is of less value to it than the life of a pig, a dog, or a chimpanzee is to the nonhuman animal. Thus while my position on the status of fetal life may

169

be acceptable to many, the implications of this position for the status of newborn life are at odds with the virtually unchallenged assumption that the life of a newborn baby is as sacrosanct as that of an adult. Indeed, some people seem to think that the life of a baby is more precious than that of an adult. Lurid tales of German soldiers bayoneting Belgian babies figured prominently in the wave of anti-German propaganda that accompanied Britain's entry into the First World War, and it seemed to be tacitly assumed that this was a greater atrocity than the murder of adults would be.

I do not regard the conflict between the position I have taken and widely accepted views about the sanctity of infant life as a ground for abandoning my position. These widely accepted views need to be challenged. It is true that infants appeal to us because they are small and helpless, and there are no doubt very good evolutionary reasons why we should instinctively feel protective towards them. It is also true that infants cannot be combatants and killing infants in wartime is the clearest possible case of killing civilians, which is prohibited by international convention. In general, since infants are harmless and morally incapable of committing a crime, those who kill them lack the excuses often offered for the killing of adults. None of this shows, however, that the killing of an infant is as bad as the killing of an (innocent) adult.

In thinking about this matter we should put aside feelings based on the small, helpless, and – sometimes – cute appearance of human infants. To think that the lives of infants are of special value because infants are small and cute is on a par with thinking that a baby seal, with its soft white fur coat and large round eyes deserves greater protection than a gorilla, who lacks these attributes. Nor can the helplessness or the innocence of the infant Homo sapiens be a ground for preferring it to the equally helpless and innocent fetal Homo sapiens, or, for that matter, to laboratory rats who are 'innocent' in exactly the same sense as the human infant, and, in view of the experimenters' power over them, almost as helpless.

If we can put aside these emotionally moving but strictly irrelevant aspects of the killing of a baby we can see that the grounds for not killing persons do not apply to newborn infants. The indirect, classical utilitarian reason does not apply, because no one capable of understanding what is happening when a newborn baby is killed could feel threatened by a policy that gave less protection to the newborn than to adults. In this respect Bentham was right to describe infanticide as 'of a nature not to give the slightest inquietude to the most timid imagination'. Once we are old enough to comprehend the policy, we are too old to be threatened by it.

Similarly, the preference utilitarian reason for respecting the life of a person cannot apply to a newborn baby. Newborn babies cannot see themselves as beings who might or might not have a future, and so cannot have a desire to continue living. For the same reason, if a right to life must be based on the capacity to want to go on living, or on the ability to see oneself as a continuing mental subject, a newborn baby cannot have a right to life. Finally, a newborn baby is not an autonomous being, capable of making choices, and so to kill a newborn baby cannot violate the principle of respect for autonomy. In all this the newborn baby is on the same footing as the fetus, and hence fewer reasons exist against killing both babies and fetuses than exist against killing those who are capable of seeing themselves as distinct entities, existing over time.

It would, of course, be difficult to say at what age children begin to see themselves as distinct entities existing over time. Even when we talk with two and three year old children it is usually very difficult to elicit any coherent conception of death, or of the possibility that someone – let alone the child herself – might cease to exist. No doubt children vary greatly in the age at which they begin to understand these matters, as they do in most things. But a difficulty in drawing the line is not a reason for drawing it in a place that is obviously wrong, any more than the notorious difficulty in saying how much hair a man has to have lost before we can call him 'bald' is a reason for saying that someone whose pate is as smooth as a billiard ball is not bald. Of course, where rights are at risk, we should err on the side of safety. There is some plausibility in the view that, for legal purposes, since birth provides the only sharp, clear and easily understood line, the law of homicide should continue to apply immediately after birth. Since this is an argument at the level of public policy and the law, it is quite compatible with the view that, on purely ethical grounds, the killing of a newborn infant is not comparable with the killing of an older child or adult. Alternatively, recalling Hare's distinction between the critical and intuitive levels of moral reasoning, one could hold that the ethical judgment we have reached applies only at the level of critical morality; for everyday decision-making, we should act as if an infant has a right to life from the moment of birth. In the next chapter, however, we shall consider another possibility: that there should be at least some circumstances in which a full legal right to life comes into force not at birth, but only a short time after birth – perhaps a month. This would provide the ample safety margin mentioned above.

If these conclusions seem too shocking to take seriously, it may be worth remembering that our present absolute protection of the lives of infants is a distinctively Christian attitude rather than a universal ethical value. Infanticide has been practised in societies ranging geographically from Tahiti to Greenland and varying in culture from the nomadic Australian aborigines to the sophisticated urban communities of ancient Greece or mandarin China. In some of these societies infanticide was not merely permitted but, in certain circumstances, deemed morally obligatory. Not to kill a deformed or sickly infant was often regarded as wrong, and infanticide was probably the first, and in several societies the only, form of population control.

We might think that we are just more 'civilised' than these 'primitive' peoples. But it is not easy to feel confident that we are more civilised than the best Greek and Roman moralists. It was not just the Spartans who exposed their infants on hillsides: both Plato and Aristotle recommended the killing of deformed infants. Romans like Seneca, whose compassionate moral sense strikes the modern reader (or me, anyway) as superior to that of the early and mediaeval Christian writers, also thought infanticide the natural and humane solution to the problem posed by sick and deformed babies. The change in Western attitudes to infanticide since Roman times is, like the doctrine of the sanctity of human life of which it is a part, a product of Christianity. Perhaps it is now possible to think about these issues without assuming the Christian moral framework that has, for so long, prevented any fundamental reassessment.

None of this is meant to suggest that someone who goes around randomly killing babies is morally on a par with a woman who has an abortion. We should certainly put very strict conditions on permissible infanticide; but these restrictions might owe more to the effects of infanticide on others than to the intrinsic wrongness of killing an infant. Obviously, in most cases, to kill an infant is to inflict a terrible loss on those who love and cherish the child. My comparison of abortion and infanticide was prompted by the objection that the position I have taken on abortion also justifies infanticide. I have admitted this charge – without regarding the admission as fatal to my position – to the extent that the *intrinsic* wrongness of killing the late fetus and the *intrinsic* wrongness of killing the newborn infant are not markedly different. In cases of abortion, however, we assume that the people most affected – the parents-to-be, or at least the mother-to-be – want to have the abortion. Thus infanticide can only be equated with abortion when those closest to the child do not want it to live. As an infant can be adopted by others in a way that a pre-viable fetus cannot be, such cases will be rare. (Some of them are discussed in the following chapter.) Killing an infant whose parents do not want it dead is, of course, an utterly different matter.

TAKING LIFE: HUMANS

IN dealing with an objection to the view of abortion presented in Chapter 6, we have already looked beyond abortion to infanticide. In so doing we will have confirmed the suspicion of supporters of the sanctity of human life that once abortion is accepted, euthanasia lurks around the next corner – and for them, euthanasia is an unequivocal evil. It has, they point out, been rejected by doctors since the fifth century B.C., when physicians first took the Oath of Hippocrates and swore 'to give no deadly medicine to anyone if asked, nor suggest any such counsel'. Moreover, they argue, the Nazi extermination programme is a recent and terrible example of what can happen once we give the state the power to kill innocent human beings.

I do not deny that if one accepts abortion on the grounds provided in Chapter 6, the case for killing other human beings, in certain circumstances, is strong. As I shall try to show in this chapter, however, this is not something to be regarded with horror, and the use of the Nazi analogy is utterly misleading. On the contrary, once we abandon those doctrines about the sanctity of human life that – as we saw in Chapter 4 – collapse as soon as they are questioned, it is the refusal to accept killing that, in some cases, is horrific.

'Euthanasia' means, according to the dictionary, 'a gentle and easy death', but it is now used to refer to the killing of those who are incurably ill and in great pain or distress, for the sake of those killed, and in order to spare them further suffering or distress. This is the main topic of this chapter. I shall also consider, however, some cases in which, though killing is not contrary to the wishes of the human who is killed, it is also not carried out specifically for the sake of that being. As we shall see, some cases involving newborn infants fall into this category. Such cases may not be 'euthanasia' within the strict meaning of the term, but they can usefully be included within the same general discussion, as long as we are clear about the relevant differences.

Within the usual definition of euthanasia there are three different types, each of which raises distinctive ethical issues. It will help our discussion if we begin by setting out this threefold distinction and then assess the justifiability of each type.

TYPES OF EUTHANASIA

Voluntary Euthanasia

Most of the groups currently campaigning for changes in the law to allow euthanasia are campaigning for voluntary euthanasia – that is, euthanasia carried out at the request of the person killed.

Sometimes voluntary euthanasia is scarcely distinguishable from assisted suicide. In *Jean's Way*, Derek Humphry has told how his wife Jean, when dying of cancer, asked him to provide her with the means to end her life swiftly and without pain. They had seen the situation coming and discussed it beforehand. Derek obtained some tablets and gave them to Jean, who took them and died soon afterwards.

Dr Jack Kevorkian, a Michigan pathologist, went one step further when he built a 'suicide machine' to help terminally ill people commit suicide. His machine consisted of a metal pole with three different bottles attached to a tube of the kind used to provide an intravenous drip. The doctor inserts the tube in the patient's vein, but at this stage only a harmless saline solution can pass through it. The patient may then flip a switch, which will allow a coma-inducing drug to come through the tube; this is automatically followed by a lethal drug contained in the third bottle. Dr Kevorkian announced that he was prepared to make the machine available to any terminally ill patient who wished to use it. (Assisting suicide is not against the law in Michigan.) In June 1990, Janet Adkins, who was suffering from Alzheimer's disease, but still competent to make the decision to end her life, contacted Dr Kevorkian and told him of her wish to die, rather than go through the slow and progressive deterioration that the disease involves. Dr Kevorkian was in attendance while she made use of his machine, and then reported Janet Adkins's death to the police. He was subsequently charged with murder, but the judge refused to allow the charge to proceed to trial, on the grounds that Janet Adkins had caused her own death. The following year Dr Kevorkian made his device available to two other people, who used it in order to end their lives.[1]

In other cases, people wanting to die may be unable to kill themselves. In 1973 George Zygmaniak was injured in a motorcycle accident near his home in New Jersey. He was taken to hospital, where he was found to be totally paralysed from the neck down. He was also in considerable pain. He told his doctor and his brother, Lester, that he did not want to live in this condition. He begged them both to kill him. Lester questioned the doctor and hospital staff about George's prospects of recovery: he was told that they were nil. He then smuggled a gun into the hospital, and said to his brother: 'I am here to end your pain, George. Is it all right with you?' George, who was now unable to speak because of an operation to assist his breathing, nodded affirmatively. Lester shot him through the temple.

The Zygmaniak case appears to be a clear instance of voluntary euthanasia, although without some of the procedural

---

1 Dr Kevorkian was again charged with murder, and with providing a prohibited substance, in connection with the latter two cases, but was once more discharged.

safeguards that advocates of the legalisation of voluntary euthanasia propose. For instance, medical opinions about the patient's prospects of recovery were obtained only in an informal manner. Nor was there a careful attempt to establish, before independent witnesses, that George's desire for death was of a fixed and rational kind, based on the best available information about his situation. The killing was not carried out by a doctor. An injection would have been less distressing to others than shooting. But these choices were not open to Lester Zygmaniak, for the law in New Jersey, as in most other places, regards mercy killing as murder, and if he had made his plans known, he would not have been able to carry them out.

Euthanasia can be voluntary even if a person is not able, as Jean Humphry, Janet Adkins, and George Zygmaniak were able, to indicate the wish to die right up to the moment the tablets are swallowed, the switch thrown, or the trigger pulled. A person may, while in good health, make a written request for euthanasia if, through accident or illness, she should come to be incapable of making or expressing a decision to die, in pain, or without the use of her mental faculties, and there is no reasonable hope of recovery. In killing a person who has made such a request, who has re-affirmed it from time to time, and who is now in one of the states described, one could truly claim to be acting with her consent.

There is now one country in which doctors can openly help their patients to die in a peaceful and dignified way. In the Netherlands, a series of court cases during the 1980s upheld a doctor's right to assist a patient to die, even if that assistance amounted to giving the patient a lethal injection. Doctors in the Netherlands who comply with certain guidelines (which will be described later in this chapter) can now quite openly carry out euthanasia and can report this on the death certificate without fear of prosecution. It has been estimated that about 2,300 deaths each year result from euthanasia carried out in this way.

Involuntary Euthanasia

I shall regard euthanasia as involuntary when the person killed is capable of consenting to her own death, but does not do so, either because she is not asked, or because she is asked and chooses to go on living. Admittedly this definition lumps two different cases under one heading. There is a significant difference between killing someone who chooses to go on living and killing someone who has not consented to being killed, but if asked, would have consented. In practice, though, it is hard to imagine cases in which a person is capable of consenting and would have consented if asked, but was not asked. For why not ask? Only in the most bizarre situations could one conceive of a reason for not obtaining the consent of a person both able and willing to consent.

Killing someone who has not consented to being killed can properly be regarded as euthanasia only when the motive for killing is the desire to prevent unbearable suffering on the part of the person killed. It is, of course, odd that anyone acting from this motive should disregard the wishes of the person for whose sake the action is done. Genuine cases of involuntary euthanasia appear to be very rare.

Non-voluntary Euthanasia

These two definitions leave room for a third kind of euthanasia. If a human being is not capable of understanding the choice between life and death, euthanasia would be neither voluntary nor involuntary, but non-voluntary. Those unable to give consent would include incurably ill or severely disabled infants, and people who through accident, illness, or old age have permanently lost the capacity to understand the issue involved, without having previously requested or rejected euthanasia in these circumstances.

Several cases of non-voluntary euthanasia have reached the courts and the popular press. Here is one example. Louis Repouille had a son who was described as 'incurably imbecile', had been bed-ridden since infancy and blind for five years. According to Repouille: 'He was just like dead all the time. . . . He couldn't walk, he couldn't talk, he couldn't do anything.' In the end Repouille killed his son with chloroform.

In 1988 a case arose that well illustrates the way in which modern medical technology forces us to make life and death decisions. Samuel Linares, an infant, swallowed a small object that stuck in his windpipe, causing a loss of oxygen to the brain. He was admitted to a Chicago hospital in a coma and placed on a respirator. Eight months later he was still comatose, still on the respirator, and the hospital was planning to move Samuel to a long-term care unit. Shortly before the move, Samuel's parents visited him in the hospital. His mother left the room, while his father produced a pistol and told the nurse to keep away. He then disconnected Samuel from the respirator, and cradled the baby in his arms until he died. When he was sure Samuel was dead, he gave up his pistol and surrendered to police. He was charged with murder, but the grand jury refused to issue a homicide indictment, and he subsequently received a suspended sentence on a minor charge arising from the use of the pistol.

Obviously, such cases raise different issues from those raised by voluntary euthanasia. There is no desire to die on the part of the infant. It may also be questioned whether, in such cases, the death is carried out for the sake of the infant, or for the sake of the family as a whole. If Louis Repouille's son was 'just like dead all the time', then he may have been so profoundly brain-damaged that he was not capable of suffering at all. That is also likely to have been true of the comatose Samuel Linares. In that case, while caring for him would have been a great and no doubt futile burden for the family, and in the Linares case, a drain on the state's limited medical resources as well, the infants were not suffering, and death could not be said to be in, or contrary to, their interests. It is therefore not euthanasia, strictly speaking, as I have defined the term. It might nevertheless be a justifiable ending of a human life.

Since cases of infanticide and non-voluntary euthanasia are the kind of case most nearly akin to our previous discussions of the status of animals and the human fetus, we shall consider them first.

JUSTIFYING INFANTICIDE AND
NON-VOLUNTARY EUTHANASIA

As we have seen, euthanasia is non-voluntary when the subject has never had the capacity to choose to live or die. This is the situation of the severely disabled infant or the older human being who has been profoundly intellectually disabled since birth. Euthanasia or other forms of killing are also nonvoluntary when the subject is not now but once was capable of making the crucial choice, and did not then express any preference relevant to her present condition.

The case of someone who has never been capable of choosing to live or die is a little more straightforward than that of a person who had, but has now lost, the capacity to make such a decision. We shall, once again, separate the two cases and take the more straightforward one first. For simplicity, I shall concentrate on infants, although everything I say about them would apply to older children or adults whose mental age is and has always been that of an infant.

Life and Death Decisions for Disabled Infants

If we were to approach the issue of life or death for a seriously disabled human infant without any prior discussion of the ethics

181

of killing in general, we might be unable to resolve the conflict between the widely accepted obligation to protect the sanctity of human life, and the goal of reducing suffering. Some say that such decisions are 'subjective', or that life and death questions must be left to God and Nature. Our previous discussions have, however, prepared the ground, and the principles established and applied in the preceding three chapters make the issue much less baffling than most take it to be.

In Chapter 4 we saw that the fact that a being is a human being, in the sense of a member of the species Homo sapiens, is not relevant to the wrongness of killing it; it is, rather, characteristics like rationality, autonomy, and self-consciousness that make a difference. Infants lack these characteristics. Killing them, therefore, cannot be equated with killing normal human beings, or any other self-conscious beings. This conclusion is not limited to infants who, because of irreversible intellectual disabilities, will never be rational, self-conscious beings. We saw in our discussion of abortion that the potential of a fetus to become a rational, self-conscious being cannot count against killing it at a stage when it lacks these characteristics – not, that is, unless we are also prepared to count the value of rational self-conscious life as a reason against contraception and celibacy. No infant – disabled or not – has as strong a claim to life as beings capable of seeing themselves as distinct entities, existing over time.

The difference between killing disabled and normal infants lies not in any supposed right to life that the latter has and the former lacks, but in other considerations about killing. Most obviously there is the difference that often exists in the attitudes of the parents. The birth of a child is usually a happy event for the parents. They have, nowadays, often planned for the child. The mother has carried it for nine months. From birth, a natural affection begins to bind the parents to it. So one important reason why it is normally a terrible thing to kill an infant is the effect the killing will have on its parents.

It is different when the infant is born with a serious disability. Birth abnormalities vary, of course. Some are trivial and have little effect on the child or its parents; but others turn the normally joyful event of birth into a threat to the happiness of the parents, and any other children they may have.

Parents may, with good reason, regret that a disabled child was ever born. In that event the effect that the death of the child will have on its parents can be a reason for, rather than against killing it. Some parents want even the most gravely disabled infant to live as long as possible, and this desire would then be a reason against killing the infant. But what if this is not the case? In the discussion that follows I shall assume that the parents do not want the disabled child to live. I shall also assume that the disability is so serious that – again in contrast to the situation of an unwanted but normal child today – there are no other couples keen to adopt the infant. This is a realistic assumption even in a society in which there is a long waiting-list of couples wishing to adopt normal babies. It is true that from time to time cases of infants who are severely disabled and are being allowed to die have reached the courts in a glare of publicity, and this has led to couples offering to adopt the child. Unfortunately such offers are the product of the highly publicised dramatic life-and-death situation, and do not extend to the less publicised but far more common situations in which parents feel themselves unable to look after a severely disabled child, and the child then languishes in an institution.

Infants are sentient beings who are neither rational nor self-conscious. So if we turn to consider the infants in themselves, independently of the attitudes of their parents, since their species is not relevant to their moral status, the principles that govern the wrongness of killing non-human animals who are sentient but not rational or self-conscious must apply here too. As we saw, the most plausible arguments for attributing a right to life to a being apply only if there is some awareness of oneself as a being existing over time, or as a continuing mental self. Nor can respect for autonomy apply where there is no capacity for autonomy. The remaining principles identified in Chapter 4 are utilitarian. Hence the quality of life that the infant can be expected to have is important.

One relatively common birth disability is a faulty development of the spine known as spina bifida. Its prevalence varies in different countries, but it can affect as many as one in five hundred live births. In the more severe cases, the child will be permanently paralysed from the waist down and lack control of bowels or bladder. Often excess fluid accumulates in the brain, a condition known as hydrocephalus, which can result in intellectual disabilities. Though some forms of treatment exist, if the child is badly affected at birth, the paralysis, incontinence, and intellectual disability cannot be overcome.

Some doctors closely connected with children suffering from severe spina bifida believe that the lives of the worst affected children are so miserable that it is wrong to resort to surgery to keep them alive. Published descriptions of the lives of these children support the judgment that these worst affected children will have lives filled with pain and discomfort. They need repeated major surgery to prevent curvature of the spine, due to the paralysis, and to correct other abnormalities. Some children with spina bifida have had forty major operations before they reach their teenage years.

When the life of an infant will be so miserable as not to be worth living, from the internal perspective of the being who will lead that life, both the 'prior existence' and the 'total' version of utilitarianism entail that, if there are no 'extrinsic' reasons for keeping the infant alive – like the feelings of the parents – it is better that the child should be helped to die without further suffering. A more difficult problem arises – and the convergence between the two views ends – when we consider disabilities that make the child's life prospects significantly less promising than those of a normal child, but not so bleak as to make the child's life not worth living. Haemophilia is probably in this category. The haemophiliac lacks the element in normal blood that makes it clot and thus risks prolonged bleeding, especially internal bleeding, from the slightest injury. If allowed to continue, this bleeding leads to permanent crippling and eventually death. The bleeding is very painful and although improved treatments have eliminated the need for constant blood transfusions, haemophiliacs still have to spend a lot of time in hospital. They are unable to play most sports and live constantly on the edge of crisis. Nevertheless, haemophiliacs do not appear to spend their time wondering whether to end it all; most find life definitely worth living, despite the difficulties they face.

Given these facts, suppose that a newborn baby is diagnosed as a haemophiliac. The parents, daunted by the prospect of bringing up a child with this condition, are not anxious for him to live. Could euthanasia be defended here? Our first reaction may well be a firm 'no', for the infant can be expected to have a life that is worth living, even if not quite as good as that of a normal baby. The 'prior existence' version of utilitarianism supports this judgment. The infant exists. His life can be expected to contain a positive balance of happiness over misery. To kill him would deprive him of this positive balance of happiness. Therefore it would be wrong.

On the 'total' version of utilitarianism, however, we cannot reach a decision on the basis of this information alone. The total view makes it necessary to ask whether the death of the haemophiliac infant would lead to the creation of another being who would not otherwise have existed. In other words, if the haemophiliac child is killed, will his parents have another child whom they would not have if the haemophiliac child lives? If they would, is the second child likely to have a better life than the one killed?

Often it will be possible to answer both these questions affirmatively. A woman may plan to have two children. If one dies while she is of child-bearing age, she may conceive another in its place. Suppose a woman planning to have two children has one normal child, and then gives birth to a haemophiliac child. The burden of caring for that child may make it impossible for her to cope with a third child; but if the disabled child were to die, she would have another. It is also plausible to suppose that the prospects of a happy life are better for a normal child than for a haemophiliac.

When the death of a disabled infant will lead to the birth of another infant with better prospects of a happy life, the total amount of happiness will be greater if the disabled infant is killed. The loss of happy life for the first infant is outweighed by the gain of a happier life for the second. Therefore, if killing the haemophiliac infant has no adverse effect on others, it would, according to the total view, be right to kill him.

The total view treats infants as replaceable, in much the same way as it treats non–self-conscious animals (as we saw in Chapter 5). Many will think that the replaceability argument cannot be applied to human infants. The direct killing of even the most hopelessly disabled infant is still officially regarded as murder; how then could the killing of infants with far less serious problems, like haemophilia, be accepted? Yet on further reflection, the implications of the replaceability argument do not seem quite so bizarre. For there are disabled members of our species whom we now deal with exactly as the argument suggests we should. These cases closely resemble the ones we have been discussing. There is only one difference, and that is a difference of timing – the timing of the discovery of the problem, and the consequent killing of the disabled being.

Prenatal diagnosis is now a routine procedure for pregnant women. There are various medical techniques for obtaining information about the fetus during the early months of pregnancy. At one stage in the development of these procedures, it was possible to discover the sex of the fetus, but not whether the fetus would suffer from haemophilia. Haemophilia is a sex-linked genetic defect, from which only males suffer; females can carry the gene and pass it on to their male offspring without themselves being affected. So a woman who knew that she carried the gene for haemophilia could, at that stage, avoid giving birth to a haemophiliac child only by finding out the sex of the fetus, and aborting all males fetuses. Statistically, only half of these male children of women who carried the defective gene would have suffered from haemophilia, but there was then no way to find out to which half a particular fetus belonged. Therefore twice as many fetuses were being killed as necessary, in order to avoid the birth of children with haemophilia. This practice was widespread in many countries, and yet did not cause any great outcry. Now that we have techniques for identifying haemophilia before birth, we can be more selective, but the principle is the same: women are offered, and usually accept, abortions in order to avoid giving birth to children with haemophilia.

The same can be said about some other conditions that can be detected before birth. Down's syndrome, formerly known as mongolism, is one of these. Children with this condition have intellectual disabilities and most will never be able to live independently, but their lives, like those of small children, can be joyful. The risk of having a Down's syndrome child increases sharply with the age of the mother, and for this reason prenatal diagnosis is routinely offered to pregnant women over 35. Again, undergoing the procedure implies that if the test for Down's syndrome is positive, the woman will consider aborting the fetus and, if she still wishes to have another child, will start another pregnancy, which has a good chance of being normal.

Prenatal diagnosis, followed by abortion in selected cases, is common practice in countries with liberal abortion laws and advanced medical techniques. I think this is as it should be. As the arguments of Chapter 6 indicate, I believe that abortion can be justified. Note, however, that neither haemophilia nor Down's syndrome is so crippling as to make life not worth living, from the inner perspective of the person with the condition. To

187

abort a fetus with one of these disabilities, intending to have another child who will not be disabled, is to treat fetuses as interchangeable or replaceable. If the mother has previously decided to have a certain number of children, say two, then what she is doing, in effect, is rejecting one potential child in favour of another. She could, in defence of her actions, say: the loss of life of the aborted fetus is outweighed by the gain of a better life for the normal child who will be conceived only if the disabled one dies.

When death occurs before birth, replaceability does not conflict with generally accepted moral convictions. That a fetus is known to be disabled is widely accepted as a ground for abortion. Yet in discussing abortion, we saw that birth does not mark a morally significant dividing line. I cannot see how one could defend the view that fetuses may be 'replaced' before birth, but newborn infants may not be. Nor is there any other point, such as viability, that does a better job of dividing the fetus from the infant. Self-consciousness, which could provide a basis for holding that it is wrong to kill one being and replace it with another, is not to be found in either the fetus or the newborn infant. Neither the fetus nor the newborn infant is an individual capable of regarding itself as a distinct entity with a life of its own to lead, and it is only for newborn infants, or for still earlier stages of human life, that replaceability should be considered to be an ethically acceptable option.

It may still be objected that to replace either a fetus or a newborn infant is wrong because it suggests to disabled people living today that their lives are less worth living than the lives of people who are not disabled. Yet it is surely flying in the face of reality to deny that, on average, this is so. That is the only way to make sense of actions that we all take for granted. Recall thalidomide: this drug, when taken by pregnant women, caused many children to be born without arms or legs. Once the cause of the abnormal births was discovered, the drug was taken off the market, and the company responsible had to pay compensation. If we really believed that there is no reason to think of the life of a disabled person as likely to be any worse than that of a normal person, we would not have regarded this as a tragedy. No compensation would have been sought, or awarded by the courts. The children would merely have been 'different'. We could even have left the drug on the market, so that women who found it a useful sleeping pill during pregnancy could continue to take it. If this sounds grotesque, that is only because we are all in no doubt at all that it is better to be born with limbs than without them. To believe this involves no disrespect at all for those who are lacking limbs; it simply recognises the reality of the difficulties they face.

In any case, the position taken here does not imply that it would be better that no people born with severe disabilities should survive; it implies only that the parents of such infants should be able to make this decision. Nor does this imply lack of respect or equal consideration for people with disabilities who are now living their own lives in accordance with their own wishes. As we saw at the end of Chapter 2, the principle of equal consideration of interests rejects any discounting of the interests of people on grounds of disability.

Even those who reject abortion and the idea that the fetus is replaceable are likely to regard possible people as replaceable. Recall the second woman in Parfit's case of the two women, described in Chapter 5. She was told by her doctor that if she went ahead with her plan to become pregnant immediately, her child would have a disability (it could have been haemophilia); but if she waited three months her child would not have the disability. If we think she would do wrong not to wait, it can only be because we are comparing the two possible lives and judging one to have better prospects than the other. Of course, at this stage no life has begun; but the question is, when does a life, in the morally significant sense, really begin? In Chapters 4 and 5 we saw several reasons for saying that life only begins in the morally significant sense when there is awareness of one's existence over time. The metaphor of life as a journey also provides a reason for holding that in infancy, life's voyage has scarcely begun.

Regarding newborn infants as replaceable, as we now regard fetuses, would have considerable advantages over prenatal diagnosis followed by abortion. Prenatal diagnosis still cannot detect all major disabilities. Some disabilities, in fact, are not present before birth; they may be the result of extremely premature birth, or of something going wrong in the birth process itself. At present parents can choose to keep or destroy their disabled offspring only if the disability happens to be detected during pregnancy. There is no logical basis for restricting parents' choice to these particular disabilities. If disabled newborn infants were not regarded as having a right to life until, say, a week or a month after birth it would allow parents, in consultation with their doctors, to choose on the basis of far greater knowledge of the infant's condition than is possible before birth.

All these remarks have been concerned with the wrongness of ending the life of the infant, considered in itself rather than for its effects on others. When we take effects on others into account, the picture may alter. Obviously, to go through the whole of pregnancy and labour, only to give birth to a child who one decides should not live, would be a difficult, perhaps heartbreaking, experience. For this reason many women would prefer prenatal diagnosis and abortion rather than live birth with the possibility of infanticide; but if the latter is not morally worse than the former, this would seem to be a choice that the woman herself should be allowed to make.

Another factor to take into account is the possibility of adoption. When there are more couples wishing to adopt than normal children available for adoption, a childless couple may be prepared to adopt a haemophiliac. This would relieve the mother of the burden of bringing up a haemophiliac child, and enable her to have another child, if she wished. Then the replaceability argument could not justify infanticide, for bringing the other child into existence would not be dependent on the death of the haemophiliac. The death of the haemophiliac would then be a straightforward loss of a life of positive quality, not outweighed by the creation of another being with a better life.

So the issue of ending life for disabled newborn infants is not without complications, which we do not have the space to discuss adequately. Nevertheless the main point is clear: killing a disabled infant is not morally equivalent to killing a person. Very often it is not wrong at all.

Other Non-voluntary Life and Death Decisions

In the preceding section we discussed justifiable killing for beings who have never been capable of choosing to live or die. Ending a life without consent may also be considered in the case of those who were once persons capable of choosing to live or die, but now, through accident or old age, have permanently lost this capacity, and did not, prior to losing it, express any views about whether they wished to go on living in such circumstances. These cases are not rare. Many hospitals care for motor accident victims whose brains have been damaged beyond all possible recovery. They may survive, in a coma, or perhaps barely conscious, for several years. In 1991, the *Lancet* reported that Rita Greene, a nurse, had been a patient at D.C. General Hospital in Washington for thirty-nine years without knowing it. Now aged sixty-three, she had been in a vegetative state since undergoing open heart surgery in 1952. The report stated that at any given time, between 5,000 and 10,000 Americans are surviving in a vegetative state. In other developed countries, where life-prolonging technology is not used so aggressively, there are far fewer long-term patients in this condition.

In most respects, these human beings do not differ importantly from disabled infants. They are not self-conscious, rational, or autonomous, and so considerations of a right to life or of respecting autonomy do not apply. If they have no experiences at all, and can never have any again, their lives have no intrinsic value. Their life's journey has come to an end. They are biologically alive, but not biographically. (If this verdict seems harsh, ask yourself whether there is anything to choose between the following options: (a) instant death or (b) instant coma, followed by death, without recovery, in ten years' time. I can see no advantage in survival in a comatose state, if death without recovery is certain.) The lives of those who are not in a coma and are conscious but not self-conscious have value if such beings experience more pleasure than pain, or have preferences that can be satisfied; but it is difficult to see the point of keeping such human beings alive if their life is, on the whole, miserable.

There is one important respect in which these cases differ from disabled infants. In discussing infanticide in the final section of Chapter 6, I cited Bentham's comment that infanticide need not 'give the slightest inquietude to the most timid imagination'. This is because those old enough to be aware of the killing of disabled infants are necessarily outside the scope of the policy. This cannot be said of euthanasia applied to those who once were rational and self-conscious. So a possible objection to this form of euthanasia would be that it will lead to insecurity and fear among those who are not now, but might come to be, within its scope. For instance, elderly people, knowing that non-voluntary euthanasia is sometimes applied to senile elderly patients, bedridden, suffering, and lacking the capacity to accept or reject death, might fear that every injection or tablet will be lethal. This fear might be quite irrational, but it would be difficult to convince people of this, particularly if old age really had affected their memory or powers of reasoning.

This objection might be met by a procedure allowing those who do not wish to be subjected to non-voluntary euthanasia under any circumstances to register their refusal. Perhaps this would suffice; but perhaps it would not provide enough reassurance. If not, non-voluntary euthanasia would be justifiable only for those never capable of choosing to live or die.

JUSTIFYING VOLUNTARY EUTHANASIA

Under existing laws in most countries, people suffering unrelievable pain or distress from an incurable illness who beg their doctors to end their lives are asking their doctors to risk a murder charge. Although juries are extremely reluctant to convict in cases of this kind the law is clear that neither the request, nor the degree of suffering, nor the incurable condition of the person killed, is a defence to a charge of murder. Advocates of voluntary euthanasia propose that this law be changed so that a doctor could legally act on a patient's desire to die without further suffering. Doctors have been able to do this quite openly in the Netherlands, as a result of a series of court decisions during the 1980s, as long as they comply with certain conditions. In Germany, doctors may provide a patient with the means to end her life, but they may not administer the substance to her.

The case for voluntary euthanasia has some common ground with the case for non-voluntary euthanasia, in that death is a benefit for the one killed. The two kinds of euthanasia differ, however, in that voluntary euthanasia involves the killing of a person, a rational and self-conscious being and not a merely conscious being. (To be strictly accurate it must be said that this is not always so, because although only rational and self-conscious beings can consent to their own deaths, they may not be rational and self-conscious at the time euthanasia is contemplated – the doctor may, for instance, be acting on a prior written request for euthanasia if, through accident or illness, one's rational faculties should be irretrievably lost. For simplicity we shall, henceforth, disregard this complication.)

We have seen that it is possible to justify ending the life of a

193

human being who lacks the capacity to consent. We must now ask in what way the ethical issues are different when the being is capable of consenting, and does in fact consent.

Let us return to the general principles about killing proposed in Chapter 4. I argued there that killing a self-conscious being is a more serious matter than killing a merely conscious being. I gave four distinct grounds on which this could be argued:

1 The classical utilitarian claim that since self-conscious beings are capable of fearing their own death, killing them has worse effects on others.

2 The preference utilitarian calculation that counts the thwarting of the victim's desire to go on living as an important reason against killing.

3 A theory of rights according to which to have a right one must have the ability to desire that to which one has a right, so that to have a right to life one must be able to desire one's own continued existence.

4 Respect for the autonomous decisions of rational agents.

Now suppose we have a situation in which a person suffering from a painful and incurable disease wishes to die. If the individual were not a person – not rational or self-conscious – euthanasia would, as I have said, be justifiable. Do any of the four grounds for holding that it is normally worse to kill a person provide reasons against killing when the individual is a person who wants to die?

The classical utilitarian objection does not apply to killing that takes place only with the genuine consent of the person killed. That people are killed under these conditions would have no tendency to spread fear or insecurity, since we have no cause to be fearful of being killed with our own genuine consent. If we do not wish to be killed, we simply do not consent. In fact, the argument from fear points in favour of voluntary euthanasia, for if voluntary euthanasia is not permitted we may, with good cause, be fearful that our deaths will be unnecessarily drawn out and distressing. In the Netherlands, a nationwide study commissioned by the government found that 'Many patients want an assurance that their doctor will assist them to die should suffering become unbearable.' Often, having received this assurance, no persistent request for euthanasia eventuated. The availability of euthanasia brought comfort without euthanasia having to be provided.

Preference utilitarianism also points in favour of, not against, voluntary euthanasia. Just as preference utilitarianism must count a desire to go on living as a reason against killing, so it must count a desire to die as a reason for killing.

Next, according to the theory of rights we have considered, it is an essential feature of a right that one can waive one's rights if one so chooses. I may have a right to privacy; but I can, if I wish, film every detail of my daily life and invite the neighbours to my home movies. Neighbours sufficiently intrigued to accept my invitation could do so without violating my right to privacy, since the right has on this occasion been waived. Similarly, to say that I have a right to life is not to say that it would be wrong for my doctor to end my life, if she does so at my request. In making this request I waive my right to life.

Lastly, the principle of respect for autonomy tells us to allow rational agents to live their own lives according to their own autonomous decisions, free from coercion or interference; but if rational agents should autonomously choose to die, then respect for autonomy will lead us to assist them to do as they choose.

So, although there are reasons for thinking that killing a self-conscious being is normally worse than killing any other kind of being, in the special case of voluntary euthanasia most of these reasons count for euthanasia rather than against. Surprising as this result might at first seem, it really does no more than reflect the fact that what is special about self-conscious beings is that they can know that they exist over time and will, unless they die, continue to exist. Normally this continued existence is fervently desired; when the foreseeable continued existence is dreaded rather than desired however, the desire to die may take the place of the normal desire to live, reversing the reasons against killing based on the desire to live. Thus the case for voluntary euthanasia is arguably much stronger than the case for non-voluntary euthanasia.

Some opponents of the legalisation of voluntary euthanasia might concede that all this follows, if we have a genuinely free and rational decision to die: but, they add, we can never be sure that a request to be killed is the result of a free and rational decision. Will not the sick and elderly be pressured by their relatives to end their lives quickly? Will it not be possible to commit outright murder by pretending that a person has requested euthanasia? And even if there is no pressure of falsification, can anyone who is ill, suffering pain, and very probably in a drugged and confused state of mind, make a rational decision about whether to live or die?

These questions raise technical difficulties for the legalisation of voluntary euthanasia, rather than objections to the underlying ethical principles; but they are serious difficulties nonetheless. The guidelines developed by the courts in the Netherlands have sought to meet them by proposing that euthanasia is acceptable only if

- It is carried out by a physician.
- The patient has explicitly requested euthanasia in a manner that leaves no doubt of the patient's desire to die.
- The patient's decision is well-informed, free, and durable.
- The patient has an irreversible condition causing protracted physical or mental suffering that the patients finds unbearable.
- There is no reasonable alternative (reasonable from the patient's point of view) to alleviate the patient's suffering.
- The doctor has consulted another independent professional who agrees with his or her judgment.

Euthanasia in these circumstances is strongly supported by the Royal Dutch Medical Association, and by the general public in the Netherlands. The guidelines make murder in the guise of euthanasia rather far-fetched, and there is no evidence of an increase in the murder rate in the Netherlands.

It is often said, in debates about euthanasia, that doctors can be mistaken. In rare instances patients diagnosed by two competent doctors as suffering from an incurable condition have survived and enjoyed years of good health. Possibly the legalisation of voluntary euthanasia would, over the years, mean the deaths of a few people who would otherwise have recovered from their immediate illness and lived for some extra years. This is not, however, the knockdown argument against euthanasia that some imagine it to be. Against a very small number of unnecessary deaths that might occur if euthanasia is legalised we must place the very large amount of pain and distress that will be suffered if euthanasia is not legalised, by patients who really are terminally ill. Longer life is not such a supreme good that it outweighs all other considerations. (If it were, there would be many more effective ways of saving life – such as a ban on smoking, or a reduction of speed limits to 40 kilometres per hour – than prohibiting voluntary euthanasia.) The possibility that two doctors may make a mistake means that the person who opts for euthanasia is deciding on the balance of probabilities and giving up a very slight chance of survival in order to avoid suffering that will almost certainly end in death. This may be a perfectly rational choice. Probability is the guide of life, and of death, too. Against this, some will reply that improved care for the terminally ill has eliminated pain and made voluntary euthanasia unnecessary. Elisabeth Kübler-Ross, whose *On Death and Dying* is perhaps the best-known book on care for the dying, has claimed that none of her patients request euthanasia. Given personal attention and the right medication, she says, people come to accept their deaths and die peacefully without pain.

Kübler-Ross may be right. It may be possible, now, to eliminate pain. In almost all cases, it may even be possible to do it in a way that leaves patients in possession of their rational faculties and free from vomiting, nausea, or other distressing side-effects. Unfortunately only a minority of dying patients now receive this kind of care. Nor is physical pain the only problem. There can also be other distressing conditions, like bones so fragile they fracture at sudden movements, uncontrollable nausea and vomiting, slow starvation due to a cancerous growth, inability to control one's bowels or bladder, difficulty in breathing, and so on.

Dr Timothy Quill, a doctor from Rochester, New York, has described how he prescribed barbiturate sleeping pills for 'Diane', a patient with a severe form of leukaemia, knowing that she wanted the tablets in order to be able to end her life. Dr Quill had known Diane for many years, and admired her courage in dealing with previous serious illnesses. In an article in the *New England Journal of Medicine*, Dr Quill wrote:

> It was extraordinarily important to Diane to maintain control of herself and her own dignity during the time remaining to her. When this was no longer possible, she clearly wanted to die. As a former director of a hospice program, I know how to use pain medicines to keep patients comfortable and lessen suffering. I explained the philosophy of comfort care, which I strongly believe in. Although Diane understood and appreciated this, she had known of people lingering in what was called relative comfort, and she wanted no part of it. When the time came, she wanted to take her life in the least painful way possible. Knowing of her desire for independence and her decision to stay in control, I thought this request made perfect sense. . . . In our discussion it became clear that preoccupation with her fear of a lingering death would interfere with Diane's getting the most out of the time she had left until she found a safe way to ensure her death.

Not all dying patients who wish to die are fortunate enough to have a doctor like Timothy Quill. Betty Rollin has described, in her moving book *Last Wish*, how her mother developed ovarian cancer that spread to other parts of her body. One morning her mother said to her:

I've had a wonderful life, but now it's over, or it should be. I'm not afraid to die, but I am afraid of this illness, what it's doing to me. . . . There's never any relief from it now. Nothing but nausea and this pain. . . . There won't be any more chemotherapy. There's no treatment anymore. So what happens to me now? I know what happens. I'll die slowly. . . . I don't want that. . . . Who does it benefit if I die slowly? If it benefits my children I'd be willing. But it's not going to do you any good. . . . There's no point in a slow death, none. I've never liked doing things with no point. I've got to end this.

Betty Rollin found it very difficult to help her mother to carry out her desire: 'Physician after physician turned down our pleas for help (How many pills? What kind?).' After her book about her mother's death was published, she received hundreds of letters, many from people, or close relatives of people, who had tried to die, failed, and suffered even more. Many of these people were denied help from doctors, because although suicide is legal in most jurisdictions, assisted suicide is not.

Perhaps one day it will be possible to treat all terminally ill and incurable patients in such a way that no one requests euthanasia and the subject becomes a non-issue; but this is now just a utopian ideal, and no reason at all to deny euthanasia to those who must live and die in far less comfortable conditions. It is, in any case, highly paternalistic to tell dying patients that they are now so well looked after that they need not be offered the option of euthanasia. It would be more in keeping with respect for individual freedom and autonomy to legalise euthanasia and let patients decide whether their situation is bearable.

Do these arguments for voluntary euthanasia perhaps give too much weight to individual freedom and autonomy? After all, we do not allow people free choices on matters like, for instance, the taking of heroin. This is a restriction of freedom but, in the view of many, one that can be justified on paternalistic grounds. If preventing people from becoming heroin addicts is justifiable paternalism, why isn't preventing people from having themselves killed?

The question is a reasonable one, because respect for individual freedom can be carried too far. John Stuart Mill thought that the state should never interfere with the individual except to prevent harm to others. The individual's own good, Mill thought, is not a proper reason for state intervention. But Mill may have had too high an opinion of the rationality of a human being. It may occasionally be right to prevent people from making choices that are obviously not rationally based and that we can be sure they will later regret. The prohibition of voluntary euthanasia cannot be justified on paternalistic grounds, however, for voluntary euthanasia is an act for which good reasons exist. Voluntary euthanasia occurs only when, to the best of medical knowledge, a person is suffering from an incurable and painful or extremely distressing condition. In these circumstances one cannot say that to choose to die quickly is obviously irrational. The strength of the case for voluntary euthanasia lies in this combination of respect for the preferences, or autonomy, of those who decide for euthanasia; and the clear rational basis of the decision itself.

NOT JUSTIFYING INVOLUNTARY EUTHANASIA

Involuntary euthanasia resembles voluntary euthanasia in that it involves the killing of those capable of consenting to their own death. It differs in that they do not consent. This difference is crucial, as the argument of the preceding section shows. All the four reasons against killing self-conscious beings apply when the person killed does not choose to die.

Would it ever be possible to justify involuntary euthanasia on paternalistic grounds, to save someone extreme agony? It might be possible to imagine a case in which the agony was so great, and so certain, that the weight of utilitarian considerations favouring euthanasia override all four reasons against killing self-conscious beings. Yet to make this decision one would have to be confident that one can judge when a person's life is so bad as to be not worth living, better than that person can judge herself. It is not clear that we are ever justified in having much confidence in our judgments about whether the life of another person is, to that person, worth living. That the other person wishes to go on living is good evidence that her life is worth living. What better evidence could there be?

The only kind of case in which the paternalistic argument is at all plausible is one in which the person to be killed does not realise what agony she will suffer in future, and if she is not killed now she will have to live through to the very end. On these grounds one might kill a person who has – though she does not yet realise it – fallen into the hands of homicidal sadists who will torture her to death. These cases are, fortunately, more commonly encountered in fiction than reality.

If in real life we are unlikely ever to encounter a case of justifiable involuntary euthanasia, then it may be best to dismiss from our minds the fanciful cases in which one might imagine defending it, and treat the rule against involuntary euthanasia as, for all practical purposes, absolute. Here Hare's distinction between critical and intuitive levels of moral reasoning (see Chapter 4), is again relevant. The case described in the preceding paragraph is one in which, if we were reasoning at the critical level, we might consider involuntary euthanasia justifiable; but at the intuitive level, the level of moral reasoning we apply in our daily lives, we can simply say that euthanasia is only justifiable if those killed either

1 lack the ability to consent to death, because they lack the capacity to understand the choice between their own continued existence or non-existence; or
2 have the capacity to choose between their own continued life or death and to make an informed, voluntary, and settled decision to die.

ACTIVE AND PASSIVE EUTHANASIA

The conclusions we have reached in this chapter will shock a large number of readers, for they violate one of the most fundamental tenets of Western ethics – the wrongness of killing innocent human beings. I have already made one attempt to show that my conclusions are, at least in the area of disabled infants, a less radical departure from existing practice than one might suppose. I pointed out that many societies allow a pregnant woman to kill a fetus at a late stage of pregnancy if there is a significant risk of it being disabled; and since the line between a developed fetus and a newborn infant is not a crucial moral divide, it is difficult to see why it is worse to kill a newborn infant known to be disabled. In this section I shall argue that there is another area of accepted medical practice that is not intrinsically different from the practices that the arguments of this chapter would allow.

I have already referred to the birth defect known as spina bifida, in which the infant is born with an opening in the back, exposing the spinal cord. Until 1957, most of these infants died young, but in that year doctors began using a new kind of valve, to drain off the excess fluid that otherwise accumulates in the head with this condition. In some hospitals it then became standard practice to make vigorous efforts to save every spina bifida infant. The result was that few such infants died – but of those who survived, many were severely disabled, with gross paralysis, multiple deformities of the legs and spine, and no control of bowel or bladder. Intellectual disabilities were also common. In short, the existence of these children caused great difficulty for their families and was often a misery for the children themselves.

After studying the results of this policy of active treatment a British doctor, John Lorber, proposed that instead of treating all cases of spina bifida, only those who have the defect in a mild form should be selected for treatment. (He proposed that the final decision should be up to the parents, but parents nearly always accept the recommendations of the doctors.) This principle of selective treatment has now been widely accepted in many countries and in Britain has been recognised as legitimate by the Department of Health and Social Security. The result is that fewer spina bifida children survive beyond infancy, but those who do survive are, by and large, the ones whose physical and mental disabilities are relatively minor.

The policy of selection, then, appears to be a desirable one: but what happens to those disabled infants not selected for treatment? Lorber does not disguise the fact that in these cases the hope is that the infant will die soon and without suffering. It is to achieve this objective that surgical operations and other forms of active treatment are not undertaken, although pain and discomfort are as far as possible relieved. If the infant happens to get an infection, the kind of infection that in a normal infant would be swiftly cleared up with antibiotics, no antibiotics are given. Since the survival of the infant is not desired, no steps are taken to prevent a condition, easily curable by ordinary medical techniques, proving fatal.

All this is, as I have said, accepted medical practice. In articles in medical journals, doctors have described cases in which they have allowed infants to die. These cases are not limited to spina bifida, but include, for instance, babies born with Down's syndrome and other complications. In 1982, the 'Baby Doe' case brought this practice to the attention of the American public. 'Baby Doe' was the legal pseudonym of a baby born in Bloomington, Indiana, with Down's syndrome and some additional problems. The most serious of these was that the passage from the mouth to the stomach – the oesophagus – was not properly formed. This meant that Baby Doe could not receive nourishment by mouth. The problem could have been repaired by surgery – but in this case the parents, after discussing the situation with their obstetrician, refused permission for surgery. Without surgery, Baby Doe would soon die. Baby Doe's father later said that as a schoolteacher he had worked closely with Down's syndrome children, and that he and his wife had decided that it was in the best interests of Baby Doe, and of their family as a whole (they had two other children), to refuse consent for the operation. The hospital authorities, uncertain of their legal position, took the matter to court. Both the local county court and the Indiana State Supreme Court upheld the parents' right to refuse consent to surgery. The case attracted national media attention, and an attempt was made to take it to the U.S. Supreme Court, but before this could happen, Baby Doe died.

One result of the Baby Doe case was that the U.S. government, headed at the time by President Ronald Reagan, who had come to power with the backing of the right-wing religious 'Moral Majority', issued a regulation directing that all infants are to be given necessary life-saving treatment, irrespective of disability. But the new regulations were strongly resisted by the American Medical Association and the American Academy of Pediatrics. In court hearings on the regulations, even Dr C. Everett Koop, Reagan's surgeon-general and the driving force behind the attempt to ensure that all infants should be treated, had to admit that there were some cases in which he would not provide life-sustaining treatment. Dr Koop mentioned three conditions in which, he said, life-sustaining treatment was not appropriate: anencephalic infants (infants born without a brain); infants who had, usually as a result of extreme prematurity, suffered such severe bleeding in the brain that they would never be able to breathe without a respirator and would never be able even to recognise another person; and infants lacking a major part of their digestive tract, who could only be kept alive by means of a drip providing nourishment directly into the bloodstream.

The regulations were eventually accepted only in a watered-down form, allowing some flexibility to doctors. Even so, a subsequent survey of American paediatricians specialising in the care of newborn infants showed that 76 percent thought that the regulations were not necessary, 66 percent considered the regulations interfered with parents' right to determine what course of action was in the best interests of their children, and 60 percent believed that the regulations did not allow adequate consideration of infants' suffering.

In a series of British cases, the courts have accepted the view that the quality of a child's life is a relevant consideration in deciding whether life-sustaining treatment should be provided. In a case called *In re B*, concerning a baby like Baby Doe, with Down's syndrome and an intestinal obstruction, the court said that surgery should be carried out, because the infant's life would not be 'demonstrably awful'. In another case, *Re C*, where the baby had a poorly formed brain combined with severe physical handicaps, the court authorised the paediatric team to refrain from giving life-prolonging treatment. This was also the course taken in the case of *Re Baby J*: this infant was born extremely prematurely, and was blind and deaf and would probably never have been able to speak.

Thus, though many would disagree with Baby Doe's parents about allowing a Down's syndrome infant to die (because people with Down's syndrome can live enjoyable lives and be warm and loving individuals), virtually everyone recognises that in more severe conditions, allowing an infant to die is the only humane and ethically acceptable course to take. The question is: if it is right to allow infants to die, why is it wrong to kill them?

This question has not escaped the notice of the doctors involved. Frequently they answer it by a pious reference to the nineteenth-century poet, Arthur Clough, who wrote:

> Thou shalt not kill; but need'st not strive
> Officiously to keep alive.

Unfortunately for those who appeal to Clough's immortal lines as an authoritative ethical pronouncement, they come from a biting satire – 'The Latest Decalogue' – the intent of which is to mock the attitudes described. The opening lines, for example, are:

> Thou shalt have one god only; who
> Would be at the expense of two.
> No graven images may be
> Worshipped except the currency.

So Clough cannot be numbered on the side of those who think it wrong to kill, but right not to try too hard to keep alive. Is there, nonetheless, something to be said for this idea? The view that there is something to be said for it is often termed 'the acts and omissions doctrine'. It holds that there is an important moral distinction between performing an act that has certain consequences – say, the death of a disabled child – and omitting to do something that has the same consequences. If this doctrine is correct, the doctor who gives the child a lethal injection does wrong; the doctor who omits to give the child antibiotics, knowing full well that without antibiotics the child will die, does not.

What grounds are there for accepting the acts and omissions doctrine? Few champion the doctrine for its own sake, as an important ethical first principle. It is, rather, an implication of one view of ethics, of a view that holds that as long as we do not violate specified moral rules that place determinate moral obligations upon us, we do all that morality demands of us. These rules are of the kind made familiar by the Ten Commandments and similar moral codes: Do not kill, Do not lie, Do not steal, and so on. Characteristically they are formulated in the negative, so that to obey them it is necessary only to abstain from the actions they prohibit. Hence obedience can be demanded of every member of the community.

An ethic consisting of specific duties, prescribed by moral rules that everyone can be expected to obey, must make a sharp moral distinction between acts and omissions. Take, for example, the rule: 'Do not kill.' If this rule is interpreted, as it has been in the Western tradition, as prohibiting only the taking of innocent human life, it is not too difficult to avoid overt acts in violation of it. Few of us are murderers. It is not so easy to avoid letting innocent humans die. Many people die because of insufficient food, or poor medical facilities. If we could assist some of them, but do not do so, we are letting them die. Taking the rule against killing to apply to omissions would make living in accordance with it a mark of saintliness or moral heroism, rather than a minimum required of every morally decent person.

An ethic that judges acts according to whether they do or do not violate specific moral rules must, therefore, place moral weight on the distinction between acts and omissions. An ethic that judges acts by their consequences will not do so, for the consequences of an act and an omission will often be, in all significant respects, indistinguishable. For instance, omitting to give antibiotics to a child with pneumonia may have consequences no less fatal than giving the child a lethal injection.

Which approach is right? I have argued for a consequentialist approach to ethics. The acts/omissions issue poses the choice between these two basic approaches in an unusually clear and direct way. What we need to do is imagine two parallel situations differing only in that in one a person performs an act resulting in the death of another human being, while in the other she omits to do something, with the same result. Here is a description of a relatively common situation, taken from an essay by Sir Gustav Nossal, an eminent Australian medical researcher:

> An old lady of 83 has been admitted [to a nursing home for the aged] because her increasing degree of mental confusion has made it impossible for her to stay in her own home, and there is no one willing and able to look after her. Over three years, her condition deteriorates. She loses the ability to speak, requires to be fed, and becomes incontinent. Finally, she cannot sit in an armchair any longer, and is confined permanently to bed. One day, she contracts pneumonia.

In a patient who was enjoying a reasonable quality of life, pneumonia would be routinely treated with antibiotics. Should this patient be given antibiotics? Nossal continues:

> The relatives are contacted, and the matron of the nursing home tells them that she and the doctor she uses most frequently have worked out a loose arrangement for cases of this type. With advanced senile dementia, they treat the first three infections with antibiotics, and after that, mindful of the adage that 'pneumonia is the old person's friend', they let nature take its course. The matron emphasises that if the relatives desire, all infections can be vigorously treated. The relatives agree with the rule of thumb. The patient dies of a urinary tract infection six months later.

This patient died when she did as a result of a deliberate omission. Many people would think that this omission was well-justified. They might question whether it would not have been better to omit treatment even for the initial occurrence of pneumonia. There is, after all, no moral magic about the number three. Would it also have been justifiable, at the time of the omission, to give an injection that would bring about the patient's death in a peaceful way?

Comparing these two possible ways of bringing about a patient's death at a particular time, is it reasonable to hold that the doctor who gives the injection is a murderer who deserves to go to jail, while the doctor who decides not to administer antibiotics is practising good and compassionate medicine? That may be what courts of law would say, but surely it is an untenable distinction. In both cases, the outcome is the death of the patient. In both cases, the doctor knows that this will be the result, and decides what she will do on the basis of this knowledge, because she judges this result to be better than the alternative. In both cases the doctor must take responsibility for her decision – it would not be correct for the doctor who decided not to provide antibiotics to say that she was not responsible for the patient's death because she did nothing. Doing nothing in this situation is itself a deliberate choice and one cannot escape responsibility for its consequences.

One might say, of course, that the doctor who withholds antibiotics does not kill the patient, she merely allows the patient to die; but one must then answer the further question why killing is wrong, and letting die is not. The answer that most advocates of the distinction give is simply that there is a moral rule against killing innocent human beings and none against allowing them to die. This answer treats a conventionally accepted moral rule as if it were beyond questioning; it does not go on to ask whether we should have a moral rule against killing (but not against allowing to die). But we have already seen that the conventionally accepted principle of the sanctity of human life is untenable. The moral rules that prohibit killing, but accept 'letting die' cannot be taken for granted either.

Reflecting on these cases leads us to the conclusion that there is no *intrinsic* moral difference between killing and allowing to die. That is, there is no difference which depends solely on the distinction between an act and an omission. (This does not mean that all cases of allowing to die are morally equivalent to killing. Other factors – extrinsic factors – will sometimes be relevant. This will be discussed further in Chapter 8.) Allowing to die – sometimes called 'passive euthanasia' – is already accepted as a humane and proper course of action in certain cases. If there is no intrinsic moral difference between killing and allowing to die, active euthanasia should also be accepted as humane and proper in certain circumstances.

Others have suggested that the difference between withholding treatment necessary to prolong life, and giving a lethal injection, lies in the intention with which the two are done. Those who take this view resort to the 'doctrine of double effect', a doctrine widely held among Roman Catholic moral theologians and moral philosophers, to argue that one action (for example, refraining from life-sustaining treatment) may have two effects (in this case, not causing additional suffering to the patient, and shortening the patient's life). They then argue that as long as the *directly intended* effect is the beneficial one that does not violate an absolute moral rule, the action is permissible. Though we foresee that our action (or omission) will result in the death of the patient, this is merely an unwanted side-effect. But the distinction between directly intended effect and side-effect is a contrived one. We cannot avoid responsibility simply by directing our intention to one effect rather than another. If we foresee both effects, we must take responsibility for the foreseen effects of what we do. We often want to do something, but cannot do it because of its other, unwanted consequences. For example, a chemical company might want to get rid of toxic waste in the most economical manner, by dumping it in the nearest river. Would we allow the executives of the company to say that all they directly intended was to improve the efficiency of the factory, thus promoting employment and keeping down the cost of living? Would we regard the pollution as excusable because it is merely an unwanted side-effect of furthering these worthy objectives?

Obviously the defenders of the doctrine of double effect would not accept such an excuse. In rejecting it, however, they would have to rely upon a judgment that the cost – the polluted river – is disproportionate to the gains. Here a consequentialist judgment lurks behind the doctrine of double effect. The same is true when the doctrine is used in medical care. Normally, saving life takes precedence over relieving pain. If in the case of a particular patient it does not, this can only be because we have judged that the patient's prospects for a future life of acceptable quality are so poor that in this case relieving suffering can take precedence. This is, in other words, not a decision based on acceptance of the sanctity of human life, but a decision based on a disguised quality of life judgment.

Equally unsatisfactory is the common appeal to a distinction between 'ordinary' and 'extraordinary' means of treatment, coupled with the belief that it is not obligatory to provide extraordinary means. Together with my colleague, Helga Kuhse, I carried out a survey of paediatricians and obstetricians in Australia and found that they had remarkable ideas about what constituted 'ordinary' and what 'extraordinary' means. Some even thought that the use of antibiotics – the cheapest, simplest, and most common medical procedure – could be extraordinary. The reason for this range of views is easy to find. When one looks at the justifications given by moral theologians and philosophers for the distinction, it turns out that what is 'ordinary' in one situation can become 'extraordinary' in another. For example, in the famous case of Karen Ann Quinlan, the young New Jersey woman who was in a coma for ten years before she died, a Roman Catholic bishop testified that the use of a respirator was 'extraordinary' and hence optional because Quinlan had no hope of recovery from the coma. Obviously, if doctors had thought that Quinlan was likely to recover, the use of the respirator would not have been optional, and would have been declared 'ordinary'. Again, it is the quality of life of the patient (and where resources are limited and could be used more effectively to save lives elsewhere, the cost of the treatment) that is determining whether a given form of treatment is ordinary or extraordinary, and therefore is to be provided or not. Those who appeal to this distinction are cloaking their consequentialist views in the robe of an absolutist ethic; but the robe is worn out, and the disguise is now transparent.

So it is not possible to appeal to either the doctrine of double effect or the distinction between ordinary and extraordinary means in order to show that allowing a patient to die is morally different from actively helping a patient to die. Indeed, because of extrinsic differences – especially differences in the time it takes for death to occur – active euthanasia may be the only humane and morally proper course. Passive euthanasia can be a slow process. In an article in the *British Medical Journal*, John Lorber has charted the fate of twenty-five infants born with spina bifida on whom it had been decided, in view of the poor

211

prospects for a worthwhile life, not to operate. It will be recalled that Lorber freely grants that the object of not treating infants is that they should die soon and painlessly. Yet of the twenty-five untreated infants, fourteen were still alive after one month, and seven after three months. In Lorber's sample, all the infants died within nine months, but this cannot be guaranteed, or at least, cannot be guaranteed without stepping over the fine line between active and passive euthanasia. (Lorber's opponents have claimed that the untreated infants under his care all die because they are given sedatives and fed only on demand. Sleepy babies do not have healthy appetites.) An Australian clinic following Lorber's approach to spina bifida found that of seventy-nine untreated infants, five survived for more than two years. For both the infants, and their families, this must be a long-drawn out ordeal. It is also (although in a society with a reasonable level of affluence this should not be the primary consideration) a considerable burden on the hospital staff and the community's medical resources.

Consider, to take another example, infants born with Down's syndrome and a blockage in the digestive system which, if not removed, will make it impossible for the baby to eat. Like 'Baby Doe', these infants may be allowed to die. Yet the blockage can be removed and has nothing to do with the degree of intellectual disability the child will have. Moreover, the death resulting from the failure to operate in these circumstances is, though sure, neither swift nor painless. The infant dies from dehydration or hunger. Baby Doe took about five days to die, and in other recorded instances of this practice, it has taken up to two weeks for death to come.

It is interesting, in this context, to think again of our earlier argument that membership of the species Homo sapiens does not entitle a being to better treatment than a being at a similar mental level who is a member of a different species. We could also have said – except that it seemed too obvious to need saying – that membership of the species Homo sapiens is not a reason for giving a being *worse* treatment than a member of a different species. Yet in respect of euthanasia, this needs to be said. We do not doubt that it is right to shoot badly injured or sick animals if they are in pain and their chances of recovery are negligible. To 'allow nature to take its course', withholding treatment but refusing to kill, would obviously be wrong. It is only our misplaced respect for the doctrine of the sanctity of human life that prevents us from seeing that what it is obviously wrong to do to a horse, it is equally wrong to do to a disabled infant.

To summarise: passive ways of ending life result in a drawn-out death. They introduce irrelevant factors (a blockage in the intestine, or an easily curable infection) into the selection of those who shall die. If we are able to admit that our objective is a swift and painless death we should not leave it up to chance to determine whether this objective is achieved. Having chosen death we should ensure that it comes in the best possible way.

THE SLIPPERY SLOPE: FROM EUTHANASIA TO GENOCIDE?

Before we leave this topic we must consider an objection that looms so large in the anti-euthanasia literature that it merits a section to itself. It is, for instance, the reason why John Lorber rejects active euthanasia. Lorber has written:

> I wholly disagree with euthanasia. Though it is fully logical, and in expert and conscientious hands it could be the most humane way of dealing with such a situation, legalizing euthanasia would be a most dangerous weapon in the hands of the State or ignorant or unscrupulous individuals. One does not have to go far back in history to know what crimes can be committed if euthanasia were legalized.

Would euthanasia be the first step down a slippery slope? In the absence of prominent moral footholds to check our descent, would we slide all the way down into the abyss of state terror and mass murder? The experience of Nazism, to which Lorber no doubt is referring, has often been used as an illustration of what could follow acceptance of euthanasia. Here is a more specific example, from an article by another doctor, Leo Alexander:

> Whatever proportions [Nazi] crimes finally assumed, it became evident to all who investigated them that they had started from small beginnings. The beginnings at first were merely a subtle shift in emphasis in the basic attitude of the physicians. It started with the acceptance of the attitude, basic in the euthanasia movement, that there is such a thing as life not worthy to be lived. This attitude in its early stages concerned itself merely with the severely and chronically sick. Gradually the sphere of those to be included in the category was enlarged to encompass the socially unproductive, the ideologically unwanted, the racially unwanted and finally all non-Germans. But it is important to realize that the infinitely small wedged-in lever from which this entire trend of mind received its impetus was the attitude toward the nonrehabilitable sick.

Alexander singles out the Nazis' so-called euthanasia program as the root of all the horrendous crimes the Nazis later committed, because that program implied 'that there is such a thing as life not worthy to be lived'. Lorber could hardly agree with Alexander on this, since his recommended procedure of not treating selected infants is based on exactly this judgment. Although people sometimes talk as if we should never judge a human life to be not worth living, there are times when such a judgment is obviously correct. A life of physical suffering, unredeemed by any form of pleasure or by a minimal level of self-consciousness, is not worth living. Surveys undertaken by health care economists in which people are asked how much they value being alive in certain states of health, regularly find that people give some states a negative value – that is, they indicate that they would prefer to be dead than to survive in that condition. Apparently, the life of the elderly woman described by Sir Gustav Nossal was, in the opinion of the matron of the nursing home, the doctor, and the relatives, not worth living. If we can set criteria for deciding who is to be allowed to die and who is to be given treatment, then why should it be wrong to set criteria, perhaps the same criteria, for deciding who should be killed?

So it is not the attitude that some lives are not worth living that marks out the Nazis from normal people who do not commit mass murder. What then is it? Is it that they went beyond passive euthanasia, and practised active euthanasia? Many, like Lorber, worry about the power that a program of active euthanasia could place in the hands of an unscrupulous government. This worry is not negligible, but should not be exaggerated. Unscrupulous governments already have within their power more plausible means of getting rid of their opponents than euthanasia administered by doctors on medical grounds. 'Suicides' can be arranged. 'Accidents' can occur. If necessary, assassins can be hired. Our best defence against such possibilities is to do everything possible to keep our government democratic, open, and in the hands of people who would not seriously wish to kill their opponents. Once the wish is serious enough, governments will find a way, whether euthanasia is legal or not.

In fact the Nazis did not have a euthanasia program, in the proper sense of the word. Their so-called euthanasia program was not motivated by concern for the suffering of those killed. If it had been, why would the Nazis have kept their operations secret, deceived relatives about the cause of death of those killed, and exempted from the program certain privileged classes, such as veterans of the armed services, or relatives of the euthanasia staff? Nazi 'euthanasia' was never voluntary, and often was involuntary rather than non-voluntary. 'Doing away with useless mouths' – a phrase used by those in charge – gives a better idea of the objectives of the program than 'mercy-killing'. Both racial origin and ability to work were among the factors considered in the selection of patients to be killed. It was the Nazi belief in the importance of maintaining a pure Aryan *Volk* – a somewhat mystical entity that was thought of as more important than mere individuals lives – that made both the so-called euthanasia program and later the entire holocaust possible. Proposals for the legalisation of euthanasia, in contrast, are based on respect for autonomy and the goal of avoiding pointless suffering.

This essential difference in the aims of Nazi 'euthanasia' and modern proposals may be granted, but the slippery slope argument could still be defended as a way of suggesting that the present strict rule against the direct killing of innocent human beings serves a useful purpose. However arbitrary and unjustifiable the distinctions between human and non-human, fetus and infant, killing and allowing to die may be, the rule against direct killing of innocent humans at least marks a workable line. The distinction between an infant whose life may be worth living, and one whose life definitely is not, is much more difficult to draw. Perhaps people who see that certain kinds of human beings are killed in certain circumstances may go on to conclude that it is not wrong to kill others not very different from the first kind. So will the boundary of acceptable killing be pushed gradually back? In the absence of any logical stopping place, will the outcome be the loss of all respect for human life?

If our laws were altered so that anyone could carry out an act of euthanasia, the absence of a clear line between those who might justifiably be killed and those who might not would pose a real danger; but that is not what advocates of euthanasia propose. If acts of euthanasia could only be carried out by a member of the medical profession, with the concurrence of a second doctor, it is not likely that the propensity to kill would spread unchecked throughout the community. Doctors already have a good deal of power over life and death, through their ability to withhold treatment. There has been no suggestion that doctors who begin by allowing severely disabled infants to die from pneumonia will move on to withhold antibiotics from racial minorities or political extremists. In fact legalising euthanasia might well act as a check on the power of doctors since it would bring into the open and under the scrutiny of another doctor what some doctors now do on their own initiative and in secret.

There is, anyway, little historical evidence to suggest that a permissive attitude towards the killing of one category of human beings leads to a breakdown of restrictions against killing other humans. Ancient Greeks regularly killed or exposed infants, but appear to have been at least as scrupulous about taking the lives of their fellow-citizens as medieval Christians or modern Americans. In traditional Eskimo societies it was the custom for a man to kill his elderly parents, but the murder of a normal healthy adult was almost unheard of. I mention these practices not to suggest that they should be imitated, but only to indicate that lines can be drawn at places different from where we now draw them. If these societies could separate human beings into different categories without transferring their attitudes from one group to another, we with our more sophisticated legal systems and greater medical knowledge should be able to do the same.

All of this is not to deny that departing from the traditional sanctity-of-life ethic carries with it a very small but nevertheless finite risk of unwanted consequences. Against this risk we must balance the tangible harm to which the traditional ethic gives rise – harm to those whose misery is needlessly prolonged. We must also ask if the widespread acceptance of abortion and passive euthanasia has not already revealed flaws in the traditional ethic that make it a weak defence against those who lack respect for individual lives. A sounder, if less clear-cut, ethic may in the long run provide a firmer ground for resisting unjustifiable killing.

8

RICH AND POOR

SOME FACTS ABOUT POVERTY

IN the discussion of euthanasia in Chapter 7, we questioned the distinction between killing and allowing to die, concluding that it is of no intrinsic ethical significance. This conclusion has implications that go far beyond euthanasia.

Consider these facts: by the most cautious estimates, 400 million people lack the calories, protein, vitamins and minerals needed to sustain their bodies and minds in a healthy state. Millions are constantly hungry; others suffer from deficiency diseases and from infections they would be able to resist on a better diet. Children are the worst affected. According to one study, 14 million children under five die every year from the combined effects of malnutrition and infection. In some districts half the children born can be expected to die before their fifth birthday.

Nor is lack of food the only hardship of the poor. To give a broader picture, Robert McNamara, when president of the World Bank, suggested the term 'absolute poverty'. The poverty we are familiar with in industrialised nations is relative poverty – meaning that some citizens are poor, relative to the wealth enjoyed by their neighbours. People living in relative poverty in Australia might be quite comfortably off by comparison with pensioners in Britain, and British pensioners are not poor in comparison with the poverty that exists in Mali or Ethiopia. Absolute poverty, on the other hand, is poverty by any standard. In McNamara's words:

Poverty at the absolute level . . . is life at the very margin of existence. The absolute poor are severely deprived human beings struggling to survive in a set of squalid and degraded circumstances almost beyond the power of our sophisticated imaginations and privileged circumstances to conceive.

Compared to those fortunate enough to live in developed countries, individuals in the poorest nations have:

An infant mortality rate eight times higher
A life expectancy one-third lower
An adult literacy rate 60 per cent less
A nutritional level, for one out of every two in the population, below acceptable standards;
And for millions of infants, less protein than is sufficient to permit optimum development of the brain.

McNamara has summed up absolute poverty as 'a condition of life so characterised by malnutrition, illiteracy, disease, squalid surroundings, high infant mortality and low life expectancy as to be beneath any reasonable definition of human decency'.

Absolute poverty is, as McNamara has said, responsible for the loss of countless lives, especially among infants and young children. When absolute poverty does not cause death, it still causes misery of a kind not often seen in the affluent nations. Malnutrition in young children stunts both physical and mental development. According to the United Nations Development Programme, 180 million children under the age of five suffer from serious malnutrition. Millions of people on poor diets suffer from deficiency diseases, like goitre, or blindness caused by a lack of vitamin A. The food value of what the poor eat is further reduced by parasites such as hookworm and ringworm, which are endemic in conditions of poor sanitation and health education.

Death and disease apart, absolute poverty remains a miserable condition of life, with inadequate food, shelter, clothing, sanitation, health services and education. The Worldwatch Institute estimates that as many as 1.2 billion people – or 23 per cent of the world's population – live in absolute poverty. For the purposes of this estimate, absolute poverty is defined as "the lack of sufficient income in cash or kind to meet the most basic biological needs for food, clothing, and shelter." Absolute poverty is probably the principal cause of human misery today.

SOME FACTS ABOUT WEALTH

This is the background situation, the situation that prevails on our planet all the time. It does not make headlines. People died from malnutrition and related diseases yesterday, and more will die tomorrow. The occasional droughts, cyclones, earthquakes, and floods that take the lives of tens of thousands in one place and at one time are more newsworthy. They add greatly to the total amount of human suffering; but it is wrong to assume that when there are no major calamities reported, all is well.

The problem is not that the world cannot produce enough to feed and shelter its people. People in the poor countries consume, on average, 180 kilos of grain a year, while North Americans average around 900 kilos. The difference is caused by the fact that in the rich countries we feed most of our grain to animals, converting it into meat, milk, and eggs. Because this is a highly inefficient process, people in rich countries are responsible for the consumption of far more food than those in poor countries who eat few animal products. If we stopped feeding animals on grains and soybeans, the amount of food saved would – if distributed to those who need it – be more than enough to end hunger throughout the world.

These facts about animal food do not mean that we can easily solve the world food problem by cutting down on animal products, but they show that the problem is essentially one of distribution rather than production. The world does produce enough food. Moreover, the poorer nations themselves could produce far more if they made more use of improved agricultural techniques.

So why are people hungry? Poor people cannot afford to buy grain grown by farmers in the richer nations. Poor farmers cannot afford to buy improved seeds, or fertilisers, or the machinery needed for drilling wells and pumping water. Only by transferring some of the wealth of the rich nations to the poor can the situation be changed.

That this wealth exists is clear. Against the picture of absolute poverty that McNamara has painted, one might pose a picture of 'absolute affluence'. Those who are absolutely affluent are not necessarily affluent by comparison with their neighbours, but they are affluent by any reasonable definition of human needs. This means that they have more income than they need to provide themselves adequately with all the basic necessities of life. After buying (either directly or through their taxes) food, shelter, clothing, basic health services, and education, the absolutely affluent are still able to spend money on luxuries. The absolutely affluent choose their food for the pleasures of the palate, not to stop hunger; they buy new clothes to look good, not to keep warm; they move house to be in a better neighbourhood or have a playroom for the children, not to keep out the rain; and after all this there is still money to spend on stereo systems, video-cameras, and overseas holidays.

At this stage I am making no ethical judgments about absolute affluence, merely pointing out that it exists. Its defining characteristic is a significant amount of income above the level necessary to provide for the basic human needs of oneself and one's dependents. By this standard, the majority of citizens of Western Europe, North America, Japan, Australia, New Zealand, and the oil-rich Middle Eastern states are all absolutely affluent. To quote McNamara once more:

'The average citizen of a developed country enjoys wealth beyond the wildest dreams of the one billion people in countries with per capita incomes under $200.' These, therefore, are the countries – and individuals – who have wealth that they could, without threatening their own basic welfare, transfer to the absolutely poor.

At present, very little is being transferred. Only Sweden, the Netherlands, Norway, and some of the oil-exporting Arab states have reached the modest target, set by the United Nations, of 0.7 per cent of gross national product (GNP). Britain gives 0.31 per cent of its GNP in official development assistance and a small additional amount in unofficial aid from voluntary organisations. The total comes to about £2 per month per person, and compares with 5.5 per cent of GNP spent on alcohol, and 3 per cent on tobacco. Other, even wealthier nations, give little more: Germany gives 0.41 per cent and Japan 0.32 per cent. The United States gives a mere 0.15 per cent of its GNP.

THE MORAL EQUIVALENT OF MURDER?

If these are the facts, we cannot avoid concluding that by not giving more than we do, people in rich countries are allowing those in poor countries to suffer from absolute poverty, with consequent malnutrition, ill health, and death. This is not a conclusion that applies only to governments. It applies to each absolutely affluent individual, for each of us has the opportunity to do something about the situation; for instance, to give our time or money to voluntary organisations like Oxfam, Care, War on Want, Freedom from Hunger, Community Aid Abroad, and so on. If, then, allowing someone to die is not intrinsically different from killing someone, it would seem that we are all murderers.

Is this verdict too harsh? Many will reject it as self-evidently absurd. They would sooner take it as showing that allowing to die cannot be equivalent to killing than as showing that living in an affluent style without contributing to an overseas aid agency is ethically equivalent to going over to Ethiopia and shooting a few peasants. And no doubt, put as bluntly as that, the verdict is too harsh.

There are several significant differences between spending money on luxuries instead of using it to save lives, and deliberately shooting people.

First, the motivation will normally be different. Those who deliberately shoot others go out of their way to kill; they presumably want their victims dead, from malice, sadism, or some equally unpleasant motive. A person who buys a new stereo system presumably wants to enhance her enjoyment of music – not in itself a terrible thing. At worst, spending money on luxuries instead of giving it away indicates selfishness and indifference to the sufferings of others, characteristics that may be undesirable but are not comparable with actual malice or similar motives.

Second, it is not difficult for most of us to act in accordance with a rule against killing people: it is, on the other hand, very difficult to obey a rule that commands us to save all the lives we can. To live a comfortable, or even luxurious life it is not necessary to kill anyone; but it is necessary to allow some to die whom we might have saved, for the money that we need to live comfortably could have been given away. Thus the duty to avoid killing is much easier to discharge completely than the duty to save. Saving every life we could would mean cutting our standard of living down to the bare essentials needed to keep us alive.[1] To discharge this duty completely would require a degree of moral heroism utterly different from that required by mere avoidance of killing.

---

1 Strictly, we would need to cut down to the minimum level compatible with earning the income which, after providing for our needs, left us most to give away. Thus if my present position earns me, say, $40,000 a year, but requires me to spend $5,000 a year on dressing respectably and maintaining a car, I cannot save more people by giving away the car and clothes if that will mean taking a job that, although it does not involve me in these expenses, earns me only $20,000.

A third difference is the greater certainty of the outcome of shooting when compared with not giving aid. If I point a loaded gun at someone at close range and pull the trigger, it is virtually certain that the person will be killed; whereas the money that I could give might be spent on a project that turns out to be unsuccessful and helps no one.

Fourth, when people are shot there are identifiable individuals who have been harmed. We can point to them and to their grieving families. When I buy my stereo system, I cannot know who my money would have saved if I had given it away. In a time of famine I may see dead bodies and grieving families on television reports, and I might not doubt that my money would have saved some of them; even then it is impossible to point to a body and say that had I not bought the stereo, that person would have survived.

Fifth, it might be said that the plight of the hungry is not my doing, and so I cannot be held responsible for it. The starving would have been starving if I had never existed. If I kill, however, I am responsible for my victims' deaths, for those people would not have died if I had not killed them.

These differences need not shake our previous conclusion that there is no intrinsic difference between killing and allowing to die. They are extrinsic differences, that is, differences normally but not necessarily associated with the distinction between killing and allowing to die. We can imagine cases in which someone allows another to die for malicious or sadistic reasons; we can imagine a world in which there are so few people needing assistance, and they are so easy to assist, that our duty not to allow people to die is as easily discharged as our duty not to kill; we can imagine situations in which the outcome of not helping is as sure as shooting; we can imagine cases in which we can identify the person we allow to die. We can even imagine a case of allowing to die in which, if I had not existed, the person would not have died – for instance, a case in which if I had not been in a position to help (though I don't help) someone else would have been in my position and would have helped.

Our previous discussion of euthanasia illustrates the extrinsic nature of these differences, for they do not provide a basis for distinguishing active from passive euthanasia. If a doctor decides, in consultation with the parents, not to operate on – and thus to allow to die – a Down's syndrome infant with an intestinal blockage, her motivation will be similar to that of a doctor who gives a lethal injection rather than allow the infant to die. No extraordinary sacrifice or moral heroism will be required in either case. Not operating will just as certainly end in death as administering the injection. Allowing to die does have an identifiable victim. Finally, it may well be that the doctor is personally responsible for the death of the infant she decides not to operate upon, since she may know that if she had not taken this case, other doctors in the hospital would have operated.

Nevertheless, euthanasia is a special case, and very different from allowing people to starve to death. (The major difference being that when euthanasia is justifiable, death is a good thing.) The extrinsic differences that *normally* mark off killing and allowing to die do explain why we *normally* regard killing as much worse than allowing to die.

To explain our conventional ethical attitudes is not to justify them. Do the five differences not only explain, but also justify, our attitudes? Let us consider them one by one:

1. Take the lack of an identifiable victim first. Suppose that I am a travelling salesperson, selling tinned food, and I learn that a batch of tins contains a contaminant, the known effect of which, when consumed, is to double the risk that the consumer will die from stomach cancer. Suppose I continue to sell the tins. My decision may have no identifiable victims. Some of those who eat the food will die from cancer. The proportion of consumers dying in this way will be twice that of the community at large, but who among the consumers died because

they ate what I sold, and who would have contracted the disease anyway? It is impossible to tell; but surely this impossibility makes my decision no less reprehensible than it would have been had the contaminant had more readily detectable, though equally fatal, effects.

2. The lack of certainty that by giving money I could save a life does reduce the wrongness of not giving, by comparison with deliberate killing; but it is insufficient to show that not giving is acceptable conduct. The motorist who speeds through pedestrian crossings, heedless of anyone who might be on them, is not a murderer. She may never actually hit a pedestrian; yet what she does is very wrong indeed.

3. The notion of responsibility for acts rather than omissions is more puzzling. On the one hand, we feel ourselves to be under a greater obligation to help those whose misfortunes we have caused. (It is for this reason that advocates of overseas aid often argue that Western nations have created the poverty of third world nations, through forms of economic exploitation that go back to the colonial system.) On the other hand, any consequentialist would insist that we are responsible for all the consequences of our actions, and if a consequence of my spending money on a luxury item is that someone dies, I am responsible for that death. It is true that the person would have died even if I had never existed, but what is the relevance of that? The fact is that I do exist, and the consequentialist will say that our responsibilities derive from the world as it is, not as it might have been.

One way of making sense of the non-consequentialist view of responsibility is by basing it on a theory of rights of the kind proposed by John Locke or, more recently, Robert Nozick. If everyone has a right to life, and this right is a right *against* others who might threaten my life, but not a right to assistance from others when my life is in danger, then we can understand the feeling that we are responsible for acting to kill but not for omitting to save. The former violates the rights of others, the latter does not.

Should we accept such a theory of rights? If we build up our theory of rights by imagining, as Locke and Nozick do, individuals living independently from each other in a 'state of nature', it may seem natural to adopt a conception of rights in which as long as each leaves the other alone, no rights are violated. I might, on this view, quite properly have maintained my independent existence if I had wished to do so. So if I do not make you any worse off than you would have been if I had had nothing at all to do with you, how can I have violated your rights? But why start from such an unhistorical, abstract and ultimately inexplicable idea as an independent individual? Our ancestors were – like other primates – social beings long before they were human beings, and could not have developed the abilities and capacities of human beings if they had not been social beings first. In any case, we are not, now, isolated individuals. So why should we assume that rights must be restricted to rights against interference? We might, instead, adopt the view that taking rights to life seriously is incompatible with standing by and watching people die when one could easily save them.

4. What of the difference in motivation? That a person does not positively wish for the death of another lessens the severity of the blame she deserves; but not by as much as our present attitudes to giving aid suggest. The behaviour of the speeding motorist is again comparable, for such motorists usually have no desire at all to kill anyone. They merely enjoy speeding and are indifferent to the consequences. Despite their lack of malice, those who kill with cars deserve not only blame but also severe punishment.

5. Finally, the fact that to avoid killing people is normally not difficult, whereas to save all one possibly could save is heroic, must make an important difference to our attitude to failure to do what the respective principles demand. Not to kill is a min-

imum standard of acceptable conduct we can require of everyone; to save all one possibly could is not something that can realistically be required, especially not in societies accustomed to giving as little as ours do. Given the generally accepted standards, people who give, say, $1,000 a year to an overseas aid organisation are more aptly praised for above average generosity than blamed for giving less than they might. The appropriateness of praise and blame is, however, a separate issue from the rightness or wrongness of actions. The former evaluates the agent: the latter evaluates the action. Perhaps many people who give $1,000 really ought to give at least $5,000, but to blame them for not giving more could be counterproductive. It might make them feel that what is required is too demanding, and if one is going to be blamed anyway, one might as well not give anything at all.

(That an ethic that put saving all one possibly can on the same footing as not killing would be an ethic for saints or heroes should not lead us to assume that the alternative must be an ethic that makes it obligatory not to kill, but puts us under no obligation to save anyone. There are positions in between these extremes, as we shall soon see.)

Here is a summary of the five differences that normally exist between killing and allowing to die, in the context of absolute poverty and overseas aid. The lack of an identifiable victim is of no moral significance, though it may play an important role in explaining our attitudes. The idea that we are directly responsible for those we kill, but not for those we do not help, depends on a questionable notion of responsibility and may need to be based on a controversial theory of rights. Differences in certainty and motivation are ethically significant, and show that not aiding the poor is not to be condemned as murdering them; it could, however, be on a par with killing someone as a result of reckless driving, which is serious enough. Finally the difficulty of completely discharging the duty of saving all one possibly can makes it inappropriate to blame those who fall short of this target as we blame those who kill; but this does not show that the act itself is less serious. Nor does it indicate anything about those who, far from saving all they possibly can, make no effort to save anyone.

These conclusions suggest a new approach. Instead of attempting to deal with the contrast between affluence and poverty by comparing not saving with deliberate killing, let us consider afresh whether we have an obligation to assist those whose lives are in danger, and if so, how this obligation applies to the present world situation.

THE OBLIGATION TO ASSIST

The Argument for an Obligation to Assist

The path from the library at my university to the humanities lecture theatre passes a shallow ornamental pond. Suppose that on my way to give a lecture I notice that a small child has fallen in and is in danger of drowning. Would anyone deny that I ought to wade in and pull the child out? This will mean getting my clothes muddy and either cancelling my lecture or delaying it until I can find something dry to change into; but compared with the avoidable death of a child this is insignificant.

A plausible principle that would support the judgment that I ought to pull the child out is this: if it is in our power to prevent something very bad from happening, without thereby sacrificing anything of comparable moral significance, we ought to do it. This principle seems uncontroversial. It will obviously win the assent of consequentialists; but non-consequentialists should accept it too, because the injunction to prevent what is bad applies only when nothing comparably significant is at stake. Thus the principle cannot lead to the kinds of actions of which non-consequentialists strongly disapprove – serious violations of individual rights, injustice, broken promises, and so on. If non-consequentialists regard any of these as comparable in moral significance to the bad thing that is to be prevented, they will automatically regard the principle as not applying in those cases in which the bad thing can only be prevented by violating rights, doing injustice, breaking promises, or whatever else is at stake. Most non-consequentialists hold that we ought to prevent what is bad and promote what is good. Their dispute with consequentialists lies in their insistence that this is not the sole ultimate ethical principle: that it is an ethical principle is not denied by any plausible ethical theory.

Nevertheless the uncontroversial appearance of the principle that we ought to prevent what is bad when we can do so without sacrificing anything of comparable moral significance is deceptive. If it were taken seriously and acted upon, our lives and our world would be fundamentally changed. For the principle applies, not just to rare situations in which one can save a child from a pond, but to the everyday situation in which we can assist those living in absolute poverty. In saying this I assume that absolute poverty, with its hunger and malnutrition, lack of shelter, illiteracy, disease, high infant mortality, and low life expectancy, is a bad thing. And I assume that it is within the power of the affluent to reduce absolute poverty, without sacrificing anything of comparable moral significance. If these two assumptions and the principle we have been discussing are correct, we have an obligation to help those in absolute poverty that is no less strong than our obligation to rescue a drowning child from a pond. Not to help would be wrong, whether or not it is intrinsically equivalent to killing. Helping is not, as conventionally thought, a charitable act that it is praiseworthy to do, but not wrong to omit; it is something that everyone ought to do.

This is the argument for an obligation to assist. Set out more formally, it would look like this.

First premise: If we can prevent something bad without sacrificing anything of comparable significance, we ought to do it.

Second premise: Absolute poverty is bad.
Third premise: There is some absolute poverty we can prevent without sacrificing anything of comparable moral significance.
Conclusion: We ought to prevent some absolute poverty.

The first premise is the substantive moral premise on which the argument rests, and I have tried to show that it can be accepted by people who hold a variety of ethical positions.

The second premise is unlikely to be challenged. Absolute poverty is, as McNamara put it, 'beneath any reasonable definition of human decency' and it would be hard to find a plausible ethical view that did not regard it as a bad thing.

The third premise is more controversial, even though it is cautiously framed. It claims only that some absolute poverty can be prevented without the sacrifice of anything of comparable moral significance. It thus avoids the objection that any aid I can give is just 'drops in the ocean' for the point is not whether my personal contribution will make any noticeable impression on world poverty as a whole (of course it won't) but whether it will prevent some poverty. This is all the argument needs to sustain its conclusion, since the second premise says that any absolute poverty is bad, and not merely the total amount of absolute poverty. If without sacrificing anything of comparable moral significance we can provide just one family with the means to raise itself out of absolute poverty, the third premise is vindicated.

I have left the notion of moral significance unexamined in order to show that the argument does not depend on any specific values or ethical principles. I think the third premise is true for most people living in industrialised nations, on any defensible view of what is morally significant. Our affluence means that we have income we can dispose of without giving up the basic necessities of life, and we can use this income to reduce absolute poverty. Just how much we will think ourselves obliged to give up will depend on what we consider to be of comparable moral significance to the poverty we could prevent: stylish clothes, expensive dinners, a sophisticated stereo system, overseas holidays, a (second?) car, a larger house, private schools for our children, and so on. For a utilitarian, none of these is likely to be of comparable significance to the reduction of absolute poverty; and those who are not utilitarians surely must, if they subscribe to the principle of universalisability, accept that at least some of these things are of far less moral significance than the absolute poverty that could be prevented by the money they cost. So the third premise seems to be true on any plausible ethical view – although the precise amount of absolute poverty that can be prevented before anything of moral significance is sacrificed will vary according to the ethical view one accepts.

Objections to the Argument

Taking care of our own. Anyone who has worked to increase overseas aid will have come across the argument that we should look after those near us, our families, and then the poor in our own country, before we think about poverty in distant places.

No doubt we do instinctively prefer to help those who are close to us. Few could stand by and watch a child drown; many can ignore a famine in Africa. But the question is not what we usually do, but what we ought to do, and it is difficult to see any sound moral justification for the view that distance, or community membership, makes a crucial difference to our obligations.

Consider, for instance, racial affinities. Should people of European origin help poor Europeans before helping poor Africans? Most of us would reject such a suggestion out of hand, and our discussion of the principle of equal consideration of interests in Chapter 2 has shown why we should reject it: people's need for food has nothing to do with their race, and if Africans need food more than Europeans, it would be a violation of the principle of equal consideration to give preference to Europeans.

The same point applies to citizenship or nationhood. Every affluent nation has some relatively poor citizens, but absolute poverty is limited largely to the poor nations. Those living on the streets of Calcutta, or in the drought-prone Sahel region of Africa, are experiencing poverty unknown in the West. Under these circumstances it would be wrong to decide that only those fortunate enough to be citizens of our own community will share our abundance.

We feel obligations of kinship more strongly than those of citizenship. Which parents could give away their last bowl of rice if their own children were starving? To do so would seem unnatural, contrary to our nature as biologically evolved beings – although whether it would be wrong is another question altogether. In any case, we are not faced with that situation, but with one in which our own children are well-fed, well-clothed, well-educated, and would now like new bikes, a stereo set, or their own car. In these circumstances any special obligations we might have to our children have been fulfilled, and the needs of strangers make a stronger claim upon us.

The element of truth in the view that we should first take care of our own, lies in the advantage of a recognised system of responsibilities. When families and local communities look after their own poorer members, ties of affection and personal relationships achieve ends that would otherwise require a large, impersonal bureaucracy. Hence it would be absurd to propose that from now on we all regard ourselves as equally responsible for the welfare of everyone in the world; but the argument for an obligation to assist does not propose that. It applies only when some are in absolute poverty, and others can help without sacrificing anything of comparable moral significance. To allow one's own kin to sink into absolute poverty would be to sacrifice something of comparable significance; and before that point had been reached, the breakdown of the system of family and community responsibility would be a factor to weigh the balance in favour of a small degree of preference for family and community. This small degree of preference is, however, decisively outweighed by existing discrepancies in wealth and property.

Property rights. Do people have a right to private property, a right that contradicts the view that they are under an obligation to give some of their wealth away to those in absolute poverty? According to some theories of rights (for instance, Robert Nozick's), provided one has acquired one's property without the use of unjust means like force and fraud, one may be entitled to enormous wealth while others starve. This individualistic conception of rights is in contrast to other views, like the early Christian doctrine to be found in the works of Thomas Aquinas, which holds that since property exists for the satisfaction of human needs, 'whatever a man has in superabundance is owed, of natural right, to the poor for their sustenance'. A socialist would also, of course, see wealth as belonging to the community rather than the individual, while utilitarians, whether socialist or not, would be prepared to override property rights to prevent great evils.

Does the argument for an obligation to assist others therefore presuppose one of these other theories of property rights, and not an individualistic theory like Nozick's? Not necessarily. A theory of property rights can insist on our *right* to retain wealth without pronouncing on whether the rich *ought* to give to the poor. Nozick, for example, rejects the use of compulsory means like taxation to redistribute income, but suggests that we can achieve the ends we deem morally desirable by voluntary means. So Nozick would reject the claim that rich people have an 'obligation' to give to the poor, in so far as this implies that the poor have a right to our aid, but might accept that giving is something we ought to do and failing to give, though within one's rights, is wrong – for there is more to an ethical life than respecting the rights of others.

The argument for an obligation to assist can survive, with only minor modifications, even if we accept an individualistic theory of property rights. In any case, however, I do not think we should accept such a theory. It leaves too much to chance to be an acceptable ethical view. For instance, those whose forefathers happened to inhabit some sandy wastes around the Persian Gulf are now fabulously wealthy, because oil lay under those sands; while those whose forefathers settled on better land south of the Sahara live in absolute poverty, because of drought and bad harvests. Can this distribution be acceptable from an impartial point of view? If we imagine ourselves about to begin life as a citizen of either Bahrein or Chad – but we do not know which – would we accept the principle that citizens of Bahrein are under no obligation to assist people living in Chad?

Population and the ethics of triage. Perhaps the most serious objection to the argument that we have an obligation to assist is that since the major cause of absolute poverty is overpopulation, helping those now in poverty will only ensure that yet more people are born to live in poverty in the future.

In its most extreme form, this objection is taken to show that we should adopt a policy of 'triage'. The term comes from medical policies adopted in wartime. With too few doctors to cope with all the casualties, the wounded were divided into three categories: those who would probably survive without medical assistance, those who might survive if they received assistance, but otherwise probably would not, and those who even with medical assistance probably would not survive. Only those in the middle category were given medical assistance. The idea, of course, was to use limited medical resources as effectively as possible. For those in the first category, medical treatment was not strictly necessary; for those in the third category, it was likely to be useless. It has been suggested that we should apply the same policies to countries, according to their prospects of becoming self-sustaining. We would not aid countries that even without our help will soon be able to feed their populations. We would not aid countries that, even with our help, will not be able to limit their population to a level they can feed. We would aid those countries where our help might make the difference between success and failure in bringing food and population into balance.

Advocates of this theory are understandably reluctant to give a complete list of the countries they would place into the 'hopeless' category; Bangladesh has been cited as an example, and so have some of the countries of the Sahel region of Africa. Adopting the policy of triage would, then, mean cutting off assistance to these countries and allowing famine, disease, and natural disasters to reduce the population of those countries to the level at which they can provide adequately for all.

In support of this view Garrett Hardin has offered a metaphor: we in the rich nations are like the occupants of a crowded lifeboat adrift in a sea full of drowning people. If we try to save the drowning by bringing them aboard, our boat will be overloaded and we shall all drown. Since it is better that some survive than none, we should leave the others to drown. In the world today, according to Hardin, 'lifeboat ethics' apply. The rich should leave the poor to starve, for otherwise the poor will drag the rich down with them.

Against this view, some writers have argued that overpopulation is a myth. The world produces ample food to feed its population, and could, according to some estimates, feed ten times as many. People are hungry not because there are too many but because of inequitable land distribution, the manipulation of third world economies by the developed nations, wastage of food in the West, and so on.

Putting aside the controversial issue of the extent to which food production might one day be increased, it is true, as we have already seen, that the world now produces enough to feed its inhabitants – the amount lost by being fed to animals itself being enough to meet existing grain shortages. Nevertheless population growth cannot be ignored. Bangladesh could, with land reform and using better techniques, feed its present population of 115 million; but by the year 2000, according to United Nations Population Division estimates, its population will be 150 million. The enormous effort that will have to go into feeding an extra 35 million people, all added to the population within a decade, means that Bangladesh must develop at full speed to stay where it is. Other low-income countries are in similar situations. By the end of the century, Ethiopia's population is expected to rise from 49 to 66 million; Somalia's from 7 to 9 million, India's from 853 to 1041 million, Zaire's from 35 to 49 million.[2]

What will happen if the world population continues to grow? It cannot do so indefinitely. It will be checked by a decline in birth rates or a rise in death rates. Those who advocate triage are proposing that we allow the population growth of some countries to be checked by a rise in death rates – that is, by increased malnutrition, and related diseases; by widespread famines; by increased infant mortality; and by epidemics of infectious diseases.

The consequences of triage on this scale are so horrible that we are inclined to reject it without further argument. How could we sit by our television sets, watching millions starve while we do nothing? Would not that be the end of all notions of human equality and respect for human life? (Those who attack the proposals for legalising euthanasia discussed in Chapter 7, saying that these proposals will weaken respect for human life, would surely do better to object to the idea that we should reduce or end our overseas aid programs, for that proposal, if

2 Ominously, in the twelve years that have passed between editions of this book, the signs are that the situation is becoming even worse than was then predicted. In 1979 Bangladesh had a population of 80 million and it was predicted that by 2000 its population would reach 146 million; Ethiopia's was only 29 million, and was predicted to reach 54 million; and India's was 620 million and predicted to reach 958 million.

implemented, would be responsible for a far greater loss of human life.) Don't people have a right to our assistance, irrespective of the consequences?

Anyone whose initial reaction to triage was not one of repugnance would be an unpleasant sort of person. Yet initial reactions based on strong feelings are not always reliable guides. Advocates of triage are rightly concerned with the long-term consequences of our actions. They say that helping the poor and starving now merely ensures more poor and starving in the future. When our capacity to help is finally unable to cope – as one day it must be – the suffering will be greater than it would be if we stopped helping now. If this is correct, there is nothing we can do to prevent absolute starvation and poverty, in the long run, and so we have no obligation to assist. Nor does it seem reasonable to hold that under these circumstances people have a right to our assistance. If we do accept such a right, irrespective of the consequences, we are saying that, in Hardin's metaphor, we should continue to haul the drowning into our lifeboat until the boat sinks and we all drown.

If triage is to be rejected it must be tackled on its own ground, within the framework of consequentialist ethics. Here it is vulnerable. Any consequentialist ethics must take probability of outcome into account. A course of action that will certainly produce some benefit is to be preferred to an alternative course that may lead to a slightly larger benefit, but is equally likely to result in no benefit at all. Only if the greater magnitude of the uncertain benefit outweighs its uncertainty should we choose it. Better one certain unit of benefit than a 10 per cent chance of five units; but better a 50 per cent chance of three units than a single certain unit. The same principle applies when we are trying to avoid evils.

The policy of triage involves a certain, very great evil: population control by famine and disease. Tens of millions would die slowly. Hundreds of millions would continue to live in absolute poverty, at the very margin of existence. Against this prospect, advocates of the policy place a possible evil that is greater still: the same process of famine and disease, taking place in, say, fifty years' time, when the world's population may be three times its present level, and the number who will die from famine, or struggle on in absolute poverty, will be that much greater. The question is: how probable is this forecast that continued assistance now will lead to greater disasters in the future?

Forecasts of population growth are notoriously fallible, and theories about the factors that affect it remain speculative. One theory, at least as plausible as any other, is that countries pass through a 'demographic transition' as their standard of living rises. When people are very poor and have no access to modern medicine their fertility is high, but population is kept in check by high death rates. The introduction of sanitation, modern medical techniques, and other improvements reduces the death rate, but initially has little effect on the birth rate. Then population grows rapidly. Some poor countries, especially in sub-Saharan Africa, are now in this phase. If standards of living continue to rise, however, couples begin to realise that to have the same number of children surviving to maturity as in the past, they do not need to give birth to as many children as their parents did. The need for children to provide economic support in old age diminishes. Improved education and the emancipation and employment of women also reduce the birth-rate, and so population growth begins to level off. Most rich nations have reached this stage, and their populations are growing only very slowly, if at all.

If this theory is right, there is an alternative to the disasters accepted as inevitable by supporters of triage. We can assist poor countries to raise the living standards of the poorest members of their population. We can encourage the governments of these countries to enact land reform measures, improve education, and liberate women from a purely child-bearing role. We can also help other countries to make contraception and sterilisation widely available. There is a fair chance that these measures will

hasten the onset of the demographic transition and bring population growth down to a manageable level. According to
United Nations estimates, in 1965 the average woman in the
third world gave birth to six children, and only 8 per cent were
using some form of contraception; by 1991 the average number
of children had dropped to just below four, and more than half
the women in the third world were taking contraceptive measures. Notable successes in encouraging the use of contraception
had occurred in Thailand, Indonesia, Mexico, Colombia, Brazil,
and Bangladesh. This achievement reflected a relatively low
expenditure in developing countries – considering the size and
significance of the problem – of $3 billion annually, with only
20 per cent of this sum coming from developed nations. So
expenditure in this area seems likely to be highly cost-effective.
Success cannot be guaranteed; but the evidence suggests that
we can reduce population growth by improving economic security and education, and making contraceptives more widely
available. This prospect makes triage ethically unacceptable. We
cannot allow millions to die from starvation and disease when
there is a reasonable probability that population can be brought
under control without such horrors.

Population growth is therefore not a reason against giving
overseas aid, although it should make us think about the kind
of aid to give. Instead of food handouts, it may be better to give
aid that leads to a slowing of population growth. This may mean
agricultural assistance for the rural poor, or assistance with education, or the provision of contraceptive services. Whatever
kind of aid proves most effective in specific circumstances, the
obligation to assist is not reduced.

One awkward question remains. What should we do about
a poor and already overpopulated country that, for religious or
nationalistic reasons, restricts the use of contraceptives and refuses to slow its population growth? Should we nevertheless
offer development assistance? Or should we make our offer
conditional on effective steps being taken to reduce the birth-

rate? To the latter course, some would object that putting conditions on aid is an attempt to impose our own ideas on
independent sovereign nations. So it is – but is this imposition
unjustifiable? If the argument for an obligation to assist is sound,
we have an obligation to reduce absolute poverty; but we have
no obligation to make sacrifices that, to the best of our knowledge, have no prospect of reducing poverty in the long run.
Hence we have no obligation to assist countries whose governments have policies that will make our aid ineffective. This could
be very harsh on poor citizens of these countries – for they may
have no say in the government's policies – but we will help
more people in the long run by using our resources where they
are most effective. (The same principles may apply, incidentally,
to countries that refuse to take other steps that could make
assistance effective – like refusing to reform systems of land
holding that impose intolerable burdens on poor tenant
farmers.)

Leaving it to the government. We often hear that overseas aid
should be a government responsibility, not left to privately run
charities. Giving privately, it is said, allows the government to
escape its responsibilities.

Since increasing government aid is the surest way of making
a significant increase to the total amount of aid given, I would
agree that the governments of affluent nations should give much
more genuine, no-strings-attached, aid than they give now. Less
than one-sixth of one per cent of GNP is a scandalously small
amount for a nation as wealthy as the United States to give.
Even the official UN target of 0.7 per cent seems much less than
affluent nations can and should give – though it is a target few
have reached. But is this a reason against each of us giving what
we can privately, through voluntary agencies? To believe that
it is seems to assume that the more people there are who give
through voluntary agencies, the less likely it is that the government will do its part. Is this plausible? The opposite view – that

if no one gives voluntarily the government will assume that its citizens are not in favour of overseas aid, and will cut its programme accordingly – is more reasonable. In any case, unless there is a definite probability that by refusing to give we would be helping to bring about an increase in government assistance, refusing to give privately is wrong for the same reason that triage is wrong: it is a refusal to prevent a definite evil for the sake of a very uncertain gain. The onus of showing how a refusal to give privately will make the government give more is on those who refuse to give.

This is not to say that giving privately is enough. Certainly we should campaign for entirely new standards for both public and private overseas aid. We should also work for fairer trading arrangements between rich and poor countries, and less domination of the economies of poor countries by multinational corporations more concerned about producing profits for shareholders back home than food for the local poor. Perhaps it is more important to be politically active in the interests of the poor than to give to them oneself – but why not do both? Unfortunately, many use the view that overseas aid is the government's responsibility as a reason against giving, but not as a reason for being politically active.

Too high a standard? The final objection to the argument for an obligation to assist is that it sets a standard so high that none but a saint could attain it. This objection comes in at least three versions. The first maintains that, human nature being what it is, we cannot achieve so high a standard, and since it is absurd to say that we ought to do what we cannot do, we must reject the claim that we ought to give so much. The second version asserts that even if we could achieve so high a standard, to do so would be undesirable. The third version of the objection is that to set so high a standard is undesirable because it will be perceived as too difficult to reach, and will discourage many from even attempting to do so.

Those who put forward the first version of the objection are often influenced by the fact that we have evolved from a natural process in which those with a high degree of concern for their own interests, or the interests of their offspring and kin, can be expected to leave more descendants in future generations, and eventually to completely replace any who are entirely altruistic. Thus the biologist Garrett Hardin has argued, in support of his 'lifeboat ethics', that altruism can only exist 'on a small scale, over the short term, and within small, intimate groups'; while Richard Dawkins has written, in his provocative book *The Selfish Gene:* 'Much as we might wish to believe otherwise, universal love and the welfare of the species as a whole are concepts which simply do not make evolutionary sense.' I have already noted, in discussing the objection that we should first take care of our own, the very strong tendency for partiality in human beings. We naturally have a stronger desire to further our own interests, and those of our close kin, than we have to further the interests of strangers. What this means is that we would be foolish to expect widespread conformity to a standard that demands impartial concern, and for that reason it would scarcely be appropriate or feasible to condemn all those who fail to reach such a standard. Yet to act impartially, though it might be very difficult, is not impossible. The commonly quoted assertion that 'ought' implies 'can' is a reason for rejecting such moral judgments as 'You ought to have saved all the people from the sinking ship', when in fact if you had taken one more person into the lifeboat, it would have sunk and you would not have saved any. In that situation, it is absurd to say that you ought to have done what you could not possibly do. When we have money to spend on luxuries and others are starving, however, it is clear that we can all give much more than we do give, and we can therefore all come closer to the impartial standard proposed in this chapter. Nor is there, as we approach closer to this standard, any barrier beyond which we cannot go. For that reason there is no basis for saying that the impartial standard is mistaken because 'ought' implies 'can' and we cannot be impartial.

The second version of the objection has been put by several philosophers during the past decade, among them Susan Wolf in a forceful article entitled 'Moral Saints'. Wolf argues that if we all took the kind of moral stance defended in this chapter, we would have to do without a great deal that makes life interesting: opera, gourmet cooking, elegant clothes, and professional sport, for a start. The kind of life we come to see as ethically required of us would be a single-minded pursuit of the overall good, lacking that broad diversity of interests and activities that, on a less demanding view, can be part of our ideal of a good life for a human being. To this, however, one can respond that while the rich and varied life that Wolf upholds as an ideal may be the most desirable form of life for a human being in a world of plenty, it is wrong to assume that it remains a good life in a world in which buying luxuries for oneself means accepting the continued avoidable suffering of others. A doctor faced with hundreds of injured victims of a train crash can scarcely think it defensible to treat fifty of them and then go to the opera, on the grounds that going to the opera is part of a well-rounded human life. The life-or-death needs of others must take priority. Perhaps we are like the doctor in that we live in a time when we all have an opportunity to help to mitigate a disaster.

Associated with this second version of the objection is the claim that an impartial ethic of the kind advocated here makes it impossible to have serious personal relationships based on love and friendship; these relationships are, of their nature, partial. We put the interests of our loved ones, our family, and our friends ahead of those of strangers; if we did not do so, would these relationships survive? I have already indicated, in the response I gave when considering the objection that we should first take care of our own, that there is a place, within an impartially grounded moral framework, for recognising some degree of partiality for kin, and the same can be said for other close personal relationships. Clearly, for most people, personal relationships are among the necessities of a flourishing life, and to give them up would be to sacrifice something of great moral significance. Hence no such sacrifice is required by the principle for which I am here arguing.

The third version of the objection asks: might it not be counterproductive to demand that people give up so much? Might not people say: 'As I can't do what is morally required anyway, I won't bother to give at all.' If, however, we were to set a more realistic standard, people might make a genuine effort to reach it. Thus setting a lower standard might actually result in more aid being given.

It is important to get the status of this third version of the objection clear. Its accuracy as a prediction of human behaviour is quite compatible with the argument that we are obliged to give to the point at which by giving more we sacrifice something of comparable moral significance. What would follow from the objection is that public advocacy of this standard of giving is undesirable. It would mean that in order to do the maximum to reduce absolute poverty, we should advocate a standard lower than the amount we think people really ought to give. Of course we ourselves – those of us who accept the original argument, with its higher standard – would know that we ought to do more than we publicly propose people ought to do, and we might actually give more than we urge others to give. There is no inconsistency here, since in both our private and our public behaviour we are trying to do what will most reduce absolute poverty.

For a consequentialist, this apparent conflict between public and private morality is always a possibility, and not in itself an indication that the underlying principle is wrong. The consequences of a principle are one thing, the consequences of publicly advocating it another. A variant of this idea is already acknowledged by the distinction between the intuitive and critical levels of morality, of which I have made use in previous chapters. If we think of principles that are suitable for the intuitive level of morality as those that should be generally advocated, these are the principles that, when advocated, will give rise to the best consequences. Where overseas aid is concerned, those will be the principles that lead to largest amount being given by the affluent to the poor.

Is it true that the standard set by our argument is so high as to be counterproductive? There is not much evidence to go by, but discussions of the argument, with students and others have led me to think it might be. Yet, the conventionally accepted standard – a few coins in a collection tin when one is waved under your nose – is obviously far too low. What level should we advocate? Any figure will be arbitrary, but there may be something to be said for a round percentage of one's income like, say, 10 per cent – more than a token donation, yet not so high as to be beyond all but saints. (This figure has the additional advantage of being reminiscent of the ancient tithe, or tenth, that was traditionally given to the church, whose responsibilities included care of the poor in one's local community. Perhaps the idea can be revived and applied to the global community.) Some families, of course, will find 10 per cent a considerable strain on their finances. Others may be able to give more without difficulty. No figure should be advocated as a rigid minimum or maximum; but it seems safe to advocate that those earning average or above average incomes in affluent societies, unless they have an unusually large number of dependents or other special needs, ought to give a tenth of their income to reducing absolute poverty. By any reasonable ethical standards this is the minimum we ought to do, and we do wrong if we do less.

9

INSIDERS AND OUTSIDERS

THE SHELTER

IT is February 2002, and the world is taking stock of the damage done by the nuclear war in the Middle East towards the close of the previous year. The global level of radioactivity now and for about eight years to come is so high that only those living in fallout shelters can be confident of surviving in reasonable health. For the rest, who must breathe unfiltered air and consume food and water with high levels of radiation, the prospects are grim. Probably 10 per cent will die of radiation sickness within the next two months; another 30 per cent are expected to develop fatal forms of cancer within five years; and even the remainder will have rates of cancer ten times higher than normal, while the risk that their children will be malformed is fifty times greater than before the war.

The fortunate ones, of course, are those who were far-sighted enough to buy a share in the fallout shelters built by real-estate speculators as international tensions rose in the late 1990s. Most of these shelters were designed as underground villages, each with enough accommodation and supplies to provide for the needs of 10,000 people for twenty years. The villages are self-governing, with democratic constitutions that were agreed to in advance. They also have sophisticated security systems that enable them to admit to the shelter whoever they decide to admit, and keep out all others.

The news that it will not be necessary to stay in the shelters for much more than eight years has naturally been greeted with joy by the members of an underground community called Fairhaven. But it has also led to the first serious friction among them. For above the shaft that leads down to Fairhaven, there are thousands of people who are not investors in a shelter. These people can be seen, and heard, through television cameras installed at the entrance. They are pleading to be admitted. They know that if they can get into a shelter quickly, they will escape most of the consequences of exposure to radiation. At first, before it was known how long it would be until it was safe to return to the outside, these pleas had virtually no support from within the shelter. Now, however, the case for admitting at least some of them has become much stronger. Since the supplies need last only eight years, they will stretch to more than double the number of people at present in the shelters. Accommodation presents only slightly greater problems: Fairhaven was designed to function as a luxury retreat when not needed for a real emergency, and it is equipped with tennis courts, swimming pools, and a large gymnasium. If everyone were to consent to keep fit by doing aerobics in their own living rooms, it would be possible to provide primitive but adequate sleeping space for all those whom the supplies can stretch to feed.

So those outside are now not lacking advocates on the inside. The most extreme, labelled 'bleeding hearts' by their opponents, propose that the shelter should admit an additional 10,000 people – as many as it can reasonably expect to feed and house until it is safe to return to the outside. This will mean giving up all luxury in food and facilities; but the bleeding hearts point out that the fate for those who remain on the outside will be far worse.

The bleeding hearts are opposed by some who urge that these outsiders generally are an inferior kind of person, for they were either not sufficiently far-sighted, or else not sufficiently wealthy, to invest in a shelter; hence, it is said, they will cause social problems in the shelter, placing an additional strain on health, welfare, and educational services and contributing to an increase in crime and juvenile delinquency. The opposition to admitting outsiders is also supported by a small group who say that it would be an injustice to those who have paid for their share of the shelter if others who have not paid benefit by it. These opponents of admitting others are articulate, but few; their numbers are bolstered considerably, however, by many who say only that they really enjoy tennis and swimming and don't want to give it up.

Between the bleeding hearts and those who oppose admitting any outsiders, stands a middle group: those who think that, as an exceptional act of benevolence and charity, some outsiders should be admitted, but not so many as to make a significant difference to the quality of life within the shelter. They propose converting a quarter of the tennis courts to sleeping accommodation, and giving up a small public open space that has attracted little use anyway. By these means, an extra 500 people could be accommodated, which the self-styled 'moderates' think would be a sensible figure, sufficient to show that Fairhaven is not insensitive to the plight of those less fortunate than its own members.

A referendum is held. There are three proposals: to admit 10,000 outsiders; to admit 500 outsiders; and to admit no outsiders. For which would you vote?

THE REAL WORLD

Like the issue of overseas aid, the situation of refugees today raises an ethical question about the boundaries of our moral community – not, as in earlier chapters, on grounds of species, stage of development, or intellectual capacities, but on nationality. The great majority of the approximately 15 million refugees in the world today are receiving refuge, at least temporarily, in the poorer and less developed countries of the world. More than 12 million refugees are in the less developed countries of Africa, Asia and Latin America. The effect on a poor country of

249

receiving a sudden influx of millions of refugees can be gauged from the experience of Pakistan during the 1980s, when it was home to 2.8 million Afghan refugees – mainly living in the North West Frontier province. Although Pakistan did get some outside assistance to feed its refugees, the effects of bearing the burden of this refugee population for seven years was easily seen around refugee villages. Whole hillsides were denuded of trees as a result of the collection of wood for fuel for the refugees.

According to Article 14 of the 1948 United Nations Declaration of Human Rights, 'Everyone has the right to seek and to enjoy in other countries asylum from persecution.' The United Nations High Commission for Refugees was established in 1950 and the commissioner entrusted with the protection of any person who is outside the country of his nationality because of a well founded fear of persecution by reason of his race, religion, nationality or political opinion, and is unwilling or unable to avail himself of the protection of his own government'. This definition was originally designed to meet the dislocation caused by the Second World War in Europe. It is a narrow one, demanding that claims to refugee status be investigated case by case. It has failed to cover the large-scale movements of people in times of war, famine, or civil disturbance that have occurred since.

Less than generous responses to refugees are usually justified by blaming the victim. It has become common to distinguish 'genuine refugees' from 'economic refugees' and to claim that the latter should receive no assistance. This distinction is dubious, for most refugees leave their countries at great risk and peril to their lives – crossing seas in leaky boats under attack from pirates, or making long journeys over armed borders, to arrive penniless in refugee camps. To distinguish between someone fleeing from political persecution and someone who flees from a land made uninhabitable by prolonged drought is difficult to justify when they are in equal need of a refuge. The UN definition, which would not classify the latter as a refugee, defines away the problem.

What are the possible durable solutions for refugees in the world today? The main options are: voluntary repatriation, local integration in the country they first flee to, and resettlement.

Probably the best and most humane solution for refugees would be to return home. Unfortunately for the majority, voluntary repatriation is not possible because the conditions that caused them to flee have not changed sufficiently. Local settlement, where refugees can remain and rebuild their lives in neighbouring countries, is too often impossible because of the inability of poor, economically struggling – and politically unstable – countries to absorb a new population when their indigenous people face a daily struggle for survival. This option works best where ethnic and tribal links cross national frontiers.

The difficulty of achieving either voluntary repatriation or local settlement leaves resettlement in a more remote country as the only remaining option. With the number of refugees needing resettlement reaching dimensions never before experienced, the main response of the industrialised countries has been to institute deterrent policies and close their doors as tight as they can. Admittedly, resettlement can never solve the problems that make refugees leave their homes. Nor is it, of itself, a solution to the world refugee problem. Only about 2 per cent of the world's refugees are permanently resettled. Nevertheless, the resettlement option is a significant one. It provides markedly better lives for a considerable number of individuals, even if not for a large proportion of the total number of refugees.

Resettlement also affects the policies of those countries to which refugees first flee. If such countries have no hope that refugees will be resettled, they know that their burden will grow with every refugee who enters their country. And countries of first refuge are among those least able to support additional people. When the resettlement option tightens, the countries to which refugees first go adopt policies to try to discourage potential refugees from leaving their country. This policy will include turning people back at the border, making the camps as unattractive as possible, and screening the refugees as they cross the border.

Resettlement is the only solution for those who cannot return to their own countries in the foreseeable future and are only welcome temporarily in the country to which they have fled; in other words for those who have nowhere to go. There are millions who would choose this option if there were countries who would take them. For these refugees, resettlement may mean the difference between life and death. It certainly is their only hope for a decent existence.

THE *EX GRATIA* APPROACH

A widely held attitude is that we are under no moral or legal obligation to accept any refugees at all; and if we do accept some, it is an indication of our generous and humanitarian character. Though popular, this view is not self-evidently morally sound. Indeed, it appears to conflict with other attitudes that are, if we can judge from what people say, at least as widely held, including the belief in the equality of all human beings, and the rejection of principles that discriminate on the basis of race or national origin.

All developed nations safeguard the welfare of their residents in many ways − protecting their legal rights, educating their children, and providing social security payments and access to medical care, either universally or for those who fall below a defined level of poverty. Refugees receive none of these benefits unless they are accepted into the country. Since the overwhelming majority of them are not accepted, the overwhelming majority will not receive these benefits. But is this distinction in the way in which we treat residents and nonresidents ethically defensible?

Very few moral philosophers have given any attention to the issue of refugees, even though it is clearly one of the major moral issues of our time and raises significant moral questions about who is a member of our moral community. Take, for example, John Rawls, the Harvard philosopher whose book, *A Theory of Justice*, has been the most widely discussed account of justice since its publication in 1971. This 500-page volume deals exclusively with justice *within* a society, thus ignoring all the hard questions about the principles that ought to govern how wealthy societies respond to the claims of poorer nations, or of outsiders in need.

One of the few philosophers who has addressed this issue is another American, Michael Walzer. His *Spheres of Justice* opens with a chapter entitled 'The Distribution of Membership' in which he asks how we constitute the community within which distribution takes place. In the course of this chapter Walzer seeks to justify something close to the present situation with regard to refugee policy. The first question Walzer addresses is: do countries have the right to close their borders to potential immigrants? His answer is that they do, because without such closure, or at least the power to close borders if desired, distinct communities cannot exist.

Given that the decision to close borders can rightfully be made, Walzer then goes on to consider how it should be exercised. He compares the political community with a club, and with a family. Clubs are examples of the *ex gratia* approach: 'Individuals may be able to give good reason why they should be selected, but no one on the outside has a right to be inside.' But Walzer considers the analogy imperfect, because states are also a bit like families. They are morally bound to open the doors of their country – not to anyone who wants to come in, perhaps, but to a particular group of outsiders, recognised as national or ethnic 'relatives.' In this way Walzer uses the analogy of a family to justify the principle of family reunion as a basis for immigration policy.

As far as refugees are concerned, however, this is not much help. Does a political community have the right to exclude destitute, persecuted, and stateless men and women simply because they are foreigners? In Walzer's view the community is bound by a principle of mutual aid and he rightly notes that this principle may have wider effects when applied to a community than when applied to an individual, because so many benevolent actions are open to a community that will only marginally affect its members. To take a stranger into one's family is something that we might consider goes beyond the requirement of mutual aid; but to take a stranger, or even many strangers, into the community is far less burdensome.

In Walzer's view, a nation with vast unoccupied lands – he takes Australia as his example, though by assumption rather than by any examination of Australia's water and soil resources – may indeed have an obligation in mutual aid to take in people from densely populated, famine-stricken lands of Southeast Asia. The choice for the Australian community would then be to give up whatever homogeneity their society possessed, or to retreat to a small portion of the land they occupied, yielding the remainder to those who needed it.

Although not accepting any general obligation on affluent nations to admit refugees, Walzer does uphold the popular principle of asylum. In accordance with this principle, any refugee who manages to reach the shores of another country can claim asylum and cannot be deported back to a country in which he may be persecuted for reasons of race, religion, nationality, or political opinion. It is interesting that this principle is so widely supported, while the obligation to accept refugees is not. The distinction drawn may reflect some of the principles discussed in previous chapters of this book. The principle of proximity clearly plays a role – the person seeking asylum is just physically closer to us than those in other countries. Perhaps our stronger support for asylum rests in part on the distinction between an act (deporting a refugee who has arrived here) and an omission (not offering a place to a refugee in a distant camp). It could also be an instance of the difference between doing something to an identifiable individual, and doing something that we know will have the same effect on someone, but we will never be able to tell on whom it has this effect. A further factor is probably the relatively small number of people who are actually able to arrive in order to seek asylum, in contrast to the much larger number of refugees of whose existence we are aware, although they are far from us. This is the 'drops in the ocean' argument that was discussed in connection with overseas aid. We can, perhaps, cope with all the asylum seekers, but no matter how many refugees we admit, the problem will still be there. As in the case of the parallel argument against giving overseas aid, this overlooks the fact that in admitting refugees, we enable specific individuals to live decent lives and thus are doing something that is worthwhile, no matter how many other refugees remain whom we are unable to help.

Moderately liberal governments, prepared to heed at least some humanitarian sentiments, act much as Walzer suggests they should. They hold that communities have a right to decide whom they will admit; the claims of family reunion come first, and those of outsiders from the national ethnic group – should the state have an ethnic identity – next. The admission of those in need is an *ex gratia* act. The right of asylum is usually respected, as long as the numbers are relatively small. Refugees, unless they can appeal to some special sense of political affinity, have no real claim to be accepted, and have to throw themselves on the charity of the receiving country. All of this is in general agreement with immigration policy in the Western democracies. As far as refugees are concerned, the *ex gratia* approach is the current orthodoxy.

THE FALLACY OF THE CURRENT APPROACH

The current orthodoxy rests on vague and usually unargued assumptions about the community's right to determine its membership. A consequentialist would hold, instead, that immigration policy should be based squarely on the interests of all those affected. Where the interests of different parties conflict, we should be giving equal consideration to all interests, which would mean that more pressing or more fundamental interests take precedence over less fundamental interests. The first step in applying the principle of equal consideration of interests is to identify those whose interests are affected. The first and most obvious group is the refugees themselves. Their most pressing and fundamental interests are clearly at stake. Life in a refugee camp offers little prospect of anything more than a bare subsistence, and sometimes hardly even that. Here is one observer's impression of a camp on the Thai–Cambodian border in 1986. At the time the camp was home for 144,000 people:

> The visit of a foreigner causes a ripple of excitement. People gather round and ask earnestly about the progress of their case for resettlement, or share their great despair at continual rejection by the selection bodies for the various countries which will accept refugees. . . . People wept as they spoke, most had an air of quiet desperation. . . . On rice distribution day, thousands of girls and women mill in the distribution area, receiving the weekly rations for their family. From the bamboo observation tower the ground below was just a swirling sea of black hair and bags of rice hoisted onto heads for the walk home. A proud, largely farming people, forced to become dependent on UN rations of water, tinned fish and broken rice, just to survive.
>
> Most of these people could hope for no significant change in their lives for many years to come. Yet I, along with the others from outside, could get into a car and drive out of the camp, return to Taphraya or Aran, drink iced water, eat rice or noodles at the roadside restaurant at the corner, and observe life passing by. Those simplest parts of life were invested with a freedom I'd never valued so highly.

At the same time, refugees accepted into another country have a good chance of establishing themselves and leading a life as satisfactory and fulfilling as most of us. Sometimes the interests of the refugees in being accepted are as basic as the interest in life itself. In other cases the situation may not be one of life or death, but it will still profoundly affect the whole course of a person's life.

The next most directly affected group is the residents of the recipient nation. How much they will be affected will vary according to how many refugees are taken, how well they will fit into the community, the current state of the national economy, and so on. Some residents will be more affected than others: some will find themselves competing with the refugees for jobs, and others will not; some will find themselves in a neighborhood with a high population of refugees, and others will not; and this list could be continued indefinitely, too.

We should not assume that residents of the recipient nation will be affected for the worse: the economy may receive a boost from a substantial intake of refugees, and many residents may find business opportunities in providing for their needs. Others may enjoy the more cosmopolitan atmosphere created by new arrivals from other countries: the exotic food shops and restaurants that spring up, and in the long run, the benefits of different ideas and ways of living. One could argue that in many ways refugees make the best immigrants. They have nowhere else to go and must commit themselves totally to their new country, unlike immigrants who can go home when or if they please. The fact that they have survived and escaped from hardship suggests stamina, initiative, and resources that would be of great benefit to any receiving country. Certainly some refugee groups, for instance the Indo-Chinese, have displayed great entrepreneurial vigour when resettled in countries like Australia or the United States.

There are also some other *possible* and more diffuse consequences that we at least need to think about. For example, it has been argued that to take large numbers of refugees from poor countries into affluent ones will simply encourage the flow of refugees in the future. If poor and over-populated countries can get rid of their surplus people to other countries, they will have a reduced incentive to do something about the root causes of the poverty of their people, and to slow population growth. The end result could be just as much suffering as if we had never taken the refugees in the first place.

Consequences also arise from *not* taking significant numbers of refugees. Economic stability and world peace depend on international co-operation based on some measure of respect and trust; but the resource-rich and not over-populated countries of the world cannot expect to win the respect or trust of the poorest and most crowded countries if they leave them to cope with most of the refugee problem as best they can.

So we have a complex mix of interests – some definite, some highly speculative – to be considered. Equal interests are to be given equal weight, but which way does the balance lie? Consider a reasonably affluent nation that is not desperately overcrowded, like Australia (I take Australia merely as an example of a country with which I am familiar; one could, with minor modifications, substitute other affluent nations.) In the early 1990s Australia is admitting about 12,000 refugees a year, at a time when there are several million refugees in refugee camps around the world, many of whom have no hope of returning to their previous country and are seeking resettlement in a country like Australia. Now let us imagine that Australia decides to accept twice as many refugees each year as it has in fact been doing. What can we say are the definite consequences of such a decision, and what are the possible consequences?

The first definite consequence would be that each year 12,000 more refugees would have been out of the refugee camps and settled in Australia, where they could expect, after a few years of struggle, to share in the material comforts, civil rights, and political security of that country. So 12,000 people would have been *very* much better off.

The second definite consequence would have been that each year Australia would have had 12,000 more immigrants, and that these additional immigrants would not have been selected on the basis of possessing skills needed in the Australian economy. They would therefore place an additional demand on welfare services. Some long-term residents of Australia may be disconcerted by the changes that take place in their neighborhood, as significant numbers of people from a very different culture move in. More refugees would make some impact on initial post-arrival services such as the provision of English language classes, housing in the first few months, job placement, and retraining. But the differences would be minor – after all, a decade earlier, Australia had accepted approximately 22,000 refugees a year. There were no marked adverse effects from this larger intake.

At this point, if we are considering the *definite* consequences of a doubled refugee intake, in terms of having a significant impact on the interests of others, we come to a halt. We may wonder if the increased numbers will lead to a revival of racist feeling in the community. We could debate the impact on the Australian environment. We might guess that a larger intake of refugees will encourage others, in the country from which the refugees came, to become refugees themselves in order to better their economic condition. Or we could refer hopefully to the contribution towards international goodwill that may flow from a country like Australia easing the burden of less well-off nations in supporting refugees. But all of these consequences are highly speculative.

Consider the environmental impact of an extra 12,000 refugees. Certainly, more people will put some additional pressure on the environment. This means that the increased number of refugees accepted will be just one item in a long list of factors that includes the natural rate of reproduction; the government's desire to increase exports by encouraging an industry based on converting virgin forests to wood-chips; the subdivision of rural land in scenic areas for holiday houses; the spurt in popularity of vehicles suitable for off-road use; the development of ski resorts in sensitive alpine areas; the use of no-deposit bottles and other containers that increase litter – the list could be prolonged indefinitely.

If as a community we allow these other factors to have their impact on the environment, while appealing to the need to protect our environment as a reason for restricting our intake of refugees to its present level, we are implicitly giving less weight to the interests of refugees in coming to Australia than we give to the interests of Australian residents in having holiday houses, roaring around the countryside in four-wheel-drive vehicles, going skiing, and throwing away their drink containers without bothering to return them for recycling. Such a weighting is surely morally outrageous, so flagrant a violation of the principle of equal consideration of interests that I trust it has only to be exposed in order to be seen as indefensible.

The other arguments are even more problematical. No one can really say whether doubling Australia's intake of refugees would have any effect at all on the numbers who might consider fleeing their own homes; nor is it possible to predict the consequences in terms of international relations. As with the similar argument linking overseas aid with increased population, in a situation in which the definite consequences of the proposed additional intake of refugees are positive, it would be wrong to decide against the larger intake on such speculative grounds, especially since the speculative factors point in different directions.

So there is a strong case for Australia to double its refugee intake. But there was nothing in the argument that relied on the specific level of refugees now being taken by Australia. If this argument goes through, it would also seem to follow that Australia should be taking not an extra 12,000 refugees, but an extra 24,000 refugees a year. Now the argument seems to be going too far, for it can then be reapplied to this new level: should Australia be taking 48,000 refugees? We can double and redouble the intakes of all the major nations of the developed world, and the refugee camps around the world will still not be empty. Indeed, the number of refugees who would seek resettlement in the developed countries is not fixed, and probably there is some truth in the claim that if all those now in refugee camps were to be accepted, more refugees would arrive to take their places. Since the interests of the refugees in resettlement in a more prosperous country will always be greater than the conflicting interests of the residents of those countries, it would seem that the principle of equal consideration of interests points to a world in which all countries continue to accept refugees until they are reduced to the same standard of poverty and overcrowding as the third world countries from which the refugees are seeking to flee.

Is this a reason for rejecting the original argument? Does it mean that if we follow the original argument through it leads to consequences that we cannot possibly accept; and therefore there must be a flaw in the argument that has led us to such an absurd conclusion? This does not follow. The argument we put forward for doubling Australia's refugee intake does not really imply that the doubled intake should then be redoubled, and redoubled again, ad infinitum. At some point in this process – perhaps when the refugee intake is four times what it now is, or perhaps when it is sixty-four times its present level – the adverse consequences that are now only speculative possibilities would become probabilities or virtual certainties.

There would come a point at which, for instance, the resident community had eliminated all luxuries that imperilled the environment, and yet the basic needs of the expanding population were putting such pressure on fragile ecological systems that a further expansion would do irreparable harm. Or there might come a point at which tolerance in a multicultural society was breaking down because of resentment among the resident community, whose members believed that their children were unable to get jobs because of competition from the hard-working new arrivals; and this loss of tolerance might reach the point at which it was a serious danger to the peace and security of all previously accepted refugees and other immigrants from different cultures. When any such point had been reached, the balance of interests would have swung against a further increase in the intake of refugees.

The present refugee intake might increase quite dramatically before any consequences like those mentioned above were reached; and some may take this as a consequence sufficiently unacceptable to support the rejection of our line of argument. Certainly anyone starting from the assumption that the status quo must be roughly right will be likely to take that view. But the status quo is the outcome of a system of national selfishness and political expediency, and not the result of a considered attempt to work out the moral obligations of the developed nations in a world with 15 million refugees.

It would not be difficult for the nations of the developed world to move closer towards fulfilling their moral obligations to refugees. There is no objective evidence to show that doubling their refugee intake would cause them any harm whatsoever. Much present evidence, as well as past experience, points the other way, suggesting that they and their present population would probably benefit.

But, the leaders will cry, what is moral is not what is politically acceptable! This is a spurious excuse for inaction. In many policy areas, presidents and prime ministers are quite happy to try to convince the electorate of what is right – of the need to tighten belts in order to balance budgets, or to desist from drinking and driving. They could just as easily gradually increase their refugee intakes, monitoring the effects of the increase through careful research. In this way they would fulfill their moral and geopolitical obligations and still benefit their own communities.

SHELTERS AND REFUGES

How would you have voted, in the referendum conducted in Fairhaven in 1998? I think most people would have been prepared to sacrifice not just a quarter, but all of the tennis courts to the greater need of those outside. But if you would have voted with the 'bleeding hearts' in that situation, it is difficult to see how you can disagree with the conclusion that affluent nations should be taking far, far more refugees than they are taking today. For the situation of refugees is scarcely better than that of the outsiders in peril from nuclear radiation; and the luxuries that we would have to sacrifice are surely no greater.

10

THE ENVIRONMENT

A river tumbles through forested ravines and rocky gorges towards the sea. The state hydro-electricity commission sees the falling water as untapped energy. Building a dam across one of the gorges would provide three years of employment for a thousand people, and longer-term employment for twenty or thirty. The dam would store enough water to ensure that the state could economically meet its energy needs for the next decade. This would encourage the establishment of energy-intensive industry thus further contributing to employment and economic growth.

The rough terrain of the river valley makes it accessible only to the reasonably fit, but it is nevertheless a favoured spot for bush-walking. The river itself attracts the more daring whitewater rafters. Deep in the sheltered valleys are stands of rare Huon Pine, many of the trees being over a thousand years old. The valleys and gorges are home to many birds and animals, including an endangered species of marsupial mouse that has seldom been found outside the valley. There may be other rare plants and animals as well, but no one knows, for scientists are yet to investigate the region fully.

SHOULD the dam be built? This is one example of a situation in which we must choose between very different sets of values. The description is loosely based on a proposed dam on the Franklin River, in the southwest of Australia's island state, Tasmania – an account of the outcome can be found in Chapter 11, but I have deliberately altered some details, and the above description should be treated as a hypothetical case. Many other examples would have posed the choice between values equally well: logging virgin forests, building a paper mill that will release pollutants into coastal waters, or opening a new mine on the edge of a national park. A different set of examples would raise related, but slightly different, issues: the use of products that contribute to the depletion of the ozone layer, or to the greenhouse effect; building more nuclear power stations; and so on. In this chapter I explore the values that underlie debates about these decisions, and the example I have presented can serve as a point of reference to these debates. I shall focus particularly on the values at issue in controversies about the preservation of wilderness because here the fundamentally different values of the two parties are most apparent. When we are talking about flooding a river valley, the choice before us is starkly clear.

In general we can say that those who favour building the dam are valuing employment and a higher per capita income for the state above the preservation of wilderness, of plants and animals (both common ones and members of an endangered species), and of opportunities for outdoor recreational activities. Before we begin to scrutinise the values of those who would have the dam build and those who would not, however, let us briefly investigate the origins of modern attitudes towards the natural world.

THE WESTERN TRADITION

Western attitudes to nature grew out of a blend of those of the Hebrew people, as represented in the early books of the Bible, and the philosophy of the ancient Greeks, particularly that of Aristotle. In contrast to some other ancient traditions, for example, those of India, both the Hebrew and the Greek traditions made human beings the centre of the moral universe – indeed not merely the centre, but very often, the entirety of the morally significant features of this world.

The biblical story of creation, in Genesis, makes clear the Hebrew view of the special place of human beings in the divine plan:

And God said, Let us make man in our image, after our like-
ness: and let them have dominion over the fish of the sea, and
over the fowl of the air, and over the earth, and over every
creeping thing that creepeth upon the earth.
So God created man in his own image, in the image of God
created he him; male and female created he them.
And God blessed them, and God said upon them, Be fruitful,
and multiply, and replenish the earth, and subdue it; and have
dominion over the fish of the sea and over the fowl of the air,
and over every living thing that moveth upon the earth.

Today Christians debate the meaning of this grant of 'dominion'; and those concerned about the environment claim that
it should be regarded not as a license to do as we will with other
living things, but rather as a directive to look after them, on
God's behalf, and be answerable to God for the way in which
we treat them. There is, however, little justification in the text
itself for such an interpretation; and given the example God set
when he drowned almost every animal on earth in order to
punish human beings for their wickedness, it is no wonder that
people should think the flooding of a single river valley is nothing worth worrying about. After the flood there is a repetition
of the grant of dominion in more ominous language: 'And the
fear of you and the dread of you shall be upon every beast of
the earth, and upon every fowl of the air, upon all that moveth
upon the earth, and upon all the fishes of the sea; into your
hands are they delivered.'

The implication is clear: to act in a way that causes fear and
dread to everything that moves on the earth is not improper;
it is, in fact, in accordance with a God-given decree.

The most influential early Christian thinkers had no doubts
about how man's dominion was to be understood. 'Doth God
care for oxen?' asked Paul, in the course of a discussion of an
Old Testament command to rest one's ox on the sabbath, but
it was only a rhetorical question – he took it for granted that
the answer must be negative, and the command was to be
explained in terms of some benefit to humans. Augustine shared

this line of thought; referring to stories in the New Testament in which Jesus destroyed a fig tree and caused a herd of pigs to drown, Augustine explained these puzzling incidents as intended to teach us that 'to refrain from the killing of animals and the destroying of plants is the height of superstition'.

When Christianity prevailed in the Roman Empire, it also absorbed elements of the ancient Greek attitude to the natural world. The Greek influence was entrenched in Christian philosophy by the greatest of the medieval scholastics, Thomas Aquinas, whose life work was the melding of Christian theology with the thought of Aristotle. Aristotle regarded nature as a hierarchy in which those with less reasoning ability exist for the sake of those with more:

> Plants exist for the sake of animals, and brute beasts for the sake of man – domestic animals for his use and food, wild ones (or at any rate most of them) for food and other accessories of life, such as clothing and various tools.
> Since nature makes nothing purposeless or in vain, it is undeniably true that she has made all animals for the sake of man.

In his own major work, the *Summa Theologica*, Aquinas followed this passage from Aristotle almost word for word, adding that the position accords with God's command, as given in Genesis. In his classification of sins, Aquinas has room only for sins against God, ourselves, or our neighbours. There is no possibility of sinning against non-human animals, or against the natural world.

This was the thinking of mainstream Christianity for at least its first eighteen centuries. There were gentler spirits, certainly, like Basil, John Chrysostom, and Francis of Assisi, but for most of Christian history they have had no significant impact on the dominant tradition. It is therefore worth emphasising the major features of this dominant Western tradition, because these features can serve as a point of comparison when we discuss different views of the natural environment.

According to the dominant Western tradition, the natural

world exists for the benefit of human beings. God gave human beings dominion over the natural world, and God does not care how we treat it. Human beings are the only morally important members of this world. Nature itself is of no intrinsic value, and the destruction of plants and animals cannot be sinful, unless by this destruction we harm human beings.

Harsh as this tradition is, it does not rule out concern for the preservation of nature, as long as that concern can be related to human well-being. Often, of course, it can be. One could, entirely within the limits of the dominant Western tradition, oppose nuclear power on the grounds that nuclear fuel, whether in bombs or power stations, is so hazardous to human life that the uranium is better left in the ground. Similarly, many arguments against pollution, the use of gases harmful to the ozone layer, the burning of fossil fuels, and the destruction of forests, could be couched in terms of the harm to human health and welfare from the pollutants, or the changes to the climate that will occur as a result of the use of fossil fuels and the loss of forest. The greenhouse effect – to take just one danger to our environment – threatens to bring about a rise in sea level that will inundate low-lying coastal areas. This includes the fertile and densely populated Nile delta in Egypt, and the Bengal delta region, which covers 80 per cent of Bangladesh and is already subject to violent seasonal storms that cause disastrous floods. The homes and livelihood of 46 million people are at risk in these two deltas alone. A rise in sea level could also wipe out entire island nations such as the Maldives, none of which is more than a metre or two above sea level. So it is obvious that even within a human-centred moral framework, the preservation of our environment is a value of the greatest possible importance.

From the standpoint of a form of civilisation based on growing crops and grazing animals, wilderness may seem to be a wasteland, a useless area that needs clearing in order to render it productive and valuable. There was a time when villages surrounded by farmland seemed like oases of cultivation amongst the deserts of forest or rough mountain slopes. Now, however, a different metaphor is more appropriate: the remnants of true wilderness left to us are like islands amidst a sea of human activity that threatens to engulf them. This gives wilderness a scarcity value that provides the basis for a strong argument for preservation, even within the terms of a human-centred ethic. That argument becomes much stronger still when we take a long-term view. To this immensely important aspect of environmental values we shall now turn.

FUTURE GENERATIONS

A virgin forest is the product of all the millions of years that have passed since the beginning of our planet. If it is cut down, another forest may grow up, but the continuity has been broken. The disruption in the natural life cycles of the plants and animals means that the forest will never again be as it would have been, had it not been cut. The gains made from cutting the forest — employment, profits for business, export earnings, and cheaper cardboard and paper for packaging — are short-term benefits. Even if the forest is not cut, but drowned to build a dam to create electricity, it is likely that the benefits will last for only a generation or two: after that new technology will render such methods of generating power obsolete. Once the forest is cut or drowned, however, the link with the past has gone for ever. That is a cost that will be borne by every generation that succeeds us on this planet. It is for that reason that environmentalists are right to speak of wilderness as a 'world heritage'. It is something that we have inherited from our ancestors, and that we must preserve for our descendants, if they are to have it at all.

In contrast to many more stable, tradition-oriented human societies, our modern political and cultural ethos has great difficulty in recognising long-term values. Politicians are notorious for not looking beyond the next election; but even if they do, they will find their economic advisers telling them that anything to be gained in the future should be discounted to such a degree as to make it easy to disregard the long-term future altogether. Economists have been taught to apply a discount rate to all future goods. In other words, a million dollars in twenty years is not worth a million dollars today, even when we allow for inflation. Economists will discount the value of the million dollars by a certain percentage, usually corresponding to the real long-term interest rates. This makes economic sense, because if I had a thousand dollars today I could invest it so that it would be worth more, in real terms, in twenty years. But the use of a discount rate means that values gained one hundred years hence rank very low, in comparison with values gained today; and values gained one thousand years in the future scarcely count at all. This is not because of any uncertainty about whether there will be human beings or other sentient creatures inhabiting this planet at that time, but merely because of the cumulative effect of the rate of return on money invested now. From the standpoint of the priceless and timeless values of wilderness, however, applying a discount rate gives us the wrong answer. There are some things that, once lost, no amount of money can regain. Thus to justify the destruction of an ancient forest on the grounds that it will earn us substantial export income is unsound, even if we could invest that income and increase its value from year to year; for no matter how much we increased its value, it could never buy back the link with the past represented by the forest.

This argument does not show that there can be no justification for cutting any virgin forests, but it does mean that any such justification must take full account of the value of the forests to the generations to come in the more remote future, as well as in the more immediate future. This value will obviously be related to the particular scenic or biological significance of the forest; but as the proportion of true wilderness on the earth dwindles, every part of it becomes significant, because the opportunities for experiencing wilderness become scarce, and the likelihood of a reasonable selection of the major forms of wilderness being preserved is reduced.

Can we be sure that future generations will appreciate wilderness? Perhaps they will be happier sitting in air-conditioned shopping malls, playing computer games more sophisticated than any we can imagine? That is possible. But there are several reasons why we should not give this possibility too much weight. First, the trend has been in the opposite direction: the appreciation of wilderness has never been higher than it is today, especially among those nations that have overcome the problems of poverty and hunger and have relatively little wilderness left. Wilderness is valued as something of immense beauty, as a reservoir of scientific knowledge still to be gained, for the recreational opportunities that it provides, and because many people just like to know that something natural is still there, relatively untouched by modern civilisation. If, as we all hope, future generations are able to provide for the basic needs of most people, we can expect that for centuries to come, they, too, will value wilderness for the same reasons that we value it.

Arguments for preservation based on the beauty of wilderness are sometimes treated as if they were of little weight because they are 'merely aesthetic'. That is a mistake. We go to great lengths to preserve the artistic treasures of earlier human civilisations. It is difficult to imagine any economic gain that we would be prepared to accept as adequate compensation for, for instance, the destruction of the paintings in the Louvre. How should we compare the aesthetic value of wilderness with that of the paintings in the Louvre? Here, perhaps, judgment does become inescapably subjective; so I shall report my own experiences. I have looked at the paintings in the Louvre, and in many of the other great galleries of Europe and the United States. I think I have a reasonable sense of appreciation of the fine arts; yet I have not had, in any museum, experiences that have filled my aesthetic senses in the way that they are filled when I walk in a natural setting and pause to survey the view from a rocky peak overlooking a forested valley, or sit by a stream tumbling over moss-covered boulders set amongst tall tree-ferns, growing in the shade of the forest canopy. I do not think I am alone in this; for many people, wilderness is the source of the greatest feelings of aesthetic appreciation, rising to an almost spiritual intensity.

It may nevertheless be true that this appreciation of nature will not be shared by people living a century or two hence. But if wilderness can be the source of such deep joy and satisfaction, that would be a great loss. To some extent, whether future generations value wilderness is up to us; it is, at least, a decision we can influence. By our preservation of areas of wilderness, we provide an opportunity for generations to come, and by the books and films we produce, we create a culture that can be handed on to our children and their children. If we feel that a walk in the forest, with senses attuned to the appreciation of such an experience, is a more deeply rewarding way to spend a day than playing computer games, or if we feel that to carry one's food and shelter in a backpack for a week while hiking through an unspoiled natural environment will do more to develop character than watching television for an equivalent period, then we ought to encourage future generations to have a feeling for nature; if they end up preferring computer games, we shall have failed.

Finally, if we preserve intact the amount of wilderness that exists now, future generations will at least have the choice of getting up from their computer games and going to see a world that has not been created by human beings. If we destroy the wilderness, that choice is gone forever. Just as we rightly spend large sums to preserve cities like Venice, even though future generations conceivably may not be interested in such architectural treasures, so we should preserve wilderness even though it is possible that future generations will care little for it. Thus we will not wrong future generations, as we have been wronged by members of past generations whose thoughtless actions have deprived us of the possibility of seeing such animals as the dodo, Steller's sea cow, or the thylacine, the Tasmanian marsupial 'tiger'. We must take care not to inflict equally irreparable losses on the generations to follow us.

Here, too, the effort to mitigate the greenhouse effect deserves the highest priority. For if by 'wilderness' we mean that part of our planet that is unaffected by human activity, perhaps it is already too late: there may be no wilderness left anywhere on our planet. Bill McKibben has argued that by depleting the ozone layer and increasing the amount of carbon dioxide in the atmosphere, we have already brought about the change encapsulated in the title of his book – *The End of Nature*: 'By changing the weather, we make every spot on earth man-made and artificial. We have deprived nature of its independence, and that is fatal to its meaning. Nature's independence is its meaning; without it there is nothing but us.'

This is a profoundly disturbing thought. Yet McKibben does not develop it in order to suggest that we may as well give up our efforts to reverse the trend. It is true that in one sense of the term, 'nature' is finished. We have passed a watershed in the history of our planet. As McKibben says, 'we live in a post-natural world'. Nothing can undo that; the climate of our planet is under our influence. We still have, however, much that we value in nature, and it may still be possible to save what is left.

Thus a human-centred ethic can be the basis of powerful arguments for what we may call 'environmental values'. Such an ethic does not imply that economic growth is more important than the preservation of wilderness; on the contrary, it is quite compatible with a human-centred ethic to see economic growth based on the exploitation of irreplaceable resources as something that brings gains to the present generation, and possibly the next generation or two, but at a price that will be paid by every generation to come. But in the light of our discussion of speciesism in Chapter 3, it should also be clear that it is wrong to limit ourselves to a human-centred ethic. We now need to consider more fundamental challenges to this traditional Western approach to environmental issues.

IS THERE VALUE BEYOND SENTIENT BEINGS?

Although some debates about significant environmental issues can be conducted by appealing only to the long-term interests of our own species, in any serious exploration of environmental values a central issue will be the question of intrinsic value. We have already seen that it is arbitrary to hold that only human beings are of intrinsic value. If we find value in human conscious experiences, we cannot deny that there is value in at least some experiences of non-human beings. How far does intrinsic value extend? To all, but only, sentient beings? Or beyond the boundary of sentience?

To explore this question a few remarks on the notion of 'intrinsic value' will be helpful. Something is of intrinsic value if it is good or desirable *in itself*; the contrast is with 'instrumental value', that is, value as a means to some other end or purpose. Our own happiness, for example, is of intrinsic value, at least to most of us, in that we desire it for its own sake. Money, on the other hand, is only of instrumental value to us. We want it because of the things we can buy with it, but if we were marooned on a desert island, we would not want it. (Whereas happiness would be just as important to us on a desert island as anywhere else.)

Now consider again for a moment the issue of damming the river described at the beginning of this chapter. If the decision were to be made on the basis of human interests alone, we would balance the economic benefits of the dam for the citizens of the state against the loss for bushwalkers, scientists, and others, now and in the future, who value the preservation of the river in its natural state. We have already seen that because this calculation includes an indefinite number of future generations, the loss of the wild river is a much greater cost than we might at first imagine. Even so, once we broaden the basis of our decision beyond the interests of human beings, we have much more to set against the economic benefits of building the dam. Into the calculations must now go the interests of all the non-human animals who live in the area that will be flooded. A few may be able to move to a neighboring area that is suitable, but wilderness is not full of vacant niches awaiting an occupant; if there is territory that can sustain a native animal, it is most likely already occupied. Thus most of the animals living in the flooded area will die: either they will be drowned, or they will starve. Neither drowning nor starvation are easy ways to die, and the suffering involved in these deaths should, as we have seen, be given no less weight than we would give to an equivalent amount of suffering experienced by human beings. This will significantly increase the weight of considerations against building the dam.

What of the fact that the animals will die, apart from the suffering that will occur in the course of dying? As we have seen, one can, without being guilty of arbitrary discrimination on the basis of species, regard the death of a non-human animal who is not a person as less significant than the death of a person, since humans are capable of foresight and forward planning in ways that non-human animals are not. This difference between causing death to a person and to a being who is not a person does not mean that the death of an animal who is not a person should be treated as being of no account. On the contrary, utilitarians will take into account the loss that death inflicts on the animals – the loss of all their future existence, and the experiences that their future lives would have contained. When a proposed dam would flood a valley and kill thousands, perhaps millions, of sentient creatures, these deaths should be given great importance in any assessment of the costs and benefits of building the dam. For those utilitarians who accept the total view discussed in Chapter 4, moreover, if the dam destroys the habitat in which the animals lived, then it is relevant that this loss is a continuing one. If the dam is not built, animals will presumably continue to live in the valley for thousands of years, experiencing their own distinctive pleasures and pains. One might question whether life for animals in a natural environment yields a surplus of pleasure over pain, or of satisfaction over frustration of preferences. At this point the idea of calculating benefits becomes almost absurd; but that does not mean that the loss of future animal lives should be dismissed from our decision making.

That, however, may not be all. Should we also give weight, not only to the suffering and death of individual animals, but to the fact that an entire species may disappear? What of the loss of trees that have stood for thousands of years? How much – if any – weight should we give to the preservation of the animals, the species, the trees and the valley's ecosystem, independently of the interests of human beings – whether economic, recreational, or scientific – in their preservation?

Here we have a fundamental moral disagreement: a disagreement about what kinds of beings ought to be considered in our moral deliberations. Let us look at what has been said on behalf of extending ethics beyond sentient beings.

REVERENCE FOR LIFE

The ethical position developed in this book is an extension of the ethic of the dominant Western tradition. This extended ethic draws the boundary of moral consideration around all sentient creatures, but leaves other living things outside that boundary. The drowning of the ancient forests, the possible loss of an entire species, the destruction of several complex ecosystems, the blockage of the wild river itself, and the loss of those rocky gorges are factors to be taken into account only in so far as they adversely affect sentient creatures. Is a more radical break with the traditional position possible? Can some or all of these aspects of the flooding of the valley be shown to have intrinsic value, so that they must be taken into account independently of their effects on human beings or non-human animals?

To extend an ethic in a plausible way beyond sentient beings is a difficult task. An ethic based on the interests of sentient creatures is on familiar ground. Sentient creatures have wants and desires. The question: 'What is it like to be a possum drowning?' at least makes sense, even if it is impossible for us to give a more precise answer than 'It must be horrible'. In reaching moral decisions affecting sentient creatures, we can attempt to add up the effects of different actions on all the sentient creatures affected by the alternative actions open to us. This provides us with at least some rough guide to what might be the right thing to do. But there is *nothing* that corresponds to what it is like to be a tree dying because its roots have been flooded. Once we abandon the interests of sentient creatures as our source of value, where do we find value? What is good or bad for nonsentient creatures, and why does it matter?

It might be thought that as long as we limit ourselves to living things, the answer is not too difficult to find. We know what is good or bad for the plants in our garden: water, sunlight, and compost are good; extremes of heat or cold are bad. The same applies to plants in any forest or wilderness, so why not regard their flourishing as good in itself, independently of its usefulness to sentient creatures?

One problem here is that without conscious interests to guide us, we have no way of assessing the relative weights to be given to the flourishing of different forms of life. Is a two-thousand-year-old Huon pine more worthy of preservation than a tussock of grass? Most people will say that it is, but such a judgment seems to have more to do with our feelings of awe for the age, size, and beauty of the tree, or with the length of time it would take to replace it, than with our perception of some intrinsic value in the flourishing of an old tree that is not possessed by a young grass tussock.

If we cease talking in terms of sentience, the boundary between living and inanimate natural objects becomes more difficult to defend. Would it really be worse to cut down an old tree than to destroy a beautiful stalactite that has taken even longer to grow? On what grounds could such a judgment be made? Probably the best known defence of an ethic that extends to all living things is that of Albert Schweitzer. The phrase he used, 'reverence for life', is often quoted; the arguments he offered in support of such a position are less well-known. Here is one of the few passages in which he defended his ethic:

> True philosophy must commence with the most immediate and comprehensive facts of consciousness. And this may be formulated as follows: 'I am life which wills to live, and I exist in the midst of life which wills to live.' . . . Just as in my own will-to-live there is a yearning for more life, and for that mysterious exaltation of the will which is called pleasure, and terror in face of annihilation and that injury to the will-to-live which is called pain; so the same obtains in all the will-to-live around me, equally whether it can express itself to my comprehension or whether it remains unvoiced.

> Ethics thus consists in this, that I experience the necessity of practising the same reverence for life toward all will-to-live, as toward my own. Therein I have already the needed fundamental principle of morality. It is good to maintain and cherish life; it is *evil* to destroy and to check life. A man is really ethical only when he obeys the constraint laid on him to help all life which he is able to succour, and when he goes out of his way to avoid injuring anything living. He does not ask how far this or that life deserves sympathy as valuable in itself, nor how far it is capable of feeling. To him life as such is sacred. He shatters no ice crystal that sparkles in the sun, tears no leaf from its tree, breaks off no flower, and is careful not to crush any insect as he

walks. If he works by lamplight on a summer evening he prefers to keep the window shut and to breathe stifling air, rather than to see insect after insect fall on his table with singed and sinking wings.

A similar view has been defended recently by the contemporary American philosopher Paul Taylor. In his book *Respect for Nature*, Taylor argues that every living thing is 'pursuing its own good in its own unique way.' Once we see this, we can see all living things 'as we see ourselves' and therefore 'we are ready to place the same value on their existence as we do on our own'.

It is not clear how we should interpret Schweitzer's position. The reference to the ice crystal is especially puzzling, for an ice crystal is not alive at all. Putting this aside, however, the problem with the defences offered by both Schweitzer and Taylor for their ethical views is that they use language metaphorically and then argue as if what they had said was literally true. We may often talk about plants 'seeking' water or light so that they can survive, and this way of thinking about plants makes it easier to accept talk of their 'will to live', or of them 'pursuing' their own good. But once we stop to reflect on the fact that plants are not conscious and cannot engage in any intentional behaviour, it is clear that all this language is metaphorical; one might just as well say that a river is pursuing its own good and striving to reach the sea, or that the 'good' of a guided missile is to blow itself up along with its target. It is misleading of Schweitzer to attempt to sway us towards an ethic of reverence for all life by referring to 'yearning', 'exaltation', 'pleasure', and 'terror'. Plants experience none of these.

Moreover, in the case of plants, rivers, and guided missiles, it is possible to give a purely physical explanation of what is happening; and in the absence of consciousness, there is no good reason why we should have greater respect for the physical processes that govern the growth and decay of living things than we have for those that govern non-living things. This being so, it is at least not obvious why we should have greater reverence for a tree than for a stalactite, or for a single-celled organism than for a mountain.

DEEP ECOLOGY

More than forty years ago the American ecologist Aldo Leopold wrote that there was a need for a 'new ethic', an 'ethic dealing with man's relation to land and to the animals and plants which grow upon it'. His proposed 'land ethic' would enlarge 'the boundaries of the community to include soils, waters, plants, and animals, or collectively, the land'. The rise of ecological concern in the early 1970s led to a revival of interest in this attitude. The Norwegian philosopher Arne Naess wrote a brief but influential article distinguishing between 'shallow' and 'deep' strands in the ecological movement. Shallow ecological thinking was limited to the traditional moral framework; those who thought in this way were anxious to avoid pollution to our water supply so that we could have safe water to drink, and they sought to preserve wilderness so that people could continue to enjoy walking through it. Deep ecologists, on the other hand, wanted to preserve the integrity of the biosphere for its own sake, irrespective of the possible benefits to humans that might flow from so doing. Subsequently several other writers have attempted to develop some form of 'deep' environmental theory.

Where the reverence for life ethic emphasises individual living organisms, proposals for deep ecology ethics tend to take something larger as the object of value: species, ecological systems, even the biosphere as a whole. Leopold summed up the basis of his new land ethic thus: 'A thing is right when it tends to preserve the integrity, stability and beauty of the biotic community. It is wrong when it tends otherwise.' In a paper published in 1984, Arne Naess and George Sessions, an American philosopher involved in the deep ecology movement, set out several principles for a deep ecological ethic, beginning with the following:

1 The well-being and flourishing of human and non-human Life on Earth have value in themselves (synonyms: intrinsic value, inherent value). These values are independent of the useful-ness of the non-human world for human purposes.
2 Richness and diversity of life forms contribute to the realisation of these values and are also values in themselves.
3 Humans have no right to reduce this richness and diversity except to satisfy *vital* needs.

Although these principles refer only to life, in the same paper Naess and Sessions say that deep ecology uses the term 'bio-sphere' in a more comprehensive way, to refer also to non-living things such as rivers (watersheds), landscapes, and ecosystems. Two Australians working at the deep end of en-vironmental ethics, Richard Sylvan and Val Plumwood, also extend their ethic beyond living things, including in it an ob-ligation 'not to jeopardise the well-being of natural objects or systems without good reason'.

In the previous section I quoted Paul Taylor's remark to the effect that we should be ready not merely to respect every living thing, but to place the same value on the life of every living thing as we place on our own. This is a common theme among deep ecologists, often extended beyond living things. In *Deep Ecology* Bill Devall and George Sessions defend a form of 'bio-centric egalitarianism':

The intuition of biocentric equality is that all things in the bio-sphere have an equal right to live and blossom and to reach their own individual forms of unfolding and self-realisation within the larger Self-realisation. This basic intuition is that all organisms and entities in the ecosphere, as parts of the interrelated whole, are equal in intrinsic worth.

If, as this quotation appears to suggest, this biocentric equality rests on a 'basic intuition', it is up against some strong intuitions that point in the opposite direction – for example, the intuition that the rights to 'live and blossom' of normal adult humans ought to be preferred over those of yeasts, and the rights of gorillas over those of grasses. If, however, the point is that humans, gorillas, yeasts, and grasses are all parts of an inter-related whole, then it can still be asked how this establishes that they are equal in intrinsic worth. Is it because every living thing plays its role in an ecosystem on which all depend for their survival? But, firstly, even if this showed that there is intrinsic worth in micro-organisms and plants *as a whole*, it says nothing at all about the value of individual micro-organisms or plants, since no individual is necessary for the survival of the ecosystem as a whole. Secondly, the fact that all organisms are part of an interrelated whole does not suggest that they are all of *intrinsic* worth, let alone of equal intrinsic worth. They may be of worth only because they are needed for the existence of the whole, and the whole may be of worth only because it supports the existence of conscious beings.

The ethics of deep ecology thus fail to yield persuasive answers to questions about the value of the lives of individual living beings. Perhaps, though, this is the wrong kind of question to ask. As the science of ecology looks at systems rather than individual organisms, so ecological ethics might be more plausible if applied at a higher level, perhaps at the level of species and ecosystems. Behind many attempts to derive values from ecological ethics at this level lies some form of holism − some sense that the species or ecosystem is not just a collection of individuals, but really an entity in its own right. This holism is made explicit in Lawrence Johnson's *A Morally Deep World*. Johnson is quite prepared to talk about the interests of a species, in a sense that is distinct from the sum of the interests of each member of the species, and to argue that the interests of a species, or an ecosystem, ought to be taken into account, along-side individual interests, in our moral deliberations. In *The Ecological Self*, Freya Mathews contends that any 'self-realising system' has intrinsic value in that it seeks to maintain or preserve itself. While living organisms are paradigm examples of self-realising systems, Mathews, like Johnson, includes species and ecosystems as holistic entities or selves with their own form of realisation. She even includes the entire global ecosystem, following James Lovelock in referring to it by the name of the Greek goddess of the earth, Gaia. On this basis she defends her own form of biocentric egalitarianism.

There is, of course, a real philosophical question about whether a species or an ecosystem can be considered as the sort of individual that can have interests, or a 'self' to be realised; and even if it can, the deep ecology ethic will face problems similar to those we identified in considering the idea of reverence for life. For it is necessary, not merely that trees, species, and ecosystems can properly be said to have interests, but that they have morally significant interests. If they are to be regarded as 'selves' it will need to be shown that the survival or realisation of that kind of self has moral value, independently of the value it has because of its importance in sustaining conscious life.

We saw in discussing the ethic of reverence for life that one way of establishing that an interest is morally significant is to ask what it is like for the entity affected to have that interest unsatisfied. The same question can be asked about self-realisation: what is it like *for the self* to remain unrealised? Such questions yield intelligible answers when asked of sentient beings, but not when asked of trees, species, or ecosystems. The fact that, as James Lovelock points out in *Gaia: A New Look at Life on Earth*, the biosphere can respond to events in ways that resemble a self-maintaining system, does not in itself show that the biosphere consciously desires to maintain itself. Calling the global ecosystem by the name of a Greek goddess seems a nice idea, but it may not be the best way of helping us to think clearly about its nature. Similarly, on a smaller scale, there is nothing that corresponds to what it feels like to be an ecosystem flooded by a dam, because there is no such feeling. In this respect trees, ecosystems, and species are more like rocks than they are like sentient beings; so the divide between sentient and non-sentient creatures is to that extent a firmer basis for a morally important boundary than the divide between living and non-living things, or between holistic entities and any other entities that we might not regard as holistic. (Whatever these other entities could be: even a single atom is, when seen from the appropriate level, a complex system that 'seeks' to maintain itself.)

This rejection of the ethical basis for a deep ecology ethic does not mean that the case for the preservation of wilderness is not strong. All it means is that one kind of argument – the argument from the intrinsic value of the plants, species, or ecosystems – is, at best, problematic. Unless it can be placed on a different, and firmer footing, we should confine ourselves to arguments based on the interests of sentient creatures, present and future, human and non-human. These arguments are quite sufficient to show that, at least in a society where no one needs to destroy wilderness in order to obtain food for survival or materials for shelter from the elements, the value of preserving the remaining significant areas of wilderness greatly exceeds the economic values gained by its destruction.

DEVELOPING AN ENVIRONMENTAL ETHIC

In the long run, the set of ethical virtues praised and the set of ethical prohibitions adopted by the ethic of specific societies will always reflect the conditions under which they must live and work in order to survive. That statement is close to being a tautology, because if a society's ethic did not take into account whatever was needed for survival, the society would cease to exist. Many of the ethical standards that we accept today can be explained in these terms. Some are universal and can be expected to be beneficial to the community in virtually any conditions in which humans live. Obviously a society in which members of the community are permitted to kill each other with impunity would not last long. Conversely, the parental virtues of caring for children, and other virtues like honesty, or loyalty to the group, would foster a stable and lasting community. Other prohibitions may reflect specific conditions: the practice among the Eskimo of killing elderly parents no longer able to fend for themselves, is often cited as a necessary response to life in a very harsh climate. No doubt the slow pace of changing climatic conditions, or of migration to different regions, allowed time for systems of ethics to make the necessary adjustment.

Now we face a new threat to our survival. The proliferation of human beings, coupled with the by-products of economic growth, is just as capable as the old threats of wiping out our society – and every other society as well. No ethic has yet developed to cope with this threat. Some ethical principles that we do have are exactly the opposite of what we need. The problem is that, as we have already seen, ethical principles change slowly and the time we have left to develop a new environmental ethic is short. Such an ethic would regard every action that is harmful to the environment as ethically dubious, and those that are unnecessarily harmful as plainly wrong. That is the serious point behind my remark in the first chapter that the moral issues raised by driving a car are more serious than those raised by sexual behaviour. An environmental ethic would find virtue in saving and recycling resources, and vice in extravagance and unnecessary consumption. To take just one example: from the perspective of an environmental ethic, our choice of recreation is not ethically neutral. At present we see the choice between motor car racing or cycling, between water skiing or windsurfing, as merely a matter of taste. Yet there is an essential difference: motor car racing and water skiing require the consumption of fossil fuels and the discharge of carbon dioxide into the atmosphere. Cycling and windsurfing do not. Once we take the need to preserve our environment seriously, motor racing and water skiing will no more be an acceptable form of entertainment than bear-baiting is today.

The broad outlines of a truly environmental ethic are easy to discern. At its most fundamental level, such an ethic fosters consideration for the interests of all sentient creatures, including subsequent generations stretching into the far future. It is accompanied by an aesthetic of appreciation for wild places and unspoiled nature. At a more detailed level, applicable to the lives of dwellers in cities and towns, it discourages large families. (Here it forms a sharp contrast to some existing ethical beliefs that are relics of an age in which the earth was far more lightly populated; it also offers a counterweight to the implication of the 'total' version of utilitarianism discussed in Chapter 4.) An environmental ethic rejects the ideals of a materialist society in which success is gauged by the number of consumer goods one can accumulate. Instead it judges success in terms of the development of one's abilities and the achievement of real fulfilment and satisfaction. It promotes frugality, in so far as that is necessary for minimising pollution and ensuring that everything that can be re-used is re-used. Carelessly to throw out material that can be recycled is a form of vandalism or the theft of our common property in the resources of the world. Thus the various 'green consumer' guides and books about things we can do to save our planet – recycling what we use and buying the most environmentally friendly products available – are part of the new ethic that is required. Even they may prove to be only an interim solution, a stepping-stone to an ethic in which the very idea of consuming unnecessary products is questioned. Wind-surfing may be better than water-skiing, but if we keep on buying new boards in order to be up to date with the latest trends in board and sail designs, the difference is only marginal.

We must re-assess our notion of extravagance. In a world under pressure, this concept is not confined to chauffeured limousines and Dom Perignon champagne. Timber that has come from a rainforest is extravagant, because the long-term value of the rainforest is far greater than the uses to which the timber is put. Disposable paper products are extravagant, because ancient hardwood forests are being converted into wood-chips and sold to paper manufacturers. 'Going for a drive in the country' is an extravagant use of fossil fuels that contributes to the greenhouse effect. During the Second World War, when petrol was scarce, posters asked: 'Is your journey really necessary?' The appeal to national solidarity against a visible and immediate danger was highly effective. The danger to our environment is less immediate and much harder to see, but the need to cut out unnecessary journeys and other forms of unnecessary consumption is just as great.

As far as food is concerned, the great extravagance is not caviar or truffles, but beef, pork, and poultry. Some 38 per cent of the world's grain crop is now fed to animals, as well as large quantities of soybeans. There are three times as many domestic animals on this planet as there are human beings. The combined weight of the world's 1.28 billion cattle alone exceeds that of the human population. While we look darkly at the number of babies being born in poorer parts of the world, we ignore the over-population of farm animals, to which we ourselves contribute. The prodigious waste of grain that is fed to intensively farmed animals has already been mentioned in Chapters 3 and 8. That, however, is only part of the damage done by the animals we deliberately breed. The energy-intensive factory farming methods of the industrialised nations are responsible for the consumption of huge amounts of fossil fuels. Chemical fertilisers, used to grow the feed crops for cattle in feedlots and pigs and chickens kept indoors in sheds, produce nitrous oxide, another greenhouse gas. Then there is the loss of forests. Everywhere, forest dwellers, both human and non-human, are being pushed out. Since 1960, 25 per cent of the forests of Central America have been cleared for cattle. Once cleared, the poor soils will support grazing for a few years; then the graziers must move on. Scrub takes over the abandoned pasture, but the forest does not return. When the forests are cleared so that cattle can graze, billions of tons of carbon dioxide are released into the atmosphere. Finally, the world's cattle are thought to produce about 20 per cent of the methane released into the atmosphere, and methane traps twenty-five times as much heat from the sun as carbon dioxide. Factory farm manure also produces methane because, unlike manured dropped naturally in the fields, it does not decompose in the presence of oxygen. All of this amounts to a compelling reason, additional to that developed in Chapter 3, for a largely plant-based diet.

The emphasis on frugality and a simple life does not mean that an environmental ethic frowns upon pleasure, but that the pleasures it values do not come from conspicuous consumption. They come, instead, from warm personal and sexual relationships, from being close to children and friends, from conversation, from sports and recreations that are in harmony with our environment instead of being harmful to it; from food that is not based on the exploitation of sentient creatures and does not cost the earth; from creative activity and work of all kinds; and (with due care so as not to ruin precisely what is valued) from appreciating the unspoiled places in the world in which we live.

11

ENDS AND MEANS

WE have examined a number of ethical issues. We have seen that many accepted practices are open to serious objections. What ought we to do about it? This, too, is an ethical issue. Here are four actual cases to consider.

Oskar Schindler was a German industrialist. During the war he ran a factory near Cracow, in Poland. At a time when Polish Jews were being sent to death camps, he assembled a labour force of Jewish inmates from concentration camps and the ghetto, considerably larger than his factory needed, and used several illegal strategems, including bribing members of the SS and other officials, to protect them. He spent his own money to buy food on the black market to supplement the inadequate official rations he obtained for his workers. By these methods he was able to save the lives of about 1,200 people.

In 1984 Dr Thomas Gennarelli directed a Head Injury Laboratory at the University of Pennsylvania, in Philadelphia. Members of an underground organisation called the Animal Liberation Front knew that Gennarelli inflicted head injuries on monkeys there and had been told that the monkeys underwent the experiments without being properly anaesthetised. They also knew that Gennarelli and his collaborators video-taped their experiments, to provide a record of what happened during and after the injuries they inflicted. They tried to obtain further information through official channels but were unsuccessful. In May 1984, they broke into the laboratory at night and found thirty-four videotapes. They then systematically destroyed laboratory equipment before leaving with the tapes. The tapes clearly showed conscious monkeys struggling as they were being strapped to an operating table where head injuries were inflicted; they also showed experimenters mocking and laughing at frightened animals about to be used in experiments. When an edited version of the tapes was released to the public, it produced widespread revulsion. Nevertheless, it took a further year of protests, culminating in a sit-in at the headquarters of the government organisation that was funding Gennarelli's experiments, before the U.S. Secretary of Health and Human Services ordered the experiments stopped.

In 1986 Joan Andrews entered an abortion clinic in Pensacola, Florida, and damaged a suction abortion apparatus. She refused to be represented in court, on the grounds that 'the true defendants, the pre-born children, received none, and were killed without due process'. Andrews was a supporter of Operation Rescue, an American organisation that takes its name, and its authority to act, from the biblical injunction to 'rescue those who are drawn toward death and hold back those stumbling to the slaughter'. Operation Rescue uses civil disobedience to shut down abortion clinics, thus, in its view, 'sparing the lives of unborn babies whom the Rescuers are morally pledged to defend'. Participants block the doors of the clinics to prevent physicians and pregnant women seeking abortion from entering. They attempt to dissuade pregnant women from approaching the clinic by 'sidewalk counselling' on the nature of abortion. Gary Leber, an Operation Rescue director, has said that, between 1987 and 1989 alone, as a direct result of such 'rescue missions', at least 421 women changed their minds about having abortions, and the children of these women, who would have been killed, are alive today.

In 1976 Bob Brown, then a young medical practitioner, rafted down the Franklin river, in Tasmania's southwest. The wild beauty of the river and the peace of the undisturbed forests around it impressed him deeply. Then, around a bend on the lower reaches of the river, he came across workers for the Hydro-Electric Commission, studying the feasibility of building a dam across the river. Brown gave up his medical practice and founded the Tasmanian Wilderness Society, with the object of protecting the state's remaining wilderness areas. Despite vigorous campaigning, the Hydro-Electric Commission recommended the building of the dam, and after some vacillation the state government, with support both from the business community and the labour unions, decided to go ahead. The Tasmanian Wilderness Society organized a non-violent blockade of the road being built to the dam site. In 1982, Brown, along with many others, was arrested and jailed for four days for trespassing on land controlled by the Hydro-Electric Commission. But the blockade became a focus of national attention, and although the Australian federal government was not directly responsible for the dam, it became an issue in the federal election that was then due. The Australian Labor Party, in opposition before the election, pledged to explore constitutional means of preventing the dam from going ahead. The election saw the Labor party elected to office, and legislation passed to stop the dam. Though challenged by the Tasmanian government, the legislation was upheld by a narrow majority of the High Court of Australia on the grounds that the Tasmanian southwest was a World Heritage area, and the federal government had constitutional powers to uphold the international treaty creating the World Heritage Commission. Today the Franklin still runs free.

Do we have an overriding obligation to obey the law? Oskar Schindler, the members of the Animal Liberation Front who took Gennarelli's videotapes, Joan Andrews of Operation Rescue, and Bob Brown and those who joined him in front of the bulldozers in Tasmania's southwest were all breaking the law. Were they all acting wrongly?

The question cannot be dealt with by invoking the simplistic formula: 'the end never justifies the means'. For all but the strictest adherent of an ethic of rules, the end sometimes does justify the means. Most people think that lying is wrong, other things being equal, yet think it right to lie in order to avoid causing unnecessary offence or embarrassment – for instance, when a well-meaning relative gives you a hideous vase for your birthday, and then asks if you really like it. If this relatively trivial end can justify lying, it is even more obvious that some important end – preventing a murder, or saving animals from great suffering – can justify lying. Thus the principle that the end cannot justify the means is easily breached. The difficult issue is not whether the end can ever justify the means, but which means are justified by which ends.

INDIVIDUAL CONSCIENCE AND THE LAW

There are many people who are opposed to damming wild rivers, to the exploitation of animals, or to abortion, but who do not break the law in order to stop these activities. No doubt some members of the more conventional conservation, animal liberation, and anti-abortion organizations do not commit illegal acts because they do not wish to be fined or imprisoned; but others would be prepared to take the consequences of illegal acts. They refrain only because they respect and obey the moral authority of the law.

Who is right in this ethical disagreement? Are we under any moral obligation to obey the law, if the law protects and sanctions things we hold utterly wrong? A clear-cut answer to this question was given by the nineteenth-century American radical,

Henry Thoreau. In his essay entitled 'Civil Disobedience' – perhaps the first use of this now-familiar phrase – he wrote:

> Must the citizen ever for a moment, or in the least degree, resign his conscience to the legislator? Why has every man a conscience, then? I think we should be men first and subjects afterwards. It is not desirable to cultivate a respect for the law, so much as for the right. The only obligation which I have a right to assume, is to do at any time what I think right.

The American philosopher Robert Paul Wolff has written in similar vein:

> The defining mark of the state is authority, the right to rule. The primary obligation of man is autonomy, the refusal to be ruled, It would seem, then, that there can be no resolution of the conflict between the autonomy of the individual and the putative authority of the state. Insofar as a man fulfills his obligation to make himself the author of his decisions, he will resist the state's claim to have authority over him.

Thoreau and Wolff resolve the conflict between individual and society in favour of the individual. We should do as our conscience dictates, as we autonomously decide we ought to do: not as the law directs. Anything else would be a denial of our capacity for ethical choice.

Thus stated, the issue looks straightforward and the Thoreau-Wolff answer obviously right. So Oskar Schindler, the Animal Liberation Front, Joan Andrews, and Bob Brown were fully justified in doing what they saw to be right, rather than what the state laid down as lawful. But is it that simple? There is a sense in which it is undeniable that, as Thoreau says, we ought to do what we think right; or, as Wolff puts it, make ourselves the authors of our decisions. Faced with a choice between doing what we think right and what we think wrong, of course we ought to do what we think right. But this, though true, is not much help. What we need to know is not whether we should do what we decide to be right, but how we should decide what is right.

Think about the difference of opinion between members of groups like the Animal Liberation Front (ALF) and more law-abiding members of an organization like Britain's Royal Society for the Prevention of Cruelty to Animals (RSPCA): ALF members think inflicting pain on animals is, unless justified by extraordinary circumstances, wrong, and if the best way to stop it is by breaking the law then they think that breaking the law is right. RSPCA members – let us assume – also think that inflicting pain on animals is normally wrong, but they think breaking the law is wrong, too, and they think that the wrongness of breaking the law cannot be justified by the goal of stopping the unjustifiable infliction of pain on animals. Now suppose there are people opposed to inflicting pain on animals who are uncertain whether they should join the militant lawbreakers or the more orthodox animal welfare group. How does telling these people to do what they think right, or to be the author of their own decisions, resolve their uncertainty? The uncertainty is an uncertainty about what is the right thing to do, not about whether to do what one has decided to be right.

This point can be obscured by talk of 'following one's conscience' irrespective of what the law commands. Some who talk of 'following conscience' mean no more than doing what, on reflection, one thinks right – and this may, as in the case of our imagined RSPCA members, depend on what the law commands. Others mean by 'conscience' not something dependent on critical reflective judgment, but a kind of internal voice that tells us that something is wrong and may continue to tell us this despite our careful reflective decision, based on all the relevant ethical considerations, that the action is not wrong. In this sense of 'conscience' an unmarried woman brought up as a strict Roman Catholic to believe that sex outside marriage is always wrong may abandon her religion and come to hold that there is no sound basis for restricting sex to marriage – yet continue to feel guilty when she has sex. She may refer to these guilt feelings as her 'conscience' but if that is her conscience, should she follow it?

To say that we should follow our conscience is unobjectionable – and unhelpful – when 'following conscience' means doing what, on reflection, one thinks right. When 'following conscience' means doing as one's 'internal voice' prompts one to do, however, to follow one's conscience is to abdicate one's responsibility as a rational agent, to fail to take all the relevant factors into account and act on one's best judgment of the rights and wrongs of the situation. The 'internal voice' is more likely to be a product of one's upbringing and education than a source of genuine ethical insight.

Presumably neither Thoreau nor Wolff wish to suggest that we should always follow our conscience in the 'internal voice' sense. They must mean, if their views are to be at all plausible, that we should follow our judgment about what we ought to do. In this case the most that can be said for their recommendations is that they remind us that decisions about obeying the law are ethical decisions that the law itself cannot settle for us. We should not assume, without reflection, that if the law prohibits, say, stealing videotapes from laboratories, it is always wrong to do so – any more than we should assume that if the law prohibits hiding Jews from the Nazis, it is wrong to do so. Law and ethics are distinct. At the same time, this does not mean that the law carries no moral weight. It does not mean that any action that would have been right if it had been legal must be right although it is in fact illegal. That an action is illegal may be of ethical, as well as legal, significance. Whether it really is ethically significant is a separate question.

LAW AND ORDER

If we think that a practice is seriously wrong, and if we have the courage and ability to disrupt this practice by breaking the law, how could the illegality of this action provide an ethical reason against it? To answer a question as specific as this, we should first ask a more general one: why have laws at all?

Human beings are social in nature, but not so social that we do not need to protect ourselves against the risk of being assaulted or killed by our fellow humans. We might try to do this by forming vigilante organizations to prevent assaults and punish those who commit them; but the results would be haphazard and liable to grow into gang warfare. Thus it is desirable to have, as John Locke said long ago, 'an established, settled, known law', interpreted by an authoritative judge and backed with sufficient power to carry out the judge's decisions.

If people voluntarily refrained from assaulting others, or acting in other ways inimical to a harmonious and happy social existence, we might manage without judges and sanctions. We would still need law-like conventions about such matters as which side of the road one drives on. Even an anarchist utopia would have some settled principles of cooperation. So we would have something rather like law. In reality, not everyone is going to voluntarily refrain from behaviour, like assaults, that others cannot tolerate. Nor is it only the danger of individual acts like assaults that make law necessary. In any society there will be disputes: about how much water farmers may take from the river to irrigate their crops, about the ownership of land, or the custody of a child, about the control of pollution, and the level of taxation. Some settled decision-procedure is necessary for resolving such disputes economically and speedily, or else the parties to the dispute are likely to resort to force. Almost any established decision-procedure is better than a resort to force, for when force is used people get hurt. Moreover, most decision-procedures produce results at least as beneficial and just as a resort to force.

So laws and a settled decision-procedure to generate them are a good thing. This gives rise to one important reason for obeying the law. By obeying the law, I can contribute to the respect in which the established decision-procedure and the laws are held. By disobeying I set an example to others that may lead them to disobey too. The effect may multiply and contribute to a decline in law and order. In an extreme case it may lead to civil war.

A second reason for obedience follows immediately from this first. If law is to be effective – outside the anarchist's utopia – there must be some machinery for detecting and penalizing law-breakers. This machinery will cost something to maintain and operate, and the cost will have to be met by the community. If I break the law the community will be put to the expense of enforcement.

These two reasons for obeying the law are neither universally applicable nor conclusive. They are not, for instance, applicable to breaches of the law that remain secret. If, late at night when the streets are deserted, I cross the road against the red light, there is no one to be led into disobedience by my example, and no one to enforce the law against so crossing. But this is not the kind of illegality we are interested in.

Where they are applicable, these two reasons for obedience are not conclusive, because there are times when the reasons against obeying a particular law are more important than the risks of encouraging others to disobey or the costs to the community of enforcing the law. They are genuine reasons for obeying, and in the absence of reasons for disobeying, are sufficient to resolve the issue in favour of obedience; but where there are conflicting reasons, we must assess each case on its merits in order to see if the reasons for disobeying outweigh these reasons for obedience. If, for instance, illegal acts were the only way of preventing many painful experiments on animals, of saving significant areas of wilderness, or of prodding governments into increasing overseas aid, the importance of the ends would justify running some risk of contributing to a general decline in obedience to law.

DEMOCRACY

At this point some will say: the difference between Oskar Schindler's heroic deeds and the indefensible illegal actions of the Animal Liberation Front, Operation Rescue, and the opponents of the Franklin dam is that in Nazi Germany there were no legal channels that Schindler could use to bring about change. In a democracy there are legal means of ending abuses. The existence of legal procedures for changing the law makes the use of illegal means unjustifiable.

It is true that in democratic societies there are legal procedures that can be used by those seeking reforms; but this in itself does not show that the use of illegal means is wrong. Legal channels may exist, but the prospects of using them to bring about change in the foreseeable future may be very poor. While one makes slow and painful progress – or perhaps no progress at all – through these legal channels, the indefensible wrongs one is trying to stop will be continuing. Prior to the successful struggle to save the Franklin River, an earlier political campaign had been fought against another dam proposed by the Tasmanian Hydro-Electric Commission. This dam was opposed because it would flood a pristine alpine lake, Lake Peddar, situated in a national park. This campaign employed more orthodox political tactics. It failed, and Lake Peddar disappeared under the waters of the dam. Dr Thomas Gennarelli's laboratory had carried out experiments for several years before the Animal Liberation Front raided it. Without the evidence of the stolen videotapes, it would probably still be functioning today. Similarly, Operation Rescue was founded after fourteen years of more conventional political action had failed to reverse the permissive legal situation regarding abortion that has existed in the United States since the Supreme Court declared restrictive abortion laws unconstitutional in 1973. During that period, according to Operation Rescue's Gary Leber, 'twenty-five million Americans have been "legally" killed'. From this perspective it is easy to see why the existence of legal channels for change does not solve the moral dilemma. An extremely remote possibility of legal change is not a strong reason against using means more likely to succeed. The most that can follow from the mere existence of legitimate channels is that, since we cannot know whether they will prove successful until we have tried them, their existence is a reason for postponing illegal acts until legal means have been tried and have failed.

Here the upholder of democratic laws can try another tack: if legal means fail to bring about reform, it shows that the proposed reform does not have the approval of the majority of the electorate; and to attempt to implement the reform by illegal means against the wishes of the majority would be a violation of the central principle of democracy, majority rule.

The militant can challenge this argument on two grounds, one factual and the other philosophical. The factual claim in the democrat's argument is that a reform that cannot be implemented by legal means lacks the approval of the majority of the electorate. Perhaps this would hold in a direct democracy, in which the whole electorate voted on each issue; but it is certainly not always true of modern representative democracies. There is no way of ensuring that on any given issue a majority of representatives will take the same view as a majority of their constituents. One can be reasonably confident that a majority of those Americans who saw, on television, excerpts from Gennarelli's videotapes would not have supported the experiments. But that is not how decisions are made in a democracy. In choosing between representatives – or in choosing between political parties – voters elect to take one 'package deal' in preference to other package deals on offer. It will often happen that in order to vote for policies they favour, voters must go along with other policies they are not keen on. It will also happen that policies voters favour are not offered by any major party. In the case of abortion in the United States, the crucial decision was not made by a majority of voters, but by the Supreme Court.

It cannot be overturned by a simple majority of the electors, but only by the Court itself, or by the complicated procedure of a constitutional amendment, which can be thwarted by a minority of the electorate.

What if a majority did approve of the wrong that the militants wish to stop? Would it then be wrong to use illegal means? Here we have the philosophical claim underlying the democratic argument for obedience, the claim that we ought to accept the majority decision.

The case for majority rule should not be overstated. No sensible democrat would claim that the majority is always right. If 49 per cent of the population can be wrong, so can 51 per cent. Whether the majority supports the views of the Animal Liberation Front or of Operation Rescue does not settle the question whether these views are morally sound.Perhaps the fact that these groups are in a minority – if they are – means that they should reconsider their means. With a majority behind them, they could claim to be acting with democratic principles on their side, using illegal means to overcome flaws in the democratic machinery. Without that majority, all the weight of democratic tradition is against them and it is they who appear as coercers, trying to force the majority into accepting something against its will. But how much moral weight should we give to democratic principles?

Thoreau, as we might expect, was not impressed by majority decision making. 'All voting,' he wrote, 'is a sort of gaming, like checkers or backgammon, with a slight moral tinge to it, a playing with right and wrong, with moral questions.' In a sense Thoreau was right. If we reject, as we must, the doctrine that the majority is always right, to submit moral issues to the vote is to gamble that what we believe to be right will come out of the ballot with more votes behind it than what we believe to be wrong; and that is a gamble we will often lose.

Nevertheless we should not be too contemptuous about voting, or gambling either. Cowboys who agree to play poker to decide matters of honour do better than cowboys who continue to settle such matters in the traditional Western manner. A society that decides its controversial issues by ballots does better than one that uses bullets. To some extent this is a point we have already encountered, under the heading 'law and order'. It applies to any society with an established, peaceful method of resolving disputes; but in a democracy there is a subtle difference that gives added weight to the outcome of the decision-procedure. A method of settling disputes in which no one has greater ultimate power than anyone else is a method that can be recommended to all as a fair compromise between competing claims to power. Any other method must give greater power to some than to others and thereby invites opposition from those who have less. That, at least, is true in the egalitarian age in which we live. In a feudal society in which people accept as natural and proper their status as lord or vassal there is no challenge to the feudal lord and no compromise would be needed. (I am thinking of an ideal feudal system, as I am thinking of an ideal democracy.) Those times, however, seem to be gone forever. The breakdown of traditional authority created a need for political compromise. Among possible compromises, giving one vote to each person is uniquely acceptable to all. As such, in the absence of any agreed procedure for deciding on some other distribution of power, it offers, in principle, the firmest possible basis for a peaceful method of settling disputes.

To reject majority rule, therefore, is to reject the best possible basis for the peaceful ordering of society in an egalitarian age. Where else should one turn? To a meritocratic franchise, with extra votes for the more intelligent or better educated, as John Stuart Mill once proposed? But could we agree on who merits extra votes? To a benevolent despot? Many would accept that – if they could choose the despot. In practice the likely outcome of abandoning majority rule is none of these: it is the rule of those who command the greatest force.

So the principle of majority rule does carry substantial moral weight. Disobedience is easier to justify in a dictatorship like Nazi Germany than in a democracy like those of North America, Europe, India, Japan, or Australia today. In a democracy we should be reluctant to take any action that amounts to an attempt to coerce the majority, for such attempts imply the rejection of majority rule and there is no acceptable alternative to that. There may, of course, be cases where the majority decision is so appalling that coercion is justified, whatever the risk. The obligation to obey a genuine majority decision is not absolute. We show our respect for the principle not by blind obedience to the majority, but by regarding ourselves as justified in disobeying only in extreme circumstances.

DISOBEDIENCE, CIVIL OR OTHERWISE

If we draw together our conclusions on the use of illegal means to achieve laudable ends, we shall find that: (1) there are reasons why we should normally accept the verdict of an established peaceful method of settling disputes; (2) these reasons are particularly strong when the decision-procedure is democratic and the verdict represents a genuine majority view; but (3) there are still situations in which the use of illegal means can be justified.

We have seen that there are two distinct ways in which one might try to justify the use of illegal means in a society that is democratic (even if imperfectly so, as, to varying degrees, existing democracies are). The first is on the grounds that the decision one is objecting to is not a genuine expression of majority opinion. The second is that although the decision is a genuine expression of the majority view, this view is so seriously wrong that action against the majority is justified.

It is disobedience on the first ground that best merits the name 'civil disobedience'. Here the use of illegal means can be regarded as an extension of the use of legal means to secure a genuinely democratic decision. The extension may be necessary because the normal channels for securing reform are not working properly. On some issues parliamentary representatives are overly influenced by skilled and well-paid special interests. On others the public is unaware of what is happening. Perhaps the abuse requires administrative, rather than legislative change, and the bureaucrats of the civil service have refused to be inconvenienced. Perhaps the legitimate interests of a minority are being ignored by prejudiced officials. In all these cases, the now-standard forms of civil disobedience – passive resistance, marches, or sit-ins – are appropriate. The blockade of the Hydro-Electric Commission's road into the site of the proposed Franklin river dam was a classic case of civil disobedience in this sense.

In these situations disobeying the law is not an attempt to coerce the majority. Instead disobedience attempts to inform the majority; or to persuade parliamentarians that large numbers of electors feel very strongly about the issue; or to draw national attention to an issue previously left to bureaucrats; or to appeal for reconsideration of a decision too hastily made. Civil disobedience is an appropriate means to these ends when legal means have failed, because, although it is illegal, it does not threaten the majority or attempt to coerce them (though it will usually impose some extra costs on them, for example for law enforcement). By not resisting the force of the law, by remaining non-violent and by accepting the legal penalty for their actions, civil disobedients make manifest both the sincerity of their protest and their respect for the rule of law and the fundamental principles of democracy.

So conceived, civil disobedience is not difficult to justify. The justification does not have to be strong enough to override the obligation to obey a democratic decision, since disobedience is an attempt to restore, rather than frustrate, the process of democratic decision making. Disobedience of this kind could be justified by, for instance, the aim of making the public aware of the loss of irreplaceable wilderness caused by the construction of a dam, or of how animals are treated in the laboratories and factory farms that few people ever see.

The use of illegal means to prevent action undeniably in accordance with the majority view is harder — but not impossible — to justify. We may think it unlikely that a Nazi-style policy of genocide could ever be approved by a majority vote, but if that were to happen it would be carrying respect for majority rule to absurd lengths to regard oneself as bound to accept the majority decision. To oppose evils of that magnitude, we are justified in using virtually any means likely to be effective.

Genocide is an extreme case. To grant that it justifies the use of illegal means even against a majority concedes very little in terms of practical political action. Yet admitting even one exception to the obligation to abide by democratic decisions raises further questions: where is the line to be drawn between evils like genocide, where the obligation is clearly overridden, and less serious issues, where it is not? And who is to decide on which side of this imaginary line a particular issue falls? Gary Leber, of Operation Rescue, has written that in the United States alone, since 1973, 'We've already destroyed four times the number of people that Hitler did.' Ronnie Lee, one of the British founders of the Animal Liberation Front, has also used the Nazi metaphor for what we do to animals, saying: 'Although we are only one species among many on earth, we've set up a *Reich* totally dominating the other animals, even enslaving them.' It is not surprising then, that these activists consider their disobedience well justified. But do they have the right to take this decision themselves? If not, who is to decide when an issue is so serious that, even in a democracy, the obligation to obey the law is overridden?

The only answer this question can have is: we must decide for ourselves on which side of the line particular cases fall. There is no other way of deciding, since the society's method of settling issues has already made its decision. The majority cannot be judge in its own case. If we think the majority decision wrong, we must make up our own minds about how gravely it is wrong.

This does not mean that any decision we make on such an issue is subjective or arbitrary. In this book, I have offered arguments about a number of moral issues. If we apply these arguments to the four cases with which this chapter began, they lead to specific conclusions. The racist Nazi policy of murdering Jews was obviously an atrocity, and Oskar Schindler was entirely right to do what he could to save some Jews from falling victim to it. (Given the personal risks he ran, he was also morally heroic to do so.) On the basis of the arguments put forward in Chapter 3 of this book, the experiments that Gennarelli conducted on monkeys were wrong, because they treated sentient creatures as mere things to be used as research tools. To stop such experiments is a desirable goal, and if breaking in to Gennarelli's laboratory and stealing his videotapes was the only way to achieve it, that seems to me justifiable. Similarly, for reasons explored in Chapter 10, to drown the Franklin valley in order to generate a relatively small amount of electricity could only have been based on values that were unjustifiable both for taking a short-term perspective, and for being overly human-centred. Civil disobedience was an appropriate means of testifying to the importance of the values that had been overlooked by those who favoured the dam.

At the same time, the arguments that lie behind Operation Rescue's activities were found to be flawed when they were examined in Chapter 6. The human fetus is not entitled to the same sort of protection as older human beings, and so those who think of abortion as morally equivalent to murder are wrong. On this basis, Operation Rescue's campaign of civil disobedience against abortion is not justifiable. But it is important to realise that the mistake lies in Operation Rescue's moral reasoning about abortion, not in their moral reasoning about civil disobedience. If abortion really were morally equivalent to murder, we all ought to be out there blocking the doors to the abortion clinics.

This makes life difficult, of course. It is not likely that members of Operation Rescue will be convinced by the arguments in this book. Their reliance on biblical quotations does not augur well for their openness to moral reasoning on non-religious grounds. So there is no easy way of convincing them that their civil disobedience is unjustified. We may regret this, but there is nothing to be done about it. There is no simple moral rule that will enable us to declare when disobedience is justifiable and when it is not, without going into the rights and wrongs of the target of the disobedience.

When we are convinced that we are trying to stop something that really is a serious moral wrong, we still have other moral questions to ask ourselves. We must balance the magnitude of the evil we are trying to stop against the possibility that our actions will lead to a drastic decline in respect for law and for democracy. We must also take into account the likelihood that our actions will fail in their objective and provoke a reaction that will reduce the chances of success by other means. (As, for instance, terrorist attacks on an oppressive regime provide the government with an ideal excuse to lock up its more moderate political opponents, or violent attacks on experimenters enable the research establishment to brand all critics of animal experimentation as terrorists.)

One result of a consequentialist approach to this issue that may at first seem odd is that the more deeply ingrained the habit of obedience to democratic rule, the more easily disobedience can be defended. There is no paradox here, however, merely another instance of the homely truth that while young plants need to be cosseted, well-established specimens can take rougher treatment. Thus on a given issue disobedience might be justifiable in Britain or the United States but not in Cambodia

306

or Russia during the period when these countries seek to establish democratic systems of government.

These issues cannot be settled in general terms. Every case differs. When the evils to be stopped are neither utterly horrendous (like genocide) nor relatively harmless (like the design for a new national flag), reasonable people will differ on the justifiability of attempting to thwart the implementation of a considered decision democratically reached. Where illegal means are used with this aim, an important step has been taken, for disobedience then ceases to be 'civil disobedience', if by that term is meant disobedience that is justified by an appeal to principles that the community itself accepts as the proper way of running its affairs. It may still be best for such obedience to be civil in the other sense of the term, which makes a contrast with the use of violence or the tactics of terrorism.

VIOLENCE

As we have seen, civil disobedience intended as a means of attracting publicity or persuading the majority to reconsider is much easier to justify than disobedience intended to coerce the majority. Violence is obviously harder still to defend. Some go so far as to say that the use of violence as a means, particularly violence against people, is never justified, no matter how good the end.

Opposition to the use of violence can be on the basis of an absolute rule, or an assessment of its consequences. Pacifists have usually regarded the use of violence as absolutely wrong, irrespective of its consequences. This, like other 'no matter what' prohibitions, assumes the validity of the distinction between acts and omissions. Without this distinction, pacifists who refuse to use violence when it is the only means of preventing greater violence would be responsible for the greater violence they fail to prevent.

Suppose we have an opportunity to assassinate a tyrant who is systematically murdering his opponents and anyone else he dislikes. We know that if the tyrant dies he will be replaced by a popular opposition leader, now in exile, who will restore the rule of law. If we say that violence is always wrong, and refuse to carry out the assassination, mustn't we bear some responsibility for the tyrant's future murders?

If the objections made to the acts and omissions distinction in Chapter 7 were sound, those who do not use violence to prevent greater violence have to take responsibility for the violence they could have prevented, Thus the rejection of the acts and omissions distinction makes a crucial difference to the discussion of violence, for it opens the door to a plausible argument in defence of violence.

Marxists have often used this argument to rebut attacks on their doctrine of the need for violent revolution. In his classic indictment of the social effects of nineteenth-century capitalism, *The Condition of the Working Class in England*, Engels wrote:

> If one individual inflicts a bodily injury upon another which leads to the death of the person attacked we call it manslaughter; on the other hand, if the attacker knows beforehand that the blow will be fatal we call it murder. Murder has also been committed if society places hundreds of workers in such a position that they inevitably come to premature and unnatural ends. Their death is as violent as if they had been stabbed or shot. . . . Murder has been committed if thousands of workers have been deprived of the necessities of life or if they have been forced into a situation in which it is impossible for them to survive. . . . Murder has been committed if society knows perfectly well that thousands of workers cannot avoid being sacrificed so long as these conditions are allowed to continue. Murder of this sort is just as culpable as the murder committed by an individual. At first sight it does not appear to be murder at all because responsibility for the death of the victim cannot be pinned on any individual assailant. Everyone is responsible and yet no one is responsible, because it appears as if the victim has died from natural causes. If a worker dies no one places the responsibility for his death on society,

though some would realize that society has failed to take steps
to prevent the victim from dying. But it is murder all the same.

One might object to Engels's use of the term 'murder'. The
objection would resemble the arguments discussed in Chapter
8, when we considered whether our failure to aid the starving
makes us murderers. We saw that there is no intrinsic significance in the distinction between acts and omissions; but from
the point of view of motivation and the appropriateness of
blame, most cases of failing to prevent death are not equivalent
to murder. The same would apply to the cases Engels describes.
Engels tries to pin the blame on 'society', but 'society' is not a
person or a moral agent, and cannot be held responsible in the
way an individual can.

Still, this is nit-picking. Whether or not 'murder' is the right
term, whether or not we are prepared to describe as 'violent'
the deaths of malnourished workers in unhealthy and unsafe
factories, Engels's fundamental point stands. These deaths are
a wrong of the same order of magnitude as the deaths of
hundreds of people in a terrorist bombing would be. It would
be one-sided to say that violent revolution is always absolutely
wrong, without taking account of the evils that the revolution-
aries are trying to stop. If violent means had been the only way
of changing the conditions Engels describes, those who opposed
the use of violent means would have been responsible for the
continuation of those conditions.

Some of the practices we have been discussing in this book
are violent, either directly or by omission. In the case of non-
human animals, our treatment is often violent by any description. Those who regard the human fetus as a moral subject will
obviously consider abortion to be a violent act against it. In the
case of humans at or after birth, what are we to say of an
avoidable situation in which some countries have infant mortality rates eight times higher than others, and a person born
in one country can expect to live twenty years more than someone born in another country? Is this violence? Again, it doesn't

really matter whether we call it violence or not. In its effects it is as terrible as violence.

Absolutist condemnations of violence stand or fall with the distinction between acts and omissions. Therefore they fall. There are, however, strong consequentialist objections to the use of violence. We have been premising our discussion on the assumption that violence might be the only means of changing things for the better. Absolutists have no interest in challenging this assumption because they reject violence whether the assumption is true or false. Consequentialists must ask whether violence ever is the only means to an important end, or, if not the only means, the swiftest means. They must also ask about the long-term effects of pursuing change by violent means.

Could one defend, on consequentialist grounds, a condemnation of violence that is in practice, if not in principle, as all-encompassing as that of the absolute pacifist? One might attempt to do so by emphasising the hardening effect that the use of violence has, how committing one murder, no matter how 'necessary' or 'justified' it may seem, lessens the resistance to committing further murders. Is it likely that people who have become inured to acting violently will be able to create a better society? This is a question on which the historical record is relevant. The course taken by the Russian Revolution must shake the belief that a burning desire for social justice provides immunity to the corrupting effects of violence. There are, admittedly, other examples that may be read the other way; but it would take a considerable number of examples to outweigh the legacy of Lenin and Stalin.

The consequentialist pacifist can use another argument – the argument I urged against the suggestion that we should allow starvation to reduce the populations of the poorest nations to the level at which they could feed themselves. Like this policy, violence involves certain harm, said to be justified by the prospects of future benefits. But the future benefits can never be certain, and even in the few cases where violence does bring about desirable ends, we can rarely be sure that the ends could not have been achieved equally soon by non-violent means. What, for instance, has been achieved by the thousands of deaths and injuries caused by more than twenty years of the Irish Republican Army bombings in Northern Ireland? Only counter-terrorism by extremist Protestant groups. Or think of the wasted death and suffering caused by the Baader-Meinhoff gang in Germany, or the Red Brigade in Italy. What did the Palestinian Liberation Organization gain from terrorism, other than a less compromising, more ruthless Israel than the one against which they began their struggle? One may sympathize with the ends some of these groups are fighting for, but the means they are using hold no promise of gaining their ends. Using these means therefore indicates callous disregard of the interests of their victims. These consequentialist arguments add up to a strong case against the use of violence as a means, particularly when the violence is indiscriminately directed against ordinary members of the public, as terrorist violence often is. In practical terms, that kind of violence would seem never justified.

There are other kinds of violence that cannot be ruled out so convincingly. There is, for instance, the assassination of a murderous tyrant. Here, provided the murderous policies are an expression of the tyrant's personality rather than part of the institutions he commands, the violence is strictly limited, the aim is the end of much greater violence, success from a single violent act may be highly probable, and there may be no other way of ending the tyrant's rule. It would be implausible for a consequentialist to maintain that committing violence in these circumstances would have a corrupting effect, or that more, rather than less, violence would result from the assassination.

Violence may be limited in a different way. The cases we have been considering have involved violence against people. These are the standard cases that come to mind when we discuss violence, but there are other kinds of violence. Animal Liberation Front members have damaged laboratories, cages, and equipment used to confine, hurt, or kill animals, but they avoid violent acts against any animal, human or non-human. (Other organizations claiming to be acting on behalf of animals have, however, injured at least two people by explosive devices. These actions have been condemned by every well-known animal liberation organization, including the Animal Liberation Front.) Earth First!, a radical American environmentalist organization, advocates 'monkeywrenching' or 'ecotage' – secret acts designed to stop or slow down processes that are harmful to the environment. Dave Foreman and Bill Haywood of Earth First! have co-edited *Ecodefense: A Field Guide to Monkeywrenching*, a book that describes techniques for disabling computers, wrecking machinery, and blocking sewerage systems. In their view:

> Monkeywrenching is a non-violent resistance to the destruction of natural diversity and wilderness. It is not aimed toward harming human beings or other forms of life. It is aimed at inanimate machines and tools. . . . Monkeywrenchers are very conscious of the gravity of what they do. They are deliberate about taking such a serious step. . . . They remember that they are engaged in the most moral of all actions: protecting life, defending the Earth.

A more controversial technique is 'spiking' trees in forests that are to be logged. Putting metal spikes in a few trees in a forest makes it dangerous to saw timber from the forest, because the workers at the sawmill can never know when the saw might hit a spike, breaking the saw and sending sharp pieces of metal flying around the working area. Ecological activists who support spiking say that they warn the timber companies that trees in a certain area have been spiked, and if they go ahead and log the forests, any injuries that occur are the responsibility of the timber company managers who made that decision. But it is the workers who will be hurt, not the managers. Can the activists really shed their responsibility in this way? More orthodox environmental activists reject such tactics.

Damage to property is not as serious a matter as injuring or killing; hence it may be justified on grounds that would not justify anything that caused harm to sentient beings. This does not mean that violence to property is of no significance. Property means a great deal to some people, and one would need to have strong reasons to justify destroying it. But such reasons may exist. The justification might not be anything so epoch-making as transforming society. As in the case of the raid on Gennarelli's laboratory, it might be the specific and short-term goal of saving a number of animals from a painful experiment, performed on animals only because of society's speciesist bias. Again, whether such an action would really be justifiable from a consequentialist point of view would depend on the details of the actual situation. Someone lacking expertise could easily be mistaken about the value of an experiment or the degree of suffering it involved. And will not the result of damaging equipment and liberating one lot of animals simply be that more equipment is bought and more animals are bred? What is to be done with the liberated animals? Will illegal acts mean that the government will resist moves to reform the law relating to animal experiments, arguing that it must not appear to be yielding to violence? All these questions would need to be answered satisfactorily before one could come to a decision in favour of, say, damaging a laboratory. A related set of questions must also be answered before one can justify damaging a bulldozer that is being used to clear an old-growth forest.

Violence is not easy to justify, even if it is violence against property rather than against sentient beings, or violence against a dictator rather than indiscriminate violence against the general public. Nevertheless, the differences between kinds of violence are important, because only by observing them can we condemn one kind of violence – the terrorist kind – in virtually absolute terms. The differences are blurred by sweeping condemnations of everything that falls under the general heading 'violence'.

12

WHY ACT MORALLY?

PREVIOUS chapters of this book have discussed what we ought, morally, to do about several practical issues and what means we are justified in adopting to achieve our ethical goals. The nature of our conclusions about these issues – the demands they make upon us – raises a further, more fundamental question: why should we act morally?

Take our conclusions about the use of animals for food, or the aid the rich should give the poor. Some readers may accept these conclusions, become vegetarians, and do what they can to reduce absolute poverty. Others may disagree with our conclusions, maintaining that there is nothing wrong with eating animals and that they are under no moral obligation to do anything about reducing absolute poverty. There is also, however, likely to be a third group, consisting of readers who find no fault with the ethical arguments of these chapters, yet do not change their diets or their contributions to overseas aid. Of this third group, some will just be weak-willed, but others may want an answer to a further practical question. If the conclusions of ethics require so much of us, they may ask, should we bother about ethics at all?

UNDERSTANDING THE QUESTION

'Why should I act morally?' is a different type of question from those that we have been discussing up to now. Questions like 'Why should I treat people of different ethnic groups equally?' or 'Why is abortion justifiable?' seek ethical reasons for acting

in a certain way. These are questions within ethics. They presuppose the ethical point of view. 'Why should I act morally?'
is on another level. It is not a question within ethics, but a
question about ethics.

'Why should I act morally?' is therefore a question about
something normally presupposed. Such questions are perplexing. Some philosophers have found this particular question so
perplexing that they have rejected it as logically improper, as
an attempt to ask something that cannot properly be asked.

One ground for this rejection is the claim that our ethical
principles are, by definition, the principles we take as overridingly important. This means that whatever principles are
overriding for a particular person are necessarily that person's
ethical principles, and a person who accepts as an ethical principle that she ought to give her wealth to help the poor must,
by definition, have actually decided to give away her wealth.
On this definition of ethics once a person has made an ethical
decision no further practical question can arise. Hence it is impossible to make sense of the question: 'Why should I act
morally?'

It might be thought a good reason for accepting the definition
of ethics as overriding that it allows us to dismiss as meaningless
an otherwise troublesome question. Adopting this definition
cannot solve real problems, however, for it leads to correspond-
ingly greater difficulties in establishing any ethical conclusion.
Take, for example, the conclusion that the rich ought to aid the
poor. We were able to argue for this in Chapter 8 only because
we assumed that, as suggested in the first two chapters of this
book, the universalisability of ethical judgments requires us to
go beyond thinking only about our own interests, and leads us
to take a point of view from which we must give equal consideration to the interests of all affected by our actions. We cannot
hold that ethical judgments must be universalisable and *at the
same time* define a person's ethical principles as whatever principles that person takes as overridingly important – for what if

I take as overridingly important some non-universalisable principle like 'I ought to do whatever benefits *me*'? If we define
ethical principles as whatever principles one takes as overriding,
then anything whatever may count as an ethical principle, for
one may take any principle whatever as overridingly important.
Thus what we gain by being able to dismiss the question:'Why
should I act morally?' we lose by being unable to use the universalisability of ethical judgments – or any other feature of
ethics – to argue for particular conclusions about what is morally
right. Taking ethics as in some sense necessarily involving a
universal point of view seems to me a more natural and less
confusing way of discussing these issues.

Other philosophers have rejected 'Why should I act morally?'
for a different reason. They think it must be rejected for the
same reason that we must reject another question, 'Why should
I be rational?' which like 'Why should I act morally?' also
questions something – in this case rationality – normally presupposed. 'Why should I be rational?' really is logically improper because in answering it we would be giving reasons for
being rational. Thus we would presuppose rationality in our
attempt to justify rationality. The resulting justification of rationality would be circular – which shows, not that rationality
lacks a necessary justification, but that it needs no justification,
because it cannot intelligibly be questioned unless it is already
presupposed.

Is 'Why should I act morally?' like 'Why should I be rational?'
in that it presupposes the very point of view it questions? It
would be, if we interpreted the 'should' as a moral 'should'.
Then the question would ask for moral reasons for being moral.
This would be absurd. Once we have decided that an action is
morally obligatory, there is no further moral question to ask. It
is redundant to ask why I should, morally, do the action that I
morally should do.

There is, however, no need to interpret the question as a
request for an ethical justification of ethics. 'Should' need not

mean 'should, morally'. It could simply be a way of asking for reasons for action, without any specification about the kind of reasons wanted. We sometimes want to ask a general practical question, from no particular point of view. Faced with a difficult choice, we ask a close friend for advice. Morally, he says, we ought to do A, but B would be more in our interests, while etiquette demands C and only D would display a real sense of style. This answer may not satisfy us. We want advice on which of these standpoints to adopt. If it is possible to ask such a question we must ask it from a position of neutrality between all these points of view, not of commitment to any one of them.

'Why should I act morally?' is this sort of question. If it is not possible to ask practical questions without presupposing a point of view, we are unable to say anything intelligible about the most ultimate practical choices. Whether to act according to considerations of ethics, self-interest, etiquette, or aesthetics would be a choice 'beyond reason' – in a sense, an arbitrary choice. Before we resign ourselves to this conclusion we should at least attempt to interpret the question so that the mere asking of it does not commit us to any particular point of view.

We can now formulate the question more precisely. It is a question about the ethical point of view, asked from a position outside it. But what is 'the ethical point of view'? I have suggested that a distinguishing feature of ethics is that ethical judgments are universalisable. Ethics requires us to go beyond our own personal point of view to a standpoint like that of the impartial spectator who takes a universal point of view.

Given this conception of ethics, 'Why should I act morally?' is a question that may properly be asked by anyone wondering whether to act only on grounds that would be acceptable from this universal point of view. It is, after all, possible to act – and some people do act – without thinking of anything except one's own interests. The question asks for reasons for going beyond this personal basis of action and acting only on judgments one is prepared to prescribe universally.

REASON AND ETHICS

There is an ancient line of philosophical thought that attempts to demonstrate that to act rationally is to act ethically. The argument is today associated with Kant and is mainly found in the writings of modern Kantians, though it goes back as least as far as the Stoics. The form in which the argument is presented varies, but the common structure is as follows:

1 Some requirement of universalisability or impartiality is essential to ethics.
2 Reason is universally or objectively valid. If, for example, it follows from the premises 'All humans are mortal' and 'Socrates is human' that Socrates is mortal, then this inference must follow universally. It cannot be valid for me and invalid for you. This is a general point about reason, whether theoretical or practical.

Therefore:

3 Only a judgment that satisfies the requirement described in (1) as a necessary condition of an ethical judgment will be an objectively rational judgment in accordance with (2). For I cannot expect any other rational agents to accept as valid for them a judgment that I would not accept if I were in their place; and if two rational agents could not accept each other's judgments, they could not be rational judgments, for the reason given in (2). To say that I would accept the judgment I make, even if I were in someone else's position and they in mine is, however, simply to say that my judgment is one I can prescribe from a universal point of view. Ethics and reason both require us to rise above our own particular point of view and take a perspective from which our own personal identity – the role we happen to occupy – is unimportant. Thus reason requires us to act on universalisable judgments and, to that extent, to act ethically.

Is this argument valid? I have already indicated that I accept the first point, that ethics involves universalisability. The second point also seems undeniable. Reason must be universal. Does the conclusion therefore follow? Here is the flaw in the argument. The conclusion appears to follow directly from the premises; but this move involves a slide from the limited sense in which it is true that a rational judgment must be universally valid, to a stronger sense of 'universally valid' that is equivalent to universalisability. The difference between these two senses can be seen by considering a non-universalisable imperative, like the purely egoistic: 'Let everyone do what is in my interests.' This differs from the imperative of universalisable egoism – 'Let everyone do what is in *her or his own* interests' – because it contains an ineliminable reference to a particular person. It therefore cannot be an ethical imperative. Does it also lack the universality required if it is to be a rational basis for action? Surely not. Every rational agent could accept that the purely egoistic activity of other rational agents is rationally justifiable. Pure egoism could be rationally adopted by everyone.

Let us look at this more closely. It must be conceded that there is a sense in which one purely egoistic rational agent – call him Jack – could not accept the practical judgments of another purely egoistic rational agent – call her Jill. Assuming Jill's interests differ from Jack's, Jill may be acting rationally in urging Jack to do A, while Jack is also acting rationally in deciding against doing A.

This disagreement is, however, compatible with all rational agents accepting pure egoism. Though they accept pure egoism, it points them in different directions because they start from different places. When Jack adopts pure egoism, it leads him to further his interests and when Jill adopts pure egoism it leads her to further her interests. Hence the disagreement over what to do. On the other hand – and this is the sense in which pure egoism could be accepted as valid by all rational agents – if we were to ask Jill (off the record and promising not to tell Jack) what she thinks it would be rational for Jack to do, she would, if truthful, have to reply that it would be rational for Jack to do what is in his own interests, rather than what is in her interests.

So when purely egoistic rational agents oppose each other's acts, it does not indicate disagreement over the rationality of pure egoism. Pure egoism, though not a universalisable principle, could be accepted as a rational basis of action by all rational agents. The sense in which rational judgments must be universally acceptable is weaker than the sense in which ethical judgements must be. That an action will benefit me rather than anyone else could be a valid reason for doing it, though it could not be an ethical reason for doing it.

A consequence of this conclusion is that rational agents may rationally try to prevent each other from doing what they admit the other is rationally justified in doing. There is, unfortunately, nothing paradoxical about this. Two salespeople competing for an important sale will accept each other's conduct as rational, though each aims to thwart the other. The same holds of two soldiers meeting in battle, or two footballers vying for the ball.

Accordingly, this attempted demonstration of a link between reason and ethics fails. There may be other ways of forging this link, but it is difficult to see any that hold greater promise of success. The chief obstacle to be overcome is the nature of practical reason. Long ago David Hume argued that reason in action applies only to means, not to ends. The ends must be given by our wants and desires. Hume unflinchingly drew out the implications of this view:

> 'Tis not contrary to reason to prefer the destruction of the whole world to the scratching of my finger. 'Tis not contrary to reason for me to choose my total ruin, to prevent the least uneasiness of an Indian or person wholly unknown to me. 'Tis as little contrary to reason to prefer even my own acknowledged lesser good to my greater, and have a more ardent affection for the former than the latter.

320

Extreme as it is, Hume's view of practical reason has stood up to criticism remarkably well. His central claim – that in practical reasoning we start from something wanted – is difficult to refute; yet it must be refuted if any argument is to succeed in showing that it is rational for all of us to act ethically irrespective of what we want.

Nor is the refutation of Hume all that is needed for a demonstration of the rational necessity of acting ethically. In *The Possibility of Altruism*, Thomas Nagel has argued forcefully that not to take one's own future desires into account in one's practical deliberations – irrespective of whether one now happens to desire the satisfaction of those future desires – would indicate a failure to see oneself as a person existing over time, the present being merely one time among others in one's life. So it is my conception of myself as a person that makes it rational for me to consider my long-term interests. This holds true even if I have 'a more ardent affection' for something that I acknowledge is not really, all things considered, in my own interest.

Whether Nagel's argument succeeds in vindicating the rationality of prudence is one question: whether a similar argument can also be used in favour of a form of altruism based on taking the desires of *others* into account is another question altogether. Nagel attempts this analogous argument. The role occupied by 'seeing the present as merely one time among others' is, in the argument for altruism, taken by 'seeing oneself as merely one person among others'. But whereas it would be extremely difficult for most of us to cease conceiving of ourselves as existing over time, with the present merely one time among others that we will live through, the way we see ourselves as a person among others is quite different. Henry Sidgwick's observation on this point seems to me exactly right:

> It would be contrary to Common Sense to deny that the distinction between any one individual and any other is real and fundamental, and that consequently 'I' am concerned with the

quality of my existence as an individual in a sense, fundamentally important, in which I am not concerned with the quality of the existence of other individuals: and this being so, I do not see how it can be proved that this distinction is not to be taken as fundamental in determining the ultimate end of rational action for an individual.

So it is not only Hume's view of practical reason that stands in the way of attempts to show that to act rationally is to act ethically; we might succeed in overthrowing that barrier, only to find our way blocked by the commonsense distinction between self and others. Taken together, these are formidable obstacles and I know of no way of overcoming them.

ETHICS AND SELF-INTEREST

If practical reasoning begins with something wanted, to show that it is rational to act morally would involve showing that in acting morally we achieve something we want. If, agreeing with Sidgwick rather than Hume, we hold that it is rational to act in our long-term interests irrespective of what we happen to want at the present moment, we could show that it is rational to act morally by showing that it is in our long-term interests to do so. There have been many attempts to argue along these lines, ever since Plato, in *The Republic*, portrayed Socrates as arguing that to be virtuous is to have the different elements of one's personality ordered in a harmonious manner, and this is necessary for happiness. We shall look at these arguments shortly; but first it is necessary to assess an objection to this whole approach to 'Why should I act morally?'

People often say that to defend morality by appealing to self-interest is to misunderstand what ethics is all about. F. H. Bradley stated this eloquently:

> What answer can we give when the question Why should I be Moral?, in the sense of What will it advantage Me?, is put to us? Here we shall do well, I think, to avoid all praises of the

322

pleasantness of virtue. We may believe that it transcends all possible delights of vice, but it would be well to remember that we desert a moral point of view, that we degrade and prostitute virtue, when to those who do not love her for herself we bring ourselves to recommend her for the sake of her pleasures.

In other words, we can never get people to act morally by providing reasons of self-interest, because if they accept what we say and act on the reasons given, they will only be acting self-interestedly, not morally.

One reply to this objection would be that the substance of the action, what is actually done, is more important than the motive. People might give money to famine relief because their friends will think better of them, or they might give the same amount because they think it their duty. Those saved from starvation by the gift will benefit to the same extent either way.

This is true but crude. It can be made more sophisticated if it is combined with an appropriate account of the nature and function of ethics. Ethics, though not consciously created, is a product of social life that has the function of promoting values common to the members of the society. Ethical judgments do this by praising and encouraging actions in accordance with these values. Ethical judgments are concerned with motives because this is a good indication of the tendency of an action to promote good or evil, but also because it is here that praise and blame may be effective in altering the tendency of a person's actions. Conscientiousness (that is, acting for the sake of doing what is right) is a particularly useful motive, from the community's point of view. People who are conscientious will, if they accept the values of their society (and if most people did not accept these values they would not be the values of the society) always tend to promote what the society values. They may have no generous or sympathetic inclinations, but if they think it their duty to give famine relief, they will do so. Moreover, those motivated by the desire to do what is right can be relied upon to act as they think right in all circumstances, whereas those who act from some other motive, like self-interest, will only do what they think right when they believe it will also be in their interest. Conscientiousness is thus a kind of multipurpose gap-filler that can be used to motivate people towards whatever is valued, even if the natural virtues normally associated with action in accordance with those values (generosity, sympathy, honesty, tolerance, humility, and so on) are lacking. (This needs some qualification: a conscientious mother may provide as well for her children as a mother who loves them, but she cannot love them because it is the right thing to do. Sometimes conscientiousness is a poor substitute for the real thing.)

On this view of ethics it is still results, not motives, that really matter. Conscientiousness is of value because of its consequences. Yet, unlike, say, benevolence, conscientiousness can be praised and encouraged only for its own sake. To praise a conscientious act for its consequences would be to praise not conscientiousness, but something else altogether. If we appeal to sympathy or self-interest as a reason for doing one's duty, then we are not encouraging people to do their duty for its own sake. If conscientiousness is to be encouraged, it must be thought of as good for its own sake.

It is different in the case of an act done from a motive that people act upon irrespective of praise and encouragement. The use of ethical language is then inappropriate. We do not normally say that people ought to do, or that it is their duty to do, whatever gives them the greatest pleasure, for most people are sufficiently motivated to do this anyway. So, whereas we praise good acts done for the sake of doing what is right, we withhold our praise when we believe the act was done from some motive like self-interest.

This emphasis on motives and on the moral worth of doing right for its own sake is now embedded in our notion of ethics. To the extent that it is so embedded, we will feel that to provide considerations of self-interest for doing what is right is to empty the action of its moral worth.

My suggestion is that our notion of ethics has become misleading to the extent that moral worth is attributed only to action done because it is right, without any ulterior motive. It is understandable, and from the point of view of society perhaps even desirable, that this attitude should prevail; nevertheless, those who accept this view of ethics, and are led by it to do what is right because it is right, without asking for any further reason, are falling victim to a kind of confidence trick – though not, of course, a consciously perpetrated one.

That this view of ethics is unjustifiable has already been indicated by the failure of the argument discussed earlier in this chapter for a rational justification of ethics. In the history of Western philosophy, no one has urged more strongly than Kant that our ordinary moral consciousness finds moral worth only when duty is done for duty's sake. Yet Kant himself saw that without a rational justification this common conception of ethics would be 'a mere phantom of the brain'. And this is indeed the case. If we reject – as in general terms we have done – the Kantian justification of the rationality of ethics, but try to retain the Kantian conception of ethics, ethics is left hanging without support. It becomes a closed system, a system that cannot be questioned because its first premise – that only action done because it is right has any moral worth – rules out the only remaining possible justification for accepting this very premise. Morality is, on this view, no more rational an end than any other allegedly self-justifying practice, like etiquette or the kind of religious faith that comes only to those who first set aside all sceptical doubts.

Taken as a view of ethics as a whole, we should abandon this Kantian notion of ethics. This does not mean, however, that we should never do what we see to be right simply because we see it to be right, without further reasons. Here we need to appeal to the distinction Hare has made between intuitive and critical thinking. When I stand back from my day-to-day ethical decisions and ask why I should act ethically, I should seek reasons in the broadest sense, and not allow Kantian preconceptions to deter me from considering self-interested reasons for living an ethical life. If my search is successful it will provide me with reasons for taking up the ethical point of view as a settled policy, a way of living. I would not then ask, in my day-to-day ethical decision making, whether each particular right action is in my interests. Instead I do it because I see myself as an ethical person. In everyday situations, I will simply assume that doing what is right is in my interests, and once I have decided what is right, I will go ahead and do it, without thinking about further reasons for doing what is right. To deliberate over the ultimate reasons for doing what is right in each case would impossibly complicate my life; it would also be inadvisable because in particular situations I might be too greatly influenced by strong but temporary desires and inclinations and so make decisions I would later regret.

That, at least, is how a justification of ethics in terms of self-interest might work, without defeating its own aim. We can now ask if such a justification exists. There is a daunting list of those who, following Plato's lead, have offered one: Aristotle, Aquinas, Spinoza, Butler, Hegel, even – for all his strictures against prostituting virtue – Bradley. Like Plato, these philosophers made broad claims about human nature and the conditions under which human beings can be happy. Some were also able to fall back on a belief that virtue will be rewarded and wickedness punished in a life after our bodily death. Philosophers cannot use this argument if they want to carry conviction nowadays; nor can they adopt sweeping psychological theories on the basis of their own general experience of their fellows, as philosophers used to do when psychology was a branch of philosophy.

It might be said that since philosophers are not empirical

scientists, discussion of the connection between acting ethically and living a fulfilled and happy life should be left to psychologists, sociologists, and other appropriate experts. The question is not, however, dealt with by any other single discipline and its relevance to practical ethics is reason enough for our looking into it.

What facts about human nature could show that ethics and self-interest coincide? One theory is that we all have benevolent or sympathetic inclinations that make us concerned about the welfare of others. Another relies on a natural conscience that gives rise to guilt feelings when we do what we know to be wrong. But how strong are these benevolent desires or feelings of guilt? Is it possible to suppress them? If so, isn't it possible that in a world in which humans and other animals are suffering in great numbers, suppressing one's conscience and sympathy for others is the surest way to happiness?

To meet this objection those who would link ethics and happiness must assert that we cannot be happy if these elements of our nature are suppressed. Benevolence and sympathy, they might argue, are tied up with the capacity to take part in friendly or loving relations with others, and there can be no real happiness without such relationships. For the same reason it is necessary to take at least some ethical standards seriously, and to be open and honest in living by them – for a life of deception and dishonesty is a furtive life, in which the possibility of discovery always clouds the horizon. Genuine acceptance of ethical standards is likely to mean that we feel some guilt – or at least that we are less pleased with ourselves than we otherwise would be – when we do not live up to them.

These claims about the connection between our character and our prospects of happiness are no more than hypotheses. Attempts to confirm them by detailed research are sparse and inadequate. A. H. Maslow, an American psychologist, asserted that human beings have a need for self-actualisation that involves growing towards courage, kindness, knowledge, love, honesty, and unselfishness. When we fulfil this need, we feel serene, joyful, filled with zest, sometimes euphoric, and generally happy. When we act contrary to our need for self-actualisation, we experience anxiety, despair, boredom, shame, emptiness and are generally unable to enjoy ourselves. It would be nice if Maslow should turn out to be right; unfortunately, the data Maslow produced in support of his theory consisted of limited studies of selected people and cannot be considered anything more than suggestive.

Human nature is so diverse that one may doubt if any generalisation about the kind of character that leads to happiness could hold for all human beings. What, for instance, of those we call 'psychopaths'? Psychiatrists use this term as a label for a person who is asocial, impulsive, egocentric, unemotional, lacking in feelings of remorse, shame, or guilt, and apparently unable to form deep and enduring personal relationships. Psychopaths are certainly abnormal, but whether it is proper to say that they are mentally ill is another matter. At least on the surface, they do not *suffer* from their condition, and it is not obvious that it is in their interest to be 'cured'. Hervey Cleckley, the author of a classic study of psychopathy entitled *The Mask of Sanity*, notes that since his book was first published he has received countless letters from people desperate for help – but they are from the parents, spouses, and other relatives of psychopaths, almost never from the psychopaths themselves. This is not surprising, for while psychopaths are asocial and indifferent to the welfare of others, they seem to enjoy life. Psychopaths often appear to be charming, intelligent people, with no delusions or other signs of irrational thinking. When interviewed they say things like: 'A lot has happened to me, a lot more will happen. But I enjoy living and I am always looking forward to each day. I like laughing and I've done a lot. I am essentially a clown at heart – but a happy one. I always take the bad with the good.' There is no effective therapy for psychopathy, which may be explained by the fact that psychopaths see nothing wrong with their behaviour and often find it extremely rewarding, at least in the short term. Of course their impulsive nature and lack of a sense of shame or guilt means that some psychopaths end up in prison, though it is hard to tell how many do not, since those who avoid prison are also more likely to avoid contact with psychiatrists. Studies have shown that a surprisingly large number of psychopaths are able to avoid prison despite grossly antisocial behaviour, probably because of their well-known ability to convince others that they are truly repentant, that it will never happen again, that they deserve another chance, and so forth.

The existence of psychopathic people counts against the contention that benevolence, sympathy, and feelings of guilt are present in everyone. It also appears to count against attempts to link happiness with the possession of these inclinations. But let us pause before we accept this latter conclusion. Must we accept psychopaths' own evaluations of their happiness? They are, after all, notoriously persuasive liars. Moreover, even if they are telling the truth as they see it, are they qualified to say that they are really happy, when they seem unable to experience the emotional states that play such a large part in the happiness and fulfilment of more normal people? Admittedly, a psychopath could use the same argument against us: how can we say that we are truly happy when we have not experienced the excitement and freedom that comes from complete irresponsibility? Since we cannot enter into the subjective states of psychopathic people, nor they into ours, the dispute is not easy to resolve.

Cleckley suggests that the psychopaths' behaviour can be explained as a response to the meaninglessness of their lives. It is characteristic of psychopaths to work for a while at a job and then just when their ability and charm have taken them to the crest of success, commit some petty and easily detectable crime. A similar pattern occurs in their personal relationships. (There is support to be found here for Thomas Nagel's account of imprudence as rational only if one fails to see oneself as a person existing over time, with the present merely one among other times one will live through. Certainly psychopathic people live largely in the present and lack any coherent life plan.)

Cleckley explains this erratic and to us inadequately motivated behaviour by likening the psychopath's life to that of children forced to sit through a performance of *King Lear*. Children are restless and misbehave under these conditions because they cannot enjoy the play as adults do. They act to relieve boredom. Similarly, Cleckley says, psychopaths are bored because their emotional poverty means that they cannot take interest in, or gain satisfaction from, what for others are the most important things in life: love, family, success in business or professional life, and the like. These things simply do not matter to them. Their unpredictable and antisocial behaviour is an attempt to relieve what would otherwise be a tedious existence. These claims are speculative and Cleckley admits that they may not be possible to establish scientifically. They do suggest, however, an aspect of the psychopath's life that undermines the otherwise attractive nature of the psychopath's free-wheeling life. Most reflective people, at some time or other, want their life to have some kind of meaning. Few of us could deliberately choose a way of life that we regarded as utterly meaningless. For this reason most of us would not choose to live a psychopathic life, however enjoyable it might be.

Yet there is something paradoxical about criticising the psychopath's life for its meaninglessness. Don't we have to accept, in the absence of religious belief, that life really is meaningless, not just for the psychopath but for all of us? And if this is so, why should we not choose – if it were in our power to choose our personality – the life of a psychopath? But is it true that, religion aside, life is meaningless? Now our pursuit of reasons for acting morally has led us to what is often regarded as the ultimate philosophical question.

HAS LIFE A MEANING?

In what sense does rejection of belief in a god imply rejection of the view that life has any meaning? If this world had been created by some divine being with a particular goal in mind, it could be said to have a meaning, at least for that divine being. If we could know what the divine being's purpose in creating us was, we could then know what the meaning of our life was for our creator. If we accepted our creator's purpose (though why we should do that would need to be explained) we could claim to know the meaning of life.

When we reject belief in a god we must give up the idea that life on this planet has some preordained meaning. Life *as a whole* has no meaning. Life began, as the best available theories tell us, in a chance combination of molecules; it then evolved through random mutations and natural selection. All this just happened; it did not happen for any overall purpose. Now that it has resulted in the existence of beings who prefer some states of affairs to others, however, it may be possible for particular lives to be meaningful. In this sense atheists can find meaning in life.

Let us return to the comparison between the life of a psychopath and that of a more normal person. Why should the psychopath's life not be meaningful? We have seen that psychopaths are egocentric to an extreme: neither other people, nor worldly success, nor anything else really matters to them. But why is their own enjoyment of life not sufficient to give meaning to their lives?

Most of us would not be able to find happiness by deliberately setting out to enjoy ourselves without caring about anyone or anything else. The pleasures we obtained in that way would seem empty and would soon pall. We seek a meaning for our lives beyond our own pleasures and find fulfilment and happiness in doing what we see to be meaningful. If our life has no meaning other than our own happiness, we are likely to find that when we have obtained what we think we need to be happy, happiness itself still eludes us.

That those who aim at happiness for happiness's sake often fail to find it, while others find happiness in pursuing altogether different goals, has been called 'the paradox of hedonism'. It is not, of course, a logical paradox but a claim about the way in which we come to be happy. Like other generalisations on this subject, it lacks empirical confirmation. Yet it matches our every-day observations and is consistent with our nature as evolved, purposive beings. Human beings survive and reproduce them-selves through purposive action. We obtain happiness and ful-filment by working towards and achieving our goals. In evolutionary terms we could say that happiness functions as an internal reward for our achievements. Subjectively, we regard achieving the goal (or progressing towards it) as a reason for happiness. Our own happiness, therefore, is a by-product of aiming at something else, and not to be obtained by setting our sights on happiness alone.

The psychopath's life can now be seen to be meaningless in a way that a normal life is not. It is meaningless because it looks inward to the pleasures of the present moment and not outward to anything more long-term or far-reaching. More normal lives have meaning because they are lived to some larger purpose.

All this is speculative. You may accept or reject it to the extent that it agrees with your own observation and introspection. My next – and final – suggestion is more speculative still. It is that to find an enduring meaning in our lives it is not enough to go beyond psychopaths who have no long-term commitments or life plans; we must also go beyond more prudent egoists who have long term plans concerned only with their own interests. The prudent egoists may find meaning in their lives for a time, for they have the purpose of furthering their own interests; but what, in the end, does that amount to? When everything in our interests has been achieved, do we just sit back and be happy? Could we be happy in this way? Or would we decide that we had still not quite reached our target, that there was something else we needed before we could sit back and enjoy it all? Most materially successful egoists take the latter route, thus escaping the necessity of admitting that they cannot find happiness in permanent holidaying. People who slaved to establish small businesses, telling themselves they would do it only until they had made enough to live comfortably, keep working long after they have passed their original target. Their material 'needs' expand just fast enough to keep ahead of their income.

The 1980s, the 'decade of greed', provided plenty of examples of the insatiable nature of the desire for wealth. In 1985 Dennis Levine was a highly successful Wall Street banker with the fastest-growing and most talked-about Wall Street firm, Drexel Burnham Lambert. But Levine was not satisfied:

> When I was earning $20,000 a year, I thought, *I can make $100,000.* When I was earning $100,000 a year, I thought, *I can make $200,000.* When I was making $1 million, I thought, *I can make $3 million.* There was always somebody one rung higher on the ladder, and I could never stop wondering: Is he really twice as good as I am.

Levine decided to take matters into his own hands and arranged with friends at other Wall Street firms to exchange confidential information that would allow them to profit by buying shares in companies that were about to become takeover targets. By this method Levine made an additional $11 million, on top of what he earned in salary and bonuses. He also ended up bringing about his own ruin, and spending time in prison. That, however, is not the relevant point here. No doubt some who use inside information to make millions of dollars do not get caught. What is less certain, however, is that they really find satisfaction and fulfilment in having more money.

Now we begin to see where ethics comes into the problem of living a meaningful life. If we are looking for a purpose broader than our own interests, something that will allow us to see our lives as possessing significance beyond the narrow confines of our own conscious states, one obvious solution is to take up the ethical point of view. The ethical point of view does, as we have seen, require us to go beyond a personal point of view to the standpoint of an impartial spectator. Thus looking at things ethically is a way of transcending our inward-looking concerns and identifying ourselves with the most objective point of view possible – with, as Sidgwick put it, 'the point of view of the universe'.

The point of view of the universe is a lofty standpoint. In the rarefied air that surrounds it we may get carried away into talking, as Kant does, of the moral point of view, 'inevitably' humbling all who compare their own limited nature with it. I do not want to suggest anything as sweeping as this. Earlier in this chapter, in rejecting Thomas Nagel's argument for the rationality of altruism, I said that there is nothing irrational about being concerned with the quality of one's own existence in a way that one is not concerned with the quality of existence of other individuals. Without going back on this, I am now suggesting that rationality, in the broad sense that includes self-awareness and reflection on the nature and point of our own existence, may push us towards concerns broader than the quality of our own existence; but the process is not a necessary one and those who do not take part in it – or, who in taking part, do not follow it all the way to the ethical point of view – are neither irrational nor in error. Psychopaths, for all I know, may simply be unable to obtain as much happiness through caring about others as they obtain by antisocial acts. Other people find collecting stamps an entirely adequate way of giving purpose to their lives. There is nothing irrational about that; but others again grow out of stamp collecting as they become more aware of their situation in the world and more reflective about their purposes. To this third group the ethical point of view offers a meaning and purpose in life that one does not grow out of.

(At least, one cannot grow out of the ethical point of view until all ethical tasks have been accomplished. If that utopia were ever achieved, our purposive nature might well leave us dissatisfied, much as egoists might be dissatisfied when they have everything they need to be happy. There is nothing paradoxical about this, for we should not expect evolution to have equipped us, in advance, with the ability to enjoy a situation that has never previously occurred. Nor is this going to be a practical problem in the near future.)

'Why act morally?' cannot be given an answer that will provide everyone with overwhelming reasons for acting morally. Ethically indefensible behaviour is not always irrational. We will probably always need the sanctions of the law and social pressure to provide additional reasons against serious violations of ethical standards. At the same time, those reflective enough to ask the question we have been discussing in this chapter are also those most likely to appreciate the reasons that can be offered for taking the ethical point of view.

APPENDIX: ON BEING SILENCED
IN GERMANY

Some scenes from academic life in Germany and Austria today:

For the 1989/1990 winter semester, Dr. Hartmut Kliemt, a professor of philosophy at the University of Duisburg, a small town in the north of Germany, offered a course in which my book *Practical Ethics* was the principal text assigned to the class. First published in English in 1979, this book has been widely used in philosophy courses in North America, the United Kingdom, and Australia and has been translated into German, Italian, Spanish, and Swedish.[1] Until Kliemt announced his course, it had never evoked anything more than lively discussion. Kliemt's course, however, was subjected to organized and repeated disruption by protesters objecting to the use of the book on the grounds that in one of its ten chapters it advocates active euthanasia for severely disabled newborn infants. When after several weeks the disruptions showed no sign of abating, Kliemt was compelled to abandon the course.

The European society for the Philosophy of Medicine and Health Care is a learned society that does just what one would expect an organization with that name to do: it promotes the study of the philosophy of medicine and health care. In 1990 it planned its fourth annual conference, to be held in Bochum,

Reprinted with Permission from the *New York Review* of *Books,* August 15, 1991.
1 Cambridge University Press, 1979; German translation, *Praktische Ethik* (Stuttgart: Reclam, 1984); Spanish translation, *Etica Practica* (Barcelona: Ariel, 1984); Italian translation, *Etica Pratica* (Naples: Liguori, 1989); Swedish translation, *Praktisk Ethik* (Stockholm: Thales, 1990).

Germany, in June. The intended theme of the conference was 'Consensus Formation and Moral Judgment in Health Care'. During the days leading up to the conference, literature was distributed in Bochum and elsewhere in Germany by the 'Anti-Euthanasia Forum', stating that 'under the cover of tolerance and the cry of democracy and liberalism, extermination strategies will be discussed. On these grounds we will attempt to prevent the Bochum Congress taking place.' On June 5, scholars who were about to attend the conference received a letter from the secretary of the society notifying them that it was being moved to Maastricht, in the Netherlands, because the German organizers (two professors from the Center for Medical Ethics at the Ruhr University in Bochum) had been confronted with 'anti-bioethics agitation, threats and intimidation', and could not guarantee the safety of the participants.

In October 1990, Dr. Helga Kuhse, senior research fellow at the Centre for Human Bioethics at Monash University in Australia and author of *The Sanctity-of-Life Doctrine in Medicine: A Critique,*[2] was invited to give a lecture at the Institute for Anatomy of the University of Vienna. A group calling itself the 'Forum of Groups for the Crippled and Disabled' announced that it would protest against the lecture, stating that 'academic freedom has ethical limits, and we expect the medical faculty to declare that human life is inviolable'. The lecture was then canceled by the faculty of medicine. The dean of the faculty, referring to Dr. Kuhse, told the press, 'We didn't know at all who that was.'[3]

The Institute for Philosophy at the University of Hamburg decided, with the agreement of faculty members and a student representative, to appoint a professor in the field of applied ethics. The list of candidates was narrowed down to six. At this point in selecting a professor in Germany, the standard proce-

2 Oxford University Press/Clarendon Press, 1987.
3 *Der Standard* (Vienna), October 10, 1990.

dure is to invite each of the candidates to give a lecture. The lectures were announced but did not take place. Students and protesters from outside the university objected to the advertising of a chair in applied ethics on the grounds that this field raised questions about whether some human lives were worth living. The protesters blocked the entrances to the lecture theaters and blew whistles to drown out any attempts by the speakers to lecture. The university canceled the lectures. A few weeks later, a new list of candidates was announced. Two philosophers active in the field of applied ethics were no longer in consideration; they were replaced by philosophers who have done relatively little work in applied ethics; one, for example, is best known for his work in aesthetics. One of those dropped from the short list was Dr. Anton Leist, author of a book that offers ethical arguments in defense of the right to abortion,[4] and also a coeditor of *Analyse & Kritik*; one of the few German journals publishing philosophy in the mode practiced in English-speaking countries. Ironically, a recent special issue of the journal was devoted to *Practical Ethics* and the issue of academic freedom in Germany.[5]

In February 1991 a round-table discussion was to be held in Frankfurt, organized jointly by the adult education sections of both the Protestant and Roman Catholic churches. The theme was 'Aid in Dying,' and among the participants was Norbert Hoerster, a highly respected German professor of jurisprudence, who has written in support of the principle of euthanasia. As the meeting was about to get underway, a group of people challenged the organizers, accusing them of giving a platform to a 'fascist' and an 'advocate of modern mass extermination'. They distributed leaflets headed 'No Discussion about Life and Death'. The meeting had to be abandoned.

---

4 *Eine Frage des Lebens: Ethik der Abtreibung and Künstlichen Befruchtung* (Frankfurt: Campus, 1990).
5 *Analyse & Kritik*, December 12, 1990.

Appendix

The International Wittgenstein Symposium, held annually at Kirchberg, in Austria, has established itself as one of the principal philosophical conferences on the continent of Europe. The fifteenth International Wittgenstein Conference was to have been held in August 1991, on the theme 'Applied Ethics'. Arrangements for the program were made by philosophers from the Institute for Philosophy at the University of Salzburg. Among those invited to speak were Professor Georg Meggle, of the University of Saarbrücken, Professor R. M. Hare, former White's Professor of Moral Philosophy at the University of Oxford, and now a professor of philosophy at the University of Florida, Gainesville, and myself. When the names of those invited became known, threats were made to the president of the Austrian Ludwig Wittgenstein Society, Dr. Adolf Hübner, that the symposium would be disrupted unless the invitations to Professor Meggle and me were withdrawn. In other public discussions with opponents of the program, the boycott threat was extended to include several other invited professors: Hare, Kliemt, Hoerster, and Professor Dietrich Birnbacher of the department of philosophy at the Gesamthochschule in Essen.[6]

Dr. Hübner is not a philosopher; he is a retired agricultural veterinarian, so he read *Practical Ethics* only after the protest arose. On reading it, however, he formed the opinion that—as he wrote in an Austrian newspaper—the protests were 'entirely justified'.[7] In a long letter to the board of directors of the Austrian Ludwig Wittgenstein Society he wrote that 'as a result of the invitations to philosophers who hold the view that ethics can be grounded and carried out in the manner of an objective critical science, an existential crisis has arisen for the Austrian

6 During the period when opposition to the Wittgenstein Symposium was being stirred up, these philosophers were all described, in terms calculated to arouse a hostile response, in a special 'euthanasia issue' of the Austrian journal *erziehung heute (education today)* (Innsbruck, 1991), p. 37.
7 Adolf Hübner, 'Euthanasie diskussion im Geiste Ludwig Wittgenstein?' *Der Standard* (Vienna), May 21, 1991.

Appendix

Wittgenstein Symposium and the Wittgenstein Society'.[8] The reference to the 'objective critical science' is striking, since Hare, in particular, has devoted much of his life to insisting on the differences between ethical judgments and statements to which notions of objective truth or falsity are standardly applied.

According to some reports, opposition groups threatened to stage a display on 'Kirchberg under the Nazis' if the invitations were not withdrawn. This threat proved so potent that innkeepers in Kirchberg were said to have stated that they would refuse to serve philosophers during the symposium.[9] To its considerable credit, the organizing committee resisted Dr. Hübner's proposal to withdraw the invitations from those philosophers against whom the protests were directed. Instead, it recommended that the entire symposium be canceled, since Dr. Hübner's public intervention in the debate had made it unlikely that it could be held without disruption. This recommendation was accepted by the committee of the Austrian Wittgenstein Society, against the will of Dr. Hübner himself. There will be no Wittgenstein Symposium in 1991.

For those who believe that there is a strong consensus throughout Western Europe supporting freedom of thought and discussion in general, and academic freedom in particular, these scenes come as a shock. How they have come about, however, is not so difficult to explain. The story has its beginnings in events in which I was directly involved. It stems from an invitation I received to speak, in June 1989, at a European Symposium on 'Bioengineering, Ethics, and Mental Disability', organized jointly by Lebenshilfe, the major German organization for parents of intellectually disabled infants, and the Bishop

8 'Die krisenhafte Situation der Österreichischen Ludwig Wittgenstein Gesellschaft, ausgelöst durch die Einladungspraxis zum Thema "Angewandte Ethik" ' (unpublished typescript).
9 Martin Stürzinger, 'Ein Tötungshelfer mit faschistischem Gedankengut?' *Die Weltwoche* (Zurich), May 23, 1991, p. 83.

Bekkers Institute, a Dutch organization in the same field. The symposium was to be held in Marburg, a German university town, under the auspices of the International League of Societies for Persons with Mental Handicap, and the International Association for the Scientific Study of Mental Deficiency. The program looked impressive; after an opening speech from the German minister of family affairs, the conference was to be addressed by leading geneticists, bioethicists, theologians, and health-care lawyers from the United States, Canada, the Netherlands, England, France, and, of course, Germany. I accepted the invitation; and since I was going to be in Germany anyway, I also accepted an invitation from Professor Christoph Anstötz, professor of special education at the University of Dortmund, to give a lecture a few days later on the subject 'Do severely disabled newborn infants have a right to life?'

My intention in these lectures was to defend a view for which I have argued in several previously published works: that the parents of severely disabled newborn infants should be able to decide, together with their physician, whether their infant should live or die. If the parents and their medical adviser are in agreement that the infant's life will be so miserable or so devoid of minimal satisfactions that it would be inhumane or futile to prolong life, then they should be allowed to ensure that death comes about speedily and without suffering. Such a decision might reasonably be reached, if, for instance, an infant was born with anencephaly (the term means 'no brain' and infants with this condition have no prospect of ever gaining consciousness); or with a major chromosomal disorder such as trisomy 18, in which there are abnormalities of the nervous system, internal organs, and external features, and death always occurs within a few months, or at most two years; or in very severe forms of spina bifida where an exposed spinal cord leads to paralysis from the waist down, incontinence of bladder and bowel, a build-up of fluid on the brain, and, often, mental retardation. (Were these conditions to be detected in prenatal examinations, many mothers would choose to have abortions and their decisions would be widely seen as understandable.)

Parents may not always be able to make an unbiased decision concerning the future of their infant, and their decisions may not be defensible. In some cases – Down's syndrome perhaps – the outlook for the child might be for a life without suffering, but the child would need much more care and attention, over a longer period, than a normal child would require. Some couples, feeling that they were not in a position to provide the care required, or that it would be harmful for their already existing family for them to try to do so, might oppose sustaining the infant's life. There may, however, be other couples willing to give the child an adequate home; or the community may be in a position to take over the responsibility of providing medical care and for ensuring that the child has reasonably good conditions for living a satisfying life and developing his or her potential. In these circumstances, given that the child will not be living a life of unredeemed misery, and the parents will not be coerced into rearing that child, they can no longer insist upon having the major role in life or death decisions for their child.[10]

This position is, of course, at odds with the conventional doctrine of the sanctity of human life; but there are well-known difficulties in defending that doctrine in secular terms, without its traditional religious underpinnings. (Why, for example, if not because human beings are made in the image of God, should the boundary of sacrosanct life match the boundary of our species?) Among philosophers and bioethicists, the view that I was to defend is by no means extraordinary; if it has not quite

10 There is a brief account of my reasons for holding this position in *Practical Ethics*, Chapter 7; and a much more detailed one in Helga Kuhse and Peter Singer, *Should the Baby Live?* (Oxford University Press, 1985). See also Peter Singer and Helga Kuhse, 'The Future of Baby Doe', *The New York Review* (March 1, 1984), pp. 17–22.

reached the level of orthodoxy, it, or at least something akin to it, is widely held, and by some of the most respected scholars in the fields of both bioethics and applied ethics.[11]

Just a day or two before I was due to leave for Germany, my invitation to speak at the Marburg conference was abruptly withdrawn. The reason given was that, by agreeing to lecture at the University of Dortmund, I had allowed opponents of my views to argue that Lebenshilfe was providing the means for me to promote my views on euthanasia in Germany. The letter withdrawing the invitation drew a distinction between my discussing these views 'behind closed doors with critical scientists who want to convince you that your attitude infringes human rights' and my promoting my position 'in public'. A postscript added that several organizations of handicapped persons were planning protest demonstrations in Marburg and Dortmund against me, and against Lebenshilfe for having invited me. (Although organizations for the disabled were prominent among the protesters, these groups were strongly supported and encouraged by various coalitions against genetic engineering and reproductive technology, and also by organizations on the left that had, apparently, nothing to do with the issue of euthanasia. The 'Anti-Atom Bureau', for instance, joined the protests, presumably neither knowing nor caring about my opposition to uranium mining and nuclear power.)

The protests soon found their way into the popular press. *Der Spiegel,* which has a position in Germany not unlike that of *Time*

---

11 Here is a selection; many more could be added: H. Tristram Engelhardt, Jr., *The Foundations of Bioethics* (Oxford University Press, 1986); R. G. Frey, *Rights, Killing and Suffering* (Blackwell, 1983); Jonathan Glover, *Causing Deaths and Saving Lives* (Penguin, 1977); John Harris, *The Value of Life* (London: Routledge and Kegan Paul, 1985); James Rachels, *The End of Life* (Oxford University Press, 1986); and *Created from Animals* (Oxford University Press, 1991); Michael Tooley, *Abortion and Infanticide* (Oxford University Press, 1983); and the book by Helga Kuhse to which I have already referred, *The Sanctity-of-Life Doctrine in Medicine: A Critique.*

and *Newsweek* in the United States, published a vehement attack on me written by Franz Christoph, the leader of the self-styled 'Cripples Movement', a militant organization of disabled people.[12] The article was illustrated with photographs of the transportation of 'euthanasia victims' in the Third Reich, and of Hitler's 'Euthanasia Order'. The article gave readers no idea at all of the ethical basis on which I advocated euthanasia, and it quoted spokespeople for groups of the disabled who appeared to believe that I questioned their right to life. I sent a brief reply in which I pointed out that I was advocating euthanasia not for anyone like themselves, but for severely disabled newborn infants, and that it was crucial to my defense of euthanasia that these infants would never have been capable of grasping that they are living beings with a past and a future. Hence my views cannot be a threat to anyone who is capable of wanting to go on living, or even of understanding that his or her life might be threatened. After a long delay, I received a letter from *Der Spiegel* telling me that, for reasons of space, they had been unable to publish my reply. Shortly afterward, however, *Der Spiegel* found space for a further highly critical account of my position on euthanasia, together with an interview, spread over four pages, with one of my leading opponents – and again, the same photograph of the Nazi transport vehicles.[13]

If Lebenshilfe had thought that they could pacify their critics by withdrawing my invitation to speak at Marburg, they had underestimated the storm that had broken loose. The protesters continued their opposition to what they were now calling the 'Euthanasia Congress'. Shortly before the symposium was due to open, Lebenshilfe and the Bishop Bekkers Institute canceled the entire event. Soon after the Faculty of Special Education at

12 Franz Christoph, '(K)ein Diskurs über "lebensunwertes Leben" ', *Der Spiegel*, No. 23/1989 (June 5, 1989).
13 'Bizarre Verquickung' and 'Wenn Mitleid tödlich wird', *Der Spiegel*, No. 34/1989 (August 21, 1989), pp. 171–6.

the University of Dortmund decided not to proceed with my scheduled lecture there.

This was not quite the end of my experiences in Germany that summer. Dr. Georg Meggle, professor of philosophy at the University of Saarbrücken, invited me to lecture at his university in order to show that it was possible to discuss the ethics of euthanasia rationally in Germany. I hoped to use this opportunity to say that, while I understood and strongly supported every effort to prevent the resurgence of Nazi ideas, my own views about euthanasia had nothing whatsoever to do with what the Nazis did. In contrast to the Nazi ideology that the state should decide who was worthy of life, my view was designed to reduce the power of the state and allow parents to make crucial life and death decisions, both for themselves and, in consultation with their doctors, for their newborn infants. Those who argued that it is always wrong to decide that a human life is not worth living would, to be consistent, have to say that we should use all the techniques of modern medical care in order to extend to the greatest possible extent the life of every infant, no matter how hopeless the infant's prospects might be and no matter how painful his or her existence. This was surely too cruel for any humane person to support.

Making this obvious point proved more difficult than I had expected. When I rose to speak in Saarbrücken I was greeted by a chorus of whistles and shouts from a minority of the audience determined to prevent me from speaking. Professor Meggle offered the protesters the opportunity to state why they thought I should not speak. This showed how completely they had misunderstood my position. Many obviously believed that I was politically on the far right. Another suggested that I lacked the experience with Nazism that Germans had had; he and others in the audience were taken aback when I told them that I was the child of Austrian-Jewish refugees, and that three of my grandparents had died in Nazi concentration camps. Some seemed to think that I was opposed to all measures that would advance the position of the disabled in society, whereas in fact, while I hold that some lives are so severely blighted from the beginning that they are better not continued, I also believe that once a life has been allowed to develop, then in every case everything should be done to make that life as satisfying and rich as possible. This should include the best possible education, adjusted to the needs of the child, to bring out to the maximum the particular abilities of the disabled person.

Another chance comment revealed a still deeper ignorance about my position. One protester quoted from a passage in which I compare the capacities of intellectually disabled humans and nonhuman animals. The way in which he left the quotation hanging, as if it were in itself enough to condemn me, made me realize that he thought that I was urging that we should treat disabled humans in the way we now treat nonhuman animals. He had no idea that my views about how we should treat animals are utterly different from those conventionally accepted in Western society. When I replied that, for me, to compare a human being to a nonhuman animal was not to say that the human being should be treated with less consideration, but that the animal should be treated with more, this person asked why I did not use my talents to write about the morality of our treatment of animals, rather than about euthanasia. Naturally I replied that I had done that, and that it was, indeed, precisely for my views about the suffering of animals raised on commercial farms, and used in medical and psychological research, and the need for animal liberation that I was best known in English-speaking countries; but I could see that a large part of the audience simply did not believe that I could be known anywhere as anything other than an advocate of euthanasia.[14]

14 My *Animal Liberation* (Random House, 1975; second revised edition, New York Review/Random House, 1990) had been published in Germany under the title *Befreiung der Tiere* (Munich: F. Hirthammer, 1982) but it is not widely known. Nevertheless, *Practical Ethics* contains two chapters sum-

Allowing these misconceptions to be stated did, at least, provide an opportunity for reply. Someone else came to the platform and said that he agreed that it was not necessary to use intensive care medicine to prolong every life, but allowing an infant to die was different from taking active steps to end the infant's life. That led to further discussion, and so in the end we had a long and not entirely fruitless debate. Some of that audience, at least, went away better informed than they had been when they arrived.[15]

The events of the summer of 1989 have had continuing repercussions on German intellectual life. On the positive side, those who had sought to stifle the controversy over euthanasia soon found that, as so often happens, the attempt to suppress ideas only ensures that the ideas gain a wider audience. Germany's leading liberal weekly newspaper, *Die Zeit,* published two articles that gave a fair account of the arguments for euthanasia, and also discussed the taboo that had prevented open discussion of the topic in Germany. For this courageous piece of journalism, *Die Zeit* also became the target of protests, with Franz Christoph, the leader of the 'Cripples Movement', chaining his wheelchair to the door of the newspaper's editorial offices. The editors of *Die Zeit* then invited Christoph to take part in a tape-recorded discussion with the editors of the newspaper and one or two others about whether the paper was right to discuss the topic of euthanasia. Christoph accepted, and the transcript was published in a further extensive article. Predictably, as in Saarbrücken, what began as a conversation about whether or not

marising my views on animals, so the response did indicate that most of the protesters had not read the book on which they based their opposition to my invitation to speak.

15 For this reason one of the protesters, reporting on the events in a student publication, made it clear that to enter into the discussion with me was a tactical error. See Holger Dorff, 'Singer in Saarbrücken,' *Unirevue* (Wintersemester, 1989/90), p. 47.

euthanasia should be discussed very soon turned into a debate on euthanasia itself.

From this point the euthanasia debate was picked up by both German and Austrian television. The outcome was that instead of a few hundred people hearing my views at lectures in Marburg and Dortmund, several million read about them or listened to them on television. The *Deutsche Ärzteblatt* – the major German medical journal – published an article by Helga Kuhse entitled 'Why the discussion of euthanasia is unavoidable in Germany too', which led to an extensive debate in subsequent issues.[16] In philosophical circles the discussion of applied ethics in general, and euthanasia in particular, is much livelier now than it was before 1989 – as is indicated by the special issue of *Analyse & Kritik* to which I have already referred. In journals of special education, as well, ethical issues are now being discussed far more frequently than they were two years ago.

The protest also revived the flagging sales of the German edition of *Practical Ethics*. The book sold more copies in the year after June 1989 than it had in all the five years it had previously been available in Germany. Now everyone involved in the debate in Germany seems to be rushing to publish a book on euthanasia. With the exception of two books by Anstötz and Leist, which contain genuine ethical arguments, those published so far are of some interest for those wishing to study the thinking of Germans opposed to free speech, but not for any other reason.[17] For the most part each of the books appears to have been written to a formula that goes something like this:

16 Helga Kuhse, 'Warum Fragen der Euthanasie auch in Deutschland unvermeidlich sind'. *Deutsche Ärzteblatt*, No. 16 (April 19, 1990), pp. 1243–9; readers' letters, and a response by Kuhse, are to be found in No. 37 (September 13, 1990), pp. 2696–704 and No. 38 (September 20, 1990), pp. 2792–6.

17 The list of books published between January 1990 and June 1991 devoted to this theme includes: C. Anstötz, *Ethik und Behinderung* (Berlin: Edition Marhold, 1990); T. Bastian, editor, *Denken, Schreiben, Töten* (Stuttgart: Hirzel, 1990); T. Bruns, U. Panselin, and U. Sierck, *Tödliche Ethik* (Hamburg:

1 Quote a few passages from *Practical Ethics* selected so as to distort the book's meaning.
2 Express horror that anyone can say such things.
3 Make a sneering jibe at the idea that this could pass for philosophy.
4 Draw a parallel between what has been quoted and what the Nazis thought or did.

But it is also essential to observe one negative aspect of the formula:

5 Avoid discussing any of the following dangerous questions: Is human life to be preserved to the maximum extent possible? If not, in cases in which the patient cannot and never has been able to express a preference, how are decisions to discontinue treatment to be made, without an evaluation of the patient's quality of life? What is the moral significance of the distinction between bringing about a patient's death by withdrawing treatment necessary to prolong life and bringing it about by active intervention? Why is advocacy of euthanasia for severely disabled infants so much worse than advocacy of abortion on request that the same people can oppose the right even to discuss the former, while themselves advocating the latter?

The irony about the recent publications, of course, is that even those who are highly critical of my own position do, by publishing their books and articles, foster a climate of debate about the topic. Even Franz Christoph, despite chaining his wheelchair to the offices of *Die Zeit* because they published reports of my views on euthanasia, has now published his own book on the topic. At the outset he protests vigorously

Verlag Libertäre Assoziation, 1990); Franz Christoph, *Tödlicher Zeitgeist* (Cologne: Kiepenheuer und Witsch, 1990); E. Klee, *Durch Zyankali Erlöst* (Frankfurt: Fischer, 1990); A. Leist, editor, *Um Leben und Tod* (Frankfurt: Suhrkamp, 1990); and O. Tolmein, *Geschätzles Leben* (Hamburg: Konkret Literatur Verlag, 1990). They will soon be joined by what is likely to be the best book on the current German debate: R. Hegselmann and R. Merkel, editors, *Zur Debatte über Euthanasie* (Frankfurt: Suhrkamp, expected September 1991).

that his book is not a contribution *to* the debate about euthanasia, but a book *against* this debate; it is self-evident, though, that one cannot publish a book on whether or not to have a debate on euthanasia without stimulating thought among one's readers and reviewers about the issue of euthanasia itself.[18]

The negative aspects of these events are, unfortunately, probably more weighty. Most threatening of all are the incidents described at the beginning of this essay, and the atmosphere of repression and intimidation that they have evoked. Anyone who offers a course based on *Practical Ethics* in Germany now risks the same protests and personal attacks that Professor Kliemt faced in Duisburg. One Berlin philosopher told me recently that it is not possible to offer a course in applied ethics in that city – whether or not it makes reference to my book – because such a course would be bound to be disrupted.

A sinister aspect of this atmosphere is a kind of self-censorship among German publishers. It has proven extraordinarily difficult to find a publisher to undertake a German edition of *Should the Baby Live?* the updated and more comprehensive account of my views (and those of my co-author Helga Kuhse) on the treatment of severely disabled newborn infants. In view of the current controversy, there seems no doubt that a German edition of the book would have good commercial prospects. Yet one after another, German publishers have declined to publish it,

18 See, for instance, the way in which Rudi Tarneden, a reviewer from an association for the disabled, and very sympathetic to Christoph's position, is drawn in the course of his review to raise such questions as: 'Aren't there in fact extreme situations of human suffering, limits to what is bearable? Am I really guilty of contempt for humanity ['*Menschenverachtung*,' a term often used in Germany to describe what I am supposed to be guilty of— PS] if I try to take this into account?' Rudi Tarneden, 'Wo alles richtig ist, kann es auch keine Schuld mehr geben' (a review of Franz Christoph, *Tödlicher Zeitgeist* and Christoph Anstötz, *Ethik und Behinderung*), *Zeitschrift für Heilpädagogik* Vol. 42, No. 4 (1991), p. 246.

even after it had been recommended by editors whose advice they normally accept without hesitation.

For those interested in studying or teaching bioethics or applied ethics in Germany, the consequences are much more serious still. Because he had invited me to lecture at the University of Dortmund, Professor Christoph Anstötz became the target of a hostile campaign aimed at having him dismissed from his teaching duties. Petitions were circulated and letters written to the minister of science and research for the state of Nordrhein-Westfalen, in which Dortmund is situated. These letters were signed by both teachers and students in special education. Although Professor Anstötz has a tenured position from which it would scarcely be possible for him to be dismissed, the government took the complaints seriously enough to ask him to explain why he had invited me, and what implications he drew from my ethical position for his work in special education.

Throughout this campaign, the rector of the University of Dortmund and his office remained silent. The highest officers of the university took no action to indicate their concern that threats of protest had forced an academic lecture to be canceled; nor did they come to the defense of one of their professors when he was under attack for inviting a colleague to give a lecture on the campus of the university. That was typical of the reaction of German professors. There was no strong reaction among them on behalf of academic freedom. With a handful of exceptions, Anstötz's colleagues in special education either joined the campaign against him, or remained silent. A number of philosophers signed declarations of support for the principle of free debate, and one of these was published in the Berlin newspaper *taz*.[19] At Professor Meggle's instigation, 180 members of the German Philosophical Association signed a similar declaration, but the association has since failed to publish the list of the signers, despite giving an undertaking to do so.

19 *taz* (Berlin), January 10, 1990.

All this does not augur well for the future of rational discussion of controversial new ethical issues in Germany and Austria. Outside the German-speaking nations, study and discussion of bioethics is expanding rapidly, in response to the recognition of the need for ethical consideration of the many new issues raised by developments in medicine and the biological sciences. Other fields of applied ethics, such as the status of animals, questions of global justice and resource distribution, environmental ethics and business ethics, are also getting much attention. In Germany and Austria, however, it now takes real courage to do work in applied ethics, and even more courage to publish something that is likely to come under the hostile scrutiny of those who want to stop debate. Academics who do not have a permanent university position must fear not merely personal attack, but also the diminished opportunity to pursue an academic career. The events in Hamburg cast a cloud over the prospects of university posts opening up in these fields. If there are no posts to be obtained, graduate students will avoid working on questions of applied ethics, for there is no sense in studying matters that offer no prospect of employment. There is even a danger that in order to avoid controversy, analytic philosophy as a whole will suffer a setback. At the present time, a large number of new university positions are being created in the universities of the former German Democratic Republic. Philosophers interested in analytic philosophy are concerned that these positions may all go to philosophers working on less sensitive subjects, for example, to those who concentrate on historical studies, or to followers of Habermas who have generally kept quiet about these sensitive ethical issues and about the obstacles to debating them in Germany today.

Germans of course are still struggling to deal with their past, and the German past is one which comes close to defying rational understanding. There is, however, a peculiar tone of fanaticism about some sections of the German debate over euthanasia that goes beyond normal opposition to Nazism, and instead begins to seem like the very mentality that made Nazism possible. To see this attitude at work, let us look not at euthanasia, but at an issue that is, for the Germans, closely related to it and just as firmly taboo: the issue of eugenics. Because the Nazis practiced eugenics, anything in any way related to genetic engineering in Germany is now smeared with Nazi associations. This attack embraces the rejection of prenatal diagnosis, when followed by selective abortion of fetuses with Down's syndrome, spina bifida, or other defects, and even leads to criticism of genetic counseling designed to avoid the conception of children with genetic defects. It has also led to the German parliament unanimously passing a law that prohibits all non-therapeutic experimentation on the human embryo. The British parliament, by contrast, recently passed by substantial majorities in both chambers a law that allows nontherapeutic embryo experimentation up to fourteen days after fertilization.

To understand how bizarre this situation is, readers in English-speaking countries must remind themselves that this opposition comes not, as it would in our countries, from right-wing conservative and religious groups, but from the left. Since women's organizations are prominent among the opposition to anything that smacks of eugenics, and also are in the forefront of the movement to defend the right to abortion, the issue of prenatal diagnosis gives rise to an obvious problem in German feminist circles. The accepted solution seems to be that a woman should have the right to an abortion, but not to an abortion based on accurate information about the future life-prospects of the fetus she is carrying.[20]

---

20 German feminists who read Franz Christoph's recent book (see note 17, above) may reconsider their support for his position; for he leaves no doubt that he is opposed to granting women a right to decide about abortion. For Christoph, 'Abortion decisions are always decisions about whether a life is worthy of being lived; the child does not fit into the woman's present life-

The rationale for this view is, at least, consistent with the rationale for opposition to euthanasia: it is the idea that no one should ever judge one life to be less worth living than another. To accept prenatal diagnosis and selective abortion, or even to select genetic counseling aimed at avoiding the conception of infants with extreme genetic abnormalities, is seen as judging that some lives are less worth living than others. To this the more militant groups of disabled people take offense; it suggests, they maintain, that they should not have been allowed to come into existence, and thus denies their right to life.

This is, of course, a fallacy. It is one thing to hold that we may justifiably take steps to ensure that the children we bring into the world do not face appalling obstacles to living a minimally decent life, and a quite different thing to deny to a living person who wants to go on living the right to do just that. If the suggestion, on the other hand, is that whenever we seek to avoid having severely disabled children, we are improperly judging one kind of life to be worse than another, we can reply that such judgments are both necessary and proper. To argue otherwise would seem to suggest that if we break a leg, we should not get it mended, because in doing so we judge the

plans. Or: the social situation is unsatisfactory. Or: the woman holds that she is only able to bear a healthy child. Whether one likes it or not: with the last example, the woman who wants an abortion confirms an objectively negative social value judgment against the handicapped' (p. 13). There is more along these lines, all in a style well-suited for quotation in the pamphlets of the anti-abortion movement.

This is, at least, more honest than the evasive maneuvering of Oliver Tolmein, who states in the foreword to his *Geschätztes Leben* that to discuss the significance of the feminist concept of self-determination in the context of prenatal diagnosis and abortion would take him 'by far' beyond the bounds of his theme (p. 9). Odd, since the crux of his vitriolic attack on all who advocate euthanasia (an attack that includes, on the very first page of the book, a statement that it is necessary to disrupt seminars on the issue) is that those who advocate euthanasia are committed to valuing some human lives as not worth living.

lives of those with crippled legs to be less worth living than our own.[21] For people to believe such a fallacious argument is bad enough; what is really frightening, however, is that people believe in it with such fanaticism that they are prepared to use force to suppress any attempt to discuss it.

If this is the case with attempts to discuss practices like genetic counseling and prenatal diagnosis, which are today very widely accepted in most developed countries, it is easy to imagine that the shadow of Nazism prevents any rational discussion of anything that relates to euthanasia. It avails little to point out that what the Nazis called 'euthanasia' had nothing to do with compassion or concern for those who were killed, but was simply the murder of people considered unworthy of living from the racist viewpoint of the German *Volk*. Such distinctions are altogether too subtle for those who are convinced that they alone know what will prevent a revival of Nazi-like barbarism.

Can anything be done? In May this year, in Zurich, I had one of the most unpleasant experiences yet in this unhappy story; but it gave, at the same time, a glimmer of hope that there may be a remedy.

I was invited by the Zoological Institute of the University of Zurich to give a lecture on 'Animal Rights'. On the following day, the philosophy department had organized a colloquium for twenty-five invited philosophers, theologians, special educationalists, zoologists, and other academics to discuss the implications for both humans and animals of an ethic that would reject the view that the boundary of our species marks a moral boundary of great intrinsic significance, and holds that non-human animals have no rights.

The lecture on animal rights did not take place. Before it began, a group of disabled people in wheelchairs, who had been

21 R. M. Hare makes a similar point in a letter published in *Die Zeit*, August 11, 1989.

admitted to the flat area at the front of the lecture theater, staged a brief protest in which they said that, while it was all the same to them whether or not I lectured on the topic of animal rights, they objected to the fact that the University of Zurich had invited such a notorious advocate of euthanasia to discuss ethical issues that also concerned the disabled. At the end of this protest, when I rose to speak, a section of the audience – perhaps a quarter or a third – began to chant: "Singer *raus!* Singer *raus!*" As I heard this chanted, in German, by people so lacking in respect for the tradition of reasoned debate that they were unwilling even to allow me to make a response to what had just been said about me, I had an overwhelming feeling that this was what it must have been like to attempt to reason against the rising tide of Nazism in the declining days of the Weimar Republic. The difference was that the chant would have been, not 'Singer *raus*', but '*Juden raus*'. An overhead projector was still functioning, and I began to write on it, to point out this parallel that I was feeling so strongly. At that point one of the protesters came up behind me and tore my glasses from my face, throwing them on the floor and breaking them.

My host wisely decided to abandon the lecture; there was nothing else that could be done. But from this distressing affair came one good sign; it was clear that the disabled people who had made the initial protest were distressed with what had happened afterward. Several said that they had not intended that the lecture should be disrupted; they had, in fact, prepared questions to ask during the discussion period that would have followed the lecture. Even while the chanting was going on, some attempted to begin a discussion with me; at which point some of the able-bodied demonstrators (presumably well aware of the way in which in Saarbrücken a discussion had broken through the initial hostility toward me) urgently remonstrated with them not to talk to me. The disabled, however, clearly had no power to do anything about the chanting.

As already noted, my views in no way threaten anyone who

is, or ever has been, even minimally aware of the fact that he or she has a possible future life that could be threatened. But there are some who have a political interest in preventing this elementary fact from becoming known. These people are now playing on the anxieties of the disabled in order to use them as a political front for different purposes. In Zurich, for instance, prominent among the nondisabled people chanting 'Singer *raus*' were the *Autonomen*, or 'Autonomists', a group that affects an anarchist, style but disdains any interest in anarchist theory. For these nondisabled political groups, preventing Singer from speaking, no matter what the topic, has become an end in itself, a way of rallying the faithful and striking at the entire system in which rational debate takes place. Disabled people have nothing to gain, and much to lose, by allowing themselves to be used by such nihilistic groups. If they can be brought to see that their interests are better served by an open discussion with those whose views they oppose, it may be possible to begin a process in which both bioethicists and the disabled address the proper concerns of the other side, and move to a dialogue that is constructive rather than destructive.

Such a dialogue would be only a beginning. To heal the damage done to bioethics and applied ethics in Germany will take much longer. There is a real danger that the atmosphere of intimidation and intolerance which has spread from the issue of euthanasia to all of bioethics, and with the events in Hamburg, to applied ethics in general, will continue to broaden. It is essential that the minority that is actively opposing the free discussion of academic ideas be isolated. Here too, what happened in Zurich may serve as an example for other German-speaking countries to follow. In sharp contrast to the silence of the rector of the University of Dortmund, or the fatuous claim that "We didn't know at all who that was" of the dean of medicine at the University of Vienna, Professor H. H. Schmid, rector of the University of Zurich, issued a statement expressing the university's 'outrage over this grave violation of academic freedom of speech'.[22] The professors of the Zoological Institute and the dean of the Faculty of Science have also unequivocally condemned the disruption, and the major German-language newspapers in Zurich gave objective coverage to the events and to my views.[23]

Meanwhile Germans and Austrians, both in academic life and in the press, have shown themselves sadly lacking in the commitment exemplified by the celebrated utterance attributed to Voltaire: 'I disapprove of what you say, but I will defend to the death your right to say it'. No one has, as yet, been asked to risk death in order to defend my right to discuss euthanasia in Germany, but it is important that many more should be prepared to risk a little hostility from the minority that is trying to silence a debate on central ethical questions.

22 'Zur Sprengung einer Vortragsveranstaltung an der Universität', *Unipresse Dienst*, Universität Zurich, May 31, 1991.
23 See, for example, 'Mit Trillerpfeifen gegen einen Philosophen', and 'Diese Probleme kann and soll man besprechen', both in *Tages-Anzeiger*, May 29, 1991; 'Niedergeschrien', *Neue Zürcher Zeitung*, May 27, 1991; and (despite the pejorative headline) 'Ein Tötungshelfer mit faschistischem Gedankengut?' *Die Weltwoche*, May 23, 1991.

NOTES, REFERENCES, AND
FURTHER READING

Preface

The quotation on comparing humans and animals is from *Ethische Grundaussagen* (Ethical foundational statements) by the Board of the Federal Association Lebenshilfe für geistig Behinderte e.V., published in the journal of the association, *Geistige Behinderung*, vol. 29 no. 4 (1990): 256.

Chapter 1: About ethics

The issues discussed in the first section – relativism, subjectivism, and the alleged dependence of ethics on religion – are dealt with in several textbooks. R. B. Brandt's *Ethical Theory* (Englewood Cliffs, N.J., 1959) is more thorough than most. See also the articles on these topics by David Wong, James Rachels, and Jonathan Berg, respectively, in P. Singer (ed.), *A Companion to Ethics* (Oxford, 1991). Plato's argument against defining 'good' as 'what the gods approve' is in his *Euthyphro*. Engels's discussion of the Marxist view of morality, and his reference to a 'really human morality' is in his *Herr Eugen Dühring's Revolution in Science*, chap. 9. For a discussion of Marx's critique of morality, see Allen Wood, 'Marx against Morality' in P. Singer (ed.), *A Companion to Ethics*. C. L. Stevenson's emotivist theory is most fully expounded in his *Ethics and Language* (New Haven, 1944). R. M. Hare's basic position is to be found in *The Language of Morals* (Oxford, 1952); *Freedom and Reason* (Oxford, 1963), and *Moral Thinking* (Oxford, 1981). For a summary statement, see Hare's essay 'Universal Prescriptivism' in P. Singer (ed.), *A Companion to Ethics*. J. L. Mackie's *Ethics: Inventing Right and Wrong* (Harmondsworth, Middlesex, 1977) defends a version of subjectivism.

The more important formulations of the universalisability principle referred to in the second section are in I. Kant, *Groundwork of the*

Metaphysic of Morals, Section II (various translations and editions); R. M. Hare, *Freedom and Reason* and *Moral Thinking*; R. Firth, 'Ethical Absolutism and the Ideal Observer', *Philosophy and Phenomenological Research*, vol. 12 (1951-2); J. J. C. Smart and B. Williams, *Utilitarianism, For and Against* (Cambridge, 1973); John Rawls, *A Theory of Justice* (Oxford, 1972); J. P. Sartre, 'Existentialism Is a Humanism', in W. Kaufmann (ed.), *Existentialism from Dostoevsky to Sartre*, 2d ed. (New York, 1975); and Jürgen Habermas, *Legitimation Crisis* (trans. T. McCarthy, London 1976), pt. 111, chaps. 2–4.

The tentative argument for a utilitarianism based on interests or preferences owes most to Hare, although it does not go as far as the argument to be found in *Moral Thinking*.

Chapter 2: Equality and its implications

Rawls's argument that equality can be based on the natural characteristics of human beings is to be found in sec. 77 of *A Theory of Justice*.

The principal arguments in favour of a link between IQ and race can be found in A. R. Jensen, *Genetics and Education* (London, 1972) and *Educability and Group Differences* (London, 1973); and in H. J. Eysenck's *Race, Intelligence and Education* (London, 1971). A variety of objections are collected in K. Richardson and D. Spears (eds.), *Race, Culture and Intelligence* (Harmondsworth, Middlesex, 1972). See also N. J. Block and G. Dworkin, *The IQ Controversy* (New York, 1976). Thomas Jefferson's comment on the irrelevance of intelligence to the issue of rights was made in a letter to Henri Gregoire, 25 February 1809.

The debate over the nature and origin of psychological differences between the sexes is soberly and comprehensively surveyed in E. Maccoby and C. Jacklin, *The Psychology of Sex Differences* (Stanford, 1974). Corinne Hutt, in *Males and Females* (Harmondsworth, Middlesex, 1972), states the case for a biological basis for sex differences. Steven Goldberg's *The Inevitability of Patriarchy* (New York, 1973) is a polemic against feminist views like those in Kate Millett's *Sexual Politics* (New York, 1971) or Juliet Mitchell's *Women's Estate* (Harmondsworth, Middlesex, 1971). A different view is presented in A. H. Eagly, *Sex Differences in Social Behavior: A Social Role Interpretation* (Hillsdale, N.J., 1987). For recent confirmation of the existence of sex differences, see Eleanor E. Maccoby, 'Gender and Relationships: A Developmental Account', *American Psychologist*, 1990, pp. 513–20; and for a popular report,

Christine Gorman 'Sizing Up the Sexes', *Time*, 20 January 1992, pp. 30–7.

For a typical defence of equality of opportunity as the only justifiable form of equality, see Daniel Bell, 'A "Just" Equality', *Dialogue* (Washington, D.C.), vol. 8, no. 2 (1975). The quotation on pp. 38–9 is from Jeffrey Gray, 'Why Should Society Reward Intelligence?' *The Times* (London), 8 September 1972. For an acute statement of the dilemmas raised by equal opportunity, see J. Fishkin, *Justice, Equal Opportunity and the Family* (New Haven, 1983).

The leading case on reverse discrimination in the United States, *Regents of the University of California v Allan Bakke*, was decided by the U.S. Supreme Court on 5 July 1978. M. Cohen, T. Nagel, and T. Scanlon have brought together some relevant essays on this topic in their anthology, *Equality and Preferential Treatment* (Princeton, 1976). See also Bernard Boxill, 'Equality, Discrimination and Preferential Treatment', in P. Singer (ed.), *A Companion to Ethics* and the same author's *Blacks and Social Justice* (Totowa, N.J., 1983).

Chapter 3: Equality for animals

My views on animals first appeared in *The New York Review of Books*, 5 April 1973, under the title 'Animal Liberation'. This article was a review of R. and S. Godlovitch and J. Harris (eds.), *Animals, Men and Morals* (London, 1972). A more complete statement was published as *Animal Liberation*, 2d ed. (New York, 1990). Richard Ryder charts the history of changing attitudes towards speciesism in *Animal Revolution* (Oxford, 1989).

Among other works arguing for a drastic revision in our present attitudes to animals are Stephen Clark, *The Moral Status of Animals* (Oxford, 1977); and Tom Regan *The Case for Animal Rights* (Berkeley, 1983). *Animal Rights and Human Obligations*, 2d ed., edited by T. Regan and P. Singer (Englewood Cliffs, N.J., 1989) is a collection of essays, old and new, both for and against attributing rights to animals or duties to humans in respect of animals. P. Singer (ed.), *In Defence of Animals* (Oxford, 1985), collects essays by both activists and theorists involved with the animal liberation movement. Steve Sapontzis, *Morals, Reason and Animals* (Philadelphia, 1987), is a detailed and sympathetic philosophical analysis of arguments about animal liberation, while R. G. Frey, *Rights, Killing and Suffering* (Oxford, 1983), and Michael Leahy, *Against Liberation* (London, 1991), offer philosophical critiques of the animal liberation position. Mary Midgley, *Animals and Why They Matter*

(Harmondsworth, Middlesex, 1983), is a readable and often penetrating account of these issues. James Rachels, *Created from Animals* (Oxford, 1990), draws the moral implications of the Darwinian revolution in our thinking about our place among the animals. Finally, Lori Gruen's 'Animals' in P. Singer (ed.), *A Companion to Ethics*, explores the predominant recent approaches to the issue.

Bentham's defence of animals, quoted in the section 'Racism and Speciesism' is from his *Introduction to the Principles of Morals and Legislation*, chap. 18, sec. 1, n.

A more detailed description of modern farming conditions can be found in *Animal Liberation*, chap. 3; and in James Mason and Peter Singer, *Animal Factories*, 2d ed. (New York, 1990). Similarly, *Animal Liberation*, chap. 2, contains a fuller discussion of the use of animals in research than is possible in this book, but see also Richard Ryder, *Victims of Science*, 2d ed. (Fontwell, Sussex, 1983). Publication details of the experiment on rhesus monkeys carried out at the U.S. Armed Forces Radiobiology Institute are: Carol Frantz, 'Effects of Mixed Neutron-gamma Total-body Irradiation on Physical Activity Performance of Rhesus Monkeys', *Radiation Research*, vol. 101 (1985): 434–41. The experiments at Princeton University on starving rats, and those by H. F. Harlow on isolating monkeys, referred to in the sub-section 'Experimenting on Animals', were originally published in *Journal of Comparative and Physiological Psychology*, vol. 78 (1972): 202, *Proceedings of the National Academy of Science*, vol. 54 (1965): 90, and *Engineering and Science*, vol. 33, no. 6 (April 1970): 8. On the continuation of Harlow's work, see *Animal Liberation*, 2d ed., pp. 34–5.

Among the objections, the claim that animals are incapable of feeling pain has standardly been associated with Descartes. But Descartes' view is less clear (and less consistent) than most have assumed. See John Cottingham, 'A Brute to the Brutes?: Descartes' Treatment of Animals', *Philosophy*, vol. 53 (1978): 551. In *The Unheeded Cry* (Oxford, 1989), Bernard Rollin describes and criticises more recent ideologies that have denied the reality of animal pain.

The source for the anecdote about Benjamin Franklin is his *Autobiography* (New York, 1950), p. 41. The same objection has been more seriously considered by John Benson in 'Duty and the Beast', *Philosophy*, vol. 53 (1978): 545–7.

Jane Goodall's observations of chimpanzees are engagingly recounted in *In the Shadow of Man* (Boston, 1971) and *Through a Window* (London, 1990); her own more scholarly account is *The Chimpanzees of Gombe* (Cambridge, Mass., 1986). For more information on the capacities of the great apes, see Paola Cavalieri and Peter Singer (eds.), *Toward a New Equality: The Great Ape Project* (forthcoming). The 'argument from marginal cases' was thus christened by Jan Narveson, 'Animal Rights', *Canadian Journal of Philosophy*, vol. 7 (1977). Of the objections to this argument discussed in the sub-section 'Differences between Humans and Animals', the first was made by Stanley Benn, 'Egalitarianism and Equal Consideration of Interests', in J. Pennock and J. Chapman (eds.), *Nomos IX: Equality* (New York, 1967), pp. 62ff.; the second by John Benson, 'Duty and the Beast', *Philosophy*, vol. 53 (the quotation from 'one reviewer of *Animal Liberation*' is from p. 536 of this article) and related points are made by Bonnie Steinbock, 'Speciesism and the Idea of Equality', *Philosophy*, vol. 53 (1978): 255–6, and at greater length by Leslie Pickering Francis and Richard Norman, 'Some Animals Are More Equal Than Others', *Philosophy*, vol. 53 (1978): 518–27. The third objection can be found in Philip Devine, 'The Moral Basis of Vegetarianism', *Philosophy*, vol. 53 (19): 496–8.

The quotation from Plato's *Republic* in the section 'Ethics and Reciprocity' is from Book 2, pp. 358–9. Later statements of a similar view include John Rawls, *A Theory of Justice*; J. L. Mackie, *Ethics* chap. 5; and David Gauthier, *Morals by Agreement* (Oxford, 1986). They exclude animals from the centre of morality, although they soften the impact of this exclusion in various ways (see, for example, *A Theory of Justice*, p. 512, and *Ethics*, pp. 193–5). Narveson also considers the reciprocity notion of ethics in 'Animal Rights'. My discussion of the looser version of the reciprocity view draws on Edward Johnson, *Species and Morality*, Ph.D. thesis, Princeton University, 1976, University Microfilms International, Ann Arbor, Michigan, 1981, p. 145.

Chapter 4: What's wrong with killing?

Andrew Stinson's treatment is described by Robert and Peggy Stinson in *The Long Dying of Baby Andrew* (Boston, 1983).

Joseph Fletcher's article 'Indicators of Humanhood: A Tentative Profile of Man' appeared in *The Hastings Center Report*, vol. 2, no. 5 (1972). John Locke's definition of 'person' is taken from his *Essay Concerning Human Understanding*, bk. 1, chap. 9, par. 29. Aristotle's views on infanticide are in his *Politics*, bk. 7, p. 1335b; Plato's are in the *Republic*, bk. 5, p. 460. Support for the claim that our present attitudes to infanticide are largely the effect of the influence of Christianity on our thought can be found in the historical material on infanticide cited in the notes on chap. 6, below. (See especially the article by W. L. Langer, pp. 353–5.) For Aquinas's statement that killing a human being offends against God as killing a slave offends against the master of the slave, see *Summa Theologica*, 2, ii, Question 64, article 5.

Hare propounds and defends his two-level view of moral reasoning in *Moral Thinking* (Oxford, 1981).

Michael Tooley's 'Abortion and Infanticide' was first published in *Philosophy and Public Affairs*, vol. 2 (1972) The passage quoted here is from a revised version in J. Feinberg (ed.), *The Problem of Abortion* (Belmont, 1973), p. 60. His book *Abortion and Infanticide* was published in Oxford in 1983.

For further discussion of respect for autonomy as an objection to killing, see Jonathan Glover, *Causing Death and Saving Lives* (Harmondsworth, Middlesex, 1977), chap. 5. and H. J. McCloskey, 'The Right to Life', *Mind*, vol. 84 (1975).

My discussion of the 'total' and 'prior existence' versions of utilitarianism owes much to Derek Parfit. I originally tried to defend the prior existence view in 'A Utilitarian Population Principle', in M. Bayles (ed.), *Ethics and Population* (Cambridge, Mass., 1976), but Parfit's reply, 'On Doing the Best for Our Children', in the same volume, persuaded me to change my mind. Parfit's *Reasons and Persons* (Oxford, 1984) is required reading for anyone wishing to pursue this topic in depth. See also his short account of some of the issues in 'Overpopulation and the Quality of Life', in P. Singer (ed.), *Applied Ethics* (Oxford, 1986). Parfit uses the term 'person-affecting' where I use 'prior existence'. The reason for the change is that the view has no special reference to persons, as distinct from other sentient creatures.

The distinction between the two versions of utilitarianism appears to have been first noticed by Henry Sidgwick, *The Methods of Ethics* (London, 1907), pp. 414–16. Later discussions include, in addition to those cited above, J. Narveson, 'Moral Problems of Population', *The Monist*, vol. 57 (1973); T. G. Roupas, 'The Value of Life', *Philosophy and Public Affairs*, vol. 7 (1978); and R. I. Sikora, 'Is It Wrong to Prevent the Existence of Future Generations', in B. Barry and R. Sikora (eds.), *Obligations to Future Generations* (Philadelphia, 1978).

Mill's famous passage comparing Socrates and the fool appeared in his *Utilitarianism* (London, 1960; first published 1863), pp. 8–9.

Chapter 5: Taking life: animals

The break-through in talking to other species was first announced in R. and B. Gardner, 'Teaching Sign Language to a Chimpanzee', *Science*, vol. 165 (1969): 664–72. Since then the literature has multiplied rapidly. The information on language use in chimpanzees, gorillas and an orangutan in the section 'Can a Non-human Animal Be a Person?' is drawn from the articles by Roger and Deborah Fouts, Francine Patterson and Wendy Gordon, and H. Lyn Miles, in Paola Cavalieri and Peter Singer (eds.), *Toward a New Equality: The Great Ape Project* (forthcoming). Erik Eckholm, 'Language Acquisition in Nonhuman Primates', in T. Regan and P. Singer (eds.), *Animal Rights and Human Obligations*, 2d ed. (Englewood Cliffs, N.J., 1989), provides a brief popular account.

The quotation in the same section from Stuart Hampshire is to be found in his *Thought and Action* (London, 1959), pp. 98–9. Others who have held related views are Anthony Kenny, in *Will, Freedom and Power* (Oxford, 1975); Donald Davidson, 'Thought and Talk', in S. Guttenplan (ed.), *Mind and Language* (Oxford, 1975); and Michael Leahy, *Against Liberation* (London, 1991).

Julia's problem-solving abilities were demonstrated by J. Döhl and B. Rensch; their work is described in Jane Goodall, *The Chimpanzees of Gombe*, p. 31. Frans de Waal reports his observations of chimpanzees in *Chimpanzee Politics* (New York, 1983). Goodall's account of Figan's thoughtful manner of obtaining his banana is taken from p. 107 of *In the Shadow of Man*. Robert Mitchell assesses the evidence for self-consciousness in apes in 'Humans, Nonhumans and Personhood', in Paola Cavalieri and Peter Singer (eds.), *Toward a New Equality: The Great Ape Project*. The anecdotal evidence of a sense of time in a guide dog comes from Sheila Hocken, *Emma and I* (London, 1978), p. 63; and the story of the feral cats is from the chapter on intelligence in Muriel Beadle, *The Cat: History, Biology and Behaviour* (London, 1977). I owe these last two references to Mary Midgley, *Animals and Why They Matter* (Harmondsworth, Middlesex, 1983), p. 58.

Goodall's estimate of the number of chimpanzees who die for every one to reach our shores alive is on p. 257 of *In the Shadow of Man*. See also Geza Teleki's account of the chimpanzee trade in Paola Cavalieri and Peter Singer (eds.), *Toward a New Equality: The Great Ape Project*.

Leslie Stephen's claim that eating bacon is kind to pigs comes from his *Social Rights and Duties* (London, 1896) and is quoted by Henry Salt in 'The Logic of the Larder', which appeared in Salt's *The Humanities of Diet* (Manchester, 1914) and has been reprinted in the first edition of T. Regan and P. Singer (eds.), *Animal Rights and Human Obligations* (Englewood Cliffs, N.J., 1976). Salt's reply is in the same article. My own earlier discussion of this issue is in Chapter 6 of the first edition of *Animal Liberation* (New York, 1975). For the example of the two women, see Derek Parfit, 'Rights, Interests and Possible People', in S. Gorovitz et al. (eds.), *Moral Problems in Medicine* (Englewood Cliffs, N.J., 1976); a variation expressed in terms of a choice between two different medical programs can be found in Parfit's *Reasons and Persons* (Oxford, 1984), p. 367. James Rachels's distinction between a biological and a biographical life comes from his *The End of Life* (Oxford, 1987). Hart's discussion of this topic in his review of the first edition of this book was entitled 'Death and Utility' and appeared in *The New York Review of Books*, 15 May 1980. My initial response appeared as a letter in the same publication, 14 August 1980. I develop the metaphor of life as a journey in 'Life's Uncertain Voyage', in P. Pettit, R. Sylvan, and J. Norman (eds.), *Metaphysics and Morality: Essays in Honour of J. J. C. Smart* (Oxford, 1987).

Chapter 6: Taking life: The embryo and fetus

The most important sections of the decision of the U.S. Supreme Court in *Roe* v. *Wade* are reprinted in J.Feinberg (ed.), *The Problem of Abortion*. Robert Edwards's speculations about taking stem cells from embryos at around seventeen days after fertilisation are from his essay 'The case for studying human embryos and their constituent tissues *in vitro*', in R. G. Edwards and J. M. Purdy (eds.), *Human Conception in Vitro* (London, 1982). The government committee referred to in the sub-section 'Not the Law's Business?' – the Wolfenden Committee – issued the *Report of the Committee on Homosexual Offences and Prostitution*, Command Paper 247 (London, 1957). The quotation is from p. 24. J. S. Mill's 'very simple principle' is stated in the introductory chapter of *On Liberty*, 3d ed. (London, 1864). Edwin Schur's *Crimes without Victims* was published in Englewood Cliffs, N.J., in 1965. Judith Jarvis Thomson's 'A Defense of Abortion' appeared in *Philosophy and Public Affairs*, vol. 1 (1971) and has been reprinted in P. Singer (ed.), *Applied Ethics*.

Paul Ramsey uses the genetic uniqueness of the fetus as an argument against abortion in 'The Morality of Abortion', in D. H. Labby (ed.), *Life or Death: Ethics and Options* (London, 1968) and reprinted in J. Rachels (ed.), *Moral Problems*, 2d ed. (New York, 1975), p. 40.

On scientific, ethical and legal aspects of embryo experimentation, see P. Singer, H. Kuhse, S. Buckle, K. Dawson, and P. Kasimba (eds.), *Embryo Experimentation* (Cambridge, England, 1990). I owe my speculations about the identity of the splitting embryo to Helga Kuhse, with whom I co-authored 'Individuals, Humans and Persons: The Issue of

Moral Status', in that volume. We were both indebted to a remarkable book by a Roman Catholic theologian that challenges the view that conception marks the beginning of the human individual: Norman Ford, *When Did I Begin?* (Cambridge, 1988). The argument about potentiality in the context of IVF was first published in P. Singer and K. Dawson, 'IVF Technology and the Argument from Potential', *Philosophy and Public Affairs*, vol. 17 (1988) and is reprinted in *Embryo Experimentation*. Stephen Buckle takes a different approach in 'Arguing from Potential', *Bioethics*, vol. 2 (1988) and reprinted in *Embryo Experimentation*. The quotation from John Noonan in the section 'The Status of the Embryo in the Laboratory' is from his 'An Almost Absolute Value in History', in John Noonan (ed.), *The Morality of Abortion* (Cambridge, Mass., 1970) pp. 56–7. On the feminist argument about IVF, see Beth Gaze and Karen Dawson, 'Who Is the Subject of Research?' and Mary Anne Warren, 'Is IVF Research a Threat to Women's Autonomy?' both in *Embryo Experimentation*.

On the use of fetuses in research and potential clinical uses, see Karen Dawson 'Overview of Fetal Tissue Transplantation', in Lynn Gillam (ed.), *The Fetus as Tissue Donor: Use or Abuse* (Clayton, Victoria, 1990). My account of the development of fetal sentience draws on research carried out by Susan Taiwa at the Centre for Human Bioethics, Monash University, and published as 'When Is the Capacity for Sentience Acquired during Human Fetal Development?' *Journal of Maternal-Fetal Medicine*, vol. 1 (1992). An earlier expert opinion came from the British government advisory group on fetal research, chaired by Sir John Peel, published as *The Use of Fetuses and Fetal Materials for Research* (London, 1972). See also Clifford Grobstein, *Science and the Unborn* (New York 1988).

Bentham's reassuring comment on infanticide, quoted in the section 'Abortion and Infanticide' is from his *Theory of Legislation*, p. 264, and is quoted by E. Westermarck, *The Origin and Development of Moral Ideas* (London, 1924), vol. 1, p. 413n. In the final part of *Abortion and Infanticide* Michael Tooley discusses the available evidence on the development in the infant of the sense of being a continuing self.

For historical material on the prevalence of infanticide see Maria Piers, *Infanticide* (New York, 1978); and W. L. Langer, 'Infanticide: A Historical Survey', *History of Childhood Quarterly*, vol. 1 (1974). An older, but still valuable survey is in Edward Westermarck, *The Origin and Development of Moral Ideas*, vol. 1, pp. 394–413. An interesting study of the use of infanticide as a form of family planning is *Nakahara: Family Farming and Population in a Japanese Village, 1717–1830*, by

Thomas C. Smith (Palo Alto, Calif., 1977). References for Plato and Aristotle were given in the notes to Chapter 4. For Seneca, see *De Ira*, 1, 15, cited by Westermarck, *The Origin and Development of Moral Ideas*, vol. 1, p. 419. Marvin Kohl (ed.), *Infanticide and the Value of Life* (Buffalo, N.Y., 1978) is a collection of essays on infanticide. A powerful argument on public policy grounds for birth as the place to draw line, can be found (by readers of German) in Norbert Hoerster, 'Kindstötung und das Lebensrecht von Personen', *Analyse & Kritik*, vol. 12 (1990): 226–44.

Further articles on abortion are collected in J. Feinberg (ed.), *The Problem of Abortion*, and in Robert Perkins (ed.), *Abortion, Pro and Con* (Cambridge, Mass., 1974). Articles with some affinity with the position I have taken include R. M. Hare, 'Abortion and the Golden Rule', *Philosophy and Public Affairs*, vol. 4 (1975); and Mary Anne Warren, 'The Moral and Legal Status of Abortion', *The Monist*, vol. 57 (1973). Don Marquis restates the conservative position in 'Why Abortion Is Immoral', *Journal of Philosophy*, vol. 86 (1989); but see also Alistair Norcross, 'Killing, Abortion and Contraception: A Reply to Marquis', *Journal of Philosophy*, vol. 87 (1990). A useful summary of the abortion issue is Mary Anne Warren's 'Abortion' in P. Singer (ed.), *A Companion to Ethics*.

Chapter 7: Taking life: Humans

Derek Humphry's account of his wife's death, *Jean's Way*, was published in London in 1978. On the death of Janet Adkins, see *New York Times*, 14 December 1990; for Jack Kevorkian's own account, see J. Kevorkian, *Prescription: Medicide* (Buffalo, N.Y., 1991). For details of the Zygmaniak case, see Paige Mitchell, *Act of Love* (New York, 1976), or the *New York Times*, 1, 3, and 6 November 1973. Louis Repouille's killing of his son was reported in the *New York Times*, 13 October 1939, and is cited by Yale Kamisar, 'Some Non-religious Views against Proposed Mercy Killing Legislation', *Minnesota Law Review*, vol. 42 (1958): 1,021. Details of the Linares case are from the *New York Times*, 27 April 1989 and the *Hastings Center Report*, July/August 1989.

Robert Reid, *My Children, My Children*, is a fine introduction to the nature of some birth defects, including spina bifida and haemophilia. For evidence of high rates of divorce and severe marital difficulties among parents of spina bifida children, see p. 127. See also Helga Kuhse and Peter Singer, *Should the Baby Live?* (Oxford, 1985), for more detailed information and references regarding the entire topic of life and death decisions for infants.

The numbers of patients in a persistent vegetative state and the duration of these states is reported in 'USA: Right to Live, or Right to Die?' *Lancet*, vol. 337 (12 January 1991).

On euthanasia in the Netherlands, see J. K. Gevers, 'Legal Developments Concerning Active Euthanasia on Request in the Netherlands, *Bioethics*, vol. 1 (1987). The annual number of cases is given in 'Dutch Doctors Call for Legal Euthanasia', *New Scientist*, 12 October 1991, p. 17. Paul J. van der Maas et al., 'Euthanasia and Other Medical Decisions Concerning the End of Life', *Lancet*, vol. 338 (14 September 1991): 669–74, at 673, gives a figure of 1900 deaths due to euthanasia each year, but this is limited to reports from doctors in general practice. The quotation in the section 'Justifying Voluntary Euthanasia' about patients' desire for reassurance comes from this article, p. 673. The case of Diane is cited from Timothy E. Quill, 'Death and Dignity: A Case of Individualized Decision Making', *New England Journal of Medicine*, vol. 324, no. 10 (7 March 1991): 691–4, while Betty Rollins describes the death of her mother in Betty Rollins, *Last Wish* (Penguin, 1987). The passage quoted is from pp. 149–50. See also Betty Rollins's foreword to Derek Humphry, *Final Exit: The Practicalities of Self-Deliverance and Assisted Suicide* (Eugene, Oreg., 1991), pp. 12–13. Yale Kamisar argues against voluntary as well as nonvoluntary euthanasia in the article cited above; he is answered by Robert Young, 'Voluntary and Nonvoluntary Euthanasia', *The Monist*, vol. 59 (1976). The view of the Roman Catholic church was presented in *Declaration on Euthanasia* published by the Sacred Congregation for the Doctrine of the Faith, Vatican City, 1980. Other useful discussions are Jonathan Glover, *Causing Death and Saving Lives*, chaps. 14 and 15; D. Humphry and A. Wickett, *The Right to Die: Understanding Euthanasia* (New York, 1986); and H. Kuhse, 'Euthanasia', in P. Singer (ed.), *A Companion to Ethics*.

The distinction between active and passive euthanasia is succinctly criticized by James Rachels, 'Active and Passive Euthanasia', *New England Journal of Medicine*, vol. 292 (1975): pp. 78–80, reprinted in P. Singer (ed.), *Applied Ethics*. See also Rachels's *The End of Life*; Kuhse and Singer, *Should the Baby Live?*, chap. 4; and for the most thorough and rigorous philosophical discussion, Helga Kuhse, *The Sanctity-of-Life Doctrine in Medicine – A Critique* (Oxford, 1987), chap. 2. An account of the Baby Doe case is given in Chapter 1 of the same book. The survey of American paediatricians was published as Loretta M. Kopelman, Thomas G. Irons, and Arthur E. Kopelman, 'Neonatologists Judge the "Baby Doe" Regulations', *New England Journal of Medicine*, vol. 318, no. 11 (17 March 1988): 677–83. The British legal cases concerning such decisions are described in Derek Morgan, 'Letting Babies Die Legally', *Institute of Medical Ethics Bulletin* (May 1989), pp. 13–18; and in 'Withholding of Life-saving Treatment', *Lancet*, vol. 336 (1991): 1121. A representative example of the pious misinterpretation of Arthur Clough's lines occurs in G. K. and E. D. Smith, 'Selection for Treatment in Spina Bifida Cystica', *British Medical Journal*, 27 October 1973, at p. 197. The entire poem is included in Helen Gardner (ed.), *The New Oxford Book of English Verse* (Oxford, 1978).

Sir Gustav Nossal's essay cited in the section 'Active and Passive Euthanasia' is 'The Right to Die: Do We Need New Legislation?' in Parliament of Victoria, Social Development Committee, *First Report on Inquiry into Options for Dying with Dignity*, p. 104. On the doctrine of double effect and the distinction between ordinary and extraordinary means of treatment, see Helga Kuhse, 'Euthanasia', in P. Singer (ed.), *A Companion to Ethics*; and for a fuller account, H. Kuhse, *The Sanctity-of-Life Doctrine in Medicine – A Critique*, chaps. 3–4.

The survey of Australian pediatricians and obstetricians referred to in the section 'Active and Passive Euthanasia' was published as P. Singer, H. Kuhse, and C. Singer, 'The Treatment of Newborn Infants with Major Handicaps', *Medical Journal of Australia*, 17 September 1983. The testimony of the Roman Catholic bishop, Lawrence Casey, in the Quinlan case is cited in the judgment, 'In the Matter of Karen Quinlan, An Alleged Incompetent', reprinted in B. Steinbock (ed.), *Killing and Letting Die* (Englewood Cliffs, N.J., 1980). John Lorber describes his practice of passive euthanasia for selected cases of spina bifida in 'Early Results of Selective Treatment of Spina Bifida Cystica', *British Medical Journal*, 27 October 1973, pp. 201–4. The statistics for survival of untreated spina bifida infants come from the articles by Lorber and G. K. and E. D. Smith, cited above. Different doctors report different figures. For further discussion of the treatment of infants with spina bifida, see Helga Kuhse and Peter Singer, *Should the Baby Live?*, chap. 3.

Lorber's objection to active euthanasia quoted at the start of the section 'The Slippery Slope' is from p. 204 of his *British Medical Journal* article cited above. The argument that Nazi crimes developed out of the euthanasia programme is quoted from Leo Alexander, 'Medical Science under Dictatorship', *New England Journal of Medicine*, vol.241 (14 July 1949): 39–47. Gitta Sereny, *Into That Darkness: From Mercy Killing to Mass Murder* (London, 1974) makes a similar claim in tracing the career of Franz Stangl from the euthanasia centres to the death camp at Treblinka; but in so doing she reveals how different the Nazi 'euthanasia' programme was from what is now advocated (see especially pp. 51–5). For an example of a survey showing that people regularly evaluate some health states as worse than death, see G. W. Torrance, 'Utility Approach to Measuring Health-Related Quality of Life', *Journal of Chronic Diseases*, vol. 40 (1987): 6.

On euthanasia among the Eskimo (and the rarity of homicide outside such special circumstances), see E. Westermarck, *The Origin and Development of Moral Ideas*, vol. 1, pp. 329–34, 387, n.1, and 392, nn. 1–3.

Chapter 8: Rich and poor

The summary of world poverty was compiled from a number of sources, including Alan B. Durning, 'Ending Poverty' in the Worldwatch Institute report edited by Lester Brown et al., *State of the World 1990* (Washington D.C., 1990); the United Nations Development Programme's *Human Development Report 1991*; and the report of the World Commission on Environment and Development, *Our Common Future* (Oxford, 1987). The first quotation from Robert McNamara in the section 'Some Facts about Poverty' is from the *Summary Proceedings* of the 1976 Annual Meeting of the World Bank/IFC/IDA, p. 14; the following quotation is from the World Bank's *World Development Report, 1978* (New York 1978), p. iii.

For the wastage involved in feeding crops to animals instead of directly to humans, see Francis Moore Lappe, *Diet for a Small Planet* (New York, 1971; 10th anniversary ed., 1982); A. Durning and H. Brough, *Taking Stock*, Worldwatch Paper 103 (Washington, D.C. 1991); and J. Rifkin, *Beyond Beef* (New York, 1991), chap. 23.

On the difference – or lack of it – between killing and allowing to die, see (in addition to the previous references to active and passive euthanasia) Jonathan Glover, *Causing Death and Saving Lives*, chap. 7; Richard Trammel, 'Saving Life and Taking Life', *Journal of Philosophy*, vol. 72 (1975); John Harris, 'The Marxist Conception of Violence', *Philosophy and Public Affairs*, vol. 3 (1974); John Harris, *Violence and Responsibility* (London, 1980); and S. Kagan, *The Limits of Morality* (Oxford, 1989).

John Locke's view of rights is developed in his *Second Treatise on Civil Government*, and Robert Nozick's in *Anarchy, State and Utopia* (New

York, 1974). Thomas Aquinas's quite different view is quoted from *Summa Theologica*, 2, ii, Question 66, article 7.

Garrett Hardin proposed his 'lifeboat ethic' in 'Living on a Lifeboat', *Bioscience*, October 1974, another version of which has been reprinted in W. Aiken and H. La Follette (eds.), *World Hunger and Moral Obligation* (Englewood Cliffs, N.J., 1977). Hardin elaborates on the argument in *The Limits of Altruism* (Bloomington, Indiana, 1977). An earlier argument against aid was voiced by W. and P. Paddock in their mistitled *Famine 1975!* (Boston 1967) but pride of place in the history of this view must go to Thomas Malthus for *An Essay on the Principle of Population* (London, 1798).

Opposition to the view that the world is over-populated comes from Susan George, *How the Other Half Dies*, rev. ed. (Harmondsworth, Middlesex, 1977), chap. 2. See also T. Hayter *The Creation of World Poverty* (London, 1981). The estimates of population in various countries by the year 2000 are taken from the *Human Development Report, 1991*. For evidence that more equal distribution of income, better education, and better health facilities can reduce population growth, see John W. Ratcliffe, 'Poverty, Politics and Fertility: The Anomaly of Kerala', *Hastings Center Report*, vol. 7 (1977); for a more general discussion of the idea of demographic transition, see William Rich, *Smaller Families through Social and Economic Progress*, Overseas Development Council Monograph no. 7 (1973); and Julian Simon, *The Effects of Income on Fertility*, Carolina Population Center Monograph (Chapel Hill, N.C., 1974). On ethical issues relating to population control, see Robert Young, 'Population Policies, Coercion and Morality', in D. Mannison, R. Routley, and M. McRobbie (eds.), *Environmental Philosophy* (Canberra, 1979).

The objection that a position such as mine poses too high a standard is put by Susan Wolf, 'Moral Saints', *Journal of Philosophy*, vol. 79 (1982): 419–39. See also the 'Symposium on Impartiality and Ethical Theory', *Ethics*, vol. 101 (July 1991): 4. For a forceful defence of impartialist ethics see S. Kagan, *The Limits of Morality* (Oxford, 1989).

For a summary of the issues, see Nigel Dower, 'World Poverty', in P. Singer (ed.), *A Companion to Ethics*. A fuller account by the same author is *World Poverty: Challenge and Response* (York, 1983). For a rights approach, see H. Shue, *Basic Rights: Subsistence, Affluence and U.S. Policy* (Princeton, 1980); and for a Kantian approach, Onora O'Neill, *Faces of Hunger* (London, 1986). A useful general collection is W. Aiken and H. La Follette (eds.), *World Hunger and Moral Obligation* (Englewood Cliffs, N.J., 1977). On the efficacy of overseas aid, see R. Riddell, *Foreign Aid Reconsidered* (Baltimore, 1987).

Chapter 9: Insiders and outsiders

Figures on refugee numbers are taken from *New Internationalist*, September 1991, pp. 18–19. The United Nations High Commission for Refugees also publishes estimates of refugee numbers, in terms of its own narrow definition of a refugee, and of numbers resettled.

Michael Walzer's views are presented in his *Spheres of Justice* (New York, 1983), pp. 9–22.

The account of the visit to the refugee camp in the section 'The Fallacy of the Current Approach' comes from Rossi van der Borch, 'Impressions of a Refugee Camp', quoted in *Asia Bureau Australia Newsletter*, no. 85 (October-December 1986).

Michael Gibney (ed.), *Open Borders? Closed Societies?* (New York 1988), is a valuable collection of essays on ethical and political aspects of the refugee issue.

Chapter 10: The environment

On the proposal to dam the Franklin River in southwest Tasmania, see James McQueen, *The Franklin: Not Just a River* (Ringwood, Victoria, 1983).

The first quotation in 'The Western Tradition' is from Genesis 1:24–8 and the second from Genesis 9:1–3. For attempts to soften the message of these passages, see, for instance, Robin Attfield, *The Ethics of Environmental Concern* (Oxford, 1983); and Andrew Linzey *Christianity and the Rights of Animals* (London 1987). The quotation from Paul comes from Corinthians 9:9–10, and that from Augustine is from his *The Catholic and Manichean Ways of Life*, trans. D. A. Gallagher and I. J. Gallagher (Boston, 1966), p. 102. For the cursing of the fig tree, see Mark 11:12–22, and for the drowning of the pigs, Mark 5:1–13. The passage from Aristotle is to be found in *Politics* (London, 1916), p. 16; for the views of Aquinas, see *Summa Theologica*, 1, ii, Question 64, article 1; 1, ii, Question 72, article 4.

For details on the alternative Christian thinkers, see Keith Thomas, *Man and the Natural World* (London, 1983), pp. 152–3; and Attfield, *The Ethics of Environmental Concern*.

For further information on the effects of global warming, see Lester Brown and others, *State of the World 1990*, Worldwatch Institute (Washington, D.C., 1990). The information on the effects of rising sea levels comes from Jodi L. Jacobson's 'Holding Back the Sea' in that volume; she in turn draws on John D. Milliman and others, 'Environmental and Economic Implications of Rising Sea Level and Subsiding Deltas: The Nile and Bengal Examples', *Ambio*, vol. 18 (1989): 6; and United Nations Environment Program, *Criteria for Assessing Vulnerability to Sea-Level Rise: A Global Inventory to High Risk Areas* (Delft, Netherlands, 1989). The quotations from Bill McKibben's *The End of Nature* (New York, 1989) are from pp. 58 and 60 of that book.

Albert Schweitzer's most complete statement of his ethical stance is *Civilisation and Ethics* (Part 2 of *The Philosophy of Civilisation*), 2d ed., trans. C. T. Campion (London, 1929). The quotation is from pp. 246–7. The quotations from Paul Taylor's *Respect for Nature* (Princeton, 1986) are from pp. 45 and 128. For a critique of Taylor, see Gerald Paske: 'The Life Principle: A (Metaethical) Rejection', *Journal of Applied Philosophy*, vol. 6 (1989).

A. Leopold's proposal for a 'land ethic' can be found in his *A Sand County Almanac, with Essays on Conservation from Round River* (New York, 1970; first published 1949, 1953); the passages quoted are from pp. 238 and 262. The classic text for the distinction between shallow and deep ecology is very brief: A. Naess, 'The Shallow and the Deep, Long-Range Ecology Movement', *Inquiry*, vol. 16 (1973): 95–100. For later works on deep ecology, see, for example, A. Naess and G. Sessions, 'Basic Principles of Deep Ecology', *Ecophilosophy*, vol. 6 (1984) (I first read the quoted passage in D. Bennet and R. Sylvan, 'Australian Perspectives on Environmental Ethics: A UNESCO Project' [unpublished, 1989]); W. Devall and G. Sessions, *Deep Ecology: Living As If Nature Mattered* (Salt Lake City, 1985) (The passage quoted is from p. 67); L. Johnson, *A Morally Deep World* (Cambridge, 1990), F. Mathews, *The Ecological Self* (London, 1991); V. Plumwood, 'Ecofeminism: An Overview and Discussion of Positions and Arguments: Critical Review', *Australasian Journal of Philosophy*, vol. 64 (1986): suppl.; and R. Sylvan, 'Three Essays upon Deeper Environmental Ethics', *Discussion Papers in Environmental Philosophy*, vol. 13 (1986) (published by the Australian National University, Canberra). James Lovelock, *Gaia: A New Look at Life on Earth*, was published in Oxford in 1979. Christopher Stone's *Earth and Other Ethics* (New York, 1987) is a tentative exploration of ways in which nonsentient beings might be included in an ethical framework.

The original *Green Consumer Guide* was by John Elkington and Julia Hailes (London 1988). Adaptations have since been published in several other countries, as have many similar guides. On the extravagance of animal production, see the references given in Chapter 8, above. Rifkin's *Beyond Beef* and Durning and Brough's *Taking Stock* both also contain information on the clearing of the rainforest and other environmental impacts of the animals we raise for food.

Roderick Nash, *The Rights of Nature* (Madison, Wis., 1989) is a useful, but not always reliable, historical account of the development of environmental ethics. Some collections of essays on this topic are R. Elliot and A. Gare (eds.), *Environmental Philosophy: A Collection of Readings* (St. Lucia, Queensland, 1983); T. Regan, *Earthbound: New Introductory Essays in Environmental Ethics* (New York, 1984); and D. VandeVeer and C. Pierce (eds.), *People, Penguins and Plastic Trees: Basic Issues in Environmental Ethics* (Belmont, Calif., 1986). Robert Elliot summarizes the issues in 'Environmental Ethics', in P. Singer (ed.), *A Companion to Ethics*.

Chapter 11: Ends and means

The story of Oskar Schindler is brilliantly told by Thomas Kenneally in *Schindler's Ark* (London, 1982). The case of Joan Andrews and the work of Operation Rescue is described by Bernard Nathanson, 'Operation Rescue: Domestic Terrorism or Legitimate Civil Rights Protest?' *Hastings Center Report*, November/December 1989, pp. 28–32. The biblical passage quoted is from Proverbs 24:11. The claim by Gary Leber about the number of children saved is in his essay 'We Must Rescue Them', *Hastings Center Report*, November/December 1989, pp. 26–7. On Gennarelli's experiments and the events surrounding them, see Lori Gruen and Peter Singer, *Animal Liberation: A Graphic Guide* (London, 1987). On the Animal Liberation Front, see also Philip Windeatt, 'They Clearly Now See the Link: Militant Voices', in P. Singer (ed.), *In Defence of Animals* (Oxford, 1985). The blockade of the Franklin River is vividly described by a participant in James McQueen, *The Franklin: Not Just a River* (Ringwood, Victoria, 1983); on the unsuccessful earlier campaign to save Lake Peddar, see Kevin Kiernan, 'I Saw My Temple Ransacked', in Cassandra Pybus and Richard Flanagan (eds.), *The Rest of the World Is Watching* (Sydney, 1990).

Henry Thoreau's 'Civil Disobedience' has been reprinted in several places, among them H. A. Bedau (ed.), *Civil Disobedience: Theory and Practice* (New York, 1969); the passage quoted is on p. 28 of this collection. The immediately following quotation is from p. 18 of R. P. Wolff's *In Defense of Anarchism* (New York, 1970). On the nature of conscience, see A. Campbell Garnett, 'Conscience and Conscientiousness', in J. Feinberg (ed.), *Moral Concepts* (Oxford, 1969).

John Locke argued for the importance of settled law in his *Second Treatise on Civil Government*, especially sections 124–6.

On the sorry history of attempts to reform the law on animal experimentation, see Richard Ryder, *Victims of Science*.

Mill's proposal for multiple votes for the better educated occurs in Chapter 8 of his *Representative Government*. The quotation from Engels's *Condition of the Working Class in England*, trans. and ed. Henderson and Chaloner (Oxford, 1958), p. 108, I owe to John Harris, 'The Marxist Conception of Violence', *Philosophy and Public Affairs*, vol. 3 (1974), which argues persuasively for regarding passive violence as a genuine form of violence. See also Harris's book, *Violence and Responsibility* (London, 1980); and Ted Honderich, *Three Essays on Political Violence* (Oxford, 1976). The quotation from Dave Foreman and Bill Haywood, *Ecodefense: A Field Guide to Monkeywrenching* (Tucson, Ariz., 1987), appears on pp. 14 and 17.

The issues dealt with in the first three sections of this chapter are more fully treated in my *Democracy and Disobedience* (Oxford, 1973). Probably the best collection of essays in this area is still J. G. Murphy (ed.), *Civil Disobedience and Violence* (Belmont, 1971), although the anthology edited by H. A. Bedau, referred to above, is valuable for its emphasis on the writings of those who practice civil disobedience rather than theorise about it from afar.

Chapter 12: Why act morally?

For attempts to reject the title question of this chapter as an improper question, see S. Toulmin, *The Place of Reason in Ethics* (Cambridge, 1961), p. 162; J. Hospers, *Human Conduct* (London, 1963), p. 194; and M. G. Singer, *Generalization in Ethics* (London, 1963), pp. 319–27. D. H. Monro defines ethical judgments as overriding in *Empiricism and Ethics* (Cambridge, 1967); see, for instance, p. 127. R. M. Hare's prescriptivist view of ethics implies that a commitment to act is involved in accepting a moral judgment, but since only universalisable judgments count as moral judgments, this view does not have the consequence that whatever judgment we take to be overriding is necessarily our moral judgment. Hare's view therefore allows us to give sense to our question. On this general issue of the definition of moral terms and the consequences of different definitions, see my 'The Triviality of the Debate over "Is–Ought" and the Definition of "Moral"', *American Philosophical Quarterly*, vol. 10 (1973).

The argument discussed in the second section is a distillation of such sources as Marcus Aurelius, *Meditations*, bk. 4, par. 4; I. Kant, *Groundwork of the Metaphysic of Morals*; H. J. Paton, *The Categorical Imperative* (London, 1963), pp. 245–6; J. Hospers, *Human Conduct* (London, 1963), pp. 584–93; and D. Gauthier, *Practical Reasoning* (Oxford, 1963), p. 118.

G. Carlson, 'Ethical Egoism Reconsidered', *American Philosophical Quarterly*, vol. 10 (1973), argues that egoism is irrational because the individual egoist cannot defend it publicly without inconsistency; but it is not clear why this should be a test of rationality, since the egoist can still defend it to himself.

Hume defends his view of practical reason in *A Treatise of Human Nature*, bk. 1, pt. iii, sec. 3. T. Nagel's objections to it are in *The Possibility of Altruism* (Oxford, 1970). For a more recent statement of Nagel's position, see his *The View from Nowhere* (New York, 1986). Sidgwick's observation on the rationality of egoism is on p. 498 of *The Methods of Ethics*, 7th ed. (London, 1907).

Bradley's insistence on loving virtue for its own sake comes from his *Ethical Studies* (Oxford, 1876; repr. 1962), pp. 61–3. The same position can be found in Kant's *Groundwork of the Metaphysic of Morals*, chap. 1, and in D. Z. Phillips, 'Does It Pay to Be Good?' *Proceedings of the Aristotelian Society*, vol. 64 (1964–5). Bradley and Kant are expounding what they take to be 'the common moral consciousness' rather than their own views. Kant himself adheres to the view of the common moral consciousness, but later in *Ethical Studies* Bradley supports a view of morality in which the subjective satisfaction involved in the moral life plays a prominent role.

My account of why we believe that only actions done for the sake of morality have moral worth is similar to Hume's view in his *Enquiry Concerning the Principles of Morals*. See also P. H. Nowell-Smith, *Ethics*, pt. 3.

Maslow presents some sketchy data in support of his theory of personality in 'Psychological Data and Value Theory', in A. H. Maslow (ed.), *New Knowledge in Human Values* (New York, 1959); see also A. H. Maslow, *Motivation and Personality* (New York, 1954). Charles Hampden-Turner, *Radical Man* (New York, 1971) contains a hotchpotch of surveys and research linking certain humanistic values with an outlook on life that is subjectively rewarding; but the data are often only tangentially relevant to the conclusions drawn from them.

On psychopaths, see H. Cleckley, *The Mask of Sanity*, 5th ed. (St. Louis, 1976). The remark about requests for help coming from relatives, not the psychopaths themselves, is on p. viii. The quotation from a happy psychopath is from W. and J. McCord, *Psychopathy and Delinquency* (New York, 1956), p. 6. On the ability of psychopaths to avoid prison, see R. D. Hare, *Psychopathy* (New York, 1970), pp. 111–12.

The 'paradox of hedonism' is discussed by F. H. Bradley in the third essay of his *Ethical Studies*; for a psychotherapist's account, see V. Frankl, *The Will to Meaning* (London, 1971), pp. 33–4.

On the relation between self-interest and ethics, see the concluding chapter of Sidgwick's *Methods of Ethics*; and for a useful anthology, D. Gauthier (ed.), *Morality and Rational Self-Interest* (Englewood Cliffs, N.J., 1970). On the more general issue of the nature of practical reasoning, see J. Raz (ed.), *Practical Reasoning* (Oxford, 1978).

The quotation from Dennis Levine is from his *Inside Out* (New York, 1991), p. 391.

INDEX